The Creation of the
First Arthurian Romance

A Quest

Claude Luttrell

NORTHWESTERN UNIVERSITY PRESS

Evanston   1974

Library of Congress Catalog Card No. 73–94432
ISBN 0–8101–0450–4
Printed in the United States of America

Contents

Author's Note

One cannot be an isolationist with the literature of the Middle Ages, and least of all when dealing with Arthurian romance. So international must be its study that Professor Eugène Vinaver, a distinguished scholar in French literature, is the editor of Malory. I appreciate the kind interest he showed when I set out on this inquiry into the beginnings of Arthurian romance, which necessarily enters the preserves of French scholarship, and I doubt whether it would have been undertaken and pursued to a conclusion without the constant encouragement given by my former colleague at Leicester, now Professor Kenneth Varty, University of Glasgow. To him and Professor Lewis Thorpe, University of Nottingham, who in turn read and criticized the book, as completed in 1971, I am indebted for performing this service. I owe my thanks for helpful discussion to various colleagues in the Department of Classics, University of Leicester, especially Dr. Wolf Liebeschuetz, who read and criticized my translations from Latin. Lastly, I pay tribute to the patience of my wife with this preoccupation, which has taken so long to bring to an end.

I

Nature

The twelfth-century renaissance brought great developments in art, literature, and thought, and the example of the Latin classics and the practice of Latin composition stimulated the birth of the French romance, as a book narrative in verse for the entertainment of the well-bred. It reached its prime in the series by Chrétien de Troyes, the father of Arthurian romance, a title which is justified whether or not he was the first to bestow the conditions of written poetic composition on what had been a form of story-telling practised by professional entertainers, the tale of adventure associated with Arthur's court. For his *Erec et Enide* is the first romance we have whose hero rides on adventure in the imagined heroic age when Arthur holds sway, and to those who came after him Chrétien was the master of the form. Much in the luxuriant growth of Arthurian story can be traced directly from him, and when derivation from tales that Chrétien drew on is assumed, the likely shape of these is in fact determined by our conception of what he did with them. Chrétien as inventor would provide quite different foundations from Chrétien as reteller for our structure of the *matière de Bretagne*, and so there is no question more crucial in the whole of Arthurian studies than that of his creative process.

His renderings of Ovid, one of which (*Philomena*) has survived, show that he was inspired by classical poetry, and scholars have looked for signs of its influence on his romances.[1] The book at Beauvais on which Chrétien says he based the story of *Cligès* is probably meant to be a Latin one,[2] and we must bear in mind the influence on his poetry of the methods taught in the schools and illustrated by the Latin manual of rhetoric. And such a man as Chrétien, not only trained in the liberal arts—as he must have been—but a poet of some classical inspiration, was also likely to show interest in Latin works of literary taste belonging to his day.[3] There is indeed a precise relationship that can be seen between Chrétien and certain Latin productions of his time, and it is the purpose of this inquiry to trace these connections and examine their bearing on *Erec et Enide* before considering the use of Arthurian matter in this first work of its genre.

1 In particular, F. E. Guyer, *Romance in the Making* (1954).

2 See A. Fourrier, *Le courant réaliste dans le roman courtois en France au moyen-âge* (1960), i, 159.

3 V. Bertolucci, "Di nuovo su 'Cligès' e 'Tristan' ", *Studi Francesi* VI (1962), 410 ff., discusses the affinities of *Cligès* with the Latin "comedy" *Lidia*. An attempt to relate Chrétien's *Perceval* to the school of Chartres has been made by L. Pollmann, *Chrétien de Troyes und der Conte del Graal* (1965), 83 ff.

I shall begin with the figure of Nature, the creator nearly always of beauty and perfection, which is often found in the romancers and the troubadours. A conventional formula, for instance, is "Nature never fashioned such a beautiful creature". This use of Nature in Old French poetry was surveyed by Gelzer, who proposed that it is due to the influence of Alain de Lille's *Anticlaudianus*, a long Latin poem dealing with the creation of a perfect human by Nature.[4] But he had overlooked the Nature topos, a rhetorical device which was employed by Latin poets throughout the twelfth century.[5] Owing to the rejection of Gelzer's theory, there has been neglect of the material he collected, which illustrates the use of the Nature topos in French and reveals developments beyond the original conventions.

By Chrétien's time many of the Latin themes of the topos were naturalized in the vernacular, as can be seen from Gelzer's collection, and so for several of his Nature topoi this poet did not have to draw on Latin models. But in French poetry before the romances *Guillaume d'Angleterre, Ille et Galeron, Ipomedon, Athis et Prophilias,* and the lay of *Narcisus,* there is not to be seen such amplitude of development with the Nature topos[6] as Chrétien exhibits already in his first Arthurian romance, as he portrays Enide:

> Molt estoit la pucele gente,
> car tote i ot mise s'antante
> Nature qui fete l'avoit;
> ele meïsmes s'an estoit
> plus de .V^c. foiz mervelliee
> comant une sole foiee
> tant bele chose fere pot;
> car puis tant pener ne se pot
> qu'ele poïst son essanplaire
> an nule guise contrefaire.
> De ceste tesmoingne Nature
> c'onques si bele criature
> ne fu veüe an tot le monde.
>
> (*Erec et Enide,* 411 ff.)[7]

This degree of amplification with the topos is striking, and one should turn to contemporary Latin literature as the source of inspiration. There the rhetorical device was employed in praise and portraiture, and instances of it may

---

4 H. Gelzer, *Nature: zum Einfluss der Scholastik auf den altfranzösischen Roman* (1917).

5 On the Nature topos, see E. R. Curtius, "Zur Literarästhetik des Mittelalters. II", *ZrP* LVIII (1938), 180 ff.; and his *European Literature and the Latin Middle Ages* (1953), 180 ff. Further reference to Curtius is to the latter.

6 The passage in *Roman de Troie,* 29827 ff., does not develop the topos of *Natura formatrix,* but brings to bear at some length *nature devine* (cf. 20803) and *nature humaine* in praising beauty.

7 For editions of texts cited, see Bibliography.

occupy four long lines, as in Matthew of Vendôme, *Milo*, 39 ff., where Nature marvels at her accomplishment, and in *Architrenius*, in which Jean de Hanville speaks of her using an exemplar:

> Consuluit Natura modum, cum sedula tantum
> Desudaret opus, ne qua delinqueret, utque
> Artificis digitos exemplar duceret, ante
> Pinxerat electi spatii mensura puellam.
>
> (*Architrenius*, ed. Wright, i, 258)

(While she toiled industriously over such a great work, Nature took counsel with Proportion lest she might go wrong in some way, and Measure had previously drawn the girl of choice proportions in order that an exemplar should guide the fingers of the artist.)

The individual themes employed by Chrétien in the Nature topos included in the portrait of Enide may be divided into traditional and non-traditional types. Nature lavishing all her pains on her handiwork is conventional in Latin, and appears in Benoît de Sainte-Maure's *Roman de Troie*, 5320. The marvelling at her own achievement, which is well illustrated in Latin, may be compared to:

> miratur in illo
> Se tantum potuisse potens Natura stupensque
> Vix opus esse suum credit quod fecerat ipsa.

(Mighty Nature is amazed that she has been able to accomplish so much in him, and, astonished, hardly believes the work to be her own which she herself had made.)

Chrétien and the Latin poet express Nature's marvelling in a comparable manner, *s'an estoit . . . mervelliee comant . . . tant bele chose fere pot* being similar to *miratur in illo se tantum potuisse*.

I have quoted this Latin passage from *Anticlaudianus*, VII, 74 ff. In Alain's poem, which might almost be described as the most amplified Nature topos of all, it is Nature's project that all effort, care, and skill should be put into a work which will be endowed with every possible gift, and this making of the perfect human takes place in a scene of creation. When the creature is formed, the very epitome of beauty (Nature) is amazed at its match on earth, and astonished at her own accomplishment. In the portrait of Enide, we hear that Nature put every effort into fashioning the heroine, was amazed at how she managed to make such a beautiful being on this one occasion, and declares that such a lovely creature has never been seen. The effect is that of a dramatic scene of creation like that of *Anticlaudianus*, with Nature expending all her care, starting back in amazement at what she has achieved, and exclaiming that the beautiful creature has no match on earth.[8] Chrétien's *une sole foiee* is reminiscent of the

---

8 For Chrétien's Nature marvelling five hundred times on one occasion, compare the five hundred times a farewell is said in *Erec*, 273 f.

continual stress laid in Alain's poem on the uniqueness of the work which Nature intends once and for all to be her most perfect achievement, to sum up her gifts in this one creation, and with this one success to redeem her failures in all the others.

In late twelfth-century romance we have another such scene of creation that also shows Nature as overwhelmed by her accomplishment and finding it unrepeatable:

> Par grant esgart, par grant esveil,
> Par grant leisir, par grant conseil
> Tres sotilment Nature asist
> Les granz beautez que en lui mist,
> Et si que puis en ot envie
> Et dist qu'ele ne porroit mie
> Feire autretel senz trop grant peinne;
> Tant i ot mis del suen demeinne.
>
> (*Athis et Prophilias*, 10165 ff.)

The other matter in this passage makes it not far from:

> Omnes divicias forme diffundit in illo
> Nature prelarga manus; post munera pauper
> Pene fuit Natura parens que dona decoris,
> Forme thesauros vultu deponit in uno.
>
> (*Anticlaudianus*, VII, 38 ff.)

(The very lavish hand of Nature spreads all the riches of beauty in it; after making the gifts Mother Nature has almost become destitute, who places the endowments of bodily charms, the treasures of beauty, in one appearance.)

How likely it is that *Athis et Prophilias* here echoes *Anticlaudianus* will be realized when we come to a second such scene, in lines 19635 ff., for this is definitely based on Alain's poem.[9] Both these texts have a long description of how a lovely being is created by Nature with the assistance of fifteen Virtues. This greatly amplified Nature topos in *Athis et Prophilias* names: Beautez, Sinplesce, Deboneiritez, Corteisie, Sens, Largesce, Avenandise, Foi, Pröesce, Enors, Cointise, Humilitez, Bontez, Lëautez, and Franchise. The romance poet has adapted to his own courtly purpose Alain's series—Concordia, Copia, Favor, Juventus, Risus, Pudor, Modestia, Racio, Honestas, Decus, Prudencia, Pietas, Fides, Largitas, and Nobilitas—and also counted them.

The drawing upon *Anticlaudianus* in the second half of *Athis et Prophilias* (main version) underlines the correspondence between the scenes in *Erec* and Alain's poem. The relation to *Anticlaudianus* in Chrétien is more specific than that of Nature's unique creation in *Ipomedon*, by Hue de Rotelande:

---

9 Gelzer, *op. cit.*, 51-4.

Puz cel tens k'Adam fut furmez
Ne li munz primes estorez,
Ne se sout tant pener Nature,
K'ele furmast tel creature,
Par estudie ne par penser,
Ke plus i poust asener,
K'unkes si bele poust faire,
Ne de bel cors ne de viaire.

(Ipomedon, 2271 ff.)

It is stressed again when we find, in the romance Chrétien composed after *Erec,* yet another Nature topos that is reminiscent of *Anticlaudianus.* Nature, in *Cligès,* is said to have put together in one creation all the gifts that she scattered separately among her creatures:

Et fu de si boene estature
Com mialz le sot feire Nature,
Que an lui mist trestot a un
Ce que par parz done a chascun.
En lui fu Nature si large
Que trestot mist en une charge,
Si li dona quanque ele ot.

(Cligès, 2739 ff.)

Compare the opening lines where Alain declares his subject, Nature's unique and perfect creation:

Solers Nature studium, que singula sparsim
Munera cuntulerat aliis, cuncludit in unum.

(Anticlaudianus, I, 3 f.)
(The skilled zeal of Nature brings together in one work the individual gifts she had bestowed here and there on others.)

This expresses a theme which is found in Latin with the topos, of Nature lavishing on a creation the gifts she had bestowed more sparingly on others. Yet it is noteworthy that Chrétien's *ce que par parz done a chascun* and *mist trestot a un* or *en une charge* are here in Alain's *que singula sparsim munera cuntulerat aliis* and *cuncludit in unum.*

So far I have been dealing with themes in Chrétien which belong to the tradition of the Nature topos, and therefore where the parallels between him and Alain do not amount to proof of connection. It is when I come to the non-traditional themes that the proper evidence for this emerges. To begin with, let us consider how Nature, after her creation of Enide, was quite unable to copy her exemplar. The conception that Nature employs an exemplar, which guides the fingers of the artist, we have already seen in Jean de Hanville's *Architrenius.* Closer to Chrétien are lines in *Ille et Galeron,* by Gautier d'Arras,

who speculates on what could have happened to the pattern (*la forme*) that
Nature had employed for the hero's shape, which she has never since used:
either it was immediately lost, or she threw it away out of reach. Never since
has she wished to apply herself to a work that could be taken from this one.
She put so much into it that she could not do more:

> Bien torna le plus biel defors
> Nature al jor qu'ele le fist.
> Ne sai u el la forme prist,
> C'onques puis ne fu mise en ués:
> U ele fu perdue lués
> U Nature le fist enpaindre
> La u on puis nel pot ataindre.
> Ainc puis ne volt a ouevre entendre
> Qui a cestui se peüst prendre;
> Tant en i mist que ne pot plus.
>
> (*Ille et Galeron*, 192 ff.)

It is this idea, that what Nature does is to copy an exemplar, which explains
the other instances of Nature the copier in Chrétien. Yvain, in a lovesick
soliloquy, thus argues that the heroine was made by God:

> "Oïl voir, bien le puis jurer,
> onques mes si desmesurer
> ne se pot an biauté Nature,
> que trespassee i a mesure,
> ou ele, espoir, n'i ovra onques.
> Comant poïst ce estre donques?
> Don fust si grant biauté venue?
> Ja la fist Dex, de sa main nue,
> por Nature feire muser.
> Tot son tans i porroit user
> s'ele la voloit contrefere,
> que ja n'en porroit a chief trere
> nes Deus, s'il s'an voloit pener,
> ce cuit, ne porroit asener
> que ja mes nule tel feïst,
> por poinne que il i meïst."
>
> (*Yvain*, 1495 ff.)

Never before was Nature able to so excel herself in creating beauty, or she,
perhaps, never worked on it. How could this be, then? From what source would
such great beauty come? Surely God made it with His own unaided hand, so
that Nature should be at a loss. If she tried to copy it, she could waste all her
time, surely, without being able to achieve the work. Not even God, it seems,
no matter what pains He took, could ever succeed in creating another like it.

The creation by God is thought of as separate from Nature's in this particular case, but elsewhere in Chrétien we find collaboration between the two creators is implied, when both God and Nature have created the being:

> Tel l'ot Deus feite que Nature
> Mien esciant i fausist bien,
> S'ele i vosist amender rien.
> ... tant bele rien ne vit nus,
> Car Nature s'an fu penee
> Plus que de nule autre rien nee,
> S'i ot tot mis quanqu'ele pot.
>
> (*Philomena*, 142 ff.)[10]

Such collaboration took place in the creation of Enide, for she is not only Nature's highest achievement but also God's:

> onques Dex ne sot fere mialz
> le nes, la boche ne les ialz.
>
> (*Erec et Enide*, 435 f.)

Again, with Soredamor, both God and Nature played their part, according to Cligès. He declares that God fashioned her, and, while He made her mouth, the sheen of the teeth, like that of ivory or silver, was Nature's work of art:

> "que vaut li remenanz,
> Qui tant est biax et avenanz,
> Et tant boens, et tant precïeus,
> Que desirranz et anvïeus
> Sui ancor de moi remirer
> El front que Dex a fet tant cler
> Que nule rien n'i feroit glace,
> Ne esmeraude, ne topace? ...
> Et de la bochete riant
> Que Dex fist tele a esciant,
> Por ce que nus ne la veïst
> Qui ne cuidast qu'ele reïst?
> Et quel sont li dant an la boche?
> Li uns de l'autre si prés toche,
> Qu'il sanble que il s'antretaingnent;
> Et por ce que mialz i avaingnent,
> I fist Nature un petit d'uevre:
> Qui verroit con la bochete oevre,
> Ne diroit mie que li dant
> Ne fussent d'ivoire ou d'argent."
>
> (*Cligès*, 795 ff.)

---

10 *Philomena* is generally accepted as by Chrétien de Troyes: see J. Frappier, *Chrétien de Troyes: nouvelle édition* (1968), 63 f., 247 f.

Similarly, in *Cligès*, 2681 ff., God fashioned Fenice, and Nature, who was unable to do like work again, must have collaborated:

> Ce fu miracles et mervoille
> C'onques a sa paroille ovrer
> Ne pot Nature recovrer.

(*Cligès*, 2692 ff.)

Though in antiquity the portrait of Theodoric by Sidonius ascribes his comeliness to both God the disposer and Nature's plan,[11] in twelfth-century French poetry it had been customary to use either the Nature topos or the parallel figure with God, and not to have the two creators together in the same rhetorical device, until we find a poet such as Peire Vidal no longer adhering to this mutual independence of the similar topoi,[12] and also romancers, Hue de Rotelande in *Protheselaus*, 2976 ff., and Chrétien several times. The break with earlier rhetorical tradition is significant when Chrétien so often associates God and Nature with the same work, and makes Nature copy. The point brought out is that her skill does not measure up to His, and this is also implied when a work is so outstanding that it is attributable to the hand of God, without any mention of Nature:

> Et fu si bele et si bien feite
> Con Dex meïsmes l'eüst feite.

(*Cligès*, 2677 f.)

Compare lines in the post-*Anticlaudianus* passage that has been pointed out in another French poet:

> Si fu mollee d'estature
> Si come Deus i mist sa cure.

(*Athis et Prophilias*, 19705 f.)

Nature thus emerges, from Chrétien's untraditional handling of the topos, as a figure who exercises her powers of creation alongside God, to whom she is subordinated as a creator with a lower standard of workmanship. And the distinctive form of her creativity is turning out copies, in *Erec* specifically of an exemplar, which in *Ille et Galeron* we have seen to be a pattern that can be thought of as lost after use or thrown away. These conceptions constitute a philosophy of Nature,[13] which demands comparison with that of the philosophers belonging to the school of Chartres.

This leads one to Alain de Lille, first of all because in his treatment of

---

11 *Epistolae*, I, ii, 1.

12 Gelzer, *op. cit.*, 13-22.

13 On the history of Nature as a personification, and expressive of philosophy, see Curtius, *op. cit.*, 106 ff., and the Appendix to J. A. W. Bennett, *The Parlement of Foules* (1957).

Nature he differs from his predecessors by his emphasis on her dependence on God and her limitations.[14] In *De planctu Naturae*, while dealing with the exercise of Nature's creative powers under the direction of God, Alain conveys at length the lesson that her work falls short of His. Nature thus recognizes her lack of competence compared with God:

"Sed ne in hac meae potestatis praerogativa Deo videar quasi arrogans derogare, certissime Summi Magistri me humilem profiteor esse discipulam. Ego enim operans operantis Dei non valeo expresse inhaerere vestigiis; sed a longe, quasi suspirans, operantem respicio. Ejus operatio simplex, mea operatio multiplex; ejus opus sufficiens, meum opus deficiens; ejus opus mirabile, meum opus mutabile; ille innascibilis, ego nata; ille faciens, ego facta; ille mei opifex operis, ego opus opificis. Ille operatur ex nihilo, ego opus mendico ex aliquo. Ille suo operatur numine, ego operor illius sub nomine. Ille rem solo nutu jubet existere, mea vero operatio operationis est nota divinae, et respectu divinae potentiae meam potentiam impotentem esse cognoscas. Meum effectum scias esse defectum, meum vigorem vilitatem esse perpendas."

(De planctu Naturae, ed. Wright, ii, 455)

("But lest in this display of my power I should seem as it were arrogantly to be detracting from the might of God, I acknowledge myself to be unquestionably the humble apprentice of the Supreme Master. For as I labour it is not within my capacity to tread closely in the steps of God as He works; but from afar, as it were sighing wistfully, I watch Him working. His operation is straightforward: mine is complicated. His work is complete in itself: mine falls short. His work is marvellous: mine is impermanent. He is the unborn: I was born. He is the Maker: I was made. He is the Creator of my work: I am the work of the Creator. He works from nothing: I beg the means to produce the work from something. He works by His divine will: I work under His name. He orders a thing to exist by a nod alone, but my activity is the sign of divine activity, and you would see that my power is impotent compared with divine power. My achievement you would recognize to be a failure, my strength you would judge to be contemptible.")

Again, when one looks in these philosophers for the form of creation that Chrétien's Nature operates, the proper parallel is to be found in Alain. The definition of Nature given by Guillaume de Conches is *vis quaedam rebus insita, similia de similia operans*,[15] "a certain power innate in things, producing like from like", which is an idea exemplified by the activity of Nature in Chrétien. As for her using an exemplar, Bernardus Silvestris states that the pattern of eternal Idea is an exemplar transmitted down the links in the chain of being,

---

14 See P. Delhaye, "La vertu et les vertus dans les oeuvres d'Alain de Lille", *Cahiers de civilisation médiévale* VI (1963), 18.

15 *Dialogus de substantiis physicis*, ed. G. Gratarolo (1567), 31.

which include Nature.[16] But it is in Alain de Lille that Nature turns out copies of exemplars and is unremitting in this activity. In *De planctu Naturae*, Nature explains her function as a creator by means of an image, that she operates like a minter stamping out coins in dies, using patterns of family likeness as exemplars from which she forms copies:

> "Me igitur tanquam sui vicariam, rerum generibus sigillandis monetariam destinavit, ut ego in propriis incudibus rerum effigies commonetans, ab incudis forma conformatum deviare non sinerem, sed mei operante solertia, ab exemplaris vultu, naturarum nullarum dotibus defraudata exemplati facies deviaret. Imperantis igitur imperio ego obtemperans, operando quasi varia rerum sigillans numismata[17] ad exemplaris rei imaginem, exempli exemplans effigiem, ex conformibus conformando conformia, singularum rerum vultus reddidi sigillatos. Ita tamen, sub divinae majestatis mysterio, ministerium hujus operationis exercui, ut meae attentionis manum dextera supernae auctoritatis dirigeret, quia meae scripturae calamus exorbitatione subita deviaret, nisi supremi suppositoris digito regeretur."

> *(De planctu Naturae,* ed. Wright, ii, 469 f.)

("He appointed me therefore as his deputy-coiner, so to speak, to stamp the family likenesses of things, with the intention that while turning out copies of things in my own dies I should not let the minted shape vary from the pattern of the die, but through the exercise of my skill the appearance of the copy should derive from the aspect of the exemplar without being cheated of the gifts of any properties. And so, obeying the order of the Commander, and in my work as it were coining the varied currency of things after the likeness of the thing which is the exemplar, reproducing the image of the model, forming like from like, I have produced stamped likenesses of each thing. Nevertheless, subject to the mysterious workings of divine majesty, I have so carried out the service of this activity that the right hand of the celestial Originator was directing my attentive hand, because the pen of my composition would have strayed in sudden deviation if it were not guided by the finger of the Supreme Supporter.")

Chrétien's Nature, working with a lower standard of execution alongside God, can be placed against the background of the figure in Alain who labours as the humble apprentice of the Supreme Master, in whose steps she cannot closely tread, because in comparison with His faultless achievement hers falls short. Again, Nature in Chrétien, who busily tries to *contrefaire son essanplaire*, is none other than she who reproduces the image of the model, forming like

16 *De mundi universitate,* 32/120 ff.: *Sicut enim divinae semper voluntatis est praegnans, sic exemplis aeternarum quas gestat imaginum noys endelechiam, endelechia naturam, natura imarmenem quid mundo debeat informavit.*

    Cf. the definition of Nature given by Hugh of St. Victor: *illud archetypum exemplar rerum omnium, quod in mente divina est, cuius ratione omnia formata sunt (Didascalicon,* I, xi).

17 R reading, which is preferable to the reading *nunc insinuata.*

from like, working industriously after the likeness of the thing which is the exemplar. But whereas in *De planctu Naturae* the philosopher was concerned with the generative function of Nature, Chrétien—the romancer—was intent on amplifying Nature topoi. These philosophical conceptions about Nature, the principle of generation, opened up for Chrétien a new range of conceits for the theme of the most beautiful creation. *Natura formatrix* acquires the office of the copier, and strays in deviation because her workmanship is imperfect and does not measure up to God's. Such turning to a rhetorical purpose, though carried out differently, can be seen in Latin with the Nature who reproduces the image of the model, and works industriously after the likeness of the thing which is the exemplar—in the passage cited from Jean de Hanville's *Architrenius*, which was composed under the influence of *De planctu Naturae*.[18]

From the earliest of the narrative poems that we possess by Chrétien there are thus treatments of the Nature topos which embody conceptions related to those in *De planctu Naturae*.[19] The traditional rhetorical device is transformed under the impact of such thought, and the interplay of philosophy and rhetoric, as Chrétien aims to develop the topos in an original manner, is most fully illustrated with the culmination of the process in *Yvain*, where for the last time he draws upon the cosmology seen in Alain de Lille. In this creation Nature has surpassed herself; no, she did not work on it, rather it was God who made it (with His superior workmanship), that Nature should be at a loss (when she came to perform her reproductive function); if Nature tried to copy it (carrying out her activity of reproducing the image of the model, forming like from like), she could waste all her time without being able to achieve the work (being unable to tread closely in the steps of God); not even God, no matter what pains He took, surely could ever succeed in creating another like it. Conjured up is a scene of God setting out to perplex Nature, as if He would delight in seeing His apprentice (who from afar, as it were sighing wistfully, watches her Master working) stand bemused at the impossibility of imitation, but ironically overdoing Himself. The lines pass from an opening of conventional rhetoric, through exploitation of philosophical ideas about Nature, to transference of expression, as God is rashly assigned the limitations of a *Natura formatrix*.

18 On *Architrenius* and its use of Nature, see P. Piehler, *The Visionary Landscape* (1971), 86–94. I have quoted the passage from *Architrenius* on p. 3.

19 In *Guillaume d'Angleterre*, which is by a Chrétien who may be our poet, the amplified Nature topos (1349 ff.) seems to have such a conception, since the idea of Nature who *Tous jors porte avoec li se sause*, one sweet and the other sour, with the effect of making a man either good or bad, resembles one of the contrasts drawn by Nature between good and bad love: *"Iste suos hospites nectare debriat non amaro; ille suos absynthii potu perimit acetoso"* (*De planctu Naturae*, ed. Wright, ii, 481). "One intoxicates his guests with nectar, which has no bitterness: the other ruins his with the sour drink of wormwood." Shortly after this Nature topos in *Guillaume d'Angleterre*, there is found the figure of the forge for the power of generation (1422), which is a fundamental one in Alain's allegory (p. 53 below).

But in Chrétien's earlier works we still have the simple conception of collaboration between God and Nature, and her inability to copy the joint work when left to herself. Here, God beautifully fashions bodily parts, and this is an idea characteristic of Chrétien alone in twelfth-century romance.[20] Moreover, in *Erec* and *Cligès* there seems to be some division of labour between God and Nature, because He creates the nose, mouth, eyes, and forehead, whereas she puts colour in the complexion and gives the teeth the sheen of ivory or silver.

In *Anticlaudianus*, though Nature is responsible for the body, God has made the soul according to a Form which acts as an exemplar in which every grace has a seat, including beauty, and like Nature in *De planctu Naturae* He uses a stamp to imprint an image (VI, 434 ff.). Nature marvels at the workmanship of the Artist (VI, 486 f.), before she starts on her own labour of working up the best material from which she fashions to the designed shape a body with all the riches of beauty (VII, 8 ff.).[21] The parts played by God and Nature in the creation of a perfect human in *Anticlaudianus*, where He provides the fine form and she clothes it with the best material, should be compared with the roles Chrétien attributes to the two creators in the fashioning of Enide and Soredamor.

It now remains to examine the mirror figure which rounds off the depiction of the heroine in *Erec*, for it has an important bearing on the connection between *Anticlaudianus* and the treatment of the Nature topos in Chrétien. The lines at first sight seem intriguing:

> Que diroie de sa biauté?
> Ce fu cele por verité
> qui fu fete por esgarder,
> qu'an se poïst an li mirer
> ausi com an un mireor.
>
> (*Erec et Enide*, 437 ff.)

How does Enide's beauty serve as a mirror in which one might see oneself reflected? Basing her comments on what has been written in recent years on the historical relationship of Chrétien's style, and about the variations on the theme of the mirror in his day, Colby explains that in Provençal literature *se mirar en* was a metaphor meaning "to use as a model", and that Chrétien was the first to introduce it into Old French verse, but apparently felt his listeners might not grasp its full significance if the resemblance of the maiden's beauty to a mirror were not adequately explained, and so he added *com an un mireor*, using *mireor* in the sense of "model", to provide a key to the riddle presented in these lines.[22]

---

20 A. M. Colby, *The Portrait in Twelfth-century French Literature* (1965), 29.

21 Cf. Bernardus Silvestris, *De mundi universitate*, 32/125 f.: *habitaculum animae corpus artifex natura de initiorum materiis et qualitate conponit.*

22 Colby, *op. cit.*, 143 f.

But the riddle is only for modern readers. The comparison of a person's beauty to a mirror is thus drawn in Latin poetry of the period:

> Pro speculo servit facies preclara tuenti;
> Qui videt hanc, a se redditur ipse sibi.
> *(Miles gloriosus,* 5 f.)

(His very beautiful face serves as a mirror to the observer; he who looks at it sees himself reflected.)

> Pro speculo vultum gerit hec preclara tuenti,
> Nam quicumque videt vultum se visus in illo
> Cernit et in speculo vultus epulatur ocellus.
> *(Anticlaudianus,* III, 395 ff.)

(This very beautiful maiden wears her face like a mirror to the observer, for whoever sees her face perceives himself visible in it, and his eye feasts in the mirror of her face.)

This figure, of beauty as a mirror one gazes at to see oneself reflected, is the same as that in *Erec,* and it conveys that a person's loveliness is such that it can be used as a mirror by which to judge one's own. Chrétien has employed a laudatory image current in Latin poetry of his day.

But Enide's beauty *fu fete por esgarder,* and we do not have this idea in the Latin mirror figure. We ask ourselves who made Enide's beauty for looking at, and find that the context supplies the answer. It is *Nature qui fete l'avoit.* So Nature made Enide's beauty to be used as a mirror. We do not have just a mirror figure of the kind illustrated, but an implied Nature topos containing it.

In *Anticlaudianus,* when Nature is putting to the Virtues her project of the perfect creation, she urges that this should be a mirror to them, so that they could observe in him what their qualities should be. The line *Sit speculum nobis, ut nos speculemur in illo* (I, 243, "let him be a mirror to us, that we may observe in him", has Chrétien's type of figure, with the Latin making the same word-play in *speculum* and *speculemur* as with *mireor* and *se mirer* in the French. Chrétien did not add *com an un mireor* to *se mirer* as a key to any riddle. It is an essential part of the figure as *Anticlaudianus* expresses it. If one applies the wording in *Erec* to the situation of *Anticlaudianus,* it fits like a glove: the perfect being there, for Nature and the Virtues, will be *fete por esgarder, qu'an se poïst an li mirer ausi com an un mireor.* The difference between the texts is only that in the one there is the creation of a model for Nature and the Virtues, whereas in the other it is implied that Enide's beauty was made to be a standard for humanity.

In order to throw light on a passage in a romance one must then place, by the side of the exemplar whose likeness Nature sets out to reproduce, the mirror that she makes for looking at, philosopher's images both.

2

Portraiture

Another topic that was considerably developed by Latin poets in the course of the twelfth century is that which often employs the Nature topos, the *descriptio puellae*. French writers took up the fashion, and Chrétien's romances, like others of the period, contain portrayals of beautiful women. Colby has studied portraits in French romances at this time, particularly in Chrétien, and her book throws light on the relation between his depictions and those of other French writers, but she has hardly taken account of those in Latin.[1] Yet there is an instance in Chrétien which stands out as being under Latin influence. It has traits that belong not to the French but the Latin literature of Chrétien's day; and further, when this description is compared with portraits in Latin a conclusion of some significance emerges.

When the heroine's father, early in *Erec et Enide*, brings her forward to meet the eyes of the hero, Chrétien launches into an extended piece of portraiture, which includes these lines:

> Por voir vos di qu'Isolz la blonde
> n'ot les crins tant sors ne luisanz
> que a cesti ne fust neanz.
> Plus ot que n'est la flors de lis
> cler et blanc le front et le vis;
> sor la blanchor,[2] par grant mervoille,
> d'une fresche color vermoille,
> que Nature li ot donee,
> estoit sa face anluminee.
> Si oel si grant clarté randoient
> que deus estoiles ressanbloient.
>
> (*Erec et Enide*, 424 ff.)

Colby has not been able to find in other writers of the period any mention of the way the rosiness of the complexion illumines the face. Obviously, when it occurs in such a work as *Li Biaus Descouneus* (c. 1200), 2232 f., a romance that makes wholesale use of Chrétien's phraseology, there has been borrowing from him. Nor has Colby seen a comparison of the kind employed in *Erec* to

---

1 A. M. Colby, *The Portrait in Twelfth-century French Literature* (1965).
2 Guiot MS. *color*, but the other MSS. *blanchor*.

describe the eyes, as being like stars, in any vernacular work of Chrétien's day. Indeed, she says that the brightness of attractive eyes is rarely likened to anything in French texts of the period.[3]

Both these traits, appearing already in this first Arthurian romance by Chrétien, affect his treatment in later works. He returns more than once to the illumination of the complexion by rosiness:

> Com la rose oscure le lis,
> Einsi come li lis esface,
> Por bien anluminer la face, . . .
>
> *(Cligès, 810 ff.)*

> La face ot blanche; de desus
> L'ot enluminee Nature
> D'une color vermeille et pure.
>
> *(Perceval, 7904 ff.)*

Compare how drops of blood on snow remind Perceval of the bright colour in his sweetheart's face:

> "en icel leu
> Avoit trois goutes de fres sanc
> Qui enluminoient le blanc:
> En l'esgarder m'estoit avis
> Que la fresche color del vis
> M'amie la bele veïsse."
>
> *(Perceval, 4450 ff.)*

In the romance that followed *Erec*, Chrétien not only remembered the illumination of the face when he came to depict Soredamor, but also Enide's eyes, which he adapted for his new heroine. Now, eyes resemble two candles instead of two stars, but they still keep their *clarté*:

> Mes an tot ce n'a riens a dire,
> Qui la clarté des ialz remire;
> Car a toz ces qui les esgardent
> Sanblent deus chandoiles qui ardent.
>
> *(Cligès, 803 ff.)*

What kind of influence Chrétien reflects is evident when one considers that glowing occurs with the rosy bloom of youth in classical Latin, and that there too are to be found eyes like stars, if not a pair of stars. In fact, both the traits that Colby lays a finger on as being distinctive are present together in a poem by Ovid:

---

3 Colby, *op. cit.*, 143.

candida candorem roseo suffusa rubore
ante fuit—niveo lucet in ore rubor. . . .
argutos habuit—radiant ut sidus ocelli.

(Amores, III, iii, 5 ff.)[4]

(Before, she was dazzling white, with her whiteness tinged by a rosy flush—the flush still shines in her snowy face. . . . She had sparkling eyes—like stars still shine the eyes.)

The classics offer this analogue. Let us now sample some portraits of beautiful women in Latin texts of the period c. 1160-85:

1 *Passio sanctae Agnetis*, by Peter Riga: ed. Migne, clxxi, 1309
2 *Milo*, by Matthew of Vendôme: lines 15-42
3 *Alda*, by William of Blois: lines 125-36
4 *Ars versificatoria*, by Matthew of Vendôme: § 56
5 *Lidia*, lines 443-8
6 *Descriptio cuiusdam puellae*, by Giraldus Cambrensis
7 *De planctu Naturae*, by Alain de Lille: ed. Wright, ii, 431 f.[5]
8 *Anticlaudianus*, by Alain de Lille: I, 271-302
9 *Architrenius*, by Jean de Hanville: ed. Wright, i, 253-60
10 *Ylias*, by Joseph of Exeter: IV, 177-92

Here it is common enough for the eyes to be like stars, and Chrétien's conceit for the colour of the complexion is paralleled in *Alda*: *ardet albetque in teneris purpura nixque genis*, "vermilion glows and snow shines white in her tender cheeks". But our notable traits in the description of Enide are particularly in the manner of Alain de Lille, who provides two of the sample portraits.

First of all, as to the light shining from Enide's eyes:

Si oel si grant clarté randoient
que deus estoiles ressanbloient.

(Erec et Enide, 433 f.)

Oculorum vero serena placiditas, amica blandiens claritate, gemelli praeferebat sideris novitatem.

(De planctu Naturae, ed. Wright, ii, 432)

(And the clear calm of the eyes, seductive with a pleasant light, produced the striking effect of a pair of stars.)

There is agreement between *clarté* and *claritate*, which is used by Alain to render a feature in the description of Philosophy by Boethius (Chaucer: *hir eien brennynge and cleer-seynge*),[6] which influenced his portrayal. The significance

---

4 The parallel with *Erec* was observed by W. A. Nitze, "The Romance of Erec, Son of Lac", *Modern Philology* XI (1913-14), 453 n. 2.

5 The passage is written in prose, but Alain's rhetoric is like that of poetry.

6 Boethius, *De consolatione Philosophiae*, Book I, prose i. The translation is given from Chaucer's *Boece*. See *The Works of Geoffrey Chaucer*, ed. F. N. Robinson (2nd edn., 1957), 321.

of this trait in the depiction of Enide is underlined by its use again with the eyes of Soredamor, as if to Chrétien it was a more memorable feature than the stars of the simile, which he altered to candles.

As for the illumination of Enide's complexion, the really close analogue is in the same portrait by Alain: *genarum ignis purpureus, rosarum succensus murice*, "in the cheeks a crimson fire [i.e. flush], lit by a rosy vermilion hue". Compare Chrétien:

> sor la blanchor, par grant mervoille,
> d'une fresche color vermoille,
> que Nature li ot donee,
> estoit sa face anluminee.

(Erec et Enide, 429 ff.)

Jean de Hanville, who was influenced by *De planctu Naturae*,[7] has the same idea as there: *flamma rosae . . . candentes vultus accendit*, "a rosy flame [i.e. flush] . . . lights up the white face". Alain uses the phrase with *succensus* elsewhere in the type of context which in French may be illustrated by *la pree d'erbe et de fleurs enluminee*:[8]

> pubescens tenera lanugine florum,
> Sideribus stellata suis, *succensa rosarum*
> *Murice*, terra novum contendit pingere celum.

(Anticlaudianus, I, 61 ff.)

(Covered with the soft down of flowers, stellated by her own stars, *lit up by the vermilion hue of roses*, earth strives to depict a new heaven.)

I shall now take the Latin samples and tabulate characteristics that correspond to those in *Erec*, but leave out the colour of the hair, which is always golden, the equivalent of French *sors* for the conventional blonde. In order to show how *Erec* compares with all these portraits in respect of the two traits I have brought out, I shall include (in brackets) the various other conceits on bright eyes and the mingling of white and red in the complexion:

1. *Passio sanctae Agnetis*: eyes shine like stars
2. *Milo*: eyes shine, (a flush struggles in the snowy face)
3. *Alda*: (rose colours) lilies in the face, vermilion glows (and snow shines white) in the cheeks
4. *Ars versificatoria*: eyes outshine stars, (a flush suffuses the face and wars against its partner, whiteness)
5. *Lidia*: eyes like a pair of stars, (a flush rising among) lilies in the face (gives it a vermilion colour)
6. *Descriptio cuiusdam puellae*: bright eyes (simulate starry gems), lilies (bloom, attended by a vermilion flush, a rosy colour strives with a snowy one) in the face

7 On Jean de Hanville, see p. 259 below.
8 *Roman de la Rose*, ed. F. Lecoy (*CFMA* 95), 9987 f.

7 *De planctu Naturae*: shining hair, forehead contending with the lily, eyes like a pair of stars and having *claritas*, in the cheeks a crimson flush, lit by a rosy vermilion hue, and tempered by a cool whiteness

8 *Anticlaudianus*: lily forehead, eyes like stars and having radiance, lilies (married to roses) in the face, with a fresh colour, (a red flush relieving the whiteness)

9 *Architrenius*: (with starry torches the eye kindles lamps, and) a rosy flush among the lilies lights up the white face

10 *Ylias*: nothing

As we have seen, in Ovid's *Amores* there are eyes that shine like stars, and the whiteness of the countenance is tinged by a rosy flush which shines in the snowy face. In addition, Ovid's *candorem*, in *candorem roseo suffusa rubore*, bears some resemblance to *sor la blanchor*, as Chrétien uses the phrase. But it belongs in him to the form of the Nature topos which is also to be found in *Roman de Thèbes:*

> Sor la blanchor, par grant conseil,
> Ot Nature assis del vermeil.
> (*Roman de Thèbes*, ed. Constans, 6081 f.)

Sufficient pointers have now been gathered to come to a conclusion. In the Latin treatment of the *descriptio puellae* in 1160-85, one portrait stands out as similar to the description of Énide. This is so in comparison with Ovid as well. Though the general characteristics in common between the depictions in *Erec* and *De planctu Naturae* are indeed found elsewhere in classical or contemporary Latin texts, it is in this allegory of Alain's that they come together, and sometimes they have there also a touch of the distinctive.

We are dealing with Alain's famous description of Nature, which includes the following traits:

> cujus crinis non mendicata luce, sed propria, scintillans, non similitudinarie radiorum praesentans effigiem, sed eorum claritate nativa naturam praeveniens. . . . Crinale vero aureum in legitimi ordinis choream, crinis aurum concilians. . . . Frons vero in amplam evagata planitiem, lacteo liliata colore, lilio videbatur contendere. . . . Oculorum vero serena placiditas, amica blandiens claritate, gemelli praeferebat sideris novitatem. . . . Genarum ignis purpureus, rosarum succensus murice, dulci flamma faciem amicabat; candore namque glaciali amicam serenabat temperiem.
> (*De planctu Naturae*, ed. Wright, ii, 431 f.)

(Her hair, shining not with borrowed light but its own, displayed the likeness of rays, not figuratively, but by their inherent brightness surpassing nature. . . . And a golden comb brought the gold of the hair into a dance of proper order. . . . But the forehead, extending over a wide and even surface, made lily-white by its milky tint, seemed to vie with the lily. . . . And the clear calm of the eyes, seductive with a pleasant light, produced the striking effect of a pair of stars. . . . In the cheeks a crimson flush, lit by a rosy vermilion hue, with a delightful blush made the face charming; for a pleasing balance resulted through the lightening effect of a cool whiteness.)

Turning from the description of Enide's features to the portrayal of her dress, one finds that this also provides a parallel between Chrétien and Alain:

> La dame s'an est hors issue
> et sa fille, qui fu vestue
> d'une chemise par panz lee,
> deliee, blanche et ridee;
> un blanc cheinse ot vestu desus,
> n'avoit robe ne mains ne plus,
> et tant estoit li chainses viez
> que as costez estoit perciez:
> povre estoit la robe dehors,
> mes desoz estoit biax li cors.
>
> (*Erec et Enide*, 401 ff.)

Enide's *chainse*, or overgarment of fine linen, is so old that it is worn out and has holes. Her chemise, or linen shift, is *deliee*, that is, of fine material. In other words, their poverty is of condition, not quality, and their state may be contrasted with the elegance of the white *chainse* and chemise which are worn by the fairy mistress in Marie de France's *Lanval*, when she comes and impresses Arthur's court with her grace and great beauty. Or with the splendour of the white *chainse*, made of perfectly new and rich material, a silk adorned with a pattern in sparkling gold, in which we see the beautiful heroine of the early thirteenth-century *Durmart le Galois*.[9] In descriptions of loveliness, when clothing is included it is typically rich, so that the garments depicted in the other portrayals of handsome persons in the French literature of the period are all attractive.[10] But Alain de Lille, who makes the dress of his allegorical personages suit symbolic purpose, provides poor clothing rather like Enide's for the beautiful maiden of his portrait in *Anticlaudianus* that has been included among my samples:

> Vestis erat filo tenui contexta, colorem
> Non mentita suum nulloque sophismate visum
> Decipit, immo rubor nativus inhebriat illum. . . .
> Sompniat hic rerum species pictura resultans,

9 *Durmart*, 1897-9. This refutes the argument of Colby, *op. cit.*, 140, that the wearing of a *chainse* by Enide makes the reader aware of her poverty, because this garment was not made of costly materials or adorned with embroidery.

10 Colby, *op. cit.*, 19 n. 1.

Quas tamen ex parte iubet expirare vetustas;[11]
Et forme veteris vestigia pauca supersunt,
Sed tamen in partes vestem diffibulat istam
In variis scissura locis.

(*Anticlaudianus*, I, 303 ff.)

(The dress was woven of fine thread, and not counterfeiting its colour it deceives the sight with no sophism, but on the contrary its natural reddish tint saturates it. ... Here the emerging picture shows dimly the semblance of things, but old age bids them partly to perish; and a few traces of the old form remain, but rents here and there split this dress into parts.)

The garment is not white, but it has no artificial colour, only the natural tint of undyed, unbleached material, and in real life one would not see a fine dress that had not even gone through bleaching. The practical equivalent of Alain's lack of dye is thus the whiteness in Chrétien. And, just like Enide's, the clothing is characterized by fine material, old age and worn and tattered state.

Alain de Lille was a master of description, and these portraits of his were influential. We have already seen that his picture of Nature in *De planctu Naturae* is distinctly related to the portrayal of Enide, and now this French *descriptio puellae* and the other most famous of Alain's depictions—Prudencia in *Anticlaudianus*—are also found to correspond, and in details of a feature, poor clothing, which is uncharacteristic of the form.

Another topic of Latin origin in Chrétien's work is the description of the Quadrivium, on which he expends many lines in a striking and imaginative portrayal of the hero's coronation robe in *Erec et Enide*. He has declared he will do his small best to depict some part of the occasion's splendour, and the highlight of his account is this lengthy treatment of the personifications Geometry, Arithmetic, Music, and Astronomy in the pictures embroidered on the garment. For this portrayal the reader is referred to an authority, and Chrétien lays special emphasis on the care and the knowledge shown by the account on which he models his own:

Lisant trovomes an l'estoire
la description de la robe,
si an trai a garant Macrobe
qui an l'estoire mist s'antante,
qui l'antendié, que je ne mante.
Macrobe m'anseigne a descrivre,
si con je l'ai trové el livre,
l'uevre del drap et le portret.

(*Erec et Enide*, 6674 ff.)

---

11 Semi-colon here, and comma in the next line, where the editor gives comma and semi-colon respectively.

The effect which Chrétien creates is of a climax with significance, coming at the highest point of the hero's career and the romance's action, and the insistent direction to Macrobius is all the more impressive since the *Commentarii in Somnium Scipionis* was a leading textbook in the schools. But when we go to Macrobius, what do we find? No personification of the Quadrivium, no robe, no embroidery that portrays the mathematical sciences. *Macrobe m'anseigne a descrivre*, says Chrétien, but it is certainly not Macrobius who taught him how to picture.

There is indeed a late classical name to be connected with Chrétien's depiction, though not Macrobius but Martianus Capella, whose *De nuptiis Philologiae et Mercurii*, another important schoolbook, introduces the Seven Liberal Arts as bridesmaids at an allegorical wedding. By describing their appearance and attributes, Capella gave a topos to medieval literature, and to the art of the Middle Ages a subject, in which appear such motifs as Geometry with her drawing-table, sphere, or measuring rod.[12] It is she, in *De nuptiis*, who wears a marvellous robe, adorned with the sizes and motions of the stars, the measurements and types of orbits, and the shadow of the earth cast in the sky. As she often lends her garment to Astronomy, there are also pictured numbers, pointers of astronomical instruments, and figures of distances, weights, and measures.[13] Between *Erec* and *De nuptiis*, in the symbolism of embroidered dress, there is thus a relation.

But pictorially we have a difference of approach. Capella's imagination is concrete, his allegorical personages with their instruments, the symbols on the robe, all are visualized, whereas Chrétien interprets rather than portrays the pictures. The embroidery shows how she observes and measures, or how she numbers; she who brings harmony, or she who wondrously inspires herself from the stars—this is the manner of his depiction. There is just one exception, in the instruments that lie before his Music, recalling the attributes of the figure in *De nuptiis* and in art. Otherwise he does not, as with Capella, lend himself to artistic representation. Where Astronomy would be gazing fixedly upwards, to Chrétien she is the one who draws all counsel from the sky.

Capella could provide little to Chrétien beyond the allegorical figures themselves and a robe adorned with mathematical symbolism. Nor does the descriptive approach differ fundamentally from Capella's either in the vision poem by Baudri de Bourgueil (c. 1100) or in a passage of the *Roman de Thèbes*, where the presentation is hardly less concrete. Baudri imagines statues of the Liberal Arts around a Countess's bed in *Adelae comitissae*, and shows the mathematical sciences carrying out their activities as if alive. On the car of Amphiaras, in the French text, the Arts are painted, and when the last two lines indicate their

12 For the Liberal Arts topos, see E. R. Curtius, *European Literature and the Latin Middle Ages* (1953), 36 ff. The subject in art is treated by E. Mâle, *L'art religieux du XIIIe siècle en France* (9th edn., 1958), 75 ff.; A. Katzenellenbogen, *The Sculptural Programs of Chartres Cathedral* (1959), 15 ff. (see also endnotes for these pages).
13 *De nuptiis Philologiae et Mercurii*, ed. A. Dick (1925), § 580 f.

functions we are simply given assertions, and not told that these activities are portrayed:

> Gramaire y est painte o ses parz,
> Dyalectique o argumenz
> Et Rethorique o jugemenz.
> L'abaque i tient Arismetique,
> par la gamme chante Musique.
> Painte y est dÿathesaron,
> dÿapainté, dÿapason.
> Unne verge ot Geometrie,
> un astreleibe, Astronomie;
> l'une en terre met sa mesure,
> l'autre es estoiles met sa cure.
>
> *(Roman de Thèbes*, 4990 ff.)

But Chrétien's style of depicting the Arts in a pictorial medium, where typification has so come to dominate, has marked similarity to that of Alain de Lille. In the allegorical poem of *Anticlaudianus*, the description of these figures occupies half of about 800 lines devoted to one of the work's most memorable episodes.[14] Beside this extensive treatment those of Capella and Baudri pale into insignificance, and so much did these allegorical personages in *Anticlaudianus* impress themselves on posterity that Alain's poem was characterized as describing the Arts.[15] Each of them is here given a pictorial dress where the whole of her branch of learning is declared, so that Alain pictures it in the same medium as Chrétien. Then, too, the Latin poet pours forth the processes conveyed by the embroidered work, which otherwise remains undescribed. For instance, the robe of Arithmetic shows how number binds all things with the bond of harmony, combines separate things, rules the world, orders the globe; how the maiden produces, giving birth remains unsoiled, while simple multiplies herself, and remains in herself uncorrupted. In Chrétien, the garment portrays how she numbers days, hours, drops of water in the sea, grains of sand, stars, or leaves in a wood. While the details are not the same, the procedure is the same, typifying how the Arts function and characterizing their skills.

What distinction there is in details is only such as might be expected from the difference between a vernacular romance and a learned work by a philosopher. And there is not only such concord in general to be perceived, but also particular agreement. This may not be striking when Alain's Music bears a cithara, with which she gives banquets to the ear, and has portrayed on her garment the complicated processes of *cantus* and how they operate, while in *Erec* she provides every kind of pleasure, has instruments as attributes, and

---

14 *Anticlaudianus*, II, 325 ff.
15 *Septenas quid alat artes describit Alanus.* See E. Faral, *Les arts poétiques du XIIe et du XIIIe siècle* (1924), 360.

functions through *chanʒ, et deschanʒ, et sanʒ descorde.* But the correspondence between the portraitures of Geometry is of quite a different order:

> L'une i portraist Geometrie
> si com ele esgarde et mesure
> con li ciax et la terre dure,
> si que de rien nule n'i faut
> et puis le bas, et puis le haut,
> et puis le lé, et puis le lonc,
> et puis esgarde par selonc
> con la mers est lee et parfonde,
> et si mesure tot le monde.

(Erec et Enide, 6684 ff.)

> Virgam virgo gerit, *qua totum circinat orbem,*
> *Qua terre spacium metitur, qua mare certis*
> *Limitibus claudit, qua circinat ardua celi.*
> Et quamvis eius vestis respersa minutim
> Pulveris imbre foret, non denigratur honestas
> Materie formeque decor, sed gramate multo
> Picturata nitet multoque superbit honore.
> Hic artem totam picture lingua recenset,
> Que mensurandi doctrinam fundit et usum
> Edocet, immensum claudit, *spatiosa refrenat*
> Parvaque consequitur, *metitur magna, profundum*
> *Scrutatur, valles habitat, conscendit in altum.*

(Anticlaudianus, III, 477 ff.)

(The maiden bears a rod, *with which she makes the circuit of the whole world, with which she measures the extent of the earth, with which she bounds the sea within defined limits, with which she makes the circuit of heaven's steeps.* And however much her robe might be finely sprinkled with a shower of dust, the nobility of the material and the beauty of the form are not adversely affected, but it is resplendent, embroidered with much delineation, and magnificent with much ornament. Here the idiom of portrayal reviews the whole art which expounds the theory and teaches the practice of measurement, imprisons infinite space, *bounds the broad* and distinguishes the small, *measures the large, scrutinises depth, abides in valleys, and mounts to the height.*)

Every feature of measurement in *Erec* has its equivalent in Alain's lists of how the rod is employed and the art is portrayed on the robe:

1 ele esgarde et mesure con li ciax et la terre dure
   = terre spacium metitur, (mare certis limitibus claudit,) circinat ardua celi
2 et puis le bas, et puis le haut
   = valles habitat, conscendit in altum
3 et puis le lé, et puis le lonc
   = spatiosa refrenat, (parvaque consequitur,) metitur magna

4 et puis esgarde par selonc con la mers est lee et parfonde
  = mare certis limitibus claudit, . . . profundum scrutatur
5 et si mesure tot le monde
  = totum circinat orbem

Furthermore, the fays who made Erec's robe and adorned it with pictures are similar to these allegorical personages in *Anticlaudianus*. Alain's description of the Arts goes on side by side with that of their activity, the construction of the car of Wisdom. Each is brought forward, first *harum prima*, described and characterized, and her dress depicted. Then he tells how she fashions her portion of the car, covering it with images of those authorities who stand for her branch of learning; thus she iconographically supplements herself—compare the twelfth-century theme, as at Chartres, that associates the Arts with their human representatives.[16] He goes on to *virgo secunda* and does the same, and in this way deals with the Arts one by one, with *tertia virgo, quarta soror*, and so on, first the Trivium, then the Quadrivium, who are responsible for the four wheels. Even as they operate in turn, each on her own *opus*, so the fays, one after the other, first *la premerainne*, then *la seconde*, and finally *la quarte, qui aprés ovra*, depicted the *uevre* of each Art. Alain makes much of the skill and powers exerted in the labour, and brings out zeal by such phrases as "alert, zealous, willing, industrious, taking pains, devoted to the work" (II, 383), or "she drives herself utterly to the endeavour, pursuing it more zealously than the rest" (III, 469). The fays lavished *grant san* and *grant mestrie* on their work, doing their best *de molt bien faire*.

But there is a difference in the order of the Quadrivium in the two descriptions; for *Erec* has Geometry, Arithmetic, Music, Astronomy, which derives from the sequence of *De nuptiis*, with the positions of Astronomy and Music reversed, while it is Arithmetic, Music, Geometry, Astronomy in *Anticlaudianus*, Alain giving the other antique order—exemplified in the mid-twelfth-century *Heptateuchon* of Thierry—which was favoured by the school of Chartres. However, this does not stand in the way of dependence. The sculptors of Chartres cathedral adopted Capella's order even while expressing in their iconography the ideas set out in the *Heptateuchon*.[17] And in fact Chrétien so alters Capella's sequence that Astronomy takes up the same position as in *Anticlaudianus*. His purpose in having Astronomy close the series is similarly to emphasize its greater importance; for even as Alain draws attention to the "last maiden", who is "first in beauty, first in elegance", and "bears the first mind within her breast" (IV, 1 f.), so Chrétien has the fourth fay depicting *la meillor des arz*.[18]

16 See Katzenellenbogen, *op. cit.*, 20 f.
17 *Ibid.*, 20.
18 To Chrétien astronomy is astrology, which came to be so prized in the second half of the twelfth century that many saw in it the most practical proof of the utility of astronomy. In *Anticlaudianus*, Astronomy portrays astrology when she embellishes her wheel with the

Chrétien says *je l'ai trové el livre, l'uevre del drap et le portret* (6680 f.). We should know what book he means, when the decoration on Erec's robe is equivalent to Alain's portrayal of the Quadrivium in symbolic dress, and the activity of the four fays upon the quarters of the garment to that of the personifications with their four wheels for the car of Wisdom.

image of Albumasar, who "consults the stars, skies, heaven, and the seven planets, and reports their counsel to the earth" (IV, 62 ff.). Comparably, in Chrétien, the fourth fay pictured:

> cele qui fet tante mervoille,
> et as estoiles s'an consoille
> et a la lune et au soloil.
> En autre leu n'an prant consoil
> de rien qui a feire li soit;
> cil la consoille bien a droit
> de quanque cele li requiert,
> et quanque fu, et quanque iert.

(Erec et Enide, 6719 ff.)

B

3

New Bearings

The portrayal of Enide has been found to be related to both of Alain's major depictions. In certain respects the features of Chrétien's heroine are described in the same way as those of Nature in *De planctu Naturae*, and her dress resembles Prudencia's in *Anticlaudianus*, corresponding in some details of an element, poor clothing, which is unconventional in descriptions of beauty. Any dependence could only lie in one direction, because Enide's features are characterized by two traits not found in any vernacular work of Chrétien's day, but present in Latin literature, and the dress of Prudencia is adapted from that of Philosophy in Boethius, *De consolatione Philosophiae*.[1]

We have also seen that the treatment of the Nature topos in Chrétien shows parallels with *Anticlaudianus*, and a philosophy which not only agrees in general with that in *De planctu Naturae*, but makes use of a specific conception to be found there—that Nature copies an exemplar in her reproductive activity. In the depiction of Enide there is another of the philosopher's images, the mirror that Nature made for looking at, in word-play like that of a line in *Anticlaudianus*. And having the amplified Nature topos in this portrayal affected by both of Alain's allegories would present the same phenomenon as the existence of their combined influence on the description of Enide's appearance.

With this portrait, therefore, the detection of Alain has been no matter of dealing with one or two points, or just a few lines, but of hearing his ring from beginning to end of the long, forty-line passage, time and time again, in every main element. The consistency with which the depiction of Enide keeps on leading us to Alain's works is sufficiently telling, and so is the relation between the description of the Liberal Arts in *Erec* and *Anticlaudianus*. The romance where the figures are pictured at length is *Erec*, and *Anticlaudianus* is the medieval work which describes them in hundreds of lines. Again there can be no question as to the direction of any influence between the two authors. The master of symbolic robe depiction is Alain, and exactly the same descriptive procedure seen with the garments of the Arts is well illustrated outside them

---

1 Compare Chaucer's *Boece*, Book I, Prose i:

Hir clothes weren makid of right delye thredes and subtil craft. . . . The whiche clothes a derknesse of a forleten and despised elde hadde duskid and dirked. . . . Natheles handes of some men hadden korve that cloth by violence or by strengthe, and everich man of hem hadde boren awey swiche peces as he myghte geten.

See *The Works of Geoffrey Chaucer*, ed. F. N. Robinson (2nd edn., 1957), 321.

in his poem. It makes use of a manner that runs through *Anticlaudianus*, the typifying of functions there being practised methodically as a means of making poetry out of philosophy and having a *summa* adumbrated in a piece of imaginative literature, so that the style in Chrétien's description of the Quad-rivium is just that which is typical of *Anticlaudianus* as a whole. The Liberal Arts, too, are integral to Alain's poem, not only because it is suffused with the influence of Martianus Capella, but since they express the essential ideal summed up in their mistress, Prudencia, next to none in the extensive part she plays.

But to see Chrétien as drawing upon the allegories of Alain de Lille entails a drastic change in our view of the period when the romancer was active. For the evidence shows that *De planctu Naturae* may well be as late as 1178-80, and that *Anticlaudianus* was composed no earlier than the second half of 1182—one can take it that the earliest likely date of publication is 1183[2]—whereas Chrétien's career is held to have begun well before this. Exactly when it did has been the subject of controversy, and discussion has advanced the dating later and later, until nowadays it is generally assumed that *Erec et Enide* was composed in 1170, *Cligès* about 1176, *Yvain* and *Le Chevalier de la Charrete* worked on alternately between 1177 and 1179 or 1181, and that Chrétien began *Perceval* after 4 May 1181.[3] But if *Erec* was composed after *Anticlaudianus*, then one has to move the dating later still—considerably so—and accept that Chrétien started on his Arthurian series about the time that scholars think he was engaged on *Perceval*, with which he ended it.

However, it cannot be denied that the evidence which has been put forward for the dating of Chrétien's romances is rather weak,[4] and scholars have clutched at straws to arrive at a chronology—or even allowed preconceptions to cloud the issue of date. Thus, Marie, wife of Henri le Libéral, Count of Champagne, was the patron of Chrétien's *Le Chevalier de la Charrete*, near the end of which (5769 f.) there is a reference to quite a number of knights at a tournament not bearing arms because they are either prisoners or *croisié se erent*, that is, they have taken the Cross—and this has been connected with the Count of Cham-pagne's expedition to the East in 1179, from which he returned to die in 1181.[5] Here a prejudgement of date has associated the passage with a time not of great crusading stir, but when only a few nobles took the Cross. The period of real commotion was after the fall of Jerusalem in 1187, when preparations for the Third Crusade began with great zeal. The beginning of 1188 saw the assump-tion of the Cross by Henry II of England, Philippe Auguste of France, the Count of Flanders (Philippe d'Alsace), and a multitude of nobles, including

2 See Appendix A.
3 For the generally-accepted view of the chronology of Chrétien's works, see *Arthurian Literature in the Middle Ages*, ed. R. S. Loomis (1959), 159.
4 See J. Misrahi, "More Light on the Chronology of Chrétien de Troyes?", *BBSIA* XI (1959), 89 ff.
5 A. Fourrier, "Encore la chronologie des oeuvres de Chrétien de Troyes", *BBSIA* II (1950), 87.

Henri, the young Count of Champagne, who left leading an advance force early in 1190.

Apart from the bearing of the Cross being so very much more in the air, there are other pointers to the later date. One is the marked difference between the dedication of *Le Chevalier de la Charrete* to Marie and that of *Eracle*, by Gautier d'Arras, the completion of which Fourrier dates to 1179-81.[6] According to the epilogue, *Eracle* was begun for Marie and her husband's brother, the Count of Blois, and Gautier gives her the appellation *le contesse Marie, fille Loëi*, which agrees with that in Latin documentary usage in the 1170s.[7] The mention of Marie is brief, and Gautier lavishes such praise on the Count of Blois, as well as the Count of Hainault, that it is evident she was less important as a patron, though somewhat more so than when the poet began the romance, for he did not think of her when he addressed his prologue solely in honour of the Count of Blois. Before her husband's death Marie played no important independent role in court life; she may have delivered rulings on love. But she is the sole patron of *Le Chevalier de la Charrete*, lays down authoritatively what is to be the romance's *matiere* and *sen*, and is given the title *ma dame de Chanpaigne*. How significant when we consider the condition of Marie after her husband died! Chrétien abandoned *Le Chevalier de la Charrete*, and it has been urged that he did so because Marie's widowhood dimmed his prospects,[8] but the occasion of Henri le Libéral's death (March 1181) was certainly not the moment to lose faith in her patronage. On the contrary, her favour was thenceforth to be considered as more promising of benefit, for now she governed Champagne as regent, and became one of the greatest figures in France. She was regent till her son Henri came of age in 1187, continued in charge at home while he served in the war against Henry II of England, and had a second regency from 1190, while her son went on the Crusade and remained in the East as designate King of Jerusalem. Chroniclers report that she ruled Champagne with vigour, and while Marie was governor we have a period of literary activity in which writers both courtly and religious looked upon her as patron.[9] She was indeed *ma dame de Chanpaigne*.

So she is termed also in the poem written for her on the psalm *Eructavit*, where she is not given the title she has in *Eracle*, of being the daughter of Louis VII of France (died 1180), but is called sister of the King, i.e. his successor Philippe Auguste. This work has been dated to Marie's first regency.[10]

Not only may the appellation of *ma dame de Chanpaigne* thus be associated

6 A. Fourrier, *Le courant réaliste dans le roman courtois en France au moyen-âge* (1960), i, 204.

7 See the phrases cited, *ibid.*, 190, 254.

8 Fourrier, *art. cit.*, 88.

9 On Marie de Champagne's role in court life and her literary patronage, see J. J. Parry, *The Art of Courtly Love* (1941), 13-21; J. F. Benton, "The Court of Champagne as a Literary Center", *Speculum* XXXVI (1961), 551 ff.; R. R. Bezzola, *Les origines et la formation de la littérature courtoise en Occident*, iii (1963), 374-85.

10 *Eructavit*, vii-xi.

with the period after the death of Henri le Libéral, but with such a later dating of *Le Chevalier de la Charrete*—where the situation of an adulterous consort is set up for courtly love and ascribed to the direct command of Marie—there is the advantage that it would not be commissioned by her as a wife. What scandal could grow up we can see from the story about Marie's cousin, Isabelle of Vermandois, who like Marie is said to have ruled on love. According to report, in 1175 she fell into disgrace, presumably through devotion to non-marital courtly love: she was accused by her husband, the Count of Flanders, of encouraging the attention of a knight as lover, who was put to death.[11]

The commissioning of *Le Chevalier de la Charrete* would also seem inappropriate at a time when Marie de Champagne had religious matters much on the mind. This makes it necessary to point out that *Eructavit* probably belongs to her second regency. The year 1187 has been adopted as the work's *terminus ad quem* because there is no reference to the fall of Jerusalem when the author speaks of the Saracen rampart from Iconium to Spain, but this is negative evidence of little value. Marie is admonished to curtail her expenses, which cause anxiety—*Deus doint que n'i aiens damage!*—and she was in such financial straits in the 1190s, through sending to her son Henri out in the East not only the revenues of Champagne but also borrowed funds, that when she died in March 1198 she was in debt.[12] I then make *Eructavit* contemporary with an extended gloss of Genesis begun for her in 1192 (and completed after her death),[13] showing how during Marie's second regency, after her son had left to be a Crusader and eventually King of Jerusalem, she was regarded as being a patron of religious verse with symbolic exegesis and moral application.[14] Thus my later dating of *Le Chevalier de la Charrete* still makes it possible to place the start on the work before the time when matters of religion could be expected to engage Marie's attention so strongly that she would not have commissioned it. And if one associates the switch of interest with the mounting of crusading zeal, it would explain why Chrétien ceased work on the romance shortly after referring to Crusaders.

Quite a case, it can be seen, has already formed for connecting those who *croisié se erent* with the crusading stir that began in 1188, rather than the

---

11 Parry, *op. cit.*, 16, 20; Bezzola, *op. cit.*, iii, 118 f., 429 f.

12 For the history of Champagne's princely family at this time, see M. H. d'Arbois de Jubainville, *Histoire des ducs et des comtes de Champagne*, vol. iv (1861).

13 On the *Genesis*, see Benton, *art. cit.*, 563-6.

14 According to M. S. Simonelli, "Sulla parafrasi francese antica del Salmo Eructavit", *Cultura Neolatina* XXIV (1964), 5 ff., the conception in *Eructavit*, 737 ff., is that of Christendom united against the Saracens, and so points to a period before the Latin massacre at Constantinople in 1182. In fact, such a conception would be fitting late in Marie de Champagne's lifetime, when it would represent the papal view. In the course of the 1190s the papacy and Byzantium moved towards each other until eventually there were negotiations between Pope Celestine and Alexis, which were followed up by the Emperor of Constantinople's embassy to Pope Innocent in January 1198, suggesting an alliance. The response was a proposal of reconciliation and unification against Islam. See A. Fliche and V. Martin, *Histoire de l'Eglise*, ix. 2 (1953), 221 f., x (1950), 47 f.

expedition a decade earlier led by Henri le Libéral. Now observe that the knights in *Le Chevalier de la Charrete* who have taken the Cross also do not bear arms. It is in fact exactly in 1188 that such a situation occurred. The Count of Flanders, the Count of Blois, and other nobles of France, when horror grew at the endless fighting which held up the launching of the Crusade as Philippe Auguste warred with Henry II in the second half of 1188, laid down their arms in the autumn and said they would never bear them against Christians until their return from the East:

> comes Flandriae et comes Theobaldus, et caeteri comites et barones de regno Franciae contra quorum consilium rex Franciae guerram fecerat, arma sua deposuerunt, dicentes se nunquam gestaturos contra Christianos donec redirent de peregrinatione Jerosolimitanae profectionis.[15]

Deprived of their aid, Philippe Auguste was forced to negotiate, and his conference with Henry II on 7 October at Châtillon was followed by another near Bonmoulins on 18 November, where a truce was arranged till a meeting on 13 January to discuss terms for a lasting peace. But the meeting was delayed, and finally the war was resumed about 1 June 1189, to be soon brought to an end with the death of Henry II. In the meantime the young Count of Champagne, who left the expedition of France after August 1188 and returned home, was called to assist Namur against Hainault, but failed to engage in the war, and did not put his army into motion again until the spring of 1189.

Here are historical circumstances which account for knights who do not bear arms because they have taken the Cross, and also, for that matter, others who cannot do so because they are prisoners. Thus the evidence suggests that Chrétien suspended work on *Le Chevalier de la Charrete* late in 1188; and as *Perceval* was commissioned by the Count of Flanders, who departed on the Crusade in 1190 and died before Acre in 1191, the romance whose hero finds his way towards a religious ideal of chivalry, and which directs attention to the life of Christ and His Passion, would be fittingly associated with the imminence of the Crusade to regain Jerusalem.

Now consider the position with *Yvain*. From line 3700 onwards there are references to events in *Le Chevalier de la Charrete*, and the last (4734 ff.) mentions the final situation in this romance, as it was left unfinished by Chrétien. Fourrier sees him as starting *Yvain*, breaking off to take up *Le Chevalier de la Charrete*, and then returning to complete *Yvain*, which is surely correct. The treatment of love puts the earlier part of *Yvain* (I), and not *Le Chevalier de la Charrete*, next to *Cligès*. According to Fourrier, the initial allusions to *Le Chevalier de la Charrete* merely announce the work to come, and the break did not take place until the point where the dénouement sets in abruptly with the story of the two heiresses (4697).[16] But it is more natural to assume

---

15 *Gesta regis Henrici secundi* (Rolls series), ii, 48 f.; similarly *Chronica Rogeri de Hoveden* (Rolls series), ii, 345.
16 Fourrier, *art. cit.*, 81-6.

that all the references to *Le Chevalier de la Charrete* were written after it was composed. And after the point where such allusions begin there soon sets in an increase in religious feeling, of which some signs are visible in *Le Chevalier de la Charrete*. Observe the contrast between the beseeching in *Erec*, 4325 ff., which is *por Deu* alone, and that in these passages:

"por ce Deu qui est filz et pere
et qui de celi fist sa mere
qui estoit sa fille et s'ancele."
(*Le Chevalier de la Charrete*, 2821 ff.)
por la reïne glorieuse
del ciel et des anges li prie,
et por Deu.
(*Yvain*, 4058 ff.)

The religiosity is stronger here in *Yvain*. Though Lancelot's heart is touched he does not give way to pity, but Yvain is so powerfully affected that he does, when he hears this adjuration:

par la reïne des ciax
de par li qui est li moiax
et la dolçors de pïeté.
(*Yvain*, 4067 ff.)

Again, we have the use in *Yvain*, 4165, of the term Saviour, which does not occur elsewhere in these romances by Chrétien except in *Perceval*. With the break in the composition of *Yvain* located before these lines, it is true to say that a growth in religious feeling—which can be placed against the background of the stir in connection with the Third Crusade[17]—takes place from *Le Chevalier de la Charrete* onwards, through the later part of *Yvain* (II) to its peak in *Perceval*.[18]

A marker for what definitely comes before the break in *Yvain* is provided by the use of the Nature topos, since Chrétien shows a predilection for this in his earlier works, whereas it is absent from *Le Chevalier de la Charrete*. The last of five instances in *Yvain* occurs in line 3419, shortly before the allusions to *Le Chevalier de la Charrete* begin. The evidence therefore points to the break being in that part of *Yvain* where the initial references to *Le Chevalier de la Charrete* are to be found. It therefore seems likely that the place of resumption

17 So too can allusions to the infidels: *ceste gent sarradine qui peior que Sarraȝin sont* (*Le Chevalier de la Charrete*, 2134 f.); *Mialȝ volsist estre pris an Perse li plus hardiȝ antre les Turs, que leanȝ estre antre les murs* (*Yvain*, 6534 ff.). Also Lancelot crying out *sainte Croiȝ* (6481), in the continuation of *Le Chevalier de la Charrete*, completed with Chrétien's permission.

18 The lines on the offerings made in church in *Erec* (including the passage 2327 ff. on the True Cross), if authentic, belong to the later Chrétien (p. 52 n. 6 below); cf. *Perceval*, 6266 ff. The piety in *Guillaume d'Angleterre* is in a different category, being intrinsic to the story.

in *Yvain* is about line 3479, the return to the Storm Fountain, at virtually the middle of the work. I shall then count half of *Yvain* as written after *Le Chevalier de la Charrete*, which means that Chrétien's career in Arthurian romance, after his allusion to Crusaders not bearing arms, had about 13000 lines to run. As reference points in time, I shall place the abandonment of *Le Chevalier de la Charrete* in the autumn of 1188, when the young Count of Champagne was home from the expedition of Philippe Auguste, and the stopping of work on *Perceval* by September 1190, when the Count of Flanders departed for the Crusade, possibly taking Chrétien with him, both never to return, like so many others who died in the epidemic during the siege of Acre. These assumptions give a tempo of composition, over *Yvain* II and *Perceval*, which is equivalent to a year for an average romance by Chrétien, who apart from *Perceval* seems to aim at a length of about 6800 lines for an Arthurian work. Between *Anticlaudianus* and the autumn of 1188 I can then easily fit *Erec*, *Cligès*, *Yvain* I, and *Le Chevalier de la Charrete*, because, if the rate of production earlier in his career was anything like that which has here been computed for the end of it, *Erec* would not need to be started before 1185.

The following would then be the dates of composition or the years within which it would fall: *Erec* 1184-86; *Cligès* 1185-87; *Yvain* I 1186-87; *Le Chevalier de la Charrete* 1187-88; *Yvain* II 1188-89; *Perceval* 1189-90. The picture thus produced is that of a poet with whom the writing of romance must have been a main employment, as one should have guessed from the number of successful works that Chrétien composed. If I include the non-Arthurian *Guillaume d'Angleterre*,[19] a romance of mixed quality but some promise, in the canon of Chrétien's works and give it a date 1181-83,[20] one would have an advance of a professional romancer[21] in the 1180s comparable with that of the professional dramatist, Shakespeare, in the 1590s, for over this space of time he went from prentice work to his height at the turn of the decade.

This later dating of Chrétien results in an apt chronology relative to other literary works. *Yvain*, for instance, which draws on a French chivalric story about a knight and a grateful lion, instead of being started several years before 1184, the date of the chronicle by Geoffrey of Vigeois in which reference is made to this tale,[22] is begun shortly after it. *Le Chevalier de la Charrete*, whose form of courtly love was evidently prescribed by Marie de Champagne, now

---

19 On *Guillaume d'Angleterre*, see J. Frappier, *Chrétien de Troyes: nouvelle édition* (1968), 73 ff., 248; M. Dominica Legge, *Anglo-Norman Literature and its Background* (1963), 141-3.

20 See p. 59 n. 34 below. Chrétien does not mention *Guillaume d'Angleterre* among his works listed at the beginning of *Cligès*, so that we would have to presume he included only those that came after it, of which one will be *Philomena*.

21 *Guillaume d'Angleterre*, 18, speaks of the author as one *qui dire seut*, i.e. who practises as a composer of narrative poetry; cf. *bien dire* in *Erec*, 12 (p. 48 below). *Cil qui de conter vivre vuelent*, decried in the prologue of *Erec*, will not be composers, but those who gain their living by relating others' tales.

22 On this chivalric story, see A. G. Brodeur, "The Grateful Lion", *PMLA* XXXIX (1924), 485 ff.

is written about the time when Andreas Capellanus gives prominence to her views on love, in a work which can be dated by its allusion to the royal Hungarian marriage that was concluded in 1186.[23] And it should be observed that the romance of *Partonopeu*, with some material resembling that in *Yvain* I and *Le Chevalier de la Charrete*, is set by Fourrier at c. 1182-85.[24] But the new picture of contemporary literary background for Chrétien can be drawn most fully and convincingly with *Cligès*, which I have brought forward from c. 1176 to the different circumstances of a decade later.

CLIGÈS AND THE NEW LITERARY CHRONOLOGY

Among the literary bearings on Chrétien are the parallels in *Orson de Beauvais*, a *chanson de geste* dated by Gaston Paris to about 1180-85. It has no linguistic feature that would make a twelfth-century dating obligatory,[25] but it displays two historico-geographical features of a date before 1191, the earlier being that of Jerusalem in Christian hands, as it was till 1187. Chrétien's claim to have drawn the story of his Arthurian-Byzantine romance *Cligès* from a book in the library of Saint Pierre at Beauvais does not have the justification of that in *Orson*, with its pretended discovery there of a manuscript providing the poet with authority for an account connected with this city.[26] Then we find together in *Orson* some material like that which in Chrétien is divided between *Erec* and *Cligès*. In *Orson* the heroine Aceline is married by force, and her original husband is thought to have died (in the East), but he returns from supposed death to strike the villain down at mealtime and to repossess his wife. One sees further resemblance to what happens at Limors in *Erec* when the presumed widow in *Orson*, as they are seated for dinner at the wedding, so absolutely refuses to eat that *elle ne maingait por les mambreȝ coper* (565). She has to be carried weeping to the bed-chamber, and her *matre chamberiere* comforts her by saying that she will obtain a certain herb which will make the unwanted husband powerless to approach her at night. This is paralleled by the scene between Fenice and Thessala, when the heroine's old nurse, on being told that Fenice has to marry the Emperor while she loves Cligès and under no circumstances will share her body and heart, assures her that she will provide a potion which shall make her husband unable to consummate the marriage.[27]

From the romances by the Anglo-Norman poet Hue de Rotelande I have cited, to compare with Chrétien's usage, a Nature topos of the well-amplified

---

23 See A. Steiner, "The Identity of the Italian 'Count' in Andreas Capellanus' *De Amore*", *Speculum* XIII (1938), 308; Parry, *op. cit.*, 21; A. Eckhardt, *De Sicambria à Sans-Souci* (1943), 113-24. *De Amore* is often taken to be composed c. 1200.
24 Fourrier, *op. cit.*, i, 384, 449 n. 15.
25 H. Suchier in a review, *Romania* XXX (1901), 132.
26 *Orson*, 2525 ff.; *Cligès*, 18 ff.
27 *Orson*, 544 ff.; *Erec*, 4732 ff.; *Cligès*, 2962 ff.

kind from *Ipomedon*, and an instance from *Protheselaus* of the rhetorical device with both Nature and God,[28] placing it after *De planctu Naturae*, which does not seem to affect the figure until 1181.[29] *Ipomedon* and its sequel, which was composed by 1190/91, on the balance of evidence are already thought to be later than 1180, and by Fourrier are dated after *Partonopeu*.[30] According to Carter, the allusion in *Ipomedon*, 8939 ff., to a Welsh king Ris, who thought he could dispose of the English border counties but was ignominiously defeated, refers to Rhys ap Griffin and the circumstances of 1186, so that the romance is to be dated with plausible accuracy to 1187-88. Hue however speaks of the king as living some time ago, and so must mean Rhys ap Tudor.[31] But the reference to this eleventh-century Welshman seems pointless unless Hue de Rotelande implies that what happened to him will surely also befall the Rhys of his own day. *Ipomedon* should therefore be no earlier than the time when Rhys ap Griffin abandoned his support of Henry II and carried out border warfare with devastation and slaughter for nearly three years, until in 1184 the situation became so serious that Henry II arrived with an army to deal with Rhys, who promptly submitted.[32] My redating of Chrétien then making *Ipomedon* and *Cligès* contemporary works, this is evidently why one thinks of *Ipomedon* when in Chrétien suspense is prolonged in the love situation of Cligès and Fenice, as the hero goes to Arthur's court. In both romances the hero, to whom the heroine has not declared her love, leaves her to seek his reputation abroad, and goes on to fight incognito in a great tourney for which he wears armour of a different colour every day. Here, *Ipomedon* has the Three Days Tournament motif, which in *Cligès* is modified to four days and four suits of armour.

Of particular interest are multiple bearings, by which one can relate *Cligès* to two or more works or versions of a work. The *Roman d'Alexandre* grew through a series of versions, a revision of a composite work, formed by the joining together of the *Alexandre décasyllabique* with a poem by Lambert le Tort, being our Archetype, of which a further revision, called here the Redaction, was used by Alexandre de Paris when he constructed his version.[33] Which of these was drawn on by Chrétien for *Cligès?* The father of the hero is called Alexandre, sets out from Greece to gain fame with twelve companions who accompany him in battle, like Alexander the Great, and he names his companions one by one in *Cligès*, 1268 ff., as Alexander the Great does when he elects the twelve companions;[34] and the knighting of Alexandre and his companions in *Cligès*, 1121 ff., is based on that of Alexander the Great, with its lustral bath in the sea, the arms, armour, and steeds provided by the King, and

---

28 See pp. 5, 8 above.   29 See p. 255 below.   30 Fourrier, *op. cit.*, i, 447 f.
31 C. H. Carter, in *Haverford Essays* (1909), 237 n. 1; Dominica Legge, *op. cit.*, 85-8.
32 *Gesta regis Henrici secundi*, i, 314.
33 This sketch of the romance's history is based on the account in *Roman d'Alexandre*, iii, 1.
34 *Roman d'Alexandre*, iii, 16, 319 f.; cf. I, 673 ff., in the version by Alexandre de Paris.

the knightly raiment sent by the Queen for the young man to put on when he comes out of the water.[35] In general we need look no later than the Redaction for Chrétien's source, but it is not till the version of this last scene by Alexandre de Paris that Alexander the Great contemptuously refuses a warm water bath that men are about to prepare, and swears *Que ja n'i avra iaue fors la sausse de mer*, to which corresponds:

> il ne vostrent ne daignierent
> Qu'an lor chaufast eve an estuve:
> De la mer firent baing et cuve.
>
> (*Cligès*, 1136 ff.)

The *Roman d'Alexandre* by Alexandre de Paris came into circulation by 1190, and the *terminus a quo* for its compilation is provided by its repeated use of William of Tyre's *Historia rerum in partibus transmarinis gestarum*, which began to be published in 1182.[36]

The Relation to Eracle and Ille et Galeron

Next, let us consider the relation of *Cligès* to the romances of Gautier d'Arras: their dates have been the subject of controversy, but Fourrier's conclusions about them are in general well founded. The poet says that he devoted himself to *Eracle* before *Ille et Galeron*, the allusions to the Cathars late in *Eracle* and early in *Ille* would suit the period from 1178, and 1184 is the *terminus ad quem*, because in this year there died the wife of Frederick Barbarossa, Beatrice of Burgundy, to whom Gautier sent a copy of his second romance. Fourrier has argued that the first part of *Eracle* was written in 1176/77-78, then the poet started on *Ille* in 1178-79, but interrupted it for the completion of *Eracle* in 1179-81, and finally the other romance was finished in 1182-84.[37] This interlarding of the two works is an attempt to account for the references to patrons in their prologues and epilogues, but they provide no such secure evidence for alternation as we have with *Yvain* and *Le Chevalier de la Charrete*.

Now *Eracle* has only the conventional employment of *Natura formatrix*, and contains neither the rhetorical device in its well-amplified form—the fashion for this in French romance was surely triggered off by *De planctu Naturae*—nor any reflection of ideas in this work of Alain's, which probably began to influence poetry in 1181.[38] Whereas from early on in *Ille* there are two such amplifications (192 ff., 4371 ff.), of which the first clearly shows the influence of *De planctu Naturae* in the conception of Nature using a pattern in her creative activity,[39] as she does an exemplar in *Erec*, and also in *Architrenius*,

---

35 *Roman d'Alexandre*, 194 ff., in the decasyllabic version; cf. I, 525 ff., in the version by Alexandre de Paris.
36 *Roman d'Alexandre*, iii, 28 f.   37 Fourrier, *op. cit.*, i, 183-204.
38 See p. 255 below.   39 See p. 6 above.

which was dedicated early in 1185.[40] Thus I support Fourrier's assumption that *Eracle* was completed by 1181, but reject his alternation between the two works. On the evidence so far, *Ille* is not likely to be before 1181.

The heroine of *Ille* is the sister and heiress of the feeble Duke Conain of Brittany, who corresponds, as Fourrier has shown, to the historic Conan IV (died 1171). On her marriage to the hero there follows his destruction of the armies led by her disappointed suitors, who on hearing of the event dispatched messages to one another, and each came in the joint invasion with the strongest force he could assemble.[41] They are the Duke of Normandy, the Count of Anjou, and the Count of Poitiers, whose titles are those belonging to the English royal family at the time, and I agree with Fourrier that the poet is alluding to Henry, Richard, and Geoffrey, the sons of Henry II.[42] However, I question the assumption that hostility against the young Plantagenets, as expressed by making the hero the adversary of figures corresponding to them, is self-explanatory in a French poet. By trouvere and troubadour they were regarded as patrons, and from 1173 the King of France supported these English princes against their father.[43] But there is a year against whose background everything falls into place.

The heiress of Conan IV was not his sister but his daughter of the same name, Constance, and she was married in 1181 to Geoffrey, son of Henry II. The same year, the Count of Flanders negotiated with the Emperor of Germany to attack the King of France and extend the Empire to the Channel, and formed a league with Blois, Champagne, Burgundy, and Hainault against Philippe Auguste. The coalition, it can be seen, represents the patrons of Gautier d'Arras. Late in 1181, when the eldest son of Henry II realized that his brother-in-law Philippe Auguste was about to be overwhelmed, he collected a large army in Normandy, Richard and Geoffrey joined forces with him, and they hastened to the aid of the young King of France. Together they reduced the Count of Sancerre (Etienne de Champagne) to submission, then they marched upon Marie de Champagne, the Duke of Burgundy and their allies and dealt them a grievous blow, and finally the war was brought to an end with the pursuit of the Count of Flanders into ignominious defeat.[44] Thus late in 1181 we have the historical circumstances to account for an antagonism in Gautier d'Arras against the sons of Henry II, as shown by his reversal of contemporary events, in the marriage of the hero to the heiress of Brittany in despite of figures corresponding to the English princes, and his utter defeat of their attack. When Gautier started the romance for the Empress, he had recently come to know

40 See p. 259 below.   41 *Ille*, 939-66.

42 Fourrier, *op. cit.*, i, 308-10. Young Henry performed the function of a Duke of Normandy at the coronation of Philippe Auguste in 1179, and Richard was Count of Poitiers. Geoffrey, who was Duke or Count of Brittany, could not be represented by this title in *Ille*, and that of Count of Anjou was ancestral.

43 Bezzola, *op. cit.*, iii, 220-46.

44 *Gesta regis Henrici secundi*, i, 283 f.; *Radulfi de Diceto opera historica* (Rolls series), ii, 8-10; cf. Fourrier, *op. cit.*, i, 203.

her for the first time, and the meeting could have taken place in the course of the negotiations between the Count of Flanders and the Emperor, or when Beatrice was at home in Burgundy during the summer of 1181.[45] It is unlikely that the allusion was written as late as the spring of 1182, as from that time the English princes were in the public eye along with their father in the Aquitanian wars;[46] and when young Henry died, in the middle of 1183, the allusion to the three princes had lost its force. I shall then place the composition of *Ille et Galeron* from late in 1181 to 1183.

With the completion of *Eracle* located in the period 1178-81, and the composition of *Ille* in 1181-83, let us now set out to see how their relation to *Cligès* is expressive of chronology. *Eracle*, a Romano-Byzantine romance, which has an Emperor whose wife manages to enjoy a lover in a secret place, invites comparison with this work of Chrétien's. However, *Cligès* is not merely Byzantine, but gives fictional European history an Arthurian setting, so that by my later dating it is fittingly grouped with comparable though reverse combinations, in non-Arthurian romances which cast matter from Breton lay or Arthurian tale into the mould of pseudo-history. *Ille et Galeron* is one of these, and others are *Partonopeu*, *Ipomedon*, *Protheselaus*, and *Florimont*, which is dated 1188.[47] Now on the one hand *Ipomedon*, *Protheselaus*, and *Florimont* show similarity to *Cligès* in being romances of the Greek world. And on the other hand both *Ille* and *Cligès* move to and fro between Bretagne (Britain or Brittany) and Greece or Rome, and have an Emperor of Germany (the Holy Roman Empire), whose daughter falls in love with the hero, whom she eventually marries when the spouse of one or the other retires into a convent (*Ille*) or dies (*Cligès*).

Like *Eracle*, again, *Cligès* belongs to the Ovidian family which the *Roman d'Eneas* established, by its treatment of love and the monologues of lovers in their throes, but it is not in *Eracle* that one should seek the points of contact with the Ovidianism in Chrétien, for it is Gautier's later romance which is more closely related to *Cligès*. Both these texts, when dilating on the topic of the heart passing into the possession of the beloved, employ the conceit of the lover's *cors sans cuer*, useless and quite empty in Gautier, while in Chrétien it is like a piece of bark without the wood. This belongs to the figure of the lover being left *sans cuer*, which is found in comparable passages of Ovidianism in *Ipomedon* and *Florimont*.[48] Then the attitude of the lovers towards each other in *Eracle*—where Parides and Athanais fall in love at sight, each does not know the other is so affected, he is with difficulty persuaded to confess his passion

45 Beatrice spent part of the summer here in 1181, as observed by Fourrier, *op. cit.*, i, 204 n. 105.

46 See p. 262 f. below.

47 On *Florimont*, see Fourrier, *op. cit.*, i, 450 ff.

48 *Ille*, 2604-30; *Cligès*, 5120-45; *Ipomedon*, 1301 ff.; *Florimont*, 7736 ff. Chrétien also has *li cors est sanz le cuer* in the passage *Yvain*, 2641 ff., and here *se li cors sanz le cuer vit* (2651) is paralleled by *Nus hons ne puet sens son cuer vivre*, in *Florimont*, 7742. Cf. *sans cuer vif* in *Cligès*, 5145.

to an intermediary, and she brings them together to meet each other for the first time—only superficially resembles that in *Cligès*, where the Queen uncovers the mutual love of Alexandre and Soredamor to each other and precipitates their marriage. Again the real analogy is in Gautier's later romance, where love grows on both sides in ignorance that it is returned, with not only the lady but also the man too delicate to let the other know what each feels, until her brother brings about the marriage. Cligès and Fenice cannot find their way to avowal until the day when they toss a heart metaphor backwards and forwards between them, with ambiguity broaching the subject of love, which reminds one of Isolt in Thomas's *Tristan*.[49] But until this occasion Cligès and Fenice are like Ille and Galeron, who become acquainted and have opportunity for avowal which they do not take, so that *l'uns de l'autre ne set mot* (790). Similarly in *Ipomedon* there is an unspoken love between the hero and heroine, and *nul de l'altre ne seit rien* (1308).[50] With Alexandre and Soredamor in Chrétien, though the lady intends to lead the man on *par sanblant et par moʒ coverʒ* (1033), the shyness is carried so far that when the couple have the chance to address each other they do not do so. But in other respects the parallel to be drawn is with *Athis et Prophilias*, a romance of Ovidianism and Graeco-Roman pseudo-antiquity, whose relation to *Cligès* is so fundamental that I must examine it in some depth.

The Relation to the Versions of Athis et Prophilias

Invented by a poet called Alexandre, as a supplement to the *Roman d'Eneas*, as it were, since the action is in the time of Romulus, *Athis et Prophilias* is named after the two faithful friends who are its subject. It exists in two forms, one being in the Tours MS. (T). The first part, based on an exemplum in Petrus Alfonsi, *Disciplina Clericalis*, is in common and announces the poet's name. It shows marriage giving way to friendship, in the surrender by Athis of his bride Cardiones to Prophilias, who marries her and takes his wife home from Athens to Rome, where Athis follows them. The second part is in two versions, and tells of the love between Athis and Gaite, sister of Prophilias, and their marriage after warfare with Bilas, King of Bile, to whom she had been promised. The T version ends with the return of Athis with Gaite to Athens, and is signed off with the poet's name. But the return is to be counted as a third part in the main form of the romance, where this section is so very long that it exceeds the length of the rest, and so alters the balance of the whole that at the end it is called the story of Athens.

---

49 *Cligès*, 5112-72. For discussion of the pun on *lamer* in Thomas, and its reflection in *Cligès*, see Fourrier, *op. cit.*, i, 69 f., 125 f., 141-3. In *Ipomedon*, 825 ff., the heroine also does some hinting, hoping that the hero would understand *la glose*.

50 Some such phrase occurred in the version of the Rivalen-Blanchefleur episode in Thomas's *Tristan*. See J. Bédier, *Le Roman de Tristan* (1902), i, 16: *et pourtant chacun des deux amants ignore l'amour de l'autre*. But in Thomas the couple soon become aware of each other's love, and in fact give way to it.

Foerster's attention was attracted by *Athis* II, which in both versions shows agreements with *Cligès*.[51] He found most of these in T, but was persuaded that Chrétien knew both forms of *Athis*. Of the few analogies that Foerster noted between the main version of II and other romances by Chrétien, the most striking is with *Perceval*, both texts having what Foerster found otherwise unparalleled, a discourse on the necessity of being on one's guard against catching cold after overheating, in which the same term is used: *sanmellez estes* (*Athis*); *on en sancmelle* (*Perceval*). From *Athis* it can be seen that this rests on a current medical theory that curdling is brought on by the flowing together of hot and cold blood.[52]

In both versions, *Athis* II has monologues marked as in *Cligès* by the stylistic trait of the echoing question,[53] but only in its main form is it characterized by lengthy descriptions, of the decorations on each quarter of Bilas's tent (this is similar to Alexander's in the *Roman d'Alexandre*, as first depicted by the Redaction),[54] of Gaite's attire and horse's equipment, when she has to leave Athis and ride out of Rome to be delivered to King Bilas, whose army is encamped before the city (compare the array of Briseida in the *Roman de Troie*, 13327 ff., when she leaves Troilus and is handed over to the Greeks), and of the wedding celebrations of Athis and Gaite as a finale. The depictions of the decorated saddle given to Enide by Guivret, and of Erec's coronation robe, with images embroidered on each quarter and a fur lining from the strange beast called *berbiolete*, have been compared to passages in one or other of the romances of antiquity, such as that on the mantle of Briseida, which is lined from the extraordinary creature the *dindialos*. But it is the main version of *Athis* II (where the lining of Gaite's mantle is from a peculiar *bestelete*) that we find a whole set in which is writ large the taste that Chrétien shows in lavishing attention on rich array in *Erec* and the crowning of its hero and heroine.[55] Again, of the amplified Nature topoi in romance at this time, it is those in *Athis* III that are nearest to the style of Chrétien's. *Athis*, 10165 ff., is partly comparable with *Erec*, 411 ff., and partly with *Cligès*, 2739 ff.; while *Athis*, 19635 ff., where the creation of each beautiful bodily part is accompanied by its description,[56] just as in *Narcisus*, 64 ff., is best compared otherwise with *Cligès*, 795 ff., in which a similar long depiction of these parts refers several times to their creation. Lastly, the main version of II shares with *Cligès*

---

51 W. Foerster, "Randglossen zum Athisroman", *ZrP* XXXVI (1912), 727 ff.

52 *Athis*, 2936 ff.; *Perceval*, 7951 ff. In the *Roman d'Alexandre* by Alexandre de Paris, I, 2388 ff., Alexander the Great falls seriously ill, with every vein full of *sanc seelé*, in the episode of the bath on a torrid day in the icy water of the Nidele.

53 This feature of Chrétien's style of Ovidianism is also frequent in *Philomena*, and the author of *Piramus et Tisbé* makes good use of it.

54 *Roman d'Alexandre*, iii, 26-8; I, 1948 ff., in the version by Alexandre de Paris.

55 *Athis*, 5607 ff., 6830 ff., 6942 ff., 8639 ff.; *Erec*, 5287 ff., 6596 ff.

56 This passage in *Athis* has the line *A chascun menbre fist son droit* (19702), which strikingly parallels *lor droit randent a chascun manbre* (*Erec*, 2036), in quite a different context.

the feature of playing on the similarity of *amors* and *amer* (itself = *amare* or *amarum*, and, in *Cligès*, punning with *la mer*, as in Thomas's *Tristan*):

Qui nome Amors, nel set nomer,
Amer le puet a droit clamer.

(*Athis et Prophilias*, 4017 f.)

An la mer sont, et d'amer vient,
Et d'amors vient li max ques tient.

(*Cligès*, 543 f.)[57]

That the longer form of *Athis* is the later emerges not only from the contradiction between III, full of heroic deeds before Athens, and I, from whose opening it is seen that Alexandre did not intend to locate chivalry at the city of learning,[58] but also from the concern with courtly love ideas. Whereas in T the love problem for Gaite is how improper it is for a lady to make the first move, in the main version of II the theme which is developed, with Gaite's internal struggle represented by her being torn between the arguments of Amors and Sans, is the choice between a rich man (Bilas) and a poor man (Athis)—the subject of a judgement by Marie de Champagne, as reported by Andreas Capellanus, and one that is dealt with by Marie de France in *Equitan*.[59] As also in *Equitan*, to bestow one's love requires a ritual, when rings are exchanged.[60] Gaite kisses hers in earnest of bestowal. Then *Athis* III has sophisticated love situations inspiring prowess. A father and son, Theseus and Pirithous, become rivals when they both fall in love with the beautiful Gaite. She is married, but such love of man for woman is accepted, so long as it is not adulterous. Thus Theseus declares his love for Gaite openly before his own wife, and Gaite and Cardiones, while remaining true to their husbands, agree to give their rings to Pirithous and Cassidorus, in sign of the *leal amie*, but *sauve l'enor*, with the injunction that the love gift should be worn without thinking of *vilenie*. This supplies a background for the platonic relationship that the hero demands in *Ipomedon* as the Queen's lover who regularly kisses her, which is accepted by the court, though they have to prevail on the King.[61] We also have in this part of *Athis* a situation to compare with the *amor de lonh* in Chrétien's *Perceval*, with a messenger similarly charged to convey a salutation of love:[62]

"il vos salue
Con lëaus druz sa leal drue.
De loing, ce dit, est vostre amis."

(*Athis et Prophilias*, 14731 ff.)

---

57 It will be seen that *Ipomedon* also exploits the resemblance between these words: *Icel' amur est trop amer* (897).

58 This intention is confirmed by *Athis*, T 5902 ff.

59 *Athis*, 3781 ff.; Parry, *op. cit.*, 169; *Equitan*, 138 ff., an exchange between a man of higher and a woman of lower rank, such as occurs in the course of Andreas's treatise.

60 *Athis*, 4557-62, 4697-4766, 4819-74, 8238 f.; *Equitan*, 181.

61 *Athis*, 14053, 14771-876; *Ipomedon*, 3005-71.

62 *Athis*, 14523-46, 14727-60; *Perceval*, 8786-8812, 9009-26.

As regards the date of *Athis* in its original form, it is significant that this invented Graeco-Roman romance shares some ground with another work illustrating Ovidianism, the Romano-Byzantine *Eracle*. Gautier d'Arras has (cf. *Athis* I) a love situation made possible by a stratagem of fabliau nature, and (cf. *Athis* II) the mutual falling in love when the couple see each other at a festival, the tormented monologues that result, the mistaken sickness of the man which causes anxiety, and an intermediary who realizes what the trouble is, promises help with obtaining the lady no matter who she may be, and happens to mention the right one in an assurance of being prepared to go even so far, which causes the young man to break down and confess that she is the object of his love.[63] Again, the port and land of Bile, which is Saracen country in *chanson de geste*, appears in *Athis*, and it must be compared in this respect with *Orson de Beauvais*, these being the texts in which Bile and its King, characterized as rich and powerful, have been made to play a part in the story, and where his name Bilas in the romance is anagrammatically related to that of Basile, who is the King of Bile and the heroine's father in the *chanson*.

The date of *Athis* in its rewritten form is indicated by III making use of *Anticlaudianus*,[64] and the main version of II having an element that sounds like an echo of the negotiations for the royal Hungarian marriage that was concluded in 1186. Henry II put off making provision for the widow of his eldest son Henry, who died in 1183. King Bela of Hungary sent ambassadors in 1184 to the young Philippe Auguste, her brother, to ask for her hand, and was required to give full proof of his income. When it came, his riches caused astonishment. What discussion there was about the marriage can be seen from Andreas Capellanus, where it is thought better for a woman to stay in France, be content with moderate means and go where she wants, than to be subject to a foreigner's power in Hungary and have riches.[65] This is presumably why the motif of the rich foreign king claiming Gaite as his bride is so treated in the main version of *Athis* that Bilas brings Bela to mind. Argument develops over the match that would offer, as the alternative to comparative poverty at home, a husband who derives rich *rantes et avoir* from his empire, but would send Gaite to a far-distant country—as her brother objects:

> Ses frere n'a corage
> Que si loing soit de lui donee,
> Mialz l'aimme asez en sa contree,
> Miauz l'eimme pres plus povremant
> Que reïne lointeignemant.
>
> (*Athis et Prophilias*, 5314 ff.)

In addition, one should observe how much there is in common between the main form of *Athis* and the romance of *Florimont*, which was usefully dated 1188 at the end by Aimon de Varennes. Besides being placed well back in

---

63 *Athis*, T 3530-42; *Eracle*, 4190-4218.
64 See p. 4 above.   65 Parry, *op. cit.*, 71 f.

antiquity, this time before the foundation of Rome by Romulus, and illustrating Ovidianism, with love sickness and complaints by the hero and the heroine in parallel, *Florimont* is centred on a Greek setting, and concerns itself very much with courtly love ideas. The resemblance that we have seen, in the revised version of Gaite's love situation, to the affair of the royal Hungarian marriage in 1186 is underlined when we find in *Florimont* a similar theme, and here in fact concerning a King of Hungary. He has demanded the princess Romadanaple as his bride, and she has a problem, whether to give her love to a poor man (Florimont), the internal struggle being represented by the arguments of Amor and Sapience. Her mother urges that she should not abase herself to a man of low rank, and points out the King of Hungary has asked for her, but the heroine argues that it is not riches which count.[66] That emphasis is laid on the high standing of Bilas in the main version of *Athis*, and of the King of Hungary in *Florimont*, is in accord with the statement in Andreas Capellanus that practically the whole world resounds with the King of Hungary's praise and glory.[67]

The stage has now been set to clarify the relations between Chrétien and each form of *Athis*. In the prologue of *Cligès*, we are told that the pre-eminence in chivalry and learning once belonged to Greece, and then chivalry passed to Rome, together with the highest learning, which has now come to France. *Athis* is introduced by the dictum that Rome had the mastery of chivalry and Athens was full of learning, which Rome later acquired.[68] It can be seen that only Greece is wanted for the events in *Cligès*, but both Rome and Athens in the Graeco-Roman romance, and the going from one to the other for chivalry and vice-versa for learning is integral to *Athis*, accounting for the exchanges which lead to the friendship of the Roman Prophilias with the Athenian Athis. Whereas in *Cligès*, the prologue having left us with Rome pre-eminent for chivalry, we find that in the narrative it is in fact Arthur's Britain where one goes in pursuit of fame.

Athis I has turned the short story of its source into a romance, which is also what has happened in the second part of *Cligès* (II), as Foerster observed. And in both cases we find the heroine's husband has no carnal knowledge of her, owing to a trick that leaves one or the other ignorant that this is so, in *Athis* the wife, because he regularly introduces his friend to the bed in his place from the nuptial night, and in *Cligès* the husband, as a result of the potion which makes him dream of sexual intercourse.

In *Athis* II, the warfare that takes place to rescue Gaite from Bilas, to whom she has been surrendered by her father in fulfilment of his promise, can be

---

66 *Florimont*, 7867 ff., 8948 ff.

67 The passage, which is in Parry, *op. cit.*, 57, is discussed by Eckhardt, *loc. cit.*

An additional point of connection between the main form of *Athis* and the romance of *Florimont* is that the use of the Nature topos in *Athis*, 19635 ff., has its closest analogue in *Narcisus*, 64 ff., and the latter here has Amors collaborating with Nature, which is a feature of *Florimont*, 9543 ff. Amors is creator in a poem by the troubadour Arnaut de Mareuil (*Uns gais amoros orguoills*).

68 *Athis*, 161-204; *Cligès*, 28-42.

compared with the part of *Cligès* II where the Duke of Saxony supports his prior claim to Fenice by war. A hundred of his men succeed in capturing Fenice, but she is rescued by Cligès through an ambuscade in a deep valley, and brought back by him while they show their love for each other, though only by glance of eye. Foerster thought that this represents a significant resemblance to *Cligès* in the main form of *Athis*, because here a nephew of Bilas plays an important part in the fighting (as does the nephew of the Duke in Chrétien), Athis and his men ambush a party who are escorting Gaite away, and a love scene follows. However, having to deal with the nephew of the main adversary is a common motif, and the situation in *Cligès* is best compared with that in *Ille et Galeron*, where the enemy has captured the heroine, a hundred of them escorting her are caught in a defile by the hero and his men, and he brings her back after a love scene.[69] Moreover, it is possible to see in *Cligès* a correspondence here rather with the T text than the main version of *Athis*. There are two separate occasions of battle in *Cligès*, first the preliminary encounter at Cologne, where the Duke's nephew and his men are pitted in combat against the party led by Cligès, and later the warfare proper, which is by the Danube. It is in the T text that we find an equivalent arrangement: the falling in love; a battle (with Frolles of Egypt) in which the hero gains fame against the Emperor's opponent; further development of the love relationship; and then warfare with the prince to whom the heroine has been promised. This means that when the victorious Athis returns to Rome after the defeat of Frolles and, as he passes below the window of Gaite, makes her a sign of favour to which she responds, at the corresponding point in Chrétien we have the victorious Cligès returning by Fenice's apartment in Cologne, and an exchange of tender glances as their eyes meet.[70]

Otherwise *Athis* II resembles the first part of *Cligès* (I), as Foerster saw, and the similarity is more striking than that between *Athis* I and *Cligès* II. It is by fighting in Arthur's domain that the Greek Alexandre makes his knightly reputation, even as the Greek Athis does at Rome, and one must set the love of Athis and Gaite beside that of Alexandre and Soredamor. On falling in love with each other at sight, they are in great distress, and at night comes the bitter moan of their monologues; they keep their feelings to themselves, but look sick; and the action of a third party, on recognizing signs of love, is necessary to bring the couple together—honourably for marriage, in contrast to *Eracle*. The parallel with *Cligès* lies in the T version when the onset of the torments is followed by warfare, with Athis serving with distinction under the Emperor Romulus against Frolles, as Cligès does under King Arthur against Angres. In both cases the love situation is then resolved, as the intermediary sets to work: Prophilias obtains confessions of love from Athis and Gaite, and in Chrétien the Queen sees that Alexandre and Soredamor must be in love with each other.

69 *Athis*, 7421-7672; *Cligès*, 3598-3874; *Ille*, 5540-5689.
70 *Athis*, T 3195-3203; *Cligès*, 2916-24.

When one comes to consider the end of *Athis* in relation to *Cligès*, there can remain no doubt as to the direct connection between Chrétien and the Graeco-Roman romance. Foerster pointed out that the return home of Alexandre with Soredamor is like the events in the T version, when Athis sets out from Rome with Gaite to claim his domain after a messenger has arrived to announce his father's death and the seizure of power by a relative. Indeed, one only has to look at the arrival at Athens in both texts, each with an embassy to the people as well as the usurper, and exchanges at court when the challenge to the rule of the domain is given, for the similarity to strike home with force.[71] Now in *Athis* the essential site of the affair is Athens, whereas in *Cligès* it turns out, when Alexandre arrives at this city, that the Emperor of Constantinople is actually (*por verité*) residing there, so that the challenge to his crown can be made on the spot.

It is evident that *Cligès* shows the influence of *Athis* in its original form, reflecting its alternation between Athens and Rome, the place of chivalry, as that between Greece and Arthur's Britain. The inversion by which *Cligès* II is related to *Athis* I, and *Cligès* I to *Athis* II, can be explained as due to a blend with Thomas's *Tristan*, in which there is a comparable account of the hero's parents and his birth before we have the tale of his illicit affair with the monarch's wife. On the other hand, the agreements of Chrétien with the rewritten rather than the earlier version of *Athis* do not suggest dependence, but are best understood as arising in work that is contemporary.

This is also how one should deal with the resemblances between *Florimont* and Chrétien.[72] It is said that *Florimont* was influenced by *Cligès* and *Yvain*, but the similar expression of sentiments proves no more than a common cultural background on the subject of love. And, because the instruction of a prince was a branch of didactic literature (developing around *The Letter of Aristotle to Alexander*), one can again suspect a common source when both Florimont and Chrétien's Alexandre are instructed by their fathers on how generosity *totes bonteʒ* (or *vertuʒ*) *enlumine*.[73] This type of situation, that of *chastoiement*, is by the way in *Cligès*, but in *Florimont* the romance revolves around it, the subject of *largesce* (or its opposite) keeps on returning, and the hero is given a long didactic analysis of the virtue that was set before him as pre-eminent.[74]

71 *Athis*, T 5712-5863; *Cligès*, 2406-87.
72 These are referred to by the editor in *Florimont*, cxiii, cxc ff.
73 *Florimont*, 1920 ff.; *Cligès*, 188 ff. The material here is not considered by M. P. Cosman, *The Education of the Hero in Arthurian Romance* (1966), but his chapter on the "Prevalence and Provenance" of the education theme in medieval romance provides background.
74 *Florimont*, 4175 ff. It is notable that Alain de Lille promulgated the virtue of Largitas. There is much matter in *De planctu Naturae* on this virtue and the corresponding vice, and W. Wetherbee, "The Function of Poetry in the 'De Planctu Naturae' of Alain de Lille", *Traditio* XXV (1969), 111 ff., writes on the setting of Largitas in a unique relation to the other virtues. Nature apostrophizes Largitas in glowing terms, in the speech beginning

Then there is a parallel here with Chrétien's *Perceval*. In both texts, the hero is taught not only by his parent but also by at least one other instructor, in *Florimont* by a figure like the hero's teacher-companion in *Tristan* and *Ipomedon*, and comparable to Aristotle as the instructor of Alexander the Great. The similarity to *Perceval* is striking when at the core of Florimont's story there lies the hero's taking of the instruction about *largesce* so to heart that he ruins his parents and his country. He becomes the Povre Perdu, protests that he has only been following the counsel he received, and has to be set right about the nature of *largesce* by his teacher's disquisition.[75] Perceval tries to carry out instructions, but goes awry through lack of understanding, and by attending overmuch to advice about care in speech he disastrously fails to ask whom the Grail serves. The hero who is lectured on how to act and what he has done wrong is surely not imitated from one of these works by the other, but is to do with what was in the air at the time. Again, the parallel between Soredamor's dwelling on the meaning of her name in *Cligès* and the heroine's interpretation of her name in *Florimont* as *Plena d'Amor* need only reveal contemporary taste.

My survey has shown how *Cligès* finds a natural place against the literary background of the 1180s. Its Ovidianism is of this period, and the literary fashion for the Greek world, from Sicily eastwards, that led to the writing of *Ipomedon*, *Protheselaus*, and *Florimont*, as well as the refurbishing of *Athis*, is clearly the same movement as caused the exploitation of *Athis* in *Cligès*. Of all Chrétien's romances, this is the one about which we should have no doubt as to the literary company it keeps.

It can be seen that I have assigned Chrétien's career in the Arthurian field to a stage in the writing of romance when its authors had progressed in the art of invention, and were practising the construction of poetic narrative out of diverse material. Gautier d'Arras is decidedly less adept at this in his earlier romance than in *Ille et Galeron*. Coming after this, Chrétien's mastery becomes more understandable. Again, the previous dating of Chrétien, which sets his first Arthurian romance at 1170, means that there is a long lapse of time before other writers of courtly romance followed his lead, and indeed Hue de Rotelande would appear to reject it when he disguised the Arthurian material he used and located it in the Mediterranean. But, if the series by Chrétien is taken to begin about 1185, the problem disappears.

O virgo, cujus architectatione praesignii humanum genus virtutum ingreditur thalamum (*De planctu Naturae*, ed. Wright, ii, 514 f., but emending *Largitas ait* to *Largitati ait*, cf. Migne, ccx, 478). From an anecdote we know that Alain, when he taught knights at Montpellier, proved *multis rationibus* that the essence of high birth and courtliness is *liberalitas dandi et benefaciendi*, see A. Lecoy de la Marche, *Anecdotes tirées du recueil inédit d'Etienne de Bourbon* (1877), 246. Alain was in Southern France in the 1180s (p. 263 below).

75 In *De planctu Naturae*, Nature spends some time insisting that the abuse of her gifts by which "a torrent of wealth is drawn off into a desert of poverty" should not be mistaken for Largitas (*De planctu Naturae*, ed. Wright, ii, 515 f.).

Disapproval of unrealistic subject-matter is evident when Gautier d'Arras repudiates the example set by unbelievable lays, and Hue de Rotelande casts a similar jibe at Walter Map, that he knows well *de mentir l'art*[76]—an allusion to his telling of fairy-tales and legends, which we find in his *De nugis curialium*. When Marie de France composed her Breton lays with their marvels, she went against this current. A similar one must have been flowing away from the production of sophisticated romance in the form of an Arthurian *conte d' aventure*, to judge by Hue de Rotelande's avoidance of it, and Chrétien's compromise with the *roman byzantin* in *Cligès*, after having already composed the purely Arthurian *Erec*. Chrétien, starting on his series when the 1180s were well under way, becomes the poet who, while other romancers of his day provided a setting that would seem historically plausible for their inventions, *les aventures k'avyndrent a l'ancien tens*,[77] considered adventure in the Arthurian world as a suitable subject for sustained treatment in courtly romance,[78] and turned the tide for the full flood thereafter.

---

76 *Ille et Galeron*, P 932-6; *Ipomedon*, 7174-86.

77 *Ipomedon*, 4 f.

78 E. Köhler, *Trobadorlyrik und höfischer Roman* (1962), 13, sees in Chrétien's attack on the retellings of the *conte Erec*, at the beginning of *Erec et Enide*, an attempt to distract criticism from his own work, as *fabula* instead of *historia*.

4

Significance

From his first Arthurian romance Chrétien was acquainted with the Latin allegories of his learned contemporary Alain de Lille, with which he was so familiar that he adapted both passages and philosophy to his purpose. Considering the strength of Alain's influence in the highlights of description that signal the climaxes of Erec's career—the first meeting with Enide, and the coronation —there is an interesting question that must now be raised. Are the resemblances to Alain in *Erec* limited to the decoration of narrative for the purpose of stressing significant stages of the romance, or are there any connections that are more fundamental?

For example, the similarity between Enide and Prudencia is not restricted to dress, but extends to innate nature. The heroine's virtues are thus described by her father:

> "Molt est bele, mez mialz asez
> vaut ses savoirs que sa biautez:
> onques Dex ne fist rien tant saige
> ne qui tant soit de franc coraige."
>
> (*Erec et Enide*, 537 ff.)

His daughter is very beautiful, but her wisdom surpasses her beauty—if she is Nature's most beautiful work, what must her wisdom then be like!—and God has never made any so wise. Beauty here decidedly takes second place to wisdom. In another romance they would have been equally superlative. What we have in *Erec* is the doubly emphatic ascription to Enide of the quality which in *Anticlaudianus* is personified by Prudencia, Mistress of the Liberal Arts, she who rolls all human accomplishments into one, and whose name and *savoir* are one and the same thing.

Wisdom is not the sole virtue that the heroine of *Erec* is said to possess to a very high degree, so that she epitomizes moral quality. The resemblance of her poor clothing to the symbolic dress of Prudencia, who like her is a most beautiful maiden, draws one's attention to this aspect, the expression of inner self in the clothes that Enide wears. Then, too, in bearing a garment embroidered with the Quadrivium, Erec at his coronation is symbolically equipped with the knowledge of the world and its workings. So with both hero and heroine there is a symbolism inherent in dress. This is the technique of Alain's allegories, where symbolic robes proliferate, and it prepares one to see in *Erec* a layer of meaning such as is present in Alain's works.

47

The Summarium of *Anticlaudianus* explains:

Ex hiis liquet que sit materia huius autoris in hoc opere. Est tamen materia duplex, una historialis, alia mistica, quod satis diligenti liquet lectori, et quia circa materiam versatur intentio, per materiam intentionis comparatur noticia. . . . Finis sive utilitas est humane nature cognitio.[1]

(From our summary it is clear what material the author deals with in this work. Now the material is of dual aspect, one narrative and the other profound, which is sufficiently evident to the careful reader, and as an intended significance is imparted to the material, from the material is obtained the notion of this significance. . . . The purpose or benefit of this book is the comprehension of human nature.)

We should compare how at the beginning of *Le Chevalier de la Charrete* Chrétien tells us that Marie de Champagne gave him the *matiere* and *sen*, in other words indicated not only what was to be the narrative subject (*materia historialis*) but also the slant to be imparted,[2] to produce the deeper subject (*materia mistica*) of the work. The *finis sive utilitas* that the Countess intended could have been the comprehension of a human nature, that of the courtly lover as Marie understood it. In the opening of *Erec*, Chrétien conveys that he is doing his best to carry out the requirements both of narrative art (*bien dire*)[3] and of effective instruction (*bien aprandre*). What notion of significance arises from the material of *Erec*, it will be shown, is in harmony with Alain's philosophy.

How such a connection can exist between the Doctor Universalis and a romance of love and adventure has to do with the kind of philosopher that Alain was. His allegories stem from the tradition of the school of Chartres, which held an important place in the classical revival of this period, and was the chief centre of medieval Platonism. The quality of Alain's humanistic thought owes much to this school. As a disciple he took over the cosmological role of Nature from Bernardus Silvestris, who had dramatized it in *De mundi universitate*. But Alain infused the figure with extra force, by making explicit a moral aspect, thus conveying that what is right and proper is so according to natural law.

In *Anticlaudianus* Alain projects the ideal of a perfect human, whose creation is shown as carried out by Nature with the help of her court, an assembly of Virtues who sum up what is best in the nature of the world and circumstances or in human nature, since what is regarded as most in harmony with Nature is the perfect. The main members of Nature's assembly are Concordia (Harmony),

1 *Anticlaudianus*, p. 201.

2 Cf. E. Vinaver, *The Rise of Romance* (1971), 16: [In Gottfried von Strassburg, *sín*, which is cognate with *sen*,] "could connote any kind of deliberate intervention on the author's part intended to give the work the sort of direction, slant, or significance that he thought appropriate".

3 Cf. the illustration of the sense "dichten" given for the verb *dire* by Tobler-Lommatzsch, *Altfranzösisches Wörterbuch*, ii (1938). We find an example of it in *Guillaume d'Angleterre*, see p. 32 n. 21 above.

Copia (Riches), Favor (Approbation), Juventus (Youth), Risus (Laughter), Pudor (Modesty), Modestia (Moderation), Racio (Reason), Honestas (Noble Nature), Decus (Honour), Prudencia (Wisdom), Pietas (Kindness), Fides (Troth), an anonymous Virtue—and so particularly important—who is Largitas (Generosity), and Nobilitas (High Birth). Nature fashions a most beautiful body, Concordia joins it to a perfect soul provided by God, and the rest of the court shower the creation with their endowments, the Liberal Arts bestowing theirs immediately after Prudencia. Thus Alain's perfect man is one who catches up ideals from the classics and contemporary society, and is a model of a *verray, parfit gentil knyght* for a twelfth-century Golden Age.

Similarly, human perfection is embodied in *Erec*. The ideals principally arise from descriptions and remarks of a direct nature, and the behaviour of the characters and the reactions of others, whereas in *Anticlaudianus* they are expressed in personifications, which are characterized and described, and shown showering the creation with their gifts. The difference in presentation is the distinction between romance and allegory. The notion of the significance is comparable.

Erec is of great renown, and he is very handsome, very valiant, very noble, and not yet twenty-five. Never has any of his age shown more valour. "What can one say of his excellencies?" We see him in the first encounter—when he accompanies Guinevere in the forest during a hunt and they meet Yder, whose dwarf strikes him—showing prudence because he himself is not armed, as he retires without a murmur:

> Folie n'est pas vaselages;
> de ce fist molt Erec que sages:
> rala s'an, que plus n'i ot fet.
>
> (*Erec et Enide*, 231 ff.)

Compare Alain, on Racio's gift: "She advises the youth with elderly admonition, and bestows an old man's character on the youth. She teaches, accordingly, that he should do nothing hastily, nor venture anything suddenly, but anticipate every deed by thought, deliberate before he acts, and carefully weigh his own actions first" (VII, 170 ff.).

Erec's valour is indeed deliberate. He explains to Guinevere his intention of following the knight until he may obtain arms and punish him, and he firmly carries out this resolve, as he pursues him all the way to Laluth and enters against him in a contest. It is an illustration of Racio again: "that he should not relapse into wavering impulses, but his resolute mind press on firmly with a single good one" (VII, 184 f.). The trait of knowing his own mind is a noteworthy characteristic of Erec, and is further illustrated by his resolute spurning of the Count of Laluth's invitation—pressed twice—because Erec will not leave his poor host, who has been good to him; and by his firm insistence, again upheld against the Count, that his host's daughter, whose hand has been given him, should come to Arthur's court wearing not borrowed fine clothes, but her own old and worn garments, so that the donation of rich dress may be reserved for Guinevere to make. Firmness of resolution is a quality that others recognize in Erec, and the Count of Laluth realizes he cannot deflect him from his resolve.

The heroine, like the perfect human in *Anticlaudianus*, is Nature's highest achievement, in an act of creation so uniquely successful that she was astonished at her own accomplishment. And this maiden's beauty was made to set a standard, to be looked at in order that one may observe oneself in it like a mirror—the purpose that in Alain's poem the work of Nature and the Virtues is meant to serve, as they judge their own qualities by its model. Yet her superlative loveliness is surpassed by her wisdom, and God has made no-one so wise nor with a nobler disposition.

She holds back and blushes at her first sight of Erec, and then, as the only child, carries out the honours due to a guest by both the sons and daughters of a well-mannered household, stabling Erec's horse with proper care, and leading the hero by the hand into the house.[4] She says nothing. It is in a poor condition that she lives, and she is dressed in fine but old and worn clothing with holes, yet she is of high lineage, and no baron in the country would not wish to marry her. But she is the apple of her father's eye, and he thinks her fit for a better match. When he bestows her on Erec, she says not a word, though she is delighted at the prospect of such a worthy, courteous, and royal husband. For the contest with the knight he had encountered in the forest—Erec's challenge takes the form of putting the maiden in against the other's lady for the beauty prize of a sparrowhawk—she duly sees to his arming, and then mounts a horse to accompany him. But unlike the elegant fairy mistress of Marie de France's *Lanval*, who rides with a rich mantle over her white *chainse* and chemise, Chrétien's heroine goes in hers without a coat, her hair loose, and with poor harness, asking for nothing.

At home, after Erec's victory, when she shows greater joy than any damsel ever had for her lord, we are given no word from her. The whole argument as to whether she should wear her old dress to Arthur's court is carried out without her expressing any opinion. She travels there just as she is, with nothing of value except the sparrowhawk Erec has won for her:

> nule autre richesce n'an porte.
>
> (*Erec et Enide*, 1424)

And the couple journey together in silence and mutual admiration.

On their arrival, Erec tells Guinevere that he brings the maiden just as she was given to him, and draws attention to her clothing. But on the ground of neither beauty nor birth does he have the right to reject her hand in marriage:

> "Ne por biauté ne por linage
> ne doi je pas le mariage
> de la pucele refuser."
>
> (*Erec et Enide*, 1545 ff.)

4 Cf. *Le Chevalier de la Charrete*, 2526-39; also *Perceval*, Second Continuation, 24474-8.

Poverty is the reason for the state of her attire, he says, and he has not wished her to wear any other garment until it is seen by Guinevere. The Queen agrees he has done right to bring the maiden to her thus. In other words, she has been brought to court in this condition in order that the Queen should fully appreciate her unique combination of beauty and high birth with humility.[5]

The maiden is richly attired by Guinevere's attendants, so that she looks even lovelier than before, and as she stands speechless before the court, blushing with shame, she is recognized by the King and Queen as the most graceful in the world, and acclaimed by all as having more beauty than the sun has radiance.

The perfection of the young couple is evident to all, whose eyes they attract, whose admiration is expressed, and these two ideal beings admire each other. They are fully equal in courtesy, beauty, and graciousness, one in manner, character, and talent, so that nobody who sees them can decide who is the better, the fairer, or the wiser. They have the same disposition and suit each other perfectly. Never have two such beautiful figures come together in marriage.

Erec dutifully presents wealth and castles to his bride's poor parents, and the wedding is celebrated with much festivity and great joy. After the occasion, Erec gives a scintillating display in a tournament, where all come to fear him and he is judged the best. He is now of such great fame that people speak of no-one but him. No man has better gifts—so runs Chrétien's panegyric—he is in looks an Absolon, in speech a Solomon, in spirit a lion, and in all to do with giving and spending an Alexander.

He takes his wife back with him to his own country, Estregales, where his father is King, and whose inhabitants receive them with great joy. There the couple go first to the church. Erec kneels in prayer before the altar of the

---

5 The Guiot MS. has:

> "Ne por biauté ne por linage
> ne quier je pas le mariage
> de la dameisele esposer."

But the reading of the other MSS. is supported by this echo:

> "Ne por biauté ne por lingnage
> ne le devés vos laissier mie."
>
> (*Li Biaus Descouneus*, 6186 f.)

As in *Erec*, beauty and birth provide no grounds for not marrying the lady, as they would if she did not possess them. The comparable passage in *Guillaume d'Angleterre*, 1158 f., is more straightforward:

> "Por pekié ne por parenté
> Ne lairai que jou ne vos prenge."

Here grounds for not marrying the lady are brushed aside.

There is some parallel between Enide and a much later paragon of moral excellence, Samuel Richardson's Pamela, a lowly heroine who is told by the squire to be "only dressed as you are" in her humble garb, so that "they will perceive you owe nothing to dress" (*Pamela*, Everyman's Library 683, i, 242).

Crucifix and makes magnificent donations, while Enide prays at the altar of Our Lady for an heir and gives her own splendid gifts,[6] with her right hand making the sign of the cross, as she retires, "in the manner of a well-educated woman". That day they are attended by knights and citizens and given many presents; no king has ever been gazed at with greater joy in his kingdom or received with such delight as is Erec, and people show even more joy with Enide, because of her great beauty and, above all, because of her noble nature.

She is seated on a silk cloth from Thessaly, surrounded by her ladies, and as the lustrous gem outshines the brown pebble, and the rose excels the poppy, so is Enide more beautiful than any lady or damsel to be found in the world, even if one were to search everywhere, so noble and worthy is she of being honoured, so wise and gracious in her words, so full of sweetness and charm. No-one can ever detect in her any folly, mischief, or villainy. She is so well-schooled in good manners that she excels in all the best qualities that a lady should have, in generosity as well as wisdom. All love her for her noble disposition, and whoever can do her a service regards himself as greatly honoured. No-one speaks ill of her, and no-one has cause to do so, for there is no lady with a better way of life. And with this encomium the idealistic opening phase of the romance is brought to a resounding close.

So with justice one can say that so far in *Erec* ideals of human perfection are projected, applied to both sexes, in the persons of the hero and the heroine, whose qualities have much in common with the *virtutes naturales* infused into the creation in *Anticlaudianus*. They are both blessed with great beauty—in Enide created in a scene and with a purpose similar to those in Alain's poem— with youth (Juventus) and with high birth (Nobilitas). They have the approbation and admiration of all (Favor), the possession of great honour (Decus), and joy (Risus) attends Erec's victory over Yder at the contest for the sparrow-hawk, the wedding ceremony, and the arrival of the wedded pair in Estregales. The marriage is endowed with princely riches (Copia) and liberality is exercised (Largitas), while the couple are in manner, character, talent, and beauty perfectly harmonious (Concordia). They are both possessed of wisdom (Prudencia), and at the end of the work we discover the symbolism of Erec's coronation robe embroidered with the Quadrivium, and described in Alain's manner. Chrétien sharpens the gift of firmness and resolution (Racio) in the man: in the woman he displays modesty (Pudor), a noble nature (Honestas), and un-assuming conduct (Modestia). The poverty in which Enide lives before her marriage, her poor dress, her humble, modest and restrained behaviour, her undemanding nature, her wordlessness, all make her the representative of the opposite pole to arrogance, ostentation and presumptuous speech.

We know how Erec exemplifies Pietas in relation to Enide from what she says near the end of the romance, that he, a prince, took her when she was

---

6 These offerings are made only in the Guiot MS., and may be due to revision of the original text by Chrétien, see *Erec*, xlix. In that case, one should associate them with the religious note that emerges later in Chrétien's career (p. 31 above).

poor and naked, and through him such honour has come that never was any such granted to a poor and helpless girl. There is Pietas again in Erec's gifts to his bride's poor parents, Enide's dutiful behaviour, her treatment of Erec as a guest, both their pious obsequies and donations to the Church, and generally in courteous conduct. This is not contradicted by Erec's forceful rejection of the Count of Laluth's repeated invitation, for "leave me in peace" is a phrase that conveys a firm man's refusal to be turned from a resolve,[7] in this case (illustrating Fides) to be faithful to his host, who has given him his daughter.

Common ground between the philosophy of *Erec* and that of Alain is not limited to *Anticlaudianus*, but also exists with *De planctu Naturae*. This allegory is aimed against the evils in human character, which are regarded as crimes against Nature, and Man's attitude towards love is treated as the crucial aspect of his behaviour. *De planctu Naturae* conveys a philosophy of love which deserves study in relation to *Erec*.

It is well illustrated in a myth of Venus narrated by Nature.[8] Even as God appointed her as His deputy, so Nature set Venus as sub-deputy, assisted by a husband Hymen and son Cupid, that she should toil hard at forming the various shapes of earthly beings, regularly applying hammers (male parts) to her anvils (female parts). Cupid has tremendous powers, brings some people into a dire state of mind, and so fills them with frenzy that they change their nature, commit crimes, and are seized by perverted love. But there is nothing wrong with the essential nature of Cupid, which goes awry through excess:

"Non enim originalem Cupidinis naturam in honestate redarguo, si circum-
scribatur frenis modestiae, si habenis temperantiae castigetur, si non geminae
excursionis limites deputatos evadat, vel in nimium tumorem ejus calor
ebulliat."

(De planctu Naturae, ed. Wright, ii, 474)
("For I do not deny that Cupid's intrinsic nature is honourable, if it is curbed by the bridle of reasonable behaviour, if it is restrained by the reins of sobriety, if it does not go beyond the limits assigned to the scope for activity by two, or its ardour boil up to too much excitement.")

Nature assigned to Venus right and proper hammers, and appointed for her employment excellent workshops, enjoining that by putting the hammers to use in these she should faithfully devote herself to making images of things, and not let the hammers stray from the anvils. But Venus, tiring of her constant work, found relaxation in adultery with Antigamus (enemy of marriage), thus debasing the nature of the act by misdirecting it:

"liberale opus in mechanicum, regulare in anomalum, civile in rusticum
inciviliter immutavit, meumque disciplinatum inficiata praeceptum, malleos
ab incudis exhaeredans consortio, adulterinis damnavit incudibus."

(De planctu Naturae, ed. Wright, ii, 480)

---

7 Cf. King Arthur in *Perceval*, 2822.   8 *De planctu Naturae*, ed. Wright, ii, 470 ff.

("She transformed a noble and spontaneous act into the vulgar and not genuine,[9] the normal into the irregular, the courteous discourteously into the boorish, and refusing to follow my instilled direction she deprived the hammers of their right to associate with the proper anvils, and made them perform their office on illicit anvils.")

So Venus gave birth to a bastard, and now had sons of very different natures. By Hymen, who is Nature's brother and of very superior stock, Venus begot Cupid; to Antigamus, of low birth, she bore Jocus (Sport).[10] In Cupid the politeness of his father Hymen's courtesy shines forth: in Jocus lurks the boorishness of Antigamus's lack of good manners. Cupid dwells by silvery springs, overlaid with the silver of white lustres: Jocus continually frequents a region suffering from perpetual drought. Jocus pitches his tents in a desert plain: a wooded valley gives great pleasure to Cupid. Jocus incessantly stays all night indoors: Cupid continues day and night in the open air. Cupid wounds whom he hunts with golden hunting-spears: Jocus pierces whom he strikes with iron darts. Cupid intoxicates his guests with nectar, which has no bitterness: Jocus's are ruined by the sour drink of wormwood.

To this myth should be added scenes packed with symbolism. Hymen arrives, and is given the seat of honour at the right hand of Nature. In his face no trace of feminine weakness stands out, but only the strength of manly authority, and yet it does not depart from any grace of beauty. His hair is skilfully combed, but arranged within due bounds, lest it should seem to sink into feminine voluptuousness, and the fringe is well trimmed so that the open forehead is not hidden. Rings, gemmed with constellations of stones, making the hands bright with an extraordinary blaze of light, give the effect of a new-risen sun. His dress is covered with embroidery, in which may be dimly perceived— through the soot of age—the holy faith of marriage, the peaceful unity of wedlock, the unbreakable yoke of a wedding, the indissoluble bond of the wedded, the ceremony of rejoicing that resounds to begin the nuptials, the sweetness of melody solemnizing them, the laughing community of guests that attend and the joy of the general public.[11] Hymen's appearance is followed by that of the Virtues—Chastity, Temperance, Generosity, and Humility—who together with Nature and Hymen form an assembly sorrowing at Man's transgressions. Then Hymen, as "excellent executor of this mission, with whom the stars of glittering eloquence shine, and the requisites of the judicial assembly are deposited",[12] bears Nature's letter to her other self, Genius, asking him to pronounce an anathema expelling from her congregation all those who break

---

9 Cf. Hugh of St. Victor, *Didascalicon*, I, x: *opus humanum, quod natura non est, sed imitatur naturam, mechanicum, id est, adulterinum nominatur.*

10 Cf. Horace, *Odes*, I, ii, 34, where Venus has two figures flying round her, Cupid and Jocus. The latter appears as an attendant of Luxuria in Prudentius, *Psychomachia*, 433, and is thus an aspect of Indulgence.

11 *De planctu Naturae*, ed. Wright, ii, 502-4.

12 *Ibid.*, ii, 510 f.

the laws of Nature. In the interlude between the departure of Hymen and his return with Genius, Nature criticizes a certain man, much endowed with her gifts, which are abused by the laxity of his morals. Such a man as this, therefore, she wants Genius to excommunicate. His curses call upon men punishments that answer to their sins, and the anathema begins:

"By the authority of the transcendent Substance, and of His eternal design, and also the approbation of the celestial band—both Nature concurring and the other subsidiary powers attending in support—let him be severed from the kiss of heavenly love, and as the fault of ingratitude demands let him be degraded from the favours of Nature, let him be isolated from the unanimous assembly of things that are natural, everyone who turns awry the course of Venus."[13]

Nature's complaint is that she has endowed men's nature with so many privileges and beauties only to have them abused with the ugliness of lust, so that she means to seek punishment answering to their crimes, and to achieve the aim of having virtuous men who honour the feature of propriety in love: *ut pudici homines pudoris characterem revereantur*.[14] Alain's charge is that marriage has fallen on evil days, because of the pre-occupation with perverted and illicit love. This is not through any condemnation of desire in itself. On the contrary, he holds that there is a genuine, normal, and rightful quality about the sexual act in marriage. But love is evil and degrading when out of control and misdirected, and the unsatisfying, sordid, lustful, and bitter nature of sexual abuse contrasts with the delight, wholesomeness, nobility, and sweetness of honourable love.

The opposition is carried into the courtly field, for by her adultery with Antigamus the act was transformed by Venus from the courteous discourteously into the boorish, and in the real Cupid the politeness of his father Hymen's courtesy shines forth, but there lurks in the pseudo-Cupid the boorishness of Antigamus's lack of good manners:

"In isto, paternae civilitatis elucescit urbanitas; in illo, paternae suburbanitatis tenebrescit rusticitas."

(De planctu Naturae, ed. Wright, ii, 481)

In other words, illicit love is stamped by its very nature as uncourtly, and real courtly love can only be connected with marriage. The figure of Hymen conveys how dignified and splendid this state should be, not voluptuous, because held within bounds, yet not lacking all the attributes of a beautiful and glorious condition of life.

Nature chooses Hymen as her means of bringing Genius to bear upon Man, and the significance of this is brought out by the symbolism of Genius's activity, who arrives tracing on a scroll the images of things which live momentarily,

13 *Ibid.*, ii, 520 f.   14 *Ibid.*, ii, 462-4.

and as often die away. As he provides them with the life of their kind, they pass from the pictured semblance to the truth of their being. With his right hand he draws images of those who exemplify good genius, but evil genius with his left, which forsakes the task of true representation to produce such an image as that of Paris subdued by the voluptuousness of lewd love.[15] Bernardus Silvestris had shown Genius, dedicated to the art and office of depicter, as applying the celestial Forms to the phenomenal world.[16] This is the pictorial art that he is exercising in De planctu Naturae, where he is assisted by Truth— born when the Eternal Idea greeted Matter, considering the reflection of Forms —and hindered by Falsehood, which mars Truth's pictures.[17] To the activity of Genius is allied that of Nature in Anticlaudianus, whose home is decorated with portraits of the great men she had made, but also of those in whose creation one might think she had amused herself or gone astray, such as Paris, his spirit broken by love and ruined in Venus's fire.[18] According to C. S. Lewis, Alain's Genius is the patron of generation, as distinct from a man's higher self, and this accounts for his interest in maintaining the laws of love.[19] However, the art of Alain's figure expresses good and evil genius, which throws a different light on the significance of having Genius pronounce the anathema. He is Nature's other self, a cosmic Genius who embodies in each person that individual's specific nature.[20] The curse of this Genius falls on men whose endowments are abused by the transgressions for which they deserve to lose the favours of Nature—and first among these sins is to turn awry the course of Venus.

It can be seen that De planctu Naturae counters the denigration of marriage and its carnal relations by the Catharist heresy,[21] as well as the idealization of illicit love. Indeed, the manifestations of the latter in the literature of that time have attracted much attention. However, the normal pattern of romance in Chrétien's day is that love leads to marriage, which is in fact often its aim in Ovid, who was regarded as the master of love literature. And, as soon as the flower of courtly love came to romance, marriage is promised on the same terms:

---

15 De planctu Naturae, ed. Wright, ii, 517 f.

16 De mundi universitate, 38/89 ff.

17 De planctu Naturae, ed. Wright, ii, 518 f.

18 Anticlaudianus, I, 119 ff.

19 C. S. Lewis, The Allegory of Love (1936), 361 ff.; Studies in Medieval and Renaissance Literature (1966), 169 ff.

20 For a survey of material bearing on Genius in De planctu Naturae, see G. Raynaud de Lage, Alain de Lille (1951), 89 ff. Writing on this figure, W. Wetherbee, "The Function of Poetry in the 'De Planctu Naturae' of Alain de Lille", Traditio XXV (1969), 112 ff., observes that Alain certainly unites the procreative function with that of the cosmic bestowal of form. Genius is like Nature's mirror, see De planctu Naturae, ed. Wright, ii, 511. In M. T. d'Alverny, Alain de Lille: textes inédits (1965), 205 n. 36, 228, are these definitions by Alain: genius enim interpretatur natura; genius enim natura vel Deus nature dicitur.

21 See p. 255 f. below.

"A femme vos esposerai,
Sor tote rien vos amerai.
Ma dame sereiz e m'amie,[22]
De mei avreiz la seignorie:
Tant entendrai a vos servir
Que tot ferai vostre plaisir."

(Roman de Troie, 1433 ff.)

Long before, in Gaimar's story of Havelok, a husband and wife are *ami* and *amie*, whom he also calls *dame*. And again it is Ovidian to treat a married couple as lovers. In the courtly *Roman de Troie* there is great love in marriage, *de fin cuer e de bone amor* (29037), and the famous lovers Paris and Helen are married. More attention is paid to marital love in *Athis et Prophilias*, in the original form of which the happy couple love each other with such a deep love (*bone amor*) that they dress alike (1817 ff.), and each husband goes out with his wife as *s'amie* (5531). In *Eracle*, the Emperor loves with true love (*fine amour*) a wife who, it is said, may be kept a *bone amie* (faithful) to him, and the later version of *Athis*, even if it gives the married heroines *amis* who bear their love gifts in battle, insists on their fidelity and their love for their husbands, which is a true love (*fine amors*) that cannot be broken.[23] In spite of all this, the treatment of marital love in *Ille et Galeron* so stands out that the reflection of *De planctu Naturae* by a Nature topos in this romance[24] assumes particular significance.

Gautier d'Arras turned a story of a husband's infidelity to his wife (cf. Marie de France's *Eliduc*) into the portrayal of their mutual loyalty and love. As Fourrier has said:

Si l'on peut douter que *Cligès* soit à tous égards un *Anti-Tristan*, il est en revanche certain qu'*Ille et Galeron* est un *Anti-Eliduc*.[25]

Gautier must have set out to contradict the courtly love theory represented by the ruling of Marie de Champagne that true love is not possible between husband and wife, and the judgement pronounced by Ermengarde of Narbonne that the affection between a married couple and the true love of lovers are of totally different nature.[26] For *Ille et Galeron* regards marriage as so fully within the domain of courtly love that not only is the operation of its principles displayed within the wedded state, but the plot is basically the application to marriage of two precepts which are also reported by Andreas Capellanus, one as a judgement by the Lady of Narbonne that a lover who suffers a grievous injury,

---

22 In the original form of *Athis*, when Bilas comes for his promised bride, *s'amie et sa dame la claime* (T 3976).

23 *Eracle*, 3017, 3050; *Athis*, 15391-8, 18903-6.

24 See p. 6 above.

25 A. Fourrier, *Le courant réaliste dans le roman courtois en France au moyen-âge* (1960), i, 285.

26 For these rulings, reported by Andreas Capellanus, see J. J. Parry, *The Art of Courtly Love* (1941), 106 f., 171.

such as the loss of an eye, while fighting bravely, far from being expected to lose the love of his lady has a claim on it; and the other as Rule of Love 31, that nothing prevents a man being loved by two women.[27]

The situation of *l'homme entre deux femmes* was in Gautier's source. *Eliduc* shows that the other woman's claim to the husband's love is superior to that of the wife, by having her recognize this fact in retiring to a convent so that he can marry his sweetheart. Gautier's own earlier romance, *Eracle*, has the lover's claim to the Emperor's wife similarly recognized as the greater, when the husband surrenders her to him. But in *Ille et Galeron* the insistence is on the inviolability of the marriage bond, and the law that husband and wife should love one another, which lovers have often broken.[28] The love of the other woman for the hero is thus not allowed to infringe on the marriage. We are given a picture of marital love deeper than any before in romance: husband and wife are not just faithful *ami* and *amie* who love each other, but there is full demonstration of their mutual love and fidelity, which is put to the test and proved. His love for her is *amor fine*, but unlike *Eracle*, where it only gives rise to jealous fears (3005 ff.), here its nature is defined as one which commands that love should be directed towards one person alone (cf. Rule of Love 3, that no-one can be bound by a double love),[29] and makes the lover cleave to the beloved. When the wife eventually carries out a vow to enter a convent, leaving the hero in a state of grief, then—even as the morning headache, after drinking wine the night before, is to be cured by more wine—only *fine amors* can take away the pain given by the loss of one's sweetheart and lover (*s'amie et sa drue*). It is thus that a mutual relationship of true love can develop with the other woman, bringing about the hero's second marriage, with another bridal night full of such delight as cannot be recounted. None would believe but lovers (*amis o amie*) who have experienced a glorious night like it.[30]

Again, *Cligès* goes beyond *Athis et Prophilias* in its treatment of marital love. Chrétien has the Queen counselling Alexandre and Soredamor to live in marriage and honour in order to preserve their love,[31] which is a rebuttal of non-marital relations. And at the end of *Cligès* there is stress on the marriage retaining all of the relationship of lovers, and even improving on it: "of his sweetheart he has made his lady, and calls her sweetheart and lady (*amie et dame*), and so she loses nothing of the state of being his sweetheart, nor does he either of being treated as hers. And each day saw their love grow stronger."[32] This explicitly contradicts the view we find in Andreas Capellanus, in his chapter on how love may come to an end, that if lovers marry love is violently put to flight; and also in the judgement which he reports, that a woman who marries her lover is no longer bound to him by love.[33] However, in *Cligès* the basic sense of propriety about love and marriage is allowed to be affected by sympathy for love in a situation of questionable morality. In *Athis et Prophilias*, where

27 See Fourrier, *op. cit.*, i, 285-9.   28 *Ille*, 3719-39.
29 Parry, *op. cit.*, 184.   30 *Ille*, 2534-43, 3892-3901, 4408-23, 5755-61.
31 *Cligès*, 2266-9.   32 *Ibid.*, 6633-9.   33 Parry, *op. cit.*, 156, 175.

one friend gives up his wife to the other from the nuptial night, the infringement of moral law is recognized: in *Cligès*, it is held to be mitigated by the married heroine managing to preserve her body for her lover alone. That he who has the heart should also have the body is a criticism both of the marriage of convenience and of carnal relations with two, but the disregard of the marriage bond in *Cligès* means that the strong moral sense of *Ille et Galeron* is lacking. To find such an outlook on love fully present in Chrétien, one must look earlier in his career.[34]

In *Erec*, the attitude to love is coloured by a distinctive element. The couple do not pass through love throes, the relationship being so curbed with propriety in the idealistic opening phase of the romance that the hero hardly addresses the heroine, she does not seem ever to have spoken to him, and he asks her hand of her father and she is not consulted. Cupid is so bridled that for a long time there is no sign of desire. The love at first indicated is only such that Erec's strength is increased at the sight of Enide praying for him during the battle against Yder for the sparrowhawk, and she rejoices at his victory and the prospect of marrying such a worthy, courteous, and royal husband. Then the ride to Arthur's court shows us not typical lovers and amorous declaration, but a picture of mutual admiration, delight, and silence. Erec cannot look at her enough, for the more he gazes at her the more she pleases him, and he cannot refrain from kissing. He feels joy in keeping close and feeding his eyes upon her nose, face, and mouth, all of which he finds so sweet that it touches his heart. He admires her all the way down to the hips, gazing at her chin and white neck, her flanks and her waist, her arms and her hands. And the damsel looks at the young man with no less interest, admiring him, as he does her, with a heart as loyal as his.

When we hear of Erec's impatience at delay, it is Cupid gathering strength just before the wedding. And then on the nuptial night Cupid exerts full power, and Chrétien launches into an epithalamium. Enide[35] is not removed from the bed and Brangien substituted. And the hunted stag panting with thirst does not so desire water, nor the famished sparrowhawk so willingly answer the call, as Erec and Enide do when it comes to the time for them to lie in each other's

---

34 The non-Arthurian romance of *Guillaume d'Angleterre*, by a Chrétien who may be our poet, has an outlook on the way to that of *Ille et Galeron*. Both have a true love between a married couple, the wife is devoted to the husband, and, when each has lost the other, one is loved by another party, and in the end the husband and the wife are happily reunited, very movingly in *Guillaume d'Angleterre*. Here the triangle is completed by another man, and a marriage takes place with him, though he does not have the heroine's heart, nor her body either, as in *Cligès*, this time because she gives the penance of chastity for a year as an excuse and he soon dies. *Guillaume d'Angleterre* shows some relation to *De planctu Naturae* (p. 11 n. 19 above), which probably began to influence poetry in 1181 (p. 255 below), and we have an old King as well as *li jovenes rois* (2057) of England, which is a phrase that was used of the crowned son of Henry II, Henry, who died in 1183. Compare 1181-83 for the date of *Ille et Galeron* (p. 37 above).

35 *Erec*, ed. Foerster, 2076: *Yseuz*.

arms. This night they make up for the time lost in waiting so long. They give each member its right. The eyes, which create the joy of love and send the message to the heart, play on what gives them such pleasure to see. After the message of the eyes comes the even greater sweetness of kisses which arouse love. Both make trial of this sweetness, and drink it in right to their hearts, so that with difficulty they separate their lips. Their sport begins with kisses, and the love between them makes the maiden so bold that she fears nothing and suffers all, no matter how much it hurts her. Before she rises, she has lost the name of maiden, and with morning she is a newly-wed lady (dame novele).

Isolt makes Brangien replace her secretly in bed with King Mark on her bridal night, because Isolt has lost her maidenhood to Tristan. With his allusion Chrétien contrasts chaste Enide with Isolt, whose adultery is an illustration of how Venus can make hammers perform their office in illicit forges. This night Erec and Enide make up for the time lost in waiting so long, that is, in restraint. With marriage, now eyes have a right to see more than Erec's had done on the ride to Arthur's court, when he could not forbear from inspecting Enide, from head to hip. Now lips have a right to what on that journey Erec had found it difficult to restrain himself from taking. And the ultimate member has its ultimate right. Erec and Enide fulfil Nature's injunction to Venus to put the right and proper hammers to use in the excellent forges.

Such hot love, so full of sexual desire, occurs nowhere else in the romance, and contrasts strongly with the earlier behaviour of the hero and the heroine. Against the background of De planctu Naturae, one sees that there has been emphasis on propriety as essential for the integrity of love, and now a prominent place given to the rightfulness of the marital act. For the romancer, embodying these ideas in narrative, there is a development in love, which grows, but is fittingly restrained, until its right and proper consummation. The scenes of the ride to Arthur's court and on the nuptial night are lyrical treatments of this theme, in which, so to speak, Cupid dwells by silvery springs overlaid with the silver of white lustres, wounding with golden hunting-spears and intoxicating with nectar, which has no bitterness.

The next stage of their love ushers in the countermotion of the romance, after the encomium on Enide sitting among her ladies in Estregales like a gem among pebbles. Everything is just perfect, until Erec begins to love Enide overmuch, and so lose all interest in martial occupations. Instead, he spends his time fondling and kissing, enjoying himself with her, and staying in bed with his wife till midday. He makes her s'amie et sa drue! Here, Chrétien has introduced a distinction that Gautier d'Arras did not make in Ille et Galeron.[36] By this phrase Chrétien means to indicate that Erec treats Enide like a paramour. With inordinate love, gone is propriety, and no longer do we have Hymen in whose countenance no trace of feminine weakness stands out, and whose hair is

36 Contrast also Guillaume d'Angleterre, 1091 ff., where the man who asks the heroine to be sa feme et s'amie, and to accept him as vostre signor et vostre ami, declares he will be all his life ses drus et ses amis.

arranged within due bounds lest it should seem to sink into voluptuousness. Erec has made his marriage a voluptuous condition, and with this abuse he becomes a Paris, that symbol of the warrior whose spirit is broken by love, and who, ruined in Venus's fire, takes love-making to be his war.[37] Now he is subject to the curse of Genius, as it were, that all who turn awry the course of Venus should be degraded from the favours of Nature, for there takes place a collapse in the whole fabric of idealism, which comes crashing about our ears. Erec's knightly reputation is lost, the love relationship wrecked when Enide rebukes him, and it is replaced by anger, menaces, and fear, as the couple are launched upon a series of dangerous adventures. A man's attitude to love is as crucial an aspect of his conduct in *Erec* as in *De planctu Naturae*.

In the course of their adventurous ride the fabric of idealism is gradually raised again, until eventually Erec shows his love for Enide once more. He embraces and kisses his wife, not in passion, but to comfort and assure her of his love. He addresses her affectionately as his sweet sister, and says he loves her more than ever before. He will be once more, as before, completely at her service. Thus is fulfilled the claim Enide made, in answer to an inquiry once whether she was Erec's wife or sweetheart, that she was both. Chrétien's distinction between *sa fame et s'amie* and *s'amie et sa drue* brings into marriage the contrast which in Alain exists between Cupid, son of Hymen, and Jocus, son of Antigamus. As Andreas Capellanus shows, it was a commonplace of theology that the too ardent lover of his own wife is an adulterer.[38] Erec has passed from such a level to one which gives all that Alain would wish. In the couple's relations there is courtesy as well as delight, wholesomeness, nobility, and sweetness in their love, as in the scene where Erec and Enide lie together in bed, full of affection such as belongs to the happily-married, embracing and kissing, and each vying with the other in pleasing the partner.

In the love theory of the troubadours the kind of behaviour towards the lady which makes the perfect lover is *mezura*. However, between it and love there is a natural tension, for the true lover, when he should be guided by *mezura*, finds himself being led instead into extravagance of feeling and behaviour.[39] Thus we see in Erec what corresponds to *mezura* when he demonstrates how courtly love exists in the wedded state. And even his previous harsh treatment of Enide finds some parallel in courtly love theory, as it is presented by Andreas Capellanus. He explains the processes by which a love may be increased after

37 *Anticlaudianus*, I, 179 f.
38 Parry, *op. cit.*, 103. Cf. C. S. Lewis, *The Allegory of Love* (1936), 15.
39 See D. R. Sutherland, "The Love Meditation in Courtly Literature", *Studies in Medieval French presented to A. Ewert* (1961), 165; F. Bogdanow, "The Love Theme in Chrétien de Troyes's 'Chevalier de la Charrette' ", *Modern Language Review* LXVII (1972), 51 f. Cf. the principle in Marie de France, *Equitan*, 17 ff.:

> Cil metent lur vie en nuncure
> Ki d'amur n'unt sen ne mesure;
> Tels est la mesure d'amer
> Que nuls n'i deit reisun garder.

it has been consummated, and one of these is when a lover shows that he is angry, for the partner falls at once into a great fear that this feeling which has arisen in the beloved may last for ever. Indeed, Andreas counsels lovers to pretend from time to time to be angry at each other, for if one lets the other see that he is angry and that something has made him indignant with his loved one, he can find out clearly how faithful the other one is. For a true lover is always in fear and trembling lest the anger of the beloved last for ever, and so, even if one lover does show that he is angry at the other without cause, this disturbance will last but a little while if they find out that their feelings for each other is really love. You must not think that by ruptures of this kind the bonds of affection and love are weakened; it is only clearing away the rust. What also increases love is pure jealousy, the nurse of love. This is not possible in marriage, as Andreas Capellanus explains, for a husband who is jealous cannot suspect his wife without the thought that such conduct on her part is shameful. In Chrétien, however, this problem is solved, for the husband entertains suspicion of his wife which is not a shameful one, because he is not jealous, and yet, just as with pure jealousy as described by Andreas, there is a true emotion whereby he greatly fears that the substance of their love may be weakened by his defect in serving the desires of the beloved, and he has anxiety lest his love may not be returned.[40]

Their great love indeed increases after all the trials Erec and Enide have experienced, he for her and she for him. These constitute their penance, in other words, for their transgressions against each other, which began with Erec breaking a law of true marital love as he discourteously altered their relationship. From now on their love is firmly grounded but not excessive. It is as if to such a harbour their course has led across an expanse where the guiding star of propriety in love brings safe passage, and the period when it was lacking stands out like a rock which caused damage that necessitated long salvage.

With their love relations thus firmly established, Erec decides to bring the adventurous ride to an end, and they set out to return to Arthur's court. But then he turns aside to undertake at Brandigan the dangerous adventure of the Joie de la Cort. They enter a marvellous garden, without wall or fence, but shut in on all sides so firmly by air that it might have been enclosed in iron. All through summer and winter there are flowers and fruits within, and the fruit is of such a magic nature that it may be eaten inside, but not taken out, because no-one can find the exit and leave the garden until the fruit is restored to its place. And there is no bird pleasing to man that does not sing there in large numbers, nor any medicinal spice or root not planted there in abundance.

Alone, Erec plunges deeper into the garden. This sight now meets his eyes, a lady of ravishing beauty sitting on a splendid couch, silver, with a cover of gold-embroidered cloth. Because he has approached her, Erec is opposed by a gigantic red knight, called Mabonagrain, whom he overcomes after a terrific

---

40 The sentiments are to be found in Parry, *op. cit.*, 102 f., 153, 158 f. Cf. pp. 230-37 below.

battle. The knight has lived with the damsel in the garden, and fought and killed all who came, but by Erec's victory this state of affairs comes to an end, and there is tremendous joy in Brandigan.

The episode is different in kind from the other adventures, because the combat takes place in a location which is unreal. The marvels impart symbolic power to the garden, and its attributes suggest a mental condition or state of life. Here, enclosed by insubstantial air, though as firmly as by iron, there is a terrestrial paradise of perpetual delights, from which no-one can issue without abandoning its fruits, only to be enjoyed inside it. The sight that meets Erec's eyes, a damsel of ravishing beauty sitting on a splendid couch, is like an emblem of a certain kind of life. We are not far from Alain's world of imagery, with its symbolic pictures and locations.

In the exchanges between the red knight and Erec after the battle, and between the damsel of the garden and Enide, we learn why it was inhabited by the mysterious couple. Mabonagrain has been at the court of Erec's father, and also at Laluth, and his lady is Enide's cousin, being the daughter of someone there who is her father's brother. The red knight says he and the damsel loved each other, and their love grew until one day, when he was dubbed knight in the garden by his uncle Evrain, King of Brandigan, she claimed a boon he had promised she could have at her own choice. She laid down that he was not to leave the garden until conquered by another knight, and in this way, because she believed him invincible, she thought to keep him imprisoned with her all the days of his life. It was thus she who forced him to act as he did. But the damsel tells quite a different story. She relates how Mabonagrain stayed at her father's house and began to love her, until he swore he would always do so and bring her to this garden. To it they stole away about a dozen years before in order to enjoy their love in secret. It was his own idea, and it pleased them both.

The only one who takes no pleasure in the ending of this state of life, the damsel of the garden, weeps many tears and is inconsolable, but shares the general joy when she has spoken with Enide. The heroine says that her *ami* married her, in such a way that her father knew all about it and her mother was greatly pleased. All her relatives were delighted. For Erec is so good a knight that better could not be found. He loves her much, she loves him more, and their love could not be greater. A prince, he took her when she was poor and naked, and through him such honour has come that never was such granted to a poor and helpless girl.

So the red knight and his damsel are comparable with Erec and Enide, and yet different. Comparison is clearly drawn. Mabonagrain had been in Estregales, the hero's homeland, and like him he went to Laluth and stayed with the father of his lady, who was Enide's cousin. But Erec married Enide, with the full approval of her parents, their love could not be greater, and through him such honour has come, whereas Mabonagrain and his damsel stole away to the secret pleasures of the garden, which he regards, in his disenchantment, as a state of bondage from which he has been released, and she, in her grief, as a promised bliss that did not last.

In the course of the adventures, other forms of love have already been illustrated. There is the amorous Count, who first tries, with attractive promises, to entice Enide to be his wife, and then takes to quite a different kind of persuasion when he threatens to kill Erec. As at the turning point with the hero, this is a case of love so affecting a man that it changes his nature, but much more detestably. When Erec is led to treat Enide as *s'amie et sa drue*, love subdues his military spirit. But so very lacking in integrity is the Count's love that not only does he make his offer to another's lady, but when she refuses he descends to threats, and even—here is the seizure by Cupid's frenzy that leads to crime[41]—goes so far as to attempt traitorous murder in order to obtain her, until, lying severely wounded at the hands of Erec, he comes to his senses, repents, and acknowledges how villainous he has been made by desire. Then there is the Count of Limors, who, when Erec is apparently dead, also proposes to make Enide his lady and will not accept her refusal, making her marry him by force. He soon threatens to punish her, because she will not obey him, and in fact strikes her, which causes the Count's own retainers to protest at their lord's behaviour. Here we have a parallel to Erec's treatment of Enide on the adventurous ride; but though the hero menaces, he never commits the crime of hitting her. Again, the Count's illogical assertion, that now they belong to each other he will do with her just as he pleases, expresses an attitude that seems to be implied by Erec's behaviour since the estrangement between himself and Enide. But the resemblance between the conduct of the hero and that of the Count is only superficial, and it is the courtly sentiment of service to the lady that Erec comes to state explicitly to his wife. And then the Count's claim that he has drawn Enide out of poverty and brought her to riches, whereby fortune has now raised her to great honour—it is Erec who has done this, and he never throws it in her face—underlines how this union mirrors that of the hero and the heroine as if in some distorting glass. These situations, in the episodes of the amorous Count and the Count of Limors, place the relations between Erec and Enide in proper perspective—they are never like these odious forms of love.

But here we have a condition of love in the garden which has its attractions. It shares features with the hero's both at the turning point and at this stage in the story, but it is neither the one nor the other, because it is outside marriage and a life of amorous dalliance co-exists with the exercise of prowess. The charmed circle of the marvellous garden, with the lady on a resplendent couch emblematic of the courtly nature of its illicit and secret delights, to the man a state of love bondage maintained as if in knightly service to the damsel, and to her a bliss promised to be lasting, an enticement that has been accepted, what is reflected in its mirror but the courtly love rejected by the Queen in *Cligès*, when she counsels Alexandre and Soredamor to live in marriage and honour

41 Compare the monstrous passion in *Philomena*, where Chrétien observes that it is no love which consists of losing one's reason: *N'est pas amors de forsener* (486).

to preserve their love? The form of courtly love that had non-marital relations exerted fascination on Chrétien's contemporaries, and that it was so attractive makes its picture the climax of Erec's adventures and the greatest danger of all.[42] Chrétien pits, as it were, the real Cupid against the pseudo-Cupid. From the episode, because it has symbolic power, the notion of such a significance arises with particular force.

Erec is well feasted and served to his heart's content with the great rejoicing in Brandigan at his victory, and all now moves towards the finale, the magnificent coronation of Erec and Enide by King Arthur, when the hero wears the robe embroidered with the Quadrivium, which symbolically crowns him with knowledge. The self-fulfilment of Erec is complete, with his nature coming into full flower in a condition of marriage which is perfect. We have now seen how Chrétien's romance is in tune with the principles of Alain's doctrine of natural love as well as with the ideals expressed by Nature's model, the work that sums up all her gifts in one creation.

---

42 L. Maranini, *Personaggi e immagini nell'opera di Chrétien de Troyes* (1966), 22-4, sees the situation of Mabonagrain as an attack on courtly love which does not understand its nature fully and omits its relationship with a married woman. We have a parody of the love theory of the troubadours, according to L. Pollmann, *Die Liebe in der hochmittelalterlichen Literatur Frankreichs* (1966), 287 f.

5

Structure

Chrétien begins *Erec et Enide* with a declaration of aim and achievement. The aim is to carry out to the utmost the requirements of narrative art and effective instruction:

> reisons est que totevoies
> doit chascuns panser et antandre
> a bien dire et a bien aprandre.
>
> (*Erec et Enide*, 10 ff.)

And his achievement is to derive from a story of adventure a very fine *conjointure* which demonstrates how it is best to give free rein to one's knowledge and skill:

> et tret d'un conte d'avanture
> une molt bele conjointure
> par qu'an puet prover et savoir
> que cil ne fet mie savoir
> qui s'escïence n'abandone
> tant con Dex la grasce l'an done.
>
> (*Erec et Enide*, 13 ff.)[1]

That tale, the *conte Erec*, is told by professional story-tellers, and has been dismembered and mangled, but now begins the account which will last as long as Christianity endures. This is Chrétien's boast.

The term *conjointure* has been the subject of much discussion.[2] It is generally taken to be some kind of suitable arrangement of the matter, in contrast to the dismembering and mangling of the tale by professional story-tellers. For

---

1 Cf. the passage that begins the prologue to the lays of Marie de France:

> Ki Deus ad duné escïence
> E de parler bone eloquence
> Ne s'en deit taisir ne celer.

Here *escïence* is also associated with literary ability. Cf. Horace, *Ars poetica*, 309: *Scribendi recte sapere est et principium et fons.*

2 See particularly W. A. Nitze, "The Romance of Erec, Son of Lac", *Modern Philology* XI (1913-14), 486-8, "*Sans* et *matière* dans les oeuvres de Chrétien de Troyes", *Romania* XLIV (1915-17), 16 f., "Arthurian Problems", *BBSIA* V (1953), 76 f.; D. W. Robertson, "Some Medieval Literary Terminology, with Special Reference to Chrétien de Troyes", *Studies in Philology* XLVIII (1951), 670 f., 684-6, 692; D. Kelly, "The Source and Meaning of Conjointure in Chrétien's *Erec* 14", *Viator* I (1970), 179 ff.; E. Vinaver, *The Rise of Romance* (1971), chapter on "Tradition and Design", 33 ff.

the interpretation of *conjointure*, Nitze drew attention to the significance of *junctura* in Horace, but this refers to style. However, one is justified in transferring the concept of arrangement and disposition from style to narrative structure, as Kelly has shown from consideration both of *Ars poetica* and of medieval writers on composition. Let us therefore look at the contexts of *junctura* in Horace:

> In verbis etiam tenuis cautusque serendis,
> dixeris egregie, notum si callida verbum
> reddiderit *iunctura* novum.
>
> (*Ars poetica*, 46 ff.)

(Moreover, with a nice taste and care in weaving words together, you will express yourself most happily, if a skilful *setting* makes a familiar word new.)[3]

> Ex noto fictum carmen sequar, ut sibi quivis
> speret idem, sudet multum frustraque laboret
> ausus idem: tantum series *iunctura*que pollet,
> tantum de medio sumptis accedit honoris.
>
> (*Ars poetica*, 240 ff.)

(My aim shall be poetry, so moulded from the familiar that anybody may hope for the same success, may sweat much and yet toil in vain when attempting the same: such is the power of order and *connection*, such the beauty that may crown the commonplace.)

Thus Horace claims that the skilful association of one element with another has the power of making fresh and beautiful what is familiar and commonplace. Chrétien similarly stresses the skill shown by his *molt bele conjointure*, and looks with the greatest pride on what he has done to a known story.

For the application of *conjointure* to narrative poetry, one can draw on Alain de Lille, in a passage of *De planctu Naturae* which Robertson brought to bear on the definition of the term:

> "in superficiali litterae cortice falsum resonat lyra poetica, sed interius, auditoribus secretum intelligentiae altioris eloquitur, ut exteriore falsitatis abjecto putamine, dulciorem nucleum veritatis secrete intus lector inveniat. Poetae tamen aliquando historiales eventus joculationibus fabulosis quadam eleganti fictura confoederant, ut ex diversorum competenti *conjunctura*,[4] ipsius narrationis elegantior pictura resultet."
>
> (*De planctu Naturae*, ed. Migne, ccx, 451)

("In the exterior surface of literature the poetic medium may utter what is not true, but within expresses to its hearers the loftier meaning which is hidden,

---

3 The translation of passages in *Ars poetica* is taken from the Loeb Classics.

4 For *fictura* and *conjunctura*, Wright, ii, 466, has *structura* and *junctura*. It makes no difference to my argument if *junctura* is what Alain wrote; its replacement by *conjunctura* would demonstrate that we are dealing with the same concept as *conjointure*. The reading *fictura* agrees with *fictum* in *Ars poetica*, 240.

in order that the reader, having cast aside the outer husk of falsity, should find the sweeter kernel of truth hidden inside. Now poets sometimes unite historical events with entertaining fancies in some splendid concoction, in order that from the harmonious *conjunction* of diversities a finer picture should emerge of the narrative itself.")

With this, Robertson compared a passage about literary works in Hugh of St. Victor's *Didascalicon*, III, iv, where the activity of certain composers is thus described: *diversa simul compilantes, quasi de multis coloribus et formis, unam picturam facere*, "bringing together diversities, to produce, as it were, one picture out of many colours and shapes". There can then be no doubt that a *conjointure* is the poet's own coherent arrangement of disparate material.

In Alain's terms, Chrétien has freely lavished his skill on making a very fine *conjunctura* as the construction of his *pictura*. Through the conception of a literary work as a *pictura*, which is Horatian (*ut pictura poesis*),[5] one can see why this should be so. Vinaver has drawn attention to a passage in the poem on Genesis begun in 1192 for Chrétien's patron, Marie de Champagne, which asserts that *cele forme, cele peinture* would be like a lantern without a light

> Se Dieus n'i meist *conjoincture*
> Tel com l'ame qui la governe.

According to Vinaver, these lines mean: "if God had not given it some such *organizing principle* as the soul which rules over it".[6] This idea that *conjointure* should govern works of fine art must be connected with that of a *conjunctura* as the construction of a *pictura* in Alain, to be thought of as applied by artists whose method is *de multis coloribus et formis unam picturam facere*. Each of the passages in the poem on Genesis and in *De planctu Naturae* stresses a different side of what is evidently a principle of dual aspect, not only that there has to be cohesion between the various elements which make up a work of art, but also that the artist should compound it out of diversities, a paradox which if not resolved makes his work like a lantern without a light. On the other hand, when he sets light to the lantern, as it were, we have the brilliance that results *ex diversorum competenti conjunctura*, which Alain speaks of with reference to narrative *pictura*. This then is the effect that Chrétien aims at and which he believes he has achieved. The operation of the artistic principle of *conjointure* in the putting together of his romance must entail the application of an overall pattern, and links between individual elements, to components which are selected and placed in association, and whose diverse origin makes their cohesion a *tour de force*.

Both Alain and Chrétien pass from consideration of the two levels of

---

5 *Ars poetica*, 361. The opening lines of *Ars poetica* sustain a comparison between painters and poets.

6 The passage is quoted by Vinaver, *op. cit.*, 36 n. 1. Its subject is the transformation of the human body into a living being.

literature to that of *conjointure*, thus giving the same two principles of composition in the same order. Chrétien's use of *conjointure* in the construction of his narrative may well have been inspired by the passage in *De planctu Naturae*, and certainly this is of great importance in elucidating the sense he must have attached to the term. But though we should have some understanding of what he means by *conjointure*, how has he gone about producing one out of the *conte Erec*? His romance cannot be just the result of the selection, filing, and polishing of heterogeneous material relative to the *conte Erec* and its fitting together within a unified action, in mere contrast to the incompetent telling of the tale by professional story-tellers, even as Thomas found the tale of Tristan to be *mult divers, E pur ço l'uni par mes vers* (D 835 f.).[7] The *conte Tristan* was clearly one basic story of which there were variations in the telling, and around which could collect accounts developing a situation in it or one that was related to the circumstances there. Of this *conte* Thomas gave in effect a sophisticated retelling, whereas what is meant by a *conjointure* must be a harmonious blend of elements which were quite distinct before being thus amalgamated. Frappier assumes there existed separate stories of Erec, and that Chrétien has combined the matter of these various tales into a composite within his *plan d'ensemble*.[8] If this is not intended to be like the derivation of Thomas's *Tristan* from the *conte*, he means the disposal of originally distinct accounts within an organized whole in such a manner that basically they remain recognizably intact—the process that Gautier d'Arras refers to in *Eracle*, 2916, as *entrelacier*. The weaving of material into the narrative is no doubt included in Chrétien's conception of *conjointure*, but the *conte Erec* should not be several distinct stories. It should be like the *conte Tristan*. More appropriate then is the conception of Brugger, that Chrétien ripped the individual episodes of the *conte Erec* apart from each other, and rearranged them into a new combination.[9] The wording of Chrétien's prologue implies that he made use of the architectonic principle of a fresh and coherent conjunction of elements as he built material from the *conte Erec* into a structure of his own, in this way moulding from the familiar the *molt bele* which will last as long as Christianity endures. How exactly he did this cannot be known until one is able to compare his work with that lost *conte Erec*, but in the meantime I can investigate the general structure of his romance.

Chrétien's emphasis on the structural aspect of *Erec et Enide*, along with his intention that the work should satisfy the twin demands of *bien dire* and *bien aprandre*, underline the import of parallels between the architecture of *Erec* and *Anticlaudianus*, whose structure serves as a vehicle for Alain's philosophy. These correspondences cannot be due to any dependence of Alain on Chrétien, because the form of *Anticlaudianus* rests on Latin models, drawing its inspiration

---

7 See the commentary of D. Kelly on "*En uni dire* (*Tristan* Douce 839) and the Composition of Thomas's *Tristan*", *Modern Philology* LXVII (1969-70), 9 ff.

8 J. Frappier, *Chrétien de Troyes: nouvelle édition* (1968), 59.

9 E. Brugger, *ZrP* LXIII (1943), 127, in his series entitled "Der Schöne Feigling in der arthurischen Literatur".

from Martianus Capella, *De nuptiis Philologiae et Mercurii*, Claudian, *In Rufinum*, Prudentius, *Psychomachia*, and Bernardus Silvestris, *De mundi universitate*.

As the full title *Anticlaudianus de Antirufino* conveys, it reverses the situation in Claudian. There the fury Allecto laments the return of the Golden Age, summons a council of the Vices, and a proposal is carried to send the fury Megaera to entrust to Rufinus the championship of the cause of evil. In Alain, Nature calls a council of the Virtues, and laments the faults in her works, which cause her decrees to be scorned and the fury Tisiphone to triumph. She puts to her council the project of creating a perfect human, as one work to redeem all (in Bernardus Silvestris, the project of Man's creation is laid upon Nature in a speech by Noys). The council of Nature and the Virtues then carry a proposal to send Prudencia to Heaven to obtain the soul from God. On the one hand Prudencia's journey is comparable to that of the bride Philology to the celestial regions in Capella, where the wedding is to take place before the Gods, and with the bridesmaids, the Liberal Arts, in attendance. But in *Anticlaudianus* Prudencia returns with the soul for the creation, a marriage of the divine to the flesh, by Nature and the Virtues along with the Liberal Arts; for on the other hand the celestial journey is related to that of Nature in Bernardus Silvestris to fetch Urania, who provides the divine element in the formation of Man. In *Anticlaudianus*, when the perfect human is created he is an Antirufinus, the champion of good, and he comes under the assault of the Vices, led by Allecto. Supported by the Virtues in a battle similar to that in *Psychomachia*, he gains the victory, which ushers in a Golden Age.

This makes clear the ancestry of *Anticlaudianus* and its grand scheme, and now the structure of the work will be compared with that of *Erec*. I shall first follow the course of each in turn and show what they have in common, up to the point where the creation takes place in Alain.

Nature intends to carry out a project, the making of a perfect man, and she summons to her council the powers of perfection and announces her proposal. Then Prudencia speaks, and points to the difficulty of carrying out the project: though they can create the body, the soul is beyond them, for it can only be provided by God. Great murmur and controversy arises at Nature's court. Racio proposes that Prudencia should go to Heaven and obtain the necessary soul from God, but Prudencia hangs back, though she finally agrees when Concordia speaks in support of Racio. Then Prudencia sets her Liberal Arts fashioning a car with which she travels to Heaven, where she receives from God the perfect soul, rich in the potential of virtues as well as beautiful form. With this she returns to Nature's court, and is welcomed with great joy, while Nature admires the soul. When the beautiful creation is fashioned, Nature makes the body, Concordia joins it to the soul in a marriage of the divine to the flesh, and the rest shower the *novus homo* with their endowments.

The idealistic opening section of *Erec* begins with Arthur intending to hunt the white stag in order to renew a custom. When he announces his intention,

Gawain immediately points to the difficulty of carrying out what the custom of the hunt requires, the giving of a kiss to the loveliest damsel at court by the hunter who has killed the stag, because each lady would have her claim to be the most beautiful sustained by her own knight. But the hunt duly takes place, in the course of which Erec has an encounter in the forest with Yder, whom he pursues to Laluth. After the hunt there is such controversy about the bestowal of the kiss that the court is in a great murmur, and a council of the greatest barons is summoned to decide what to do. They accept the proposal of Guinevere to put off the giving of the kiss until Erec's return. Erec reaches Laluth, where he meets and is betrothed to Enide, and after the contest for the sparrowhawk he returns with her to Arthur's court. He is received with great joy, and Enide's beauty is greatly praised. On her, to the approval of all, Arthur bestows the kiss, and there follows the marriage of the hero and the heroine, the wedding night, after which Enide rises a *dame novele*, and eventually the tournament at which Erec magnificently distinguishes himself. The couple depart to Estregales, where Erec's father is King, the inhabitants welcome their *novel seignor*, and finally we have the resplendent picture of Enide as a noble married lady.

This section of the romance corresponds to the allegory in the following ways. The head of a court announces an intention to carry out a project, and then the most perceptive member of the court[10] points out that the project entails the performance of an act too difficult to accomplish. At both courts there is controversy and murmur over the carrying out of this part of the project, and a council deliberating about its difficulty. Then in both it is proposed that the accomplishment of the project be suspended until a member of the court returns from a quest, and this is agreed. The course of the quest is related, and then the quester comes back with a being rich in virtues as well as beautiful form, who makes the accomplishment of the project possible; they are received with joy and the being is praised. In *Anticlaudianus*, there is Prudencia returning with the soul: in *Erec*, the hero arrives with Enide looking like Prudencia. Now the perfect human can be fashioned in *Anticlaudianus*, and his creation is a marriage of the divine to the flesh: now Arthur can bestow the kiss, and there follows the wedding of Erec and Enide. And even as in *Anticlaudianus* there comes into existence *novus homo*, so Enide rises, after the wedding night, a *dame novele*, and the inhabitants of Estregales assemble to see their *novel seignor*.

These parallels are so striking, when one considers how much influence has already been shown to be exerted by *Anticlaudianus* on *Erec*, that coincidence must be ruled out. And not only can a reflection of Alain's poem be thus perceived in the events of *Erec* here, but the comparison has brought out an analogy in significance. It is the marriage in the romance that is similar to the *novus homo*, with the ideals of perfection and the perfect match embodied in

10 Chrétien endows Gawain with *sens*, see W. A. Nitze, "The Character of Gauvain in the Romances of Chrétien de Troyes", *Modern Philology* L (1953), 223 f.

the hero and the heroine both before the wedding and during their early married life, as far as the encomium on Enide. With the equivalent of Nature's creation being the marriage in *Erec*, upon it can come to bear the philosophies of both *Anticlaudianus* and *De planctu Naturae*.

We are at the stage where the creation has been completed and endowed, the perfect human in Alain and in Chrétien the perfect marriage. A turning point has been reached in both works. Now in the allegory the perfect Man is assaulted by the Vices, who stand for what is evil in the nature of the world and circumstances or in human nature. The Virtues range themselves at the side of the Man to support him in his battle, which he eventually wins. In *Erec*, now the perfect marriage is marred, with the hero and the heroine showing imperfections which contradict the qualities previously possessed, and they are launched upon a series of dangerous adventures, the outcome of which is the re-establishment of their love and perfections more firmly than ever. Let me render in Alain's terms what happens in the romance.

Erec infringes the rule of Modestia, who regulates the whole man, tempers his acts and restrains the emotions, warning earnestly that he should do nothing of which to be ashamed, and through which disrepute might cause damage to his reputation.[11] For Erec begins to love Enide inordinately, leaving Pudor for Luxuries to treat her like a paramour, through abandonment of Racio when he gives way to desire and devotes himself to the pleasure of fondling his wife (Voluptas). And he turns his back on Prudencia by his idleness (Occia) in ceasing to practise the knightly occupation of tourneying, but instead preferring to enjoy a frivolous pastime (Ludus), and slothfully not to get up from bed till after midday (Ignavia, Sompni). Sorrow (Tristicies) fills everyone at Erec's change of nature, they blame him for being too much in love and having no further interest in bearing arms (Murmur), and call him recreant (Contemptus, Infamia, Dedecus). Grief (Luctus) causes Enide to open her mouth, producing the first words from her that Chrétien gives, and she tells Erec what they say about him. Now she who has been a model of moderation and unassuming conduct goes too far (Excessus), so that later she accuses herself of arrogance and presumption (Fastus). For Modestia measures words and weighs silences, and shows what words to use to whom, when they are not fit to be spoken, and what is proper to say, lest one blurts out things best not mentioned.[12] Enide indeed later blames herself for not recognizing that a well-judged silence harms no one, whereas speech is often fatal. And she who was said to be the epitome of wisdom speaks what she comes to realize are the words of a fool (Stulticia). She goes so far that they become reproaches (Convicia), for she says what causes her most affliction is that his becoming an object of derision has given rise to the accusation that she has so entangled him in her net as to make him lose his prowess and desire no other occupation; and she tells him to bring this slander to an end by recovering his knightly reputation. The result is

11 *Anticlaudianus*, VIII, 121-6.
12 *Ibid.*, VII, 122, 127-30.

that disharmony (Discordia) arises between them, and anger (Ira), harshness (Impietas), and hatred (Odium) from now on are shown towards Enide by Erec, causing fear (Timor) and sadness (Tristicies).

Erec sets out to re-establish his reputation by going on an adventurous ride, and takes Enide with him, plunging himself into dangers as he proves his prowess. A test therefore of Favor, but also of Fides, for on the ride Enide undergoes trials of her devotion at the same time as Erec tries to expunge disgrace by gaining approbation. He waits to see whether she will warn him against attackers, which is a sign that he who holds another dear seeks to trust himself entirely to her.[13] But Erec is cruel to Enide, because with the onset of Impietas the constancy of a strong mind deviates from the right,[14] and he strains her devotion to the full by threatening her whenever, by warning him, she violates his command to be silent. There are the attacks of Discordia's band, in Erec's continued anger and declared hatred, and Enide's fear, and in the assaults upon the hero, the fights he is engaged in, and the attempts to murder him, with the resulting exhaustion, injury, suffering, and apparent death; the company of Luctus, in Enide's sorrow, lamentation, tears, and anguish, both at the treatment she receives from Erec and at his dangers and the condition to which they reduce him, until eventually he appears to be dead; and Fraus, in the amorous Count's attempt to persuade the heroine to betray Erec. As in *Anticlaudianus* the Man's mettle is tested when the Vices set out to destroy him, so in the romance the marriage is threatened with destruction, by trials initiated with the reversal of the opening idealism, and continued as Erec and Enide undergo their adventures together.

The Virtues fight by the side of the *novus homo* against the Vices, in one of the works: in the other the new marriage is defended by its endowments. Erec never loses his quality of Largitas, the core of courtliness, because even in his disastrous fall from perfection he sends his knights richly provided for and equipped to the tournaments he ceases attending. Pietas towards Enide lurks beneath his harsh exterior, when before departing on the ride he makes arrangements with his father to look after her in case he fails to survive. With his decision to go adventuring he regains that aspect of Racio which is firmness of resolution, and throughout the rest of the romance he is not to be deflected from his determination to re-establish his reputation, with an unshakeable purpose which becomes explicit. He refuses an invitation from Guivret to go with him and have his wounds seen to. Then he forcibly resists Kay's attempt to bring him to Arthur and his company in the forest, so that he should have the rest he obviously needs. "You do not know what I have to do", the hero tells him, "I must go much further. Let me go, because I stay too long. The day is still far from its end." And when the courteous Gawain prevails on him, with great difficulty and only by a trick, to come to Arthur, Erec insists that he should continue his ride the next morning, in spite of his severe wounds, declaring

13 *Ibid.*, VII, 371: *Querat cui possit se totum credere.*
14 *Ibid.*, VII, 335 f.: *firme constancia mentis Deviet a recto.*

that nothing can hold him, he has so undertaken this enterprise that he will not stay on any account.

In Enide, it is Fides that is demonstrated many times, and not only when she keeps on warning Erec against assailants, in spite of his menaces because she disobeys him by not keeping silent. She is faithful to Erec in resisting two men who try to gain possession of her, the amorous Count with his enticement and threat, and the Count of Limors who marries her by force but, in the presence of Erec's apparently lifeless body, fails to get her to obey his order to be merry and eat, even though he menaces and beats her. She saves Erec from the amorous Count's attempt to murder him, and Prudencia enables her to outmanoeuvre the Count by pretending to fall in with his intentions, so that she gains time to put the hero out of his reach. And she, too, returns to her former outstanding characteristic, Modestia, by humble behaviour, and saying and doing everything in the proper place and at the proper time.

As Fides defeats Odium, so does recognition of Enide's loyalty cause Erec no longer to declare hatred. Pax wins the upper hand over Ira, and similarly Erec's anger makes way for reconciliation. Impietas is overcome by Pietas, even as Erec comes to end his harsh treatment of Enide and shows courtesy and affection; he also demonstrates Pietas when he responds to a maiden's plea to deliver her knight from giants who cruelly ill-treat him. The outcome of the narrative is to produce a contrast between Erec's present responsible behaviour and the trifling of which he has been guilty (Seria/Ludus), between the esteem in which he comes to be held and the former derision (Honor/Contemptus), and between propriety in love and the over-indulgence that caused Erec's fall (Pudor/Luxuries), as well as between Enide's correct behaviour and her lapse (Modestia/Excessus) that accompanied his. And when Erec finally undertakes of his own accord the dangerous adventure of the Joie de la Cort, this illustrates the full flowering of that aspect of Racio which is the hero's resolution, and one can say that zeal (Studium) has conquered the idleness (Occia) he once exhibited, and that the tremendous joy which attends his victory, after the sorrow shown at the prospect of his likely death, shows how Tristicies has been utterly destroyed by Gaudia.

This last of the adventures brings the great moment which corresponds to the final victory of Nature's creation over the Vices. Chrétien emphasizes the important place that the Joie de la Cort holds in the architecture of *Erec* by bringing it on the scene as if by trumpet blasts and drum rolls. With the love relations of the couple fully re-established, Erec has at last brought the adventurous ride to a rest, being now willing to stay until his wounds are healed; and they remain with Guivret at his castle until the time when they set out to return to Arthur's court. With physical as well as mental wounds healed, to all appearance the story is coming to an end. But then Erec turns aside deliberately to undertake a most intimidating task. He learns that in Brandigan, a place that comes into sight, and which is impregnably fortified and surrounded by a rushing and perilous torrent, there is a dangerous adventure from which no-one has returned alive. He asks only for the name, and it is the Joie de la Cort, the Joy of the Court. Now nothing can restrain Erec from seeking the Joy, both because of its peril and its name, for in joy he sees nothing but good, joy is what he seeks, and from the Joy, he believes, there may come great gain.

All in Brandigan pity him and are full of grief, because this admirable knight will be killed like his predecessors, and Evrain, the King, when Erec demands of him the Joie de la Cort—there is nothing the hero desires so much—warns him to avoid that which has caused sorrow to many a man. But Erec insists he be given the Joie, until Evrain grants it, declaring that if he emerges with joy from this, he will have gained honour such as no-one could gain more.

They enter that marvellous garden, without wall or fence, but shut in on all sides so firmly by air that it might have been enclosed in iron, a terrestrial paradise of perpetual delights whose fruits are of such nature that they can only be enjoyed inside and never taken out. The pleasurable song of the birds puts Erec in mind of the Joy, the thing he longs for most. Then he sees what would arouse fear in the bravest man, stakes each bearing a severed head, apart from that which awaits the next and carries a blast horn. King Evrain informs him that no-one has ever been able to blow the horn, but he who would succeed, his fame and honour would surpass that of all others, and the feat would bring him such glory that all would come to do him honour and hold him to be the best. Others have failed, but Erec will not draw back one step from the task he has undertaken. First he comforts Enide, who is in great distress—though she says nothing—at the dangers of the Joie, and, alone, he plunges deeper into the garden.

Then this sight meets his eyes, a lady of ravishing beauty sitting on a splendid couch, silver, with a cover of gold-embroidered cloth, and Erec is opposed by a gigantic red knight whom he overcomes after a terrific battle. His defeated antagonist, Mabonagrain, informs him that by this victory he has gained no small honour. Erec has given great joy to the court of his uncle King Evrain and his friends, for now Mabonagrain will be released from the garden, and because those who will come to the court will rejoice at this, they who have waited for this joy call it the Joy of the Court. They have waited so long for it, and now they will receive it from Erec, who has won it. But Mabonagrain is not to issue from the garden until the horn is blown; only then will Erec have released him from imprisonment, and then the Joy will begin. Whoever hears the sound, nothing can prevent him from coming immediately to the court. And when Erec takes the horn and blows it, there ensues a tremendous joy. But it is disappointing for the damsel of the garden, for no-one can prevent Mabonagrain from leaving, now that the hour and the time has come.

Enide rejoices, and so does King Evrain and his people. All are merry and sing, never was such rejoicing made, and as the news spreads throughout the country the people hasten to the court, on foot, on horse, without waiting for each other. Great is the gathering and the press, everyone, high and low, rich and poor, strives to see Erec, each thrusting before the other, and they all salute him and bow, saying constantly: "May God save him through whom joy and gladness revive in our court! God save the most blessed man whom God has ever taken pains to make!" Thus they bring him to the court, and all kinds of musical instruments sound in accompaniment. Erec is well feasted and served to his heart's content with the Joy that he has sought and won.

The combat takes place, as I have already stressed, in a locality of symbolic power. Its significance is underlined by the deliberate turning aside of Erec when the couple are on their way back to Arthur's court for the arresting of the action, by the effect that the name of the adventure has on Erec, the play on this name, the intimidations of the task, and the hero's resolve to let nothing deter him from gaining the Joy. It is emphasized by the declaration of Evrain that if the hero succeeds he will gain honour such as no-one could gain more; and the tremendous joy which attends Erec's victory, whose import is such that the people hail him as the most blessed man whom God has ever taken pains to make.

There are those who have been disappointed to find, after all these signals of a most significant accomplishment, that Erec, apart from bringing to an end the evil custom of exposing the heads of slain challengers, has achieved nothing but the release of a knight from a delightful garden where he has enjoyed the pleasant company of his love. The tremendous joy, along with the great honour accorded to Erec, is indeed a mystery if this is all he accomplishes. Mystery should not be surprising in the poet who was later to treat of the Grail story; but the Joie de la Cort has meaning, as we have seen, on the level where the encounter between Erec and Mabonagrain pits the real Cupid against the pseudo-Cupid. Thus, with the hero's victory, the charm of a false ideal of love is broken and shown to be spurious. Placed against the background of *Anticlaudianus*, the Joie de la Cort parallels what there ushers in the Golden Age. "Battle ceases, Victory falls to the young man, Virtue springs up, Vice succumbs, Nature triumphs."[15] The *novus homo*, the most perfect man whom Nature has ever taken pains to make, has become *ille beatus homo*, that blessed man, who brings to the world the reign of Nature and her Virtues. Even so Erec, the most blessed man whom God has ever taken pains to make, he who along with Enide has been endowed with perfection and fully tested by the assault of evil, he who now is fitted to be the champion of ideal marriage, and the answer to Nature's complaint in *De planctu Naturae*, only he—almost a Prometheus, imbued with a sense of mission to gain a great good through peril—can be the destroyer of the false ideal. Men have been waiting for such a man to succeed in the task at which all others have failed. With Erec's victory the protagonist of non-marital courtly love is released from its dominion—and

15 *Anticlaudianus*, IX, 384 f.

similarly his partner by Enide's example—which brings about the Joy of the Court, with such rejoicing as has never been made. The Joie de la Cort rises above the level of adventure in being infused with such overtones of suggestion.[16]

The adventures are now over, the perfection of the marriage fully established, the hero and the heroine love each other greatly and with propriety, adversities of circumstance and taints on Erec's reputation have been overcome, and unhappy moods and imperfections of character are gone. As in *Anticlaudianus*, "Love reigns, nowhere is Disharmony", and "Now the Virtues take up abode on earth, acquire kingdoms, and rule the world".[17] For Pietas, Modestia, and Honestas exercise power, Favor holds sway, Racio governs, and the rule of Prudencia is symbolized by the Quadrivium embroidered on Erec's robe, as the triumph is celebrated in the magnificent coronation of hero and heroine at Arthur's court, with the reign of joyful Risus, rich Copia, high Nobilitas, and resplendent Decus at its height. Without taking us back to Estregales, the romance leaves us on this blaze of glory, giving the effect of a Golden Age inaugurated which serves as a model for Chrétien's day.

Structural comparison between *Erec* and *Anticlaudianus* confirms that Chrétien's romance is the mirror of marriage. Every illustration of an ideal, every sin against it, every circumstance favourable or unfavourable, all is to be related to this theme. To hold that from *Erec* one learns that marriage collides with courtly love and knightly accomplishment[18] is as valid as to say that *Anticlaudianus* teaches that life is destructive of perfection, when Alain is concerned with defining the perfect courtly life. According to Nature in *De planctu Naturae*, she has set a continual hostility between man's *sensualitas* and *ratio*, the one leading the human mind down the decline of vices, the other to ascend to the virtues, producing a war of opposition between these antagonists in which the victory of reason will not be without its following reward, for prizes won by victories shine more finely than other gifts, and endowments acquired by efforts are more delightfully brilliant than all those that are free.[19] The battle in *Anticlaudianus* expresses this truth, and the ideal marriage in Chrétien is as subject to evil as Nature's perfect creation. The principle underlying the master-plan that *Erec* inherits from *Anticlaudianus* also has some parallel in the Felix Culpa, the Fortunate Fall of Adam and Eve. For without

---

16 Cf. L. Pollmann, *Die Liebe in der hochmittelalterlichen Literatur Frankreichs* (1966), 287:

> Der Ritter Erec befreit Maboagrain aus den Fesseln seiner knechtischen Liebe, und es ist u. E. als Distanzierung von den Theorien der Trobadors zu verstehen, wenn Chrétien de Troyes in dieser Befreiung des Maboagrain aus den Fesseln einer in einen ideologischen Engpass führenden Liebe die Voraussetzung für die "Joie de la Cort" sieht.

17 *Anticlaudianus*, IX, 386, 391 f.
18 So R. R. Bezzola, *Le sens de l'aventure et de l'amour* (1947), 79 f., 140 f.
19 *De planctu Naturae*, ed. Wright, ii, 451 f.

good there can be no evil, and without evil there can be no good. The one depends on the other. Adam and Eve knew neither good nor evil in Paradise. But, with the Fall, they came to know the nature of Evil and so of Good.

Erec's lapse, which makes Enide subject to the accusation that she is his tempting Eve, is not the result of his married condition, but of his own action within it, in which the betrayal of its ideals leads to the collapse of the love relationship. Thus is paradise lost, not to be regained until the marital state has been put on a right basis, when its support makes Erec fit for the climactic moment when he wins his greatest glory. As he is about to penetrate to the dangers of the marvellous garden, he turns to Enide and makes this significant declaration. She is in distress for nothing, he says, since she should know for certain that even if there were no valour in him but such as her love gives, he would not fear in battle, face to face, anyone alive. So we learn, as fully from the crisis of the turning point as from the idealistic opening phase and Erec's final victory, that knightly accomplishment is both a prerequisite and a consequence of the married state at its most perfect.

Such are the insights to be obtained by going from the allegory to the romance. C. S. Lewis delivered the dictum that Chrétien can hardly turn to the inner world without at the same time turning to allegory,[20] but what we have been considering is the converse of this conventional approach, with aspects of events and human nature, in allegory represented by personifications and their actions, here appearing embodied in the course of a narrative and the behaviour of its characters. This is achieved not by way of close reproduction of Alain's mechanism, but through drawing on its inspiration for the shaping of the story. With *Anticlaudianus* behind him, it may be said that Chrétien gives a form to the narrative which makes it fall into the general pattern employed by Alain for his poem, and threads into it motifs to which we can attach such labels as Fides/Odium, Studium/Occia, Honor/Contemptus, Seria/Ludus, Gaudia/Tristicies, Pudor/Luxuries, or Modestia/Excessus, as part of a grand scheme comparable to Alain's.[21]

This, then, is the splendid structure into which Chrétien built his *conjointure* of material to make a particularly fine *pictura* of a narrative. No wonder he prides himself on the composition of *Erec*, and boasts that it will last as long as Christianity endures! He has brought about a remarkable achievement, successfully embodying, in romance, ideals like those of lofty philosophical works by a learned contemporary, and by means of a master-plan drawn from one of them[22]—a Latin poem belonging to quite a different genre—so that

---

20 C. S. Lewis, *The Allegory of Love* (1936), 30.

21 Observe that the comparison with a *psychomachia* automatically excludes the interpretation of Erec's opponents as representing vices, such as is carried out by S. Bayrav, *Symbolisme médiéval* (1957), 95-7.

22 It seems likely that when Chrétien set out to emphasize significance by an appeal to a learned authority, in his reference to Macrobius, he chose not to reveal his true source because that would have given away the secret of much else.

through the medium of an Arthurian tale comparable aspirations about behaviour in a Christian society should be instilled into a more general audience. We put down *Erec et Enide* with the impression that marriage is ideally a dignified and splendid condition, not voluptuous, but possessing all the attributes of a beautiful, courtly, and glorious state of life. To achieve this effect, Chrétien has put together a splendid vehicle that gives a new meaning to love in romance, and leads to the comprehension of how marriage can go through this dangerous world and bring out the best in human nature. With such a *finis sive utilitas* and such a calculated structure was composed the first Arthurian romance that we have.

6

The Fair Unknown

According to his prologue, Chrétien based *Erec* on a *conte d'aventure*. How much reshaping was necessary to make the story have so much in common with Alain's works? An answer cannot be given without exact knowledge of the *conte* he used.

This brings one up against the familiar problem, the *Mabinogionfrage* which has so engrossed scholars, of the relationship between Chrétien and certain Welsh tales. The latter evidently derive from French originals, but (to quote Loomis) "was Chrétien the sole source of the corresponding portions of the Welsh tales? Was Chrétien only one of the sources of the Welsh tales? Was there a common source for each of the three pairs of romances?" The answer of Loomis was that there existed in each case a common source, a lost French work by X for *Erec* and the Welsh *Gereint*, another by Y for *Yvain* and the Welsh *Owein*, and closely-related streams of tradition for *Perceval* and the Welsh *Peredur*. For *Le Chevalier de la Charrete* there is no such close cognate as to give Loomis any ground for assuming a comparable common source, but he judged that all four of Chrétien's "traditional" romances are to be regarded as based on long accounts in French prose manuscripts,[1] whose narrative material Chrétien followed on the whole with some fidelity, displaying little originality (except with *Le Chevalier de la Charrete*) in the composition and shaping of his stories, though he treated the sources with considerable freedom as to details.[2]

In the case of *Erec* and *Gereint*, several scholars have argued that there was a common original, not only from what they claimed to be original features in the Welsh tale, but also from instances where Hartmann von Aue's German adaptation of *Erec* goes with *Gereint* against Chrétien. There are also agreements against him between Hartmann and *Erex saga*, a Norse condensation of the French romance, which led to the assumption that Hartmann used, in addition to Chrétien, two independent versions of the story, one a source in common with *Gereint*, and another which also influenced the saga. It has even been contended that not only *Gereint* but also Hartmann or the saga is the sole text preserving an original motif. Or the critic may prefer to perceive what lies

1 On this view that sources in the form of French prose manuscripts were available to Chrétien, see the critical remarks of F. Koenig, *Romance Philology* XIX (1965-6), 116 f., in a review of B. Woledge and H. P. Clive, *Répertoire des plus anciens textes en prose française* (1964).

2 R. S. Loomis, *Arthurian Tradition and Chrétien de Troyes* (1949), 23 f., 32-8, 463-7.

behind them all. Sparnaay visualized a body of stories about Erec, resulting in one tale of adventure impelled by the hero's desire to re-establish his prowess, and another where he is driven by jealousy to ride forth with the heroine, the coalescence of the two producing a double pattern such as we have in *Gereint*, while Chrétien emphasized the former motif.[3]

However, if the foreign redactions reflect the existence of versions varying from Chrétien, there is no reason why these should not have been derived from his romance. The professional retellers, whom he castigates in a passage which is tantamount to a declaration of monopoly in a story of Erec superior to all, would no doubt recognize its greater merits, and with the arrival of the new creation it is likely that the old tale would be no longer told about Erec, and only Chrétien's account be henceforth associated with the name of this hero. We know of piracy by *jongleur* rivals producing their own versions of a successful work, and, according to the Second Continuation of *Perceval*, some gave a false account which would be in prose (*sanʒ rimer*), and which masqueraded as a genuine retelling. In the romance of *Flamenca* (thirteenth century) we find a picture of *jongleurs* relating stories that include those by Chrétien.[4] The oral transmission of a French tale abroad is illustrated by the case of the German *Wigalois* (c. 1210), which was based on a report given by a squire to the poet. A Welshman would have easy access to the recitation of French tales, and *Gereint* may be the product of an oral process, in which the methods Chrétien decries would be apparent in the retelling of his own story:

> d'Erec, li fil Lac, est li contes,
> que devant rois et devant contes
> depecier et corronpre suelent
> cil qui de conter vivre vuelent.
>
> (*Erec et Enide*, 19 ff.)

Certainly, there is some weakness in the logic which presumes that all the foreign redactions made use of accounts that varied from *Erec*, and accepts at the same time the dependence on Chrétien of Hartmann and the saga, while rejecting it with *Gereint*. As for the evidence that Loomis presented for a common original, this is not only scanty but very doubtful, and the point he emphasized as definite proof that the Welsh tale is not derived from Chrétien entails a premise that would in fact contradict his own thesis. He assumed that both Chrétien and the Welsh redactor misread a hypothetic *li cons uials* "the old count", for Enide's father, and understood a name, "Liconuials" in one instance, and, in the other, *niuls* instead of *uials*, thus producing "Nywl".[5]

3 R. Edens, *Erec-Geraint* (1910); R. Zenker, "Weiteres zur Mabinogionfrage", *ZfSL* XLV (1917-19), 47 ff., XLVIII (1925-6), 386 ff.; H. Sparnaay, *Hartmann von Aue, Studien ʒu einer Biographie* (1933), i, 72-125.

4 H. J. Chaytor, *From Script to Print* (1945), 119-29; *Perceval*, Second Continuation, 26086 ff.; *Flamenca*, 662 ff.

5 Loomis, *op. cit.*, 35 f.

Two authors both misreading the same phrase as containing a name, and a different one in each case? An extraordinary coincidence! With Loomis's own premise, that process of misreading, we should come to quite a different conclusion, that *Gereint* is derived from *Erec*, for with a "Nywl" due to the use of a manuscript in which the name of Enide's father, of which there are variant spellings, appeared in the form "Liconuials" instead of "Liconaus", etc.,[6] there would be no need to play with coincidence.

Another approach seeks evidence for the derivation of *Erec* and *Gereint* from a common source by adopting Philipot's view, that *Erec* is an altered form of the Fair Unknown story,[7] and seeing some instances where *Gereint* is closer than Chrétien's romance to this tale.[8] However, the points made by M. Mills are as doubtful as any that have been brought to bear on the *Mabinogion-frage*. Many rest on passages in *Gereint* which must be ruled out because they are merely instances of a stylistic habit that the author possesses, of repetition or the use of set formulas that keep on turning up in similar situations; or are unreliable as evidence, for instance because the motif that *Gereint* shares with a version of the Fair Unknown story is trite, while Chrétien has a distinctive one. And when Mills perceives the most sustained similarity between *Gereint* and the tale of the Fair Unknown, in the description of a combat, in reality the Welsh text agrees with the latter no more significantly than *Erec* does.

A positive objection that I can now bring against the theory of a common source arises from the fact that the Welsh tale is sufficiently close to Chrétien's account to make a source for both stories have much agreement with Alain. For Chrétien to have had a tale to hand that lent itself so very readily not only to a master-plan, but also to an introductory framework based on that of *Anticlaudianus*, would be a remarkable coincidence. This reinforces the impression that the evidence for the common derivation of *Erec* and *Gereint* is as insubstantial as the set of clothes for the Emperor.[9]

To disregard the Welsh redaction in seeking to define the Arthurian source material for *Erec* releases one from an unwarranted constraint, but at the same time the freedom won is dangerous. In spite of the confidence shown by such a commentator as Loomis, the comparative literary methods that have been applied to the establishment of Arthurian source material for Chrétien are typically very open to criticism, source relationships being claimed that cannot be substantiated, because the procedure used amounts to no more than guess-

6 This has been suggested by R. Harris, "*Et Liconaus ot non ses pere*", *Medium Aevum* XXVI (1957), 32 ff.

7 E. Philipot, "Un épisode d'*Erec et Enide*: La Joie de la Cour—Mabon l'enchanteur", *Romania* XXV (1896), 258 ff.

8 M. Mills, "The Huntsman and the Dwarf in *Erec* and *Libeaus Desconus*", *Romania* LXXXVII (1966), 33 ff. See also *Lybeaus Desconus*, pp. 55 n. 3, 60.

9 For another instance of dubious argumentation for a common source, see D. D. R. Owen, *The Evolution of the Grail Legend* (1968), 110-21, where there is an excursus on *Erec* and *Gereint*, as well as on *Yvain* and *Owein*.

work (or even biased judgement), with analogues interrelated according to no convincing criteria. This fundamental weakness afflicts so much of the influential work of Loomis, for instance, that it is necessary to separate the grain from the chaff in his contributions to Arthurian studies. The principle that should regulate as far as possible the defining of Chrétien's source material is the discovery of what must unavoidably be compared, with the truth as well as the nature of the relationship demonstrable with conviction. But how can one ensure properly-orientated comparison of the truly comparable? I shall try to solve this problem with regard to the derivation of *Erec et Enide*, and the workings now begin, necessarily long, as the logic of a comparative method unfolds and guides me across an extensive Arthurian panorama.

When Philipot declared in 1896 that *Erec* and the versions of the Fair Unknown story stem from a common original, he did not attempt to sustain his view by any detailed demonstration, except with the Joie de la Cort episode. Two other episodes in each story (the sparrowhawk contest and the rescue from two giants) are known to have much in common, and a certain parallelism between the relations of the hero and his lady companion on the ride was pointed out by Philipot. Matter in another episode of the Fair Unknown story (the encounter with a huntsman) has been compared by Mills to various parts of Chrétien's romance. Unfortunately, the assumption that *Erec* and *Gereint* have a common source disturbed his results, and led Mills to think that he was dealing with the end-product of a series of redactions each bringing further accidental and deliberate changes, as the story evolved away from the tale of the Fair Unknown. This is nothing but one speculation piled on another.

Let us set out on a reconnaissance, to locate strategic features of the relations between the tale of the Fair Unknown and *Erec*. To begin with, comparison will be carried out to establish common ground, rather than to demonstrate dependence. It will be found that an important aspect of my comparative method is the pursuit of the order in which episodes occur.

There are several versions of the Fair Unknown story, one being Renaut de Beaujeu's *Li Biaus Descouneus* (c. 1200), a most important text, but with which we must be on our guard against distortion of the original, through two causes. One is the influence of Chrétien, as Renaut's work is permeated with the phraseology of *Erec*. The other is the writer's purpose: Renaut composed the romance for his lady-love, and he had her in mind when dealing with the mistress of the Ile d'Or.[10] *Giglan* is an account in prose of the Fair Unknown (interlaced with another Arthurian tale) in a sixteenth-century print, and follows the version by Renaut,[11] on whose text (preserved in a single manuscript) it throws some light. Renaut and the English *Lybeaus Desconus*, of the fourteenth century, represent one form of the tale, and for the designation of its two basic versions I shall draw on the short names of their heroes, Li Descouneus

10 W. Schofield, *Studies on the Libeaus Desconus* (1895), 60 ff., 108 f.
11 See *Li Biaus Descouneus*, xi.

(Renaut) and Lybeaus, which are offered by the texts themselves. In these accounts the hero, who is brought up in ignorance of his name and origin, is given the appellation of "the Fair Unknown" (modern French Le Bel Inconnu) by Arthur when he arrives at his court. From a source with a somewhat different form of the story come two other works: in German, Wirnt von Gravenberg's *Wigalois* (c. 1210), based on a French *conte d'aventure* of which a report was given to the author by a squire;[12] and a French prose romance, *Le Chevalier du Papegau*, probably of the fourteenth rather than the fifteenth century. In three of these four basic versions the hero is the son of Gawain, and his real name is Guinglain in *Descouneus* and *Lybeaus* (Giglan in the print), while Wigalois is likely to be a reformation of this; *Papegau* makes its hero the young King Arthur. There is also the Italian *Carduino* (fourteenth century), which gives an account related to the tale in *Descouneus* and *Lybeaus*. However, far from having the hero as the son of Gawain, he is Gawain's enemy, reflecting the same situation as that of Perceval in the *Prose Tristan*.[13] The study of the Fair Unknown story must be founded on these five basic versions, but we also have heroes like the Fair Unknown elsewhere, tales allied to the Fair Unknown story, and material of the Fair Unknown type (or allied to it) in other accounts.[14]

The order of the episodes in *Descouneus*, with the labels and names that I assign to them for use as tools of analysis hereafter, is as follows (Roman numerals being employed for the adventures):

    AA Arrival at Arthur's Court
    DA Departure from Arthur's Court
    I Encounter at the Perilous Bridge[15]
    II Rescue from Two Giants
    RS Reconciliation Scene
    III Attack by Three Avengers
    IV Encounter with a Huntsman
    V Sparrowhawk Contest
    VI Ile d'Or Episode
    VII Jousting for Hospitality
    VIII Accomplishment of the Mission
    WQ Wedding to a Queen

In addition, *Lybeaus*, *Carduino*, and *Wigalois* have an introduction telling of the hero's upbringing, the Enfances (**E**).

12 F. Saran, "Ueber Wirnt von Grafenberg und den Wigalois", *Beiträge zur Geschichte der deutschen Sprache und Literatur* XXI (1896), 281-4.

13 Schofield, *op. cit.*, 183-9; Loomis, *op. cit.*, 399-403.

14 E. Brugger, "Der Schöne Feigling in der arthurischen Literatur", *ZrP* 1941-51 (for full details see the Bibliography), contributes to our knowledge of matter connected with the tale of the Fair Unknown.

15 In *Descouneus*, replaced by a Perilous Ford, as gathered from the section on the Encounter at the Perilous Bridge (p. 87 f. below).

From the order in *Descouneus* there are two deviations in *Lybeaus*, one involving the position of **IV** in relation to **V**, and the other, said to provide the original sequence,[16] of **II** in relation to the group **RS III**:

Lybeaus: E AA DA I RS III II V IV VI VII VIII WQ

In *Carduino*, **VI** has a distinctive location, which has been held to be due to a displacement:[17]

Carduino: E AA DA VI I II VIII WQ

Apart from the position of **RS**, the sequence of corresponding episodes in *Wigalois* and *Papegau* agrees with that in *Descouneus*, whose location of **IV** before **V** is supported by *Wigalois* against the reverse order in *Lybeaus*. But the omission of **III** leaves open the question of this episode's proper place. *Wigalois* and *Papegau* are however distinctive in that part of the story which is devoted to the domain that is the goal of the hero's ride. In the **VII VIII** account, when the hero reaches it he is first opposed, and then welcomed as the champion sent by Arthur, at the stronghold of **VII**, and the lady in distress is held prisoner by the magician(s) at her palace of **VIII**, where the hero destroys the magician(s) and releases her. Whereas in *Wigalois* and *Papegau* the hero has two combats, the Encounter at the Narrow Passage (**VIIa**) and the Encounter before La Roche (**VIIb**), before being welcomed as the champion sent by Arthur, in the Arrival at the Lady's Stronghold (**ALS**), where she has taken refuge from the usurper. From here the hero goes to the former capital of the region, in the Approach to the Abandoned Castle (**AAC**), and then he sets out for the usurper's stronghold. He has an Encounter at the Gateway of the Magician's Castle (**VIIc**), and destroys this usurper within in the Accomplishment of the Mission (**VIIIa**). Other adventures in this section, and any found elsewhere that do not correspond to episodes in *Descouneus*, *Lybeaus*, and *Carduino*, will be disregarded in the following schematic representation of the accounts in *Wigalois* and *Papegau*:

Wigalois: E AA DA I II IV V   VIIa RS VIIb ALS AAC VIIc VIIIa WQ
Papegau: DA (II)   V VI VIIa   VIIb ALS AAC VIIc VIIIa

The examination of the Fair Unknown story in relation to *Erec et Enide* will begin with the Departure from Arthur's Court, as Chrétien gives no account of Erec's arrival there, nor of his upbringing, only that he is the son of King Lac.

DA   DEPARTURE FROM ARTHUR'S COURT[18]

In *Lybeaus*, *Carduino*, and *Wigalois*, the hero has come to Arthur's court to be knighted. The knighting takes place on the day of his arrival in *Lybeaus*, and

---

16 Schofield, *op. cit.*, 15. Cf. *Lybeaus*, p. 61.   17 Schofield, *op. cit.*, 15 n. 1.

18 *Descouneus*, 133-320; *Lybeaus*, 72-252; *Carduino*, i, 32/1 to ii, 8/5; *Wigalois*, 1593-1927; *Papegau*, 1/5-3/8. Schofield, *op. cit.*, 6-12, 237; Saran, *op. cit.*, 307-10.

on that very day he embarks on the mission in *Descouneus, Lybeaus,* and *Carduino*; but in *Wigalois* there has been a period of probation under the supervision of Gawain, and the hero is not knighted until a later feast day.

King Arthur and his court are seated at a meal in the hall, when there comes a maiden, Helie (*Descouneus*), Elene (*Lybeaus*), Nereja (*Wigalois*), or La Belle sans Villenie (*Papegau*), with an attendant dwarf. She is an emissary from a lady in distress who asks for a champion to deliver her. Instead of assigning one of his knights of prowess, Arthur provides the unknown youth, Descouneus or Lybeaus having claimed the adventure on the ground of a boon granted by the King when the hero arrived at the court, of the first request or the first fight.[19] In *Descouneus* and *Lybeaus* the emissary protests, objecting that the hero is too young for the undertaking,[20] which is what she also feels in *Wigalois*. She departs furiously with her dwarf in *Descouneus* and *Wigalois*, leaving the hero behind, who is now armed at the court as a knight in *Lybeaus* and *Wigalois* (in *Descouneus*, where he is already a knight, he demands his own arms), mounts and hastens after the emissary in *Descouneus* and *Wigalois* (Descouneus spurring his horse along a valley), and catches her up.

These features are paralleled in Malory's tale of *Sir Gareth,* which is the story of Beawmaynes, a hero like the Fair Unknown whose real name is Gareth. Here, the emissary Lynet also departs in anger, arms are brought for the hero, and after being armed he sets out and overtakes the damsel.[21] There is a comparable tale of La Cote Mal Taillie, another hero like the Fair Unknown, of which we have only a fragment, but an adapted version was incorporated into the *Prose Tristan* (from which comes the account of La Cote Male Tayle in Malory), where his real name is Brunor. On the day that he is knighted by Arthur, the Damoisele Mesdisant arrives asking for a champion to undertake a quest, and she departs annoyed, finding it ridiculous that she should be given the hero and not wanting to have him; but arms are brought, and after arming he follows fast after her and catches her up.[22] Again, in the non-Arthurian romance of *Ipomedon*, where we also have a situation resembling that in the Fair Unknown story, the emissary Ismeine departs angrily without the hero, who arms, and catches up with the damsel and her attendant dwarf.[23]

In Chrétien, Erec has been three years at Arthur's court, and in contrast to the Fair Unknown he has achieved a great reputation there and is a knight of the Round Table. Then the departure of Erec from the court is managed quite differently from that of the Fair Unknown. But now we meet with a feature of equivalence: the hero catches up with a lady and her attendant who have left the court first, and he wishes to join her. In *Erec*, instead of the emissary

19 In *Papegau*, the young King Arthur claims the mission for himself, as the first adventure which has come to his court.
20 In *Carduino* it is the dwarf who protests, at having the *uomo selvagio*.
21 Malory, VII, c. 2 to c. 5. Here the dwarf attendant serves the hero.
22 E. Löseth, *Le roman en prose de Tristan* (1891), § 68 f.; Malory, IX, c. 1 f.
23 *Ipomedon*, 7935-8176.

and her dwarf departing from Arthur's court we have Guinevere and a maiden
going to the forest to follow the hunt of the white stag. After them comes
galloping Erec, who catches up with them and asks if he may accompany the
Queen.[24] Similarly, Descouneus says that he wishes to accompany the damsel,
and Wigalois asks permission to join her.

I ENCOUNTER AT THE PERILOUS BRIDGE[25]

In *Lybeaus*, the manuscripts locate this adventure by either a *Castell Aunterous*
or a *Chapell Auntours*, and the opponent is on either a *Vale Perylous* or a
Poynte Perylous; for the latter there is a variant reading *bridge of perrill* (MS. P).
The encounter takes place at a bridge, so that a *Pont Perillous* is indicated. A
water crossing is also the site of the combat in *Descouneus*, but here we have
a *Gué Perilleus*, or Perilous Ford, defended by an adversary who waits beside
it in a shelter. This is a conventional site for a combat, compare the defended
ford, with the antagonist's tent beside it, where Gawain is opposed by Lieoniax
in the First Continuation of *Perceval*, or the similar *Gué Amoros* in the Second
Continuation, at which Perceval encounters the White Knight.[26]

In *Descouneus* and *Lybeaus*, the adventure is a combat with an adversary
whose custom is to oppose passing knights. He informs Lybeaus that the only
alternative is for him to give up his arms, while *Wigalois* incorporates here the
Jousting for Hospitality custom; the penalty for the knight who fails is in this
case the loss of all his belongings (p. 100).[27] The threat of dispossession is also
in *Carduino*, where the opponent comes riding towards the hero and demands
that the emissary be given over to him, or otherwise he will lose his head.

As soon as the adversary sees Descouneus coming, he gives orders to his
two attendants to bring him his steed and his arms, because he will fight with
the knight who approaches with a lady companion. They prepare him for battle,
he mounts his steed, and the combat takes place when Descouneus has crossed.
The opponent in *Lybeaus* is also waiting at the crossing, but here ready on
the bridge. In *Wigalois*, however, he looks out from his castle and sees the hero
approaching, orders his armour, his attendants bring him arms and his steed,
he mounts, and starts off at once to attack Wigalois outside the castle ditches,
expecting to deal with him as he has done with others before.[28]

This bears on the First Encounter with Guivret in Chrétien. Erec and Enide
pass across a bridge in front of the little king's castle, which is enclosed by
a wall and a moat, but they have not gone far before Guivret espies them.

24 *Erec*, 77-114.
25 *Descouneus*, 321-592; *Lybeaus*, 253-444; *Carduino*, ii, 20/5-25/8; *Wigalois*, 1968-2013.
Schofield, *op. cit.*, 12-16.
26 *Perceval*, First Continuation, 8030-84; Second Continuation, 21980-22160.
27 Cross-references to other passages in this book will henceforth be provided to
facilitate comparison, appearing simply as bracketed page numbers.
28 In a derivative of the Encounter at the Perilous Bridge to be found in *Le Livre
d'Artus*, the opponent also comes from a castle (p. 137 f.).

Wishing to oppose the armed knight he sees passing in front of his castle, Guivret orders his horse and his arms, which are brought by two attendants, goes through the gate as quickly as possible and comes tearing down upon Erec, who charges when he sees him, the clash occurring *au chief del pont*, that is, at the end of the bridge.[29]

The adversary bears three gold lions on his shield in *Lybeaus*, while in Chrétien his saddle is decorated with gold lions. The course of the combat in *Erec* is similar to that in *Descouneus* and *Lybeaus*, particularly the latter, but with a significant distinction. At the first shock, Descouneus or Lybeaus smites Blioblieris or Wylleam Selebraunche so fiercely that his lance pierces him, and he falls down off his horse. The same happens in Chrétien, but to both Erec and Guivret, who do this to each other. In *Descouneus* and *Lybeaus*, as in *Erec*, the combat continues on foot, with both the antagonists so battering each other's helmets with their swords that sparks fly. Lybeaus splits his opponent's shield and goes as far as his bare flesh, and the same happens in Chrétien, but again Erec and Guivret do it to each other. In both *Lybeaus* and *Erec*, when the adversary returns a blow he breaks his sword, and is left defenceless begging for mercy, as being weaponless. The conquered antagonist, in *Descouneus* and *Lybeaus*, has been grievously wounded: so is Guivret, but again also Erec. In all three texts, the opponent in return for mercy yields himself as prisoner, but in the tale of the Fair Unknown he gives his word to go to Arthur's court.

II   RESCUE FROM TWO GIANTS[30]

The equivalence of an episode in *Erec* to the Rescue from Two Giants in the Fair Unknown story is obvious enough. In both, the hero goes alone (except in *Descouneus*) to the rescue after hearing a maiden's cry for help in the forest,[31] and later returns to the lady who accompanies him. The course of the fight is also basically similar. The hero strikes the first giant dead with his spear, and the other giant attacks him. Like Lybeaus, Erec receives a tremendous blow from him on his shield, and then, before the giant can deliver another, kills him with his sword. But in the tale of the Fair Unknown this happens at night—with the moon shining in *Descouneus* and *Wigalois*—the hero and his lady companion have taken up quarters in the forest country, the giants are by a fire with one of them roasting meat, and the hero rescues a maiden. Whereas in Chrétien he is travelling in the daytime through the forest with his lady companion, and saves a person who is not in the Fair Unknown story at all, the maiden's lover, who is found being ill-treated by the giants.[32]

---

29 *Erec*, 3653-3913.
30 *Descouneus*, 593-828; *Lybeaus*, 541-651; *Carduino*, ii, 26/1-36/8; *Wigalois*, 2014-2185, cf. *Papegau*, 3/9-15. Schofield, *op. cit.*, 18-22; Saran, *op. cit.*, 316-18.
31 In *Lybeaus*, the maiden's cry for help is first heard as the hero approaches her.
32 *Erec*, 4280-4551. Loomis, *op. cit.*, 82, 160.

The Rescue from Two Giants follows the First Encounter with Guivret in *Erec*, though not immediately, as there intervenes the Meeting with Arthur and his Company in the forest.

RS RECONCILIATION SCENE[33]

The emissary is convinced of the prowess of Descouneus, Lybeaus, or Wigalois, and openly admits this to him. In *Descouneus* and *Lybeaus*, she regrets having slandered the hero's valour (*dis vilonnie* or *spak vylanye*), begs his mercy, and he forgives her, in *Lybeaus* for the offence (*trespas*). There are comparable scenes in allied tales. In Chrétien, Enide was full of regret, ever since she committed the fault, for having spoken words that implied such slander, and at the reconciliation the hero declares that he forgives her for the offence (*forfet*).[34]

Episodes **II RS III** occur in the course of a single night in *Descouneus*. The reconcilement is here associated with a meal during the night, which they enjoy with the rescued maiden, while the dwarf and Robert (the squire who doubles the role of the dwarf in this version) busily attend to the serving. But this festive occasion, which is authentic, since it also happens when Carduino has returned with the rescued damsel to his companions after his victory over the giants, is absent from *Lybeaus*, where we find instead a sudden departure, without attention by the author to any passage from night to day, when the hero takes the rescued maiden back to her father, Earl Antore. This corresponds to the morning departure of this damsel along with the hero and his companions in *Carduino*; and in *Descouneus* one of the opponents conquered in the Attack by Three Avengers (**III**) escorts her back to her father.[35] *Lybeaus* does however possess a Reconciliation Scene, and we should note how much its circumstances resemble those in *Descouneus* in spite of the difference in location within the sequence of episodes: it is at night, when they have a meal, and they make that night *game and greet solas*, while the dwarf serves them with all that is necessary. Thus the reconciliation in *Lybeaus* is also associated with a joyful meal at night. But it is not consequent upon a deed, and it follows episode **I**, with the Rescue from Two Giants (**II**) still to come (p. 85). We shall find confirmation that it is *Descouneus* which has the correct order of episodes here.

The Reconciliation Scene in *Erec* is also at night, and follows the Rescue from Two Giants here too, though not immediately, as there intervenes the Refusal to Eat at Limors. But it is significant that we have found a sequence in *Erec* corresponding to the series **I II RS** in the tale of the Fair Unknown.

33 *Descouneus*, 829-958; *Lybeaus*, 445-53, 652-75; *Carduino*, ii, 37/1-39/2; *Wigalois*, 3608-19. Schofield, *op. cit.*, 14 f., 22-4.
34 *Erec*, 4879-97.
35 *Lybeaus*, 676-705; *Carduino*, 39/3-6. Cf. *Descouneus*, 1227-30.

D

III   ATTACK BY THREE AVENGERS[36]

In the Encounter at the Perilous Bridge, the opponent is killed in *Wigalois* and *Carduino*, where the emissary or the dwarf is aghast at the hero's deed, and she urges Wigalois to ride on in order to avoid an attack. This materializes in *Descouneus* and *Lybeaus*, in which three avengers (the adversary has three brothers in *Carduino*) set out in pursuit of the hero, who has left the vanquished knight bleeding profusely, Descouneus having given him a most debilitating wound.[37]

Willaume de Salebrant, Elins de Graies, and the Sire de Saies (*Descouneus*), or Gower and his two brothers, nephews of the conquered knight (*Lybeaus*), now launch their attack. There is obvious correspondence in *Descouneus* with the assault by the first band in Chrétien's Encounters with Marauders.[38] Not only are there also three opponents, but as in *Erec* the three come in turn at the hero, the same explanation is given for this, and the knights are called robbers:

> Vinrent poingnant li robeor
> Les le roce de Valcolor.
>
> (*Li Biaus Descouneus*, 1003 f.)

Schofield concluded that Renaut de Beaujeu had *Erec*'s Encounters with Marauders in mind.[39] Yet, in order that the sequence of corresponding episodes which I have been tracing may continue, it is not the Encounters with Marauders but something after the Reconciliation Scene in *Erec* that has to be reminiscent of the Attack by Three Avengers, and it is soon found, in what follows the reconcilement in Chrétien, the Second Encounter with Guivret.

The First Encounter ends with Erec and Guivret becoming friends, and the little king promises the hero that he will go to aid him with all the assistance he can command, should he have any need of help. Having heard of the events at Limors, Guivret now arrives with an army of rescuers, but he fails to recognize Erec in the dark and attacks him. One can see here certain functions related to those of the Attack by Three Avengers. Their assault draws its cause from the Encounter at the Perilous Bridge, the equivalent of which in *Erec*, the First Encounter with Guivret, contains the seed from which springs the Second Encounter. The Attack by Three Avengers is connected with the Encounter at the Perilous Bridge across the intervening adventure of the Rescue from Two Giants, just as the Second Encounter with Guivret is linked with the First Encounter right across intervening episodes, including the Rescue from Two Giants. And the assault on Erec by Guivret in the Second Encounter is the result of the little king's arrival with a band of rescuers, which is the reverse

36 *Descouneus*, 959-1236; *Lybeaus*, 454-540. Schofield, *op. cit.*, 16-18.
37 *Descouneus*, 517-91; *Lybeaus*, 385-441; *Carduino*, ii, 21/1 f., 24/1 f.; *Wigalois*, 2008-13.
38 *Erec*, 2791-2909.
39 Schofield, *op. cit.*, 113-16.

of the motif in the Attack by Three Avengers but also leads to an onslaught, which has to be motivated by mistake. All this makes particularly significant the following resemblances between these attacks in *Descouneus* and *Erec*.

The avengers come upon Descouneus at night, with the moon shining, as it has been for the Rescue from Two Giants earlier the same night. Descouneus has been disarmed, the reconciliation has taken place with the emissary, when the avengers arrive at a gallop and catch him unarmed. The first avenger is just about to assault Descouneus, when the emissary appeals to him not to attack an unarmed man, because that would be shameful and wrong conduct, and he should not set about doing something for which he would gain disgrace, for never was there an offence so unseemly. Descouneus has no strength against the three of them, and it would be more fitting to take him armed. This concern of hers for Descouneus is perfectly in tune with the mood of the moment, for she has just been reconciled with the hero. Her appeal succeeds, and the assault is suspended while Descouneus arms himself.

In Chrétien, Erec and Enide flee from Limors at night, have their Reconciliation Scene, and soon after encounter the force led by Guivret hastening to the rescue in the shining moonlight. The moon having just gone behind a cloud, Erec and Guivret do not recognize each other. Catching sight of Erec from a distance, Guivret comes towards him at a gallop, launching an attack right away, though he does not even know who he is. The hero is struck down. Enide immediately appeals to Guivret to stop his assault, for it is on a man who is alone and exhausted, in pain and mortally wounded, and with such injustice. He should be generous and courteous and kindly cease his attack, for his reputation would be no better for having killed or captured a knight who does not have the strength to rise.[40] Her appeal succeeds. The material here in the two texts is thus very similar, the distinction being principally that between an unarmed and a wounded hero.

The sequence of episodes in *Erec* corresponding to one in the tale of the Fair Unknown has now grown to four, in the order **I II RS III**.

IV ENCOUNTER WITH A HUNTSMAN[41]

A stag (*Descouneus*) or a hind (*Lybeaus*) appears in the forest (in *Giglan* in a glade),[42] pursued by hounds, and a beautiful dog comes past, which is white with black ears and so small that it is not much larger than a stoat (*Descouneus*), or it is a hunting dog with as many colours as the flowers (*Lybeaus*). A lovely little white dog, with one red ear, also runs by in *Wigalois*. The emissary expresses a wish to have it in *Lybeaus* and *Wigalois*, and the hero catches the

---

40 *Erec*, 4898-5008.
41 *Descouneus*, 1276-1496; *Lybeaus*, 1000-1220; *Wigalois*, 2207-2318. Schofield, *op. cit.*, 32-6; Saran, *op. cit.*, 318 f. Cognates are given on pp. 115, 189, 246.
42 *Giglan*, m ii *verso*.

dog and gives it to her; in *Descouneus* she seizes it herself and says she will take it to her lady. Its owner, who in *Descouneus* and *Lybeaus* is the huntsman, called Orguillous de la Lande (*Descouneus*) or Otes de Lyle (*Lybeaus*), arrives (carrying his horn in *Descouneus*, and blowing his bugle in *Lybeaus*) and claims his dog, there is a dispute when its return is refused, and the stranger departs angrily to his castle to arm himself and return to fight the hero. On the defeat of the opponent, Descouneus or Lybeaus makes him promise to go to Arthur as his prisoner. Then the hero and the emissary continue their ride with the dog in her possession.

M. Mills has shown how this episode is like the first adventure in *Erec*, the Encounter with Yder, but with a different distribution of roles. In Chrétien, Guinevere is accompanied by a damsel and the unarmed Erec when she follows Arthur and his company to the hunt of the white stag, and in the forest the Queen encounters Yder with a damsel and an attendant dwarf. Guinevere asks her maiden to summon the unknown knight to her, but the dwarf bars the way and refuses to let her address Yder, and when she insists he strikes her with his scourge. He repeats the treatment with Erec when he attempts in his turn to disregard the dwarf's refusal to allow the Queen's request to be conveyed to Yder. On the departure of Yder and his companions, Erec decides to pursue the knight until he can obtain arms with which to avenge the insult.[43] In relation to the Encounter with a Huntsman, Erec is the unarmed huntsman[44] who departs in search of arms to obtain revenge, and the knight accompanied by a damsel and an attendant dwarf is not the hero but Yder.[45] The refusal to allow Erec to convey a request to Yder is comparable with the refusal to accede to the demand for the return of the dog.

The sequence of episodes in *Erec* corresponding to one in the tale of the Fair Unknown has now been broken, as we revert to the first adventure in Chrétien.

V   SPARROWHAWK CONTEST[46]

Descouneus, Wigalois, or Arthur comes across a maid of surpassing beauty with whom he enters the contest for the bird, but their meeting is not like that of Erec with Enide in the equivalent episode.[47] In the tale of the Fair Unknown,

---

43 *Erec*, 115-274.

44 R. R. Bezzola, *Le sens de l'aventure et de l'amour* (1947), 96, remarks: "*pourquoi ne s'est-il même pas habillé pour la chasse?*" As the escort of a lady following the hunt, Erec is not properly a huntsman, but in a sense takes part in the hunt, and resembles a huntsman in being only armed with the sword; cf. the huntsman-knight in *Sir Gawain and the Green Knight*, 1584, 1901. Erec wears silk socks on which his golden spurs are fastened without shoes, like that same figure in *Sir Gawain*, 158-60, in his guise as an unarmed Green Knight.

45 Mills, *art. cit.* 34-6.

46 *Descouneus*, 1497-1869; *Lybeaus*, 706-999; *Wigalois*, 2349-3285; *Papegau*, 5/11-12/15. Schofield, *op. cit.*, 25-32, 164-70; Saran, *op. cit.*, 319 f., 346-62; *Papegau*, xxxiii-xxxix.

47 *Erec*, 342-1458.

the damsel is found on the approach to the city, riding alone,[48] and she wears rich apparel. It is she who informs the hero about the contest. These features are all present as well in *Durmart le Galois* (early thirteenth century), with the distinction that here the maiden is going to the city, and not coming away from it.[49] Lybeaus, however, enters the contest with the emissary.

The contest takes place at Becleus, against Giflet le fils Do, with Rose Espanie as his *amie*, while the damsel is Margerie, sister of a king of Scotland (*Descouneus*); the site is Cardevyle, and the combat against Gyffroun le Flowdous (*Lybeaus*); the opponent is called Hojir von Mannesvelt, and the damsel eventually turns out to be Elamie, Queen of Tyre (*Wigalois*); the location is Causuel, the antagonist Lion sans Mercy, and the damsel La Dame sans Orgueil (*Papegau*); or the contest is at Landoc, the adversary's name Cardroain li Ros, his *amie* being Ydain de Landoc, and the damsel, as we later discover, is Fenise, a Queen in Ireland (*Durmart*). In *Wigalois* and *Papegau* the bird is not a hawk but a parrot, after winning which the hero of the latter romance is called the Chevalier du Papegau.

The damsel is full of grief in *Descouneus* and *Wigalois*. She relates the cause of her sorrow to the hero, and according to *Wigalois* she has just taken part in a beauty competition, which was attended by knights each accompanied by his *amie*. They judged her to be the most beautiful, but when she went to take the prize a Red Knight drew it away and gave it to his own *amie*, and none dared to oppose him. Wigalois offers to champion the damsel's cause and set right the wrong. But in *Descouneus* she is weeping because her *ami* was killed in the contest, when he took part in it on her behalf against a knight whose shield was silver, with red roses, a colour combination which is to be compared with that in *Lybeaus*, where the adversary's shield is red, with silver owls. Descouneus offers to enter the contest to obtain for her both the sparrowhawk and vengeance for the slaying of her *ami*. This loss of the prize through the defeat of an *ami* must be authentic. The damsel in *Wigalois* was strangely without an escort at the contest, in *Papegau* she has just had her *ami* killed,[50] and in *Durmart* we find this pattern: when the hero comes across the lady, she is looking for the knight (Nogant) who is to take part in the contest on her behalf, she finds him, and they ride to the place (the hero goes with them); her champion fails her (through cowardice) against an opponent whose shield is red, with a silver eagle (cf. *Lybeaus*), who is termed *li ros*, i.e. with red hair, and who stays there in a tent with his *amie*, these last two traits also occurring with the adversary in *Wigalois*; the damsel dissolves into tears, and the hero then champions her cause and fights in the contest.

None of this is in *Erec*. Here the hero is told about the contest by his host,

---

48 In *Papegau*, by amalgamation with the previous episode, she is being chased by a knight.

49 The Sparrowhawk Contest is in *Durmart*, 1885-2768; cf. 3965-4020, 10593-630.

50 She is here made the lady saved in the previous episode from the knight who has killed her *ami*.

and not by the maiden, nor before he enters the town. But what he learns about its terms is paralleled in *Descouneus* and *Durmart*. However, though their authors knew their Chrétien well, the distinction apparent between them and him, as to whether it is the lady or the knight who has the initiative, shows that they are not drawing on *Erec*.

The maid informs Descouneus or Durmart that it is the lady who will wish to win the prize, and she will bring with her a knight to support her claim, in *Descouneus* specifically to be the most beautiful, against the adversary as the champion of his own *amie*. The proving of beauty by combat is nothing but the extension of a medieval practice. In Chrétien's *Yvain*, the hero is brought to support a younger sister's claim to an inheritance, in battle against Gawain, the champion of her elder sister. Judicial combat was carried out before spectators assembled for the occasion, and there was a ritual to be followed, which included formal declarations by the combatants of what each set out to prove. Thus, in Chrétien's *Le Chevalier de la Charrete*, the accuser Meleagant asserts the adultery of Kay with Guinevere, and the defender Lancelot challenges the accusation. Comparably, in *Descouneus* and *Durmart*, the champion of one lady will lead her to the sparrowhawk on a perch in the open before spectators, tell her to take the hawk from the perch, and she will begin to take possession of it. Then the adversary, advancing with his own *amie*, will challenge her right to take the bird and defend his damsel's claim to it, in *Descouneus* maintaining against the other knight that it is his own *amie* who is the more beautiful, and saying he is ready to prove his challenge in combat. In *Durmart* we find instead that the supporter of the first lady's claim has the duty of declaring his damsel's beauty surpasses that of the antagonist's *amie*, and that he is ready to fight him. The combat ensues, after the knights have defied each other, and the victor, according to *Durmart*, has conquered the sparrowhawk (cf. *Erec*, 661), takes it into his possession, and gives it to his damsel.

The situation in *Wigalois* is not far from this, because the prize is offered to the lady, and its removal from her by a knight to give to his own *amie* corresponds to upholding the denial of her claim, while the principle that the damsel requires a supporter to maintain her right is illustrated when the hero undertakes the task. Compare an episode in the thirteenth-century romance of *Cristal et Clarie* which has traits of the Sparrowhawk Contest, including the meeting with a weeping maiden.[51] She is not alone but accompanied by her knight, and informs the hero that she had an excellent sparrowhawk, but, when they encountered a knight with a beautiful damsel, he demanded the bird for his own lady. Her *ami* refused, but was defeated when they jousted for the sparrowhawk, which was taken away by the other knight and given to his own *amie*. Cristal declares he will avenge her sorrow, goes and defeats the knight, and returns the hawk to its owner.

In *Papegau*, which has no loss of the prize through the defeat of the damsel's

51 *Cristal et Clarie*, 3772-4086.

ami in a combat, she proposes that the hero should be her champion in the contest to prove that she is more beautiful than the antagonist's *amie*. We have another proposition to the hero by a lady which results in such a contest in Andreas Capellanus, whose Latin treatise on love incorporates an Arthurian tale in Book II, c. 8.

One of the knights of Bretagne, when he asks for the love of a lady, is told he can never obtain it unless he first brings for her the hawk which is on a golden perch at Arthur's court; the sparrowhawk is on a perch of gold in *Descouneus* and *Durmart*, too, but of silver in *Erec*. The knight goes on his way to Arthur, and in the forest he comes upon a damsel of marvellous beauty sitting on a horse. Like the maiden that the Fair Unknown meets in similar circumstances, she informs him about the conditions of the contest. He cannot obtain the hawk unless he proves in combat that he enjoys the love of a more beautiful lady than any man at Arthur's court. The knight asks her to permit him to claim, as she is directing him, that he enjoys the love of such a lady, and she grants him his request and gives him the kiss of love before she dispatches him on his mission. Thus he obtains the hawk for one damsel, but fights in the contest as the *ami* of another.

The hero eventually reaches Arthur's court, where he finds the approach to the hawk guarded by twelve knights, as it is also in *Durmart*. When pressed by Arthur's knights to explain his purpose, the hero in Andreas declares that he has come to carry off the bird, which is like Erec in Chrétien, who announces that *cest esprevier sui venuȝ querre* (844). One of the knights at court asks Andreas's hero why, to which he replies it is because he enjoys the love of a more beautiful woman than any knight at court; and the other answers that before he takes the hawk away he will have to fight to prove that assertion. Here we have what corresponds to the ritual of claim and challenge that has been observed.

In this version the ladies do not take part in the contest, and there is another version without the combat. In *Meraugis de Portlesgueȝ* (c. 1200), by Raoul de Houdenc, a tournament is held after which a sparrowhawk, exposed on the branch of a tree, is to be awarded to the most beautiful lady, and all recognize that the heroine is entitled to take possession of the bird. When she does so, there is a potential supporter of her right to it, for a knight who falls in love with her declares that for her sake he would dare to prove she is the most beautiful in the world.[52] By his reference to the possibility that the prize could be gained even by one with dress *perciee as cotes* (182), Raoul shows he bears in mind the account by Chrétien, but that he makes use of Fair Unknown material can be seen elsewhere.[53]

In contrast to the examples I have cited, in *Erec* a lady is put in for the contest by her *ami*, and, according to its terms, the prize is apparently not to be hers but his. For the hero learns, not that it will be a damsel who engages

<hr />

52 *Meraugis*, 157-383.
53 See pp. 118 n. 39, 123 n. 57, 159, 217 below.

a knight to support her claim, but that the knight who will have the hawk must possess a lovely *amie*, and he proposes to enter the contest. So he does, too, in *Lybeaus*, after hearing that a knight will gain the prize if he brings a fairer lady than the opponent's sweetheart, but if his own damsel is judged to be less beautiful he must fight him for it. The hawk can thus be won here on the ground of either the lady's beauty or her champion's prowess, which is an alteration of the original terms, and the offering of the prize to the knight is to be linked with the absence of a damsel met on the way, Lybeaus entering the contest with the emissary. Again, in *Papegau* we find that the prize is offered to the knight who has the most beautiful *amie* and can demonstrate it by force of arms, despite the fact that it is the damsel who proposes that the hero should enter the contest.

By putting *Wigalois* together with *Papegau*, it can be seen that their common source must have had, like *Descouneus*, *Durmart*, and *Cristal et Clarie*, the damsel's *ami* who failed her against the adversary, and the hero avenging her sorrow by conquering the bird for her. The original situation in the tale of the Fair Unknown was thus one where the lady brings a knight she has engaged as her champion, but for the second contest the initiative is the hero's. This accounts for what we have in texts where the hero is the damsel's only champion. There is overlapping in *Papegau*, and in Andreas the lady splits into two, one who proposes that the hawk should be obtained for her, and the other who receives the proposal that the hero should fight in the contest as her *ami*. Where a lady is put in for the contest by one who wishes to gain the bird, this develops from the situation of the hero having the initiative, and when he wins the prize for himself in *Lybeaus* and *Papegau* we are far from the world of judicial combat. In Chrétien, though a knight there also enters the contest because he would gain the hawk, we have the ritual of claim and challenge in support of each lady's cause, and the silent testimony of the prize that Erec wins becoming the property of Enide.

After his meeting with the maiden, in the tale of the Fair Unknown the hero rides to the town with her, and Descouneus arrives in the evening, even as Erec is seen to be there late in the day. As in Chrétien—but here he arrives alone—so too in *Lybeaus* the hero finds lodgings in the town; Wigalois stays overnight where the tents are. In the morning Erec attends early mass before the contest, and indeed the time appointed for it is after mass in *Wigalois*, while in *Descouneus* the previous contestant is said to have been killed *aprés messe cantant* that morning. In the tale of the Fair Unknown, as in *Erec*, the hero rides to the contest with the lady,[54] but unlike Enide she is splendidly dressed. The contest takes place in *Descouneus* and *Lybeaus* with the lord of the castle, who has a hawk that is to be claimed, in *Lybeaus* explicitly at any time. On the other hand, in *Wigalois*, *Papegau*, and *Durmart*, as in Chrétien, the event is a festive occasion for which large numbers of knights and ladies have assembled

---

54 In *Wigalois* she is present at the combat.

at the town, the antagonist comes to it,[55] and it has been held annually in *Papegau* and *Durmart* as well as *Erec*. But, when the hero enters the contest, there appears a critical distinction between *Erec* and the tale of the Fair Unknown.

We have a reversal of roles, for in Chrétien the contest opens not with the hero but with Yder telling his *amie* to take the hawk from the perch, and Erec, with his own damsel, hurrying up to challenge, as the opponent does in the Fair Unknown story. This alters the function of the adversary. In *Lybeaus* and *Durmart* the contest is established by him for the love of his *amie*, and the custom is maintained in *Descouneus* by the defender of the bird; in *Wigalois* the antagonist has gained possession of the prize, which accompanies him to the place of combat in *Papegau*; and also in Andreas Capellanus there is a challenger to the hero's right to carry off the hawk. But Erec is the defender of the bird in Chrétien, while the opponent is like the Fair Unknown, because his arms are azure,[56] he arrives and seeks lodgings in the town together with a damsel and a dwarf, and the next day puts forward her claim to the sparrowhawk. On the other hand, he corresponds to the antagonist in the tale of the Fair Unknown in having won the prize before and achieved a domination over other knights. The adversary in *Lybeaus* and *Wigalois* has never been defeated, in *Papegau* he has conquered all previous opponents over a period of fifteen years and more, and made everyone regularly acknowledge that his lady is the most beautiful, while in *Durmart* he has killed a knight on each of the seven years that he has already defended the sparrowhawk on behalf of his *amie*, and this time he expects no opposition. The situation, as Chrétien arranges it, is that the prize for the most beautiful lady has been obtained by Yder for his own damsel on two previous occasions without anyone daring to oppose him, and, if he has it this time as well, he will have conquered it for ever. But now he is challenged by Erec, and the course of the ritual is paralleled in particular by *Descouneus*, where it is the challenger—there the adversary—who asserts that his *amie* is more beautiful than the other knight's lady. Then Erec passes from challenger to supporter of a claim, as he tells Enide to advance and take the hawk to which her beauty entitles her. As a result the two knights defy each other, Yder being roused to high words, like the opponent we see in *Durmart*, who also charges the hero with folly in bringing the danger upon himself.

The combat follows, and its course reveals resemblances between *Erec* and the other versions. It is true that in the romances blending of the Sparrowhawk Contest of *Erec* with that in the tale of the Fair Unknown would not be surprising. But the position with Andreas Capellanus is not quite the same, and his treatise provides a reflection of the episode in the Fair Unknown story which is contemporary with *Erec*. We find points of resemblance in the fighting of the Sparrowhawk Contest that draw attention to the relation between *Erec*

---

55 This is so in *Papegau* even though the opponent turns out to possess the castle of Causuel.

56 *Descouneus*, 73; *Erec*, 585.

and Andreas Capellanus in particular. There are seven versions, and almost without exception at the first shock the lances of the contestants are shattered or their shields are split, and in four of them (*Erec, Descouneus, Papegau, Durmart*) both are unhorsed and lie on the ground. The battle continues with the sword (*Erec, Descouneus, Wigalois, Papegau*, Andreas), and they smite each other violently, until eventually the hero brings the combat to an end. In Andreas Capellanus, the vision of the adversary, whom the hero has struck on the head with two shrewd blows in rapid succession, begins to be so disturbed that he can see almost nothing, and the hero, perceiving this, leaps boldly upon him and quickly strikes him down.[57] Erec hits his antagonist on the head with three blows in quick succession and penetrates to the bone, which causes him to totter, and while he is unsteady the hero knocks him down. Finally, in *Descouneus, Wigalois*, and *Papegau*, as in *Erec*, after his defeat the adversary is made to give his word to go to Arthur's court.[58]

Like Erec and Enide, the hero and the damsel, together with the prize, which belongs to her in *Descouneus, Wigalois*, and *Durmart*, as also in Chrétien, depart from the city as companions. But now *Erec* and the tale of the Fair Unknown diverge. The damsel invites Wigalois or Durmart to come with her to her own country, and Wigalois refuses. She and Descouneus, Wigalois, or the Chevalier du Papegau take leave of each other, and he continues on his mission with the emissary. In *Descouneus* the damsel goes home with her sparrowhawk, as she does too after the later separation in *Durmart*.

The Sparrowhawk Contest in *Erec* follows immediately after the Encounter with Yder, and so we have started another sequence of episodes corresponding to one in the tale of the Fair Unknown, this time in the order **IV V**.

VI ILE D'OR EPISODE[59]

In *Descouneus* and *Lybeaus* there is a city called Ile d'Or, which is the Amoureuse Cité in *Papegau*. It is by the sea in *Descouneus* and *Papegau*, and the region is ruled by a lady, the Pucele as Blances Mains (*Descouneus*), the Dame d'Amore (*Lybeaus*), or La Dame aux Cheveux Blons (*Papegau*). The hero arrives and on the approach slays a redoubtable opponent. In *Descouneus*, the combat takes

---

57 In *Descouneus*, we also have this final striking down with a great blow: the opponent falls stunned, and *ses vis trestos en torbla* (by his face hitting a stone).

58 *Wigalois* and *Papegau* have some individual parallels with Chrétien. In *Wigalois*, the maid gives the hero his spear when he mounts to go to the contest, she offers up prayer for him during the combat, on hearing which he fights with renewed energy, and after the contest the defeated opponent leaves immediately with his *amie* for Arthur's court. In *Papegau*, the lord of the castle (the opponent) orders people to clear the place for the combat, and the exchange of blows which ends the battle is like one in the course of Erec's fight.

59 *Descouneus*, 1870-2491; *Lybeaus*, 1231-1458; *Carduino*, ii, 8/6-20/4 (lacks the combat); *Papegau*, 14/20-44/16. Schofield, *op. cit.*, 36-42; here the spelling *Ile d'Or* is used, with which I conform, though *Ille d'Or* is the usual spelling in *Descouneus*.

place between the bridge and the city, in full view of the people and their lady, who watches from the castle, and the adversary is Malgiers li Gris, the lady's suitor, on whom she has imposed the task of defending the approach for seven years in order to succeed in his suit. Maugys in *Lybeaus* is similarly the defender of the bridge and slain in sight of the inhabitants, but he is a hideous and black giant besieger of the lady, and in *Papegau* the Poisson Chevalier is a hideous and monstrous giant knight who ravages her people and her domain.

On his victory, the inhabitants of the city and their mistress, who is a beautiful fay, welcome the hero as their deliverer. She offers Descouneus or Lybeaus her domain and herself, in *Descouneus* and *Papegau* falling in love with him on sight. After supper, the emissary takes Descouneus aside and rebukes him: he should not commit a shameful act and forget her lady in distress. This causes him to set off again on his mission next morning, after a night on which the fay comes to his bed, but frustrates his desire and returns to her room. The hero's stay is also only one frustrating night in the equivalent adventure of *Carduino*, but it is prolonged in *Papegau*, and in *Lybeaus* lasts a year and more. Lybeaus lapses into amorous indolence, being so frustrated and fascinated by the fay that he cannot leave and forgets his mission, till the emissary brings him to his senses by upbraiding him with being false of faith and committing great dishonour for the love of a woman. When he hears her words, his heart wellnigh breaks for sorrow and shame. In *Papegau*, where the hero has become wrapped up in a love affair with the fay, the emissary reminds him of his promise to deliver her lady, and, because of the negligence of his duty, he is filled with shame.[60]

This bears on the Lapse into Amorous Indolence in Chrétien, when Erec leaves off valorous pursuits and earns dishonour, all for the love of a woman, and receives a rebuke from Enide that impels him to carry out his martial duty by going in quest of exploits.[61] Erec's negligence follows the Sparrowhawk Contest, though various episodes intervene, in the Arrival at Arthur's Court, the Wedding of Erec and Enide, and the Return to Estregales, none of which comprises an adventure. The new sequence of episodes corresponding to one in the tale of the Fair Unknown has now grown to three, in the order **IV V VI**.

VII JOUSTING FOR HOSPITALITY[62]

The Fair Unknown, the emissary, and the dwarf[63] come in sight of the domain that is their goal, and they see a fine stronghold. Lybeaus asks the emissary about it, and Descouneus inquires whether they are to lodge there. She tells the hero of a custom practised by the lord of the castle they have come to,

---

60 This is the second emissary, who comes to the hero at the Amoureuse Cité.

61 *Erec*, 2430-2791.

62 *Descouneus*, 2492-2740; *Lybeaus*, 1459-1737; *Wigalois*, 1928-67. Schofield, *op. cit.*, 15, 42-7, 226-30; Saran, *op. cit.*, 320-22.

63 After the Ile d'Or, the dwarf is replaced by a squire Gyfflet in *Lybeaus*.

referred to later in *Descouneus* as *la costume male*. Lanpart (called Lambard in *Lybeaus*) does not give lodging unless he is first vanquished in jousting; victory gains a knight hospitality, in *Descouneus* with great honour, but if he is defeated he must depart in disgrace, without his horse in *Descouneus*. The inhabitants will hurl a shower of refuse at the conquered knight as he leaves, according to *Giglan* treating him with the greatest dishonour (*luy font la plus grand honte qu'ilʒ peuvent*), and crying out "*ha! lasche chevalier vaincu!*"[64] In *Wigalois*, where the custom is attached to the Encounter at the Perilous Bridge, the emissary tells the hero that if he asks for lodgings he will first have to joust with the lord of the castle, victory gaining hospitality with honour, but the penalty for defeat being departure with the loss of all belongings. Descouneus is advised by the emissary not to undertake the adventure, which others have suffered to their cost, and she warns Wigalois to seek lodgings elsewhere. But the hero will not desist, and in all three versions he goes to ask for lodgings. The porter lets Lybeaus in and reports his arrival to Lambard, but Descouneus passes through the town, on the way to the castle meets Lanpart sitting down in the open, and is told that he is willing to give hospitality according to the custom he practises.

Then Lanpart (Lambard) arms himself and jousts with the hero, in the field before the castle gate in *Lybeaus*; similarly, the jousting would be *ûf dem velde*, according to *Wigalois*.[65] By his victory, Descouneus or Lybeaus gains hospitality from his opponent, who turns out to be the seneschal or steward of the lady in distress. He welcomes the hero with joy as the champion come from Arthur for the delivery of his lady, having first recognized and embraced the emissary in *Descouneus*. Synadoun is the name of the lady's city in *Lybeaus*, but in *Descouneus* her capital is Senaudon, and they are at Galigan, her seneschal's stronghold. Compare episode **VIIb** in *Wigalois*, where the lady's steward is met before Roimunt as the hero approaches, and jousts with Wigalois. Soon recognizing the hero's merit, he welcomes him to Roimunt in the kingdom of Korntin, the name of its capital, sees the emissary, salutes her warmly for having accomplished her mission, and they all go to enter Roimunt. Now, in the Arrival at the Lady's Stronghold, there is joy, all welcome Wigalois as the champion sent by Arthur for the delivery of the lady from her oppressor, and he is given hospitality with great honour.[66]

At the evening meal, Lybeaus asks Lambard about the adventure, and is told of the circumstances in the land. The lady of Synadoun is held captive by two brother-magicians, Maboun and Yrayn, who are trying to force her to do Maboun's will and yield him her kingdom. She is in an enchanted palace which no-one dares to enter, and from it she is often heard to cry out, but cannot be seen. Wigalois, who is told of the circumstances in the land by the emissary in the Reconciliation Scene, looks out at Roimunt and sees the castle of Korntin, inquires about it, and is informed that from Korntin at night cries

64 *Giglan*, n iii *verso*.   65 It is in a hall in *Descouneus*.
66 *Wigalois*, 3885-4007.

can be heard, but all is quiet during the day.[67] Both Lybeaus and Wigalois express their zeal to accomplish the mission and win the lady.[68] Descouneus is however not told of the circumstances that account for the state of Senaudon until he achieves the mission, when the lady, who is Blonde Esmeree, Queen of Gales (Wales), informs him that the magicians Mabon and Evrain, of whom the former is the senior, enchanted the city and herself to try to force her to marry Mabon. In *Carduino*, where the host is lacking, along with the Jousting for Hospitality episode, the dwarf tells the hero before the enchanted city that a magician keeps it and its inhabitants in such a condition because the princess will not love him.[69]

The equivalent in Chrétien is the Arrival at Brandigan.[70] Erec, Enide, and the little king Guivret come in sight of this fine stronghold, and the hero asks not Enide but Guivret about it. It is evening, and Erec decides to take lodgings there, but Guivret is distressed, explaining that they should not visit the place, because it has a very dangerous passage (*molt mal trespas*). In spite of the warning, Erec insists on going there. He is then informed that no-one can enter the stronghold with the intention of staying without being received by Evrain, King of Brandigan, who has forbidden the citizens to give lodgings to anyone entering the fortress. The King wants to do the honour himself. Thus instead of the Jousting for Hospitality custom we have an unavoidable reception by the lord of the stronghold, who is so noble-minded that he wishes to give all visitors to the city the honour of his hospitality. *Descouneus* therefore echoes Chrétien when it says the citizens do not give lodgings because Lanpart wishes to do the honour to all. This contrasts with the declaration of Descouneus that he will joust with the knight who so thinks by his threat to prevent anyone from lodging with him, the emissary's statement in *Lybeaus* that no knight obtains lodgings there for fear of the steward,[71] and her remark in *Wigalois* that the lord of the castle has a custom whereby he withholds his hospitality.

They enter Brandigan, and without the Jousting for Hospitality custom the *molt mal trespas* refers to the climactic adventure. Evrain comes to meet them in the street, even as Lanpart is found in the open, and when the King of Brandigan welcomes them he pays particular attention to Enide, whom he salutes and leads by the hand into the palace, which reminds one of the steward's warm welcome for the emissary in *Descouneus* and *Wigalois*.[72] Then, again like the steward, Evrain gives excellent hospitality. At the evening meal, Erec asks him not about but for the adventure, and the King speaks of it, doing his best to put Erec off by conveying how dangerous it is, but leaving the hero ignorant of its particulars. However, Erec expresses his zeal to undertake the adventure.

The location of the Arrival at Brandigan, in relation to that of the Lapse

---

67 *Ibid.*, 4297-4318.   68 *Ibid.*, 4182-91.
69 *Descouneus*, 3303-70; *Carduino*, ii, 47/4-6.   70 *Erec*, 5319-5623.
71 The other reading *for love of* means "on account of" the steward.
72 This special welcoming of Enide has attracted the attention of R. R. Bezzola, *Le sens de l'aventure et de l'amour* (1947), 209.

into Amorous Indolence, means that once more we have a break in the sequence of episodes which corresponds to a series in the tale of the Fair Unknown.

VIII   ACCOMPLISHMENT OF THE MISSION[73]

The next morning, in *Descouneus*, the host acts as guide, riding with the hero, the emissary, and the dwarf to the enchanted location; he also goes there with Lybeaus. Outside, Lanpart instructs the hero as to what he will see inside and how he should await the adventure; the dwarf does this in *Carduino*, where the host is lacking. Then the hero in all versions enters the enchanted location alone. Similarly, in the Encounter with Mabonagrain,[74] the morning after the Arrival at Brandigan, Evrain rides with Erec, Enide, and the little king Guivret to the magic locality. Though they enter it together, Erec has to penetrate the place further by himself, after Evrain has instructed him, pointing out the menace of the empty stake beside the others bearing severed heads, and speaking of how no-one has ever been able to blow the horn that was hung upon it, but leaving the hero ignorant of what is to happen, as before.

However, in the tale of the Fair Unknown the adventure itself is different from that in Chrétien. It does not take place in a garden, but in the hall of a palace, which Descouneus enters on horseback; Lybeaus dismounts and leads in his steed, while Carduino does not go into the palace at all, but remains in the space before it. Except in *Lybeaus*, we have a ruined city, which is a wondrously beautiful but desolate Cité Gaste in *Descouneus*, and in *Carduino* so devastated that it is hardly recognizable and full of animals who are the enchanted inhabitants. Descouneus finds the gate broken down, and like Carduino he rides along the main street to the palace. But the picture is obscure in *Lybeaus*, where the hero is led by Lambard to the castle gate, which is found open (the only castle that has been mentioned is the steward's), and he rides into the palace. It is clear enough that in *Lybeaus*, as in Chrétien, the magic locality is nearby, whereas in *Descouneus* it is a day's journey from the steward's stronghold. We also have an entry by the hero into a beautiful castle, and his penetration into a hall or palace, in episode **VIIIa** of *Wigalois* (at Glois) and *Papegau* (at Chastel Perilleux), but he is not on horseback.[75]

Suddenly Descouneus or Carduino is attacked by a knight who rides out from a door, but he is repelled and retreats through the door again, and soon after a knight on horseback again comes charging out of the room in *Descouneus* —in *Carduino* from the other door in the palace—and assails the hero. The combat ends with Descouneus or Lybeaus slaying Mabon (Maboun), in *Descouneus* the two magicians having each delivered an assault from the door in turn (Lybeaus goes out into the open and fights both his opponents together); but there is only a single magician in *Carduino*, destroyed in his second attack.

---

73 *Descouneus*, 2741-3503; *Lybeaus*, 1738-2097; *Carduino*, ii, 39/7-66/8. Schofield, *op. cit.*, 47-53; Saran, *op. cit.*, 406-9.

74 *Erec*, 5624-6341.   75 *Wigalois*, 7259-7312; *Papegau*, 74/3-5.

We also have one adversary in episode **VIIIa** of *Wigalois* (the magician Roaz) and *Papegau* (the Marshal), who comes out of a door to oppose the hero in the hall and after a battle on foot is killed.[76] The enchanted lady of *Descouneus*, *Lybeaus*, and *Carduino* is now transformed from serpent shape into a most beautiful woman, the disenchantment being performed by a kiss, in *Carduino* given by the hero, but received by him in *Descouneus* and *Lybeaus*. This is the *Fier Baissier*, the "serpent-kiss". There is a sound like a stroke of thunder in *Carduino* as the lady resumes her shape and all the enchantments are dispelled.

In spite of the differences between the adventures in Chrétien and in the tale of the Fair Unknown, there are certain elements in common. In both, the hero penetrates into an enchanted location, pauses, and is attacked by a knight who comes against him on horseback. In Chrétien he is called Mabonagrain, a name like that of the main adversary in *Descouneus* and *Lybeaus*, while the name of the other opponent there is also significant, in relation to that of Erec's host. But the sequel, like the introduction, provides greater similarity.

In *Descouneus* the host, the emissary, and the dwarf come with great joy at the delivery of their lady, as in *Carduino* the emissary and the dwarf hasten into the city when they realize the hero has been successful. There is a joyful celebration by the inhabitants in *Descouneus*, *Lybeaus*, and *Carduino*. And also in *Papegau*, where the lady has not been enchanted, but is at her sole remaining stronghold of La Roche sans Paour, under the oppression of the Marshal's seizure of power in the kingdom, there is great joy made by the inmates of Chastel Perilleux and the inhabitants of the land at the destruction of the Marshal[77]

Similarly, in Chrétien, as soon as Evrain, Enide, and those with them realize Erec has been successful, they rejoice and hurry to disarm him. There is a tremendous joy among the inhabitants, and their great rejoicing results from a similar cause, the release of Mabonagrain from *prison*, imprisonment. In the tale of the Fair Unknown a champion has been required from Arthur's court because:

> "Mi lady of Synadowne
> Is brought in stronge prison."
>
> (*Lybeaus Desconus*, L 160 f.)

And when Descouneus accomplishes the mission the delivered Queen declares: "*Jetee m'avés de prison.*" How firmly the term *prison* is attached to the tale can be seen when it is applied to the circumstances in *Papegau*, where the emissary says that her lady *est imprisonnee a moult grant tort*, and asks the hero to come to the Queen and her daughter *pour les oster de la prison ou elles sont a moult grant tort*.[78] Thus, while Mabonagrain in the combat is to be compared with Mabon, as a captive released by the hero from *prison* in an enchanted location he seems to correspond to the Queen.

76 *Wigalois*, 7313-7672; *Papegau*, 74/6-75/19.   77 *Papegau*, 75/21-77/33.
78 *Descouneus*, 3306; *Papegau*, 25/23 f., 26/19 f.

The Encounter with Mabonagrain being equivalent to the Accomplishment of the Mission, we have started yet another sequence of episodes in Chrétien corresponding to one in the Fair Unknown story, in the order **VII VIII.**

WQ   WEDDING TO A QUEEN[79]

Except in *Papegau*, the hero has gained both a bride and a domain. *Lybeaus* and *Carduino* agree in having him go with her to Arthur's court, where the King gives the lady to the hero as wife, after which the couple return to their own domain, a kingdom in *Lybeaus* (L 1785). In *Wigalois*, however, it is in her own land that the lady Larie becomes Queen with the wedding and coronation, though the couple do eventually go to Arthur's court at Nantes, from which they return to Korntin.

Descouneus will not accept the offer of marriage from Blonde Esmeree, Queen of Wales, until he has had Arthur's permission, but what in fact happens is a long interruption. She departs for Arthur's court without him, he sets off to pay a second visit to the fay of the Ile d'Or, and eventually has to be lured to Arthur by the proclamation of a tournament. After Descouneus has won every encounter, they go to London, and Arthur tells the hero that he will give Blonde Esmeree to him as wife and arrange to crown him. But it does not happen, because she prefers to have this done in her own land, and the couple return there for the wedding and coronation.

In similar fashion to *Lybeaus* and *Carduino*, in *Erec* the hero and heroine leave the land to go to King Arthur, and their coronation takes place at his court (at Nantes).[80] The princely hero now has a Queen for his land, even as the royal lady in the Fair Unknown story brings a King for her domain back from Arthur's court. With this, the last sequence of episodes in Chrétien corresponding to one in the tale of the Fair Unknown has grown to three, in the order **VII VIII WQ.**

Erec et Enide, in relation to the episodes in the Fair Unknown story, turns out to possess equivalents in the following order:

Erec: **DA IV V VI I II RS III VII VIII WQ**

This is a significant result, for from the series in *Descouneus* it differs in only one respect, the location of the block **I II RS III.**

79 *Descouneus*, 3504-3908, 6145-6246; *Lybeaus*, 2098-2127; *Carduino*, ii, 67/1-71/8; *Wigalois*, 8497-9798, 11392-705. Schofield, *op. cit.*, 53-6; Saran, *op. cit.*, 409 f.
80 *Erec*, 6342-6878.

7

Source Relationships

My comparison has brought me to a similar stage as when it emerged that passages of decoration in *Erec* bear a significant relationship to the works of Alain de Lille. Now that it can be seen in what manner the episodes in *Erec* and in the tale of the Fair Unknown run in parallel, there can be no doubt that the two stories are closely connected. The sustained resemblance of the kind I have traced must be due to the dependence of one narrative on the other or both on a common original.

I can narrow the choice between the alternatives, for when I look upon *Erec* as a transformation of a *conte d'aventure* like that of the Fair Unknown the inspiration of Alain stands out. On matter which contains a straightforward departure of the hero from Arthur's court and a string of his exploits, we can see imposed Arthur's project, whose accomplishment has to attend on the return of the hero; the King's proposal arranged to result in the hero's first adventure, from which his departure has been made to arise; the hero's meeting with a maiden, in the next episode, utilized to provide the person necessary for the completion of the project and the partner of a perfect union; and when, for the love of a woman, he neglects his duty to carry out deeds of prowess, receives the rebuke, launches into a ride and goes through the rest of the adventures, the events have been shaped to form the trials to which the marriage becomes subject. The more complex construction, which we have in *Erec*, is thus the complication of the simpler.

The reconnaissance leads to an advance in force towards the prospect which has opened up before us. Observe how the fitting to a pattern from *Anticlaudianus* swallows up some adventures into an introduction before the ride, and explains the postponement of the thread running through which is basically the same in *Erec* as in the tale of the Fair Unknown, as well as stories sharing with the latter the type of motivation that is its mark. With the ride, we have the young and handsome hero who journeys through perilous adventures accompanied by a lady who has disparaged his valour just before they set off. She regrets having cast aspersions on his prowess (in the tale of the Fair Unknown and allied stories, this regret is expressed on a particular occasion), and he forgives her for the fault. Through his adventures he develops into a knight of great valour, and becomes a glorious hero by his culminating encounter.

Now in the tale of the Fair Unknown, and stories with the same type of motivation, the emissary's disparagement of the hero before the ride is only the first instance of *mesdisance*. In *Descouneus*, *Wigalois*, *La Cote Mal Taillie*, and *Ipomedon*, when the hero catches up with the emissary in the departure from the court, she refuses to have his company. And when the hero in *Descouneus* asks her for permission to go to the Rescue from Two Giants she says that she does not care what he does, as in *Wigalois* she tells him curtly to do what he likes. In *Lybeaus* the *mesdisance* is more severe, for we are told she continually chides him for some time, and she calls him *lorell* and *kaytyf*, declaring that he will lose his pride when he comes upon the knight of the Encounter at the Perilous Bridge, against whom she warns him.[1] The full development of the *mesdisance* is to be seen in *Sir Gareth* and *La Cote Mal Taillie*, where the damsel's scorn is prolonged, and there is also a maiden, taken by Gawain as his companion in the course of his quest in Chrétien's *Perceval*, who similarly persists in humiliating the hero. It is in these stories, and not in *Descouneus* and *Lybeaus*—where the motif is soon brought to an end—that she is properly a Damoisele Mesdisant, as *La Cote Mal Taillie* calls the lady who, while accompanying the hero on his adventures, refuses not only to consider him fit for them but also to recognize the prowess he displays. She goes on mocking and chiding La Cote Mal Taillie, and tries to make him turn back. Such an attitude is so well maintained in *Sir Gareth* that *ever she chydde hym and wolde nat reste*, and *ever she rode chydyng hym in the fowleste maner wyse that she cowde*. She constantly warns him of opponents and advises him to turn again, and he complains that she always treats him as a coward.[2]

Counterbalancing the *mesdisance* by the damsel is the hero's determination not to be made to turn back, and his constant seeking of danger to prove his prowess in despite of the damsel's unwillingness to consider him fit for the mission, even as Erec would not be deflected from continuing to pursue the adventurous ride to re-establish his reputation. Then, too, apart from casting aspersions on the hero's valour by what she says in the bedroom scene, on the ride Enide keeps on warning Erec of opponents, which causes him to accuse her of holding him in little esteem. And, just as the Fair Unknown type of hero keeps on following the emissary (against her will),[3] so also Erec rides continuously behind Enide. The resemblance of Erec and Enide to the Fair Unknown type of hero and emissary is evident enough, but at the same time Enide's harsh treatment by Erec so contrasts with the patient and courteous manner of that kind of hero towards his difficult companion. Here I have opposed only to draw attention to where the similarity lies: the *mesdisance* on the ride

---

1 *Descouneus*, 279-320, 670-78; *Lybeaus*, 256-70; *Wigalois*, 1884-1921, 2046-53; E. Löseth, *Le roman en prose de Tristan* (1891), § 69; *Ipomedon*, 8128-76. The motif of *mesdisance* is lacking in *Carduino* and *Papegau*.

2 Malory, VII, c. 6 f., c. 10.

3 This is explicit in *Giglan*, e i *recto*, n iv *recto*; Löseth, *op. cit.*, § 69 f.; Malory, VII, c. 6 f. Note how in *Carduino*, ii, 8/5, where the motif of *mesdisance* is lacking, we still have the pattern of a ride in which one figure follows, though here it is the emissary.

is carried out by Erec.[4] With the roles of the hero and the lady in this way reversed, it is now a Chevalier Mesdisant who has been angered, he it is who humiliates his companion, and it is she who preserves the greatest patience and gentleness of speech under this treatment. The result of this reversal is that we have La Cote Mal Taillie following the emissary, refusing to turn back in spite of her continual mockery and chiding, and the Fair Unknown type of hero not deterred by her from taking on his opponents, while in Chrétien we find Enide riding ahead of Erec and continuing to warn him against assailants in spite of his menaces and repeated command not to speak. It is Enide who is demonstrating the quality which at first her companion is convinced she lacks, then refuses to recognize, and finally admits she possesses, when he declares that he is sure she loves him, and shows his love for her. The gradual though only implicit change in Erec's attitude towards Enide, until it becomes explicit, should be compared with that of the emissary in respect of the youth whom she accompanies. In *Wigalois* she shifts over the course of the ride from initial anger and scorn, then coldness towards the hero and lack of trust in his prowess, to friendliness and faith in his heroism, which she acknowledges eventually when fully persuaded of his valour. Thus she still doubts his *manheit* just before the contest for the parrot, and she has no faith in it yet, after his victory, but she desists now from anger.[5] In *La Cote Mal Taillie* and *Ipomedon*, the emissary's scorn is also seen to diminish before she comes to hold the hero in esteem. As we can see from the emissary privately admitting to the dwarf the hero's prowess after his first victory, but not to the hero himself until after his second, there is even postponement of open recognition by her in *Descouneus*, with its abbreviated theme of *mesdisance*.[6]

This kind of development in the tale of the Fair Unknown and allied stories, with its swelling flow bursting out into the open in the scene where the emissary fully recognizes the hero's valour, makes the adventures not just a string of deeds, but directly confers on them the function of mounting proof of prowess for her, even as the parallel theme in Chrétien, in respect of Enide's loyalty towards Erec, has a comparable effect on the adventures side by side with that exerted by Erec's concern to demonstrate his heroism after the original *mesdisance*, that by Enide. The treatment in *Wigalois* leads up to the occasion, in the Arrival at the Lady's Stronghold, when the emissary relates the deeds and praises the prowess of the hero who has been joyfully received there as the champion fetched from Arthur's court. Compare, in *Lybeaus*, the scene (after Lambard has welcomed the hero as the champion come from Arthur) of the emissary giving the steward an account of the hero's deeds on the journey,

---

4 Cf. E. Brugger, *ZrP* LXIII (1943), 327, in his series entitled "Der Schöne Feigling in der arthurischen Literatur".

5 See F. Saran, "Ueber Wirnt von Grafenberg und den Wigalois", *Beiträge zur Geschichte der deutschen Sprache und Literatur* XXI (1896), 309-15.

6 *Descouneus*, 488-504; Löseth, *op. cit.*, §§ 73, 93; *Ipomedon*, 8336-60, 8547-82. Along with the *mesdisance*, the reconciliation is lacking in *Carduino* and *Papegau*.

which rejoices him. Similarly, in *Descouneus*, she tells him that she has looked for thorough proof of the hero's prowess on the ride, in the combats in which she has seen him take part:

> "Bien l'ai en la voie esprové
> Es grans estors u veü l'ai."
> *(Li Biaus Descouneus, 2720 f.)*

And she praises his valour, causing Lanpart great joy.[7] But in these last two versions the emissary has openly admitted the hero's prowess early on the journey, so that we do not have an effect of building up to the arrival at the destination. Early recognition of the hero's valour also makes the reference in *Descouneus* to his having fully convinced her seem out of place in comparison with the thorough proof required by the emissary in *La Cote Mal Taillie*, where in the later course of the ride *son mépris pour Brunor a diminué; cependant, elle désire l'éprouver encore.*[8] This motif is paralleled in *Erec*, for here, in addition to the hero's declaration to the heroine that he has fully tried her—*"bien vos ai de tot essaiee"* (4883)—Chrétien comments that Erec has looked for thorough proof of her worth and found great love for him:

> bien l'a esprovee:[9]
> vers li a grant amor trovee.
> *(Erec et Enide, 5097 f.)*

Compare, in relation to Erec's prowess, Enide's statement that she is now more fully aware of it, because (like the emissary) *"ge l'ai veü a mes ialz"* (3108), which supplies the rest of the parallel to the lines quoted from *Descouneus*.

A late position of the Reconciliation Scene in a tale with the Fair Unknown type of motivation is obviously more effective, as it keeps the story longer related to a tension between the hero and his companion, and successfully leads up to the point when at the destination he is regarded as a knight of great prowess, completely fit to undertake the difficult task for which a champion was sought from King Arthur. And in fact it turns out that the development of the relationship between the hero and his companion during the adventurous ride in *Erec* corresponds, given the reversal of roles, to that not in *Descouneus* and *Lybeaus* but in those stories with sustained treatment of the theme that has been observed, and particularly in *La Cote Mal Taillie*, with its Damoisele Mesdisant who keeps up her scorn of the hero until he has been fully tested. This raises the question whether the Reconciliation Scene, in what I may call the *Descouneus/Lybeaus* tale, has undergone a shift to the early part of the ride. As a result, attention is drawn to the location of the block **I II RS III**, which

---

7 *Descouneus*, 2711-28; *Lybeaus*, 1648-74; *Wigalois*, 3973-4054.

8 Löseth, *op. cit.*, § 73.

9 In support of her translation "he has had full proof of her worth", Z. P. Zaddy, "Chrétien de Troyes and the verb *esprover*", *Medium Aevum* XXXVII (1968), 263 ff., surveys the use of this verb in him. But see p. 236 f. below.

in *Erec* comes after **VI**. In other words, does the series we have found in *Erec* reflect that of the common original (O), which has been altered, in the *conte d'aventure* that was the source of *Descouneus* and *Lybeaus*, by the transfer of the block **I II RS III** to the beginning of the ride? This would then be why *Carduino* cannot be reconciled with the sequence in *Descouneus*, but fits into that revealed by *Erec*:

Erec:	**DA IV V VI I II RS III VII VIII WQ**		
Carduino:	**E AA DA**	**VI I II**	**VIII WQ**

But how could one then explain the later position of the Reconciliation Scene in *Wigalois*, where **I II** come at the beginning of the ride (p. 85), as in *Descouneus*? In this way: the source of *Wigalois* and *Papegau* derived the sequence followed in the earlier part from the *Descouneus/Lybeaus* tale, but that of the later section, from **VIIa** onwards, represents another version (X) of the story. The combination of *conte d'aventure* X with the *Descouneus/Lybeaus* tale (Y) would make available two variants of the material in common,[10] and two **RS** locations to choose from, of which the later one, that in *conte d'aventure* X, has been retained in the *Wigalois/Papegau* version (Z). Along with this position of the Reconciliation Scene, reflecting its late type of location in the original form of the story, there would come from *conte d'aventure* X the protracted theme of the emissary passing from lack of trust in the hero's prowess to its open recognition. But treatment of her to the full as a Damoisele Mesdisant would be inhibited in the *Wigalois/Papegau* version by the limitation of such behaviour to the early part of the ride in the *Descouneus/Lybeaus* tale, which passes straight from the emissary's anger in the Departure from Arthur's Court to her abating scorn in the later part of the original account. A table of descent, based on the order of episodes, would in this way take the shape shown overleaf.[11]

I shall now restrict the term "the tale of the Fair Unknown" to the *Descouneus/Lybeaus* narrative (Y), because this appellation for the hero does not exist in *Carduino*, *Wigalois*, or *Papegau*. The modern French title of *Le Bel Inconnu* is suitable for the Y form of the story, but I shall not use it, as it has been traditionally applied to Renaut's romance.[12] I shall assign "the Fair Unknown type" as a label to the group in the table, which emphasizes the

10 Conflicting with the account from **VIIa** onwards, *Wigalois* has a motif from **VII** which is astray (p. 100), and *Papegau* refers to the imprisonment of **VIII** (p. 103). But these elements need not derive from the common source, as they may be due to the direct influence of Y.

11 Tables of descent expressing the views of various scholars are given by M. Tyssens, "Les sources de Renaut de Beaujeu", *Mélanges offerts à Jean Frappier* (1970), ii, 1042 ff. From my table it can be seen, for instance, how in the Rescue from Two Giants *Wigalois* can go with *Descouneus* and *Lybeaus* against *Carduino* in having the party go to bed without supper, but with *Carduino* against *Descouneus* and *Lybeaus* in the hero attacking first the giant roasting meat at the fire and not the one about to rape the abducted maiden.

12 To speak of "Renaut's version of *Le Bel Inconnu*" would be appropriate.

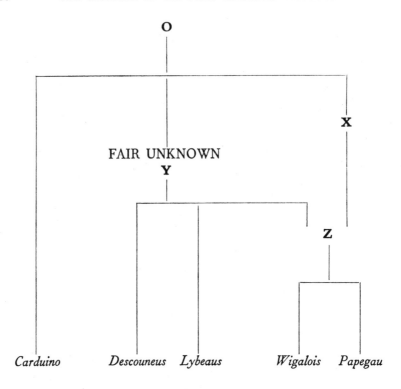

O

FAIR UNKNOWN
Y

X

Z

Carduino   Descouneus   Lybeaus   Wigalois   Papegau

new viewpoint that the relative order of episodes has led me to adopt. The next step will be to examine some tales allied to the Fair Unknown type, in order to establish their relation to it and to see whether they support my assumptions. The survey will also allow me to assemble material in readiness for the unravelling of the *conjointure* in *Erec*.

IPOMEDON[13]

The non-Arthurian romance of *Ipomedon* is contemporary with *Erec et Enide*. Its story may be divided into two parts, I and II, of which only the second is related to the Fair Unknown type of tale. Here, disguised as a fool, Ipomedon goes to King Meleager's court, and obtains from him the grant of the first request for a champion that will be made. On the same day, under circumstances which correspond to those of the Fair Unknown type (p. 86), Ipomedon leaves on a mission to deliver the lady La Fiere, after her emissary Ismeine has come for a champion to save her mistress from Leonin, the unwanted suitor who besieges her and has devastated her country. In the company of Ismeine and her attendant dwarf, the damsel at first hostile and the dwarf pleading with

13 Brugger, *op. cit.*, ZrP LXIII, 147-62, discusses the relation of *Ipomedon* to the Fair Unknown type of tale.

her on behalf of the hero as he does in *Descouneus* and *Wigalois*,[14] Ipomedon
has a series of three similar encounters on the ride, one a day, in each of which
he defeats a cousin, nephew, or brother of Leonin's, called Malgis, Creon,
and Leander respectively. This repetitive pattern is reinforced by a series of
three night-lodgings. After Ipomedon's first victory, Ismeine will not acknowledge his prowess, but after the second she repents. Up till now the tension
between them has kept the hero and the emissary apart, so that he always
dismounted at a distance whenever they halted, and did not eat with her. But
Ismeine's change of attitude towards Ipomedon causes her to invite him to
join her at dinner where they are in the open. He refuses, but at their lodgings
that evening, when she begs him to pardon her great folly, he does so and they
have food and drink together. Henceforth she not only sits with him, but is
even in love with the hero. Such is the anguish of her love that with amorous
intent she comes to his bedside in a mantle on the second and third nights,
but he puts her off. Ipomedon reaches his destination, accomplishes the mission
by defeating Leonin in single combat, and the wedding and coronation of
Ipomedon and La Fiere brings the story to an end.

Material of the Fair Unknown Type

The King grants the hero, on his arrival at court,[15] a *don* that will give him
the right to undertake the mission when the emissary turns up, and it is that
same day, as in *Descouneus*, *Lybeaus*, and *Carduino*, that he departs on it. Not
only do the circumstances of the departure correspond to the Fair Unknown
type, but so do the relations between hero, emissary, and dwarf for much of
the journey. One should note in particular how the Reconciliation Scene is
followed by a meal at night, which is associated with it in the tale of the Fair
Unknown (p. 89), and how, before apologizing, Ismeine confesses to the dwarf
that she has been guilty of folly, even as the emissary in *Descouneus* tells him
that she will now ask pardon of the hero for her bad behaviour.[16] Even Ismeine's
falling in love with the hero is explicable from the Fair Unknown type of story,
as a transfer from another damsel there, because what happens in *Ipomedon* II
takes place in *Wigalois*, though in different circumstances. In the anguish of
love, Ismeine goes to Ipomedon at night and begs him to come home with her
to Burgundy, where he can have both her and the land, as she is the Duke's
heir. Ipomedon will not answer her plea on the first occasion, but the next
night replies that he has come to carry out a combat, and his reputation would
suffer greatly if he abandoned the undertaking. Similarly, at the parting with
the damsel for whom Wigalois fought in the contest for the beauty prize
(p. 98), in distress she begs the hero to come home with her to her land, where
the death of her father will bring him reward, and Wigalois rejects her proposal

14 *Ipomedon*, 8113-17, 8144-52, 8190, 8337-42, 8389-91; *Descouneus*, 307-16, 490-97,
830-40; *Wigalois*, 1890-98, 2204-6.
15 On Ipomedon's dress, see p. 167 below.
16 *Ipomedon*, 8665-84; *Descouneus*, 829-59, 901-48.

on the ground that he has undertaken the adventure of Korntin and his reputation would suffer a blow if he gave up on the way.[17] Again, when Ismeine
goes through agonies of hesitation about approaching the hero's bed, and
eventually succumbs to temptation only to suffer repulse—once she has her
hand bitten and the second time he draws his sword—with reversal of sex
her experience is like that suffered by the Fair Unknown with the mistress of
the Ile d'Or, who repels him by her spells (p. 133). In *Ipomedon*, we have two
such successive nights instead of the two successive occasions on one night in
Descouneus.[18]

The adventures fall into a pattern which is not that of the Fair Unknown
type, but Brugger explained that the encounters on the ride have been thoroughly
transformed from that kind of story and assimilated to each other, and the
delivery of La Fiere from her besieger is a rationalizing of the enchantment
motif.[19] However, his contention utterly lacks conviction, and in fact what
common ground there is between the combat with the besieger Leonin and the
Fair Unknown type of material lies there in the Ile d'Or Episode (p. 98 f.),
where each of the versions has some of the following traits: a city by the sea,
at which the hero fights in full view of the people and their lady against her
suitor, a giant who besieges the lady and ravages her people and her domain.
The description of Leonin is like that of Maugys in *Lybeaus*, and both wear
black armour.[20] But a distinctive feature of the Ile d'Or Episode is lacking,
the night when the hero's desire is frustrated by the lady, and this adventure
does not lead to the Wedding to a Queen.

Yet features which occur in the Fair Unknown type of tale do appear in the
course of Ipomedon's ride, however much the repetitive encounters with
Malgis, Creon, and Leander differ from the adventures of the Fair Unknown
type. On each occasion, Ipomedon and his companions have halted during
the heat of the day for dinner and repose, a knight appears out of the forest and
tries to abduct the emissary Ismeine, and Ipomedon goes to the rescue and
vanquishes him. The parallels are with the night of the Rescue from Two
Giants, the Reconciliation Scene, and the Attack by Three Avengers (p. 88 ff.).[21]
In *Ipomedon* II, the dwarf occupies himself with the hero's steed, the disarming
of the hero, and the preparation and excellent serving of the meal, like the
squire Robert, the dwarf's doublet in *Descouneus*; the opponents, abductors of
a maiden, belong to a family of gigantic knights; and they are three in number,
relatives of another adversary, and suddenly turn up. On the third occasion,
in the heat of the day the forest is resounding with bird-song at the halting
place, just as in *Descouneus* and *Wigalois* nightingales are heard singing where

17 *Ipomedon*, 8864-92, 9179-94; *Wigalois*, 3194-3221.

18 *Ipomedon*, 8683-8854, 9109-58; *Descouneus*, 4482-4662.

19 Brugger, *op. cit.*, ZrP LXIII, 156, LXV, 140 f.

20 *Ipomedon*, 7700-10; *Lybeaus*, 1249-54, 1273 f., L 1305-16.

21 *Ipomedon*, 8179-8326, 8384-8616, 8901-9016; *Descouneus*, 593-1226; *Lybeaus*, 548-675,
followed by 445-537; *Carduino*, ii, 26/4-39/3; *Wigalois*, 2015-2185.

they stop on the evening of the Rescue from Two Giants. The meal being prepared by the dwarf on the second day is interrupted by the frightening arrival of the gigantic Creon, Ipomedon goes to the rescue of Ismeine, defeats Creon, Ismeine repents and gives Ipomedon an invitation to join her at the meal (he refuses), and it is now that they eat (separately, as before). The sequence of events corresponds, not to that in *Descouneus*, *Lybeaus*, and *Wigalois*, where they go to bed without supper before the adventure and the laying of the meal occurs at the place where Descouneus has fought and killed the giants,[22] but to what happens in *Carduino*. Here the dwarf lays the meal when they halt, and before they can start eating there is the frightening interruption of the voice crying out in the forest, the hero goes to the rescue of the maiden, from which he returns after his victory, and they set to and eat. The invitation by Ismeine corresponds to the moment in *Descouneus* when the hero has disarmed after his defeat of the giants and the Reconciliation Scene begins, but in *Ipomedon* II this portion of the action is not completed until they are at their lodgings that evening, a phenomenon of suspension which is also illustrated by the two occasions when Ismeine begs Ipomedon to go home with her. As for the first day, Malgis comes upon Ismeine asleep after the meal and she is suddenly awakened: in the Attack by Three Avengers, Descouneus is so caught out. The parallelism continues when Ipomedon immediately strikes Malgis off his horse onto the ground, and the dwarf comes forward and exchanges his own mount (a *roncin* or inferior type of horse) for the adversary's steed, as this is just what we see happening when Lybeaus disposes of the first avenger. Finally, the name Malgis for one of the adversaries on the ride, those of the others being classical, is identical with the name Maugys of the giant besieger in the Ile d'Or Episode of *Lybeaus*.

The dispersion of motifs over a repetitive pattern in *Ipomedon* II, which in the Fair Unknown type of tale are found in natural concentration on a single night, points to the derivation of the former set of motifs from the latter. A corollary results from such a conclusion, that the agreement of *Ipomedon* II, in its sequence of events, with the meal after the Rescue from Two Giants in *Carduino* against the other versions, suits my table of descent (p. 110), with *Carduino* in this respect representing the original story, and the others that of the *Descouneus/Lybeaus* account.

DURMART LE GALOIS[23]

One must distinguish *Ipomedon* II from the Fair Unknown type of tale, whatever their resemblances, by the form of the hero's mission as well as by the repetitive

---

22 In *Giglan*, m i *recto*, after the meal by the giants' fire, they are shown going back to the original meadow to sleep.

23 Brugger, *op. cit.*, ZrP LXIII, 162-72, discusses the relation of *Durmart* to both *Ipomedon* and the Fair Unknown type of tale.

pattern of the encounters on the ride. In the early thirteenth-century romance of *Durmart*, we again find the delivery of a lady from her besieger as the climax, but coupled with adventure undeniably of the Fair Unknown type.

Like the hero in *Ipomedon* I, Durmart is a very handsome young man, brought up excellently by his royal parents, who lapses into not caring for deeds of arms during a period when he is away from their court. In the case of Ipomedon, after hearing about the incomparable La Fiere he sets out to enter her service incognito, and during his three years at her court he devotes himself to hunting and not to arms, so that he is looked on as a coward. All find it sad that he lacks valour, and La Fiere laments that destiny has given him beauty but not prowess, for she is enamoured of him—as he is of her—but does not reveal her love, since she has made a vow to marry a man of the greatest valour. Then for her sake Ipomedon decides to leave and change his manner of life to one of chivalry, and he returns to his father's court, to set out from there and win fame in many lands. Durmart, on the other hand, is given into the care of a seneschal, with whose young wife he has a love affair which causes him to sink into amorous indolence for three years. But otherwise his situation is analogous to that of Ipomedon. People speak disparagingly of Durmart, saying there has never been such a handsome coward. Then, like Ipomedon, but merely by a sudden decision, Durmart leaves the lady and changes his manner of life, returning to his father's court, where he is knighted.

On the same day, Durmart meets a pilgrim who tells him about a beautiful Queen in Ireland, whose love he urges him to seek in spite of the dangers to be overcome, and the hero falls in love on hearing of her and her beauty. He goes straight to the palace, demands of the King that he should undergo the arming ceremony, and sets out to seek this Queen in Ireland, so that the hero's departure from court is caused by falling in love from afar, as in *Ipomedon* I, and not by any necessity to rescue the lady from her gigantic besieger, as in *Ipomedon* II. But in fact this is just what Durmart does eventually find it necessary to do.

The place of the siege in the plan of *Durmart* corresponds to that in *Fergus*, another early thirteenth-century romance. As in *Durmart*, though in different circumstances, we have the hero meeting the heroine in the course of a quest, when she falls in love with him; then he loses her and goes in search of his lost love; until one day he finds himself in her domain, harasses her besiegers daily from a fortress nearby, and is at hand to be her champion against the besieging king when this becomes necessary. The comparisons with *Ipomedon* and *Fergus* define the framework of *Durmart*, and make clear that Brugger was wrong in equating its climax with the Fair Unknown type.[24] The material of this origin is only that which partly fills this framework.

24 In addition to Brugger's main treatment of *Durmart*, see *ZrP* LXV, 141. He follows his usual practice, which we have already seen with *Ipomedon* (p. 112), of regarding the delivery of the lady from her besieger as a rationalizing of the enchantment motif in the Fair Unknown type of tale.

Material of the Fair Unknown Type

Like the hero of the Fair Unknown type, dissatisfied with his life, the young Durmart decides to go to court, enters the hall—the courtiers are all struck by his beauty—goes before the King, and then joins in the meal. He is knighted, like Wigalois, on a feast day following his arrival at court. He reminds us again of the Fair Unknown type of hero when, in undertaking a quest for a lady on the same day as the knighting, he demands the provision of arms, is immediately armed at court, and sets out at once (cf. p. 85 f.).[25]

On landing in Ireland, Durmart's first adventure is an encounter in a glade with a knight who has a greyhound. He defies the hero for daring to seek the Queen's hand without having accomplished deeds of prowess, and Durmart must either give up his intention or fight him. The hero defeats his opponent, makes him promise to betake himself as prisoner to Durmart's mother, Queen of Wales (the hero of the Fair Unknown type sends vanquished adversaries to Arthur), and is given the hunting dog to lead him to the Queen he seeks. Durmart, following the animal, meets a damsel who unknown to him is this Queen. He asks her about the Queen, she says that she will test whether he truly loves her, demands the dog from him—as a guarantee of good faith—he gives it to her, and they ride on together to the Sparrowhawk Contest, in which he conquers the prize for the damsel.[26]

The adventure of the greyhound bears some resemblance to the Encounter with a Huntsman (p. 91 f.), but it has been objected that the motif of the dog which leads the hero to a lady points rather to the influence of the Second Continuation of *Perceval*, which is apparent elsewhere in *Durmart*.[27] In the Second Continuation, the little white dog has been regained by Perceval for a lady after a combat disputing its possession with a huntsman, who arrived blowing a horn and following the dog, which was pursuing an exhausted stag that appeared before the hero in the forest.[28] This is equivalent to the Encounter with a Huntsman. Now, absent from the Second Continuation, but in common between the adventures in *Durmart* and the Encounter with a Huntsman, is this: the damsel sees a dog, expresses a desire to have it, and the hero delivers it to her on the spot and they ride on together with the animal. There has evidently been some blending here in *Durmart* between material from the Second Continuation and that properly of the Fair Unknown type, and the correspondence of the episode in *Durmart* with the Encounter with a Huntsman (**IV**) is clinched by its location, immediately before the Sparrowhawk Contest (**V**). The absence of a damsel accompanying the hero accounts for the difference in the subject under dispute with the antagonist, which in the Encounter with a Huntsman is the delivery of his dog to her by the hero. It also allows the author of *Durmart*

25 *Durmart*, 591-1470.
26 *Ibid.*, 1575-1774, 1885-2003.
27 *Ibid.*, ii, 57, 62 f.
28 *Perceval*, Second Continuation, 20272, 20291, 24842-25043.

to merge the motif of her receiving the hound not only with that of the guiding dog but also with the starting point of the next adventure, in the meeting with a solitary and beautiful maiden riding alone towards the hero.

In this way, too, the lady of the Sparrowhawk Contest can have the role of the damsel who acquires a dog and accompanies the hero on his ride in the Fair Unknown type of tale. By the time Durmart meets her, he has already come across a dwarf, who is singing lustily: in *Wigalois*, when the dwarf arrives at Arthur's court and the hero first sees him, he is singing a song beautifully. With a dwarf and a lady on the ride with the hero, we now have a semblance of the cavalcade in the Fair Unknown type of story, but there is no tension between the damsel and Durmart. However, as in *Ipomedon* II, we find a knight who eats apart when they halt (p. 111). This is the hero in *Ipomedon* II, but in *Durmart* it is an additional member of the party, a gigantic knight called Nogant, who later is the besieger of the lady, and whose function just now is to be the lady's *ami* who fails at the contest for the sparrowhawk, an episode in *Durmart* which has already been considered (p. 93 ff.). After the contest, Durmart departs with the damsel carrying the bird he has won for her. As in *Wigalois*, to repay what the hero has done she invites him to come with her to her own country, but, instead of refusing the invitation on the ground of having to pursue his quest, Durmart accepts, because the damsel says that she will indicate to him the Queen he seeks.[29] Later, after Durmart has failed to find his way back to where he had left her, he learns that the damsel was overcome by grief at being separated from him. This is because she is in love with Durmart, and one should compare how at the parting with Wigalois the maiden for whom he has conquered the bird offers marriage, and is in tears with grief when the hero does not accept her proposal and they have to separate.[30]

Durmart had left the lady with the damsel of the Red Tent, who was found sitting on a rich couch combing her hair before a mirror which was held for her. She has suffered a forcible identification by Brugger with the fay of the Ile d'Or, because he was looking for the Sparrowhawk Contest to be followed by material from the Ile d'Or Episode (**VI**: p. 98 f.), and the damsel of the Red Tent looked like a fay to him.[31] But, alas, there is no matter resembling that of the Ile d'Or Episode until later on in *Durmart*. When the hero rescues Guinevere from Brun de Morois, the adversary's castle has battered shields hung on the battlements, the trophies of his victories over knights who had fought him. Durmart is told that his shield will join the others, and the head of his companion Yder will be fixed on a spear; but this does not deter the hero, who engages in combat with Brun de Morois and defeats him. Here is to be recognized a parallel to the exposure of heads on stakes by Malgiers li Gris, the opponent at the

---

29 *Durmart*, 1775-2768; *Wigalois*, 1727-36, 3194-3233.

30 *Durmart*, 5293-5304. In *Descouneus*, 1843-66, the damsel is in a similar state of distress at the parting, though here because she and the emissary have come to realize they are relatives.

31 Brugger, *op. cit.*, *ZrP* LXIII, 170.

Ile d'Or in *Descouneus*,[32] and there are other respects in which this adventure in *Durmart* has made use of **VI**, as we shall see from the section on The Horn to be Blown as Challenge (p. 124).

Ile d'Or material does not come shortly after the Sparrowhawk Contest in *Durmart* because the latter episode is here used as the first leg of a pair corresponding to the complex formed by the Encounter at the Perilous Bridge (**I**: p. 87 f.) and the Attack by Three Avengers (**III**: p. 90 f.). After his victory over Cardroain at the Sparrowhawk Contest, Durmart is warned to depart, as his opponent's brother Brun de Morois would want to avenge him when he hears what has happened. In *Descouneus*, the Rescue from Two Giants (**II**) intervenes before the avengers arrive: similarly, Durmart first has another fight, with the gigantic Nogant, and then Brun de Morois arrives at a gallop. What does Durmart then do but stop his assault by appealing to him somewhat in the manner of the emissary on behalf of Descouneus as the first avenger attacks! You would be foolish and cowardly to assail me just now, Durmart says, because I am mortally wounded, and if I were so lucky as to win the fight, everyone would find fault with you. In *Descouneus*, the appeal is on the ground that the hero is unarmed. As there, a respite before the combat is granted to the hero in *Durmart*, not to arm himself, however, but to fight another day when he has recovered from his wound.[33] The weakened condition of Durmart is due to the wound streaming with blood that he received in the combat with Cardroain, whereas in the Encounter at the Perilous Bridge such a debilitating wound flowing with blood is suffered by the opponent (p. 137). Durmart next meets the damsel of the Red Tent, and during his stay with her she heals his wound, but there is no such healing at the corresponding point in the versions of the Fair Unknown type.[34]

I have now traced a sequence which may be represented, in relation to the Fair Unknown type of tale, as **AA DA IV V/I (II) III**, with **VI** reflected later. There is also a displacement of traits corresponding to those of the night's stay in the forest during which occur the Rescue from Two Giants, the Reconciliation Scene, and the Attack by Three Avengers (**II RS III**: p. 88 ff.). In *Lybeaus* and *Wigalois*, the hero and his companions lodge at the town on the night before the contest for the bird, but in *Durmart* they take up quarters instead in the forest country. When they halt in the evening, the dwarf sets a cloth on the grass with food and wine, and busies himself with serving. The scene is like that which is fully described in *Descouneus* in connection with **RS**, but it is in *Carduino* (in **II**) that as in *Durmart* we have the fire lit when they halt, followed by the laying for supper.[35] Carduino sees one of the giants by a great fire roasting a deer in preparation for their meal (so does Giglan,

---

32 *Durmart*, 4453-4516; *Descouneus*, 1956-2003.
33 *Durmart*, 2596-2954.
34 The location of the stay corresponds to that of the arrival at the home of the maiden saved in the Rescue from Two Giants (p. 140 n. 35).
35 *Carduino*, ii, 27/1-7.

and there is a similar scene in *Lybeaus*), and a comparable sight lies before Durmart as he rides up to the halting place: the hideous dwarf is roasting a large piece of meat at a great fire in preparation for their meal.[36] Durmart and his companions listen to the birds singing in the forest, and bird-song is also heard at the place where the party halts in *Descouneus*, *Wigalois*, and *Ipomedon* II (p. 112 f.). The moon is shining when the damsel goes to Durmart towards morning, finds him sleeping, and wakes him up to warn him not to be caught asleep by Nogant, who would kill him.[37] This may be compared with the waking up and warning of Descouneus, when the avengers who are out to slay him arrive that moonlit night, catch him off his guard, and the last of them is conquered just as day breaks.[38] In *Descouneus* it is Robert, i.e. originally the dwarf, who does this service to the hero, the dwarf of the Fair Unknown type being an admirable figure, *cortois, gent, bel* (*Descouneus*), and *grazioso* (*Carduino*), which makes him distinctive. In *Durmart*, however, the dwarf is a figure of fun, hideous and discourteous, the horrid dwarf of Arthurian tradition.[39]

The Source of the Fair Unknown Type

Both the *Descouneus/Lybeaus* and the *Wigalois/Papegau* tales are ruled out on the grounds that in the latter the bird is a parrot and in the former the contest for the hawk is against the lord of the castle, to whom the bird belongs and from whom it is to be claimed, in *Lybeaus* explicitly at any time. Whereas in *Durmart*, as in *Wigalois* and *Papegau*, and also *Erec*, the event is a festive occasion for which large numbers of knights and ladies have assembled at the town, the adversary comes to it, and it has been held annually in *Durmart* as well as in *Papegau* and *Erec* (p. 96 f.). In Andreas Capellanus, too, the contest for the hawk is not with the lord of the castle (p. 95). Furthermore, the camping out of Durmart and his companions in the forest is to be classed with that in *Carduino* and *Ipomedon* II, where the meal is laid by the dwarf when they halt, and not that in *Descouneus*, *Lybeaus*, and *Wigalois*, where they go to bed without supper (p. 113). Taking *Erec*, Andreas, and *Ipomedon* II to rest here on the original story of the Fair Unknown type, and following the table of descent which has been given (p. 110), it can be seen that to *conte d'aventure* X are to be attributed features in Z (*Wigalois/Papegau*) which agree with *Erec* and Andreas against Y (*Descouneus/Lybeaus*), and from it are to be excluded those in Z that go with Y against *Carduino* and *Ipomedon* II. Thus the evidence so far would be consistent with having either the original story or *conte d'aventure* X as the tale of the Fair Unknown type drawn on by *Durmart*.

36 Observe the similarity between *Durmart*, 2140-46 and *Descouneus*, 705 f., 717-20; the latter, where there is a gap, is to be supplemented by *Giglan*, l iv *recto*.

37 *Durmart*, 2135-2283.

38 *Descouneus*, 983-94, 1157-9, 1193 f.

39 Compare the somewhat similar ugly dwarf in *Meraugis*, 1274 ff. He comes to Arthur to propose a quest, which the hero undertakes; the dwarf's departure without the hero, who catches him up, and their ride together with a lady indicate a Fair Unknown type of origin (cf. p. 86).

I have already given some instances when it was *Wigalois* that had to be compared with *Durmart*, and now I point to agreements between them in the contest for the beauty prize. The traits of red hair and staying in a tent with his *amie* are attached to the opponent only in these two versions (p. 93). Again, the holding of the contest in the meadowland before the city in *Durmart* is the picture found in *Wigalois* and *Papegau*, whereas in *Descouneus* and *Lybeaus*, as also in *Erec*, the combat takes place in the town.[40] Finally, as Brugger saw, *Durmart*'s first adventure in Ireland bears a resemblance to those with Schaffilun in *Wigalois* and the Chevalier du Passage in *Papegau*.[41] This has to do with *Durmart*'s replacement for the subject of dispute in the Encounter with a Huntsman, when the author formed from it the adventure of the grey-hound. There the argument was over the possession of a dog, but in *Durmart* it is whether the hero has sufficient merit to continue his quest for the Queen, and this has to be settled by combat. In *Papegau* the hero is opposed by the Chevalier du Passage, whom he tells of his mission, but the Chevalier refuses to let him through and advises him to go back, and whether he can pass is settled by jousting. Closer to *Durmart* is *Wigalois*, where the hero has a similar opponent in Schaffilun, whom he also informs of his mission. Schaffilun tells him that he is too young and lacking in prowess for it, and proposes a combat to settle whether Wigalois is to ride on to accomplish the quest. Comparably, *Durmart* tells the knight with the greyhound that he is seeking the Queen, whom he loves, and in reply is asked what brave deeds he has carried out to be worthy of her. *Durmart* has to confess that he has not yet done so, whereupon the knight declares the hero must give up his presumptuous intention, or otherwise have to fight him.[42] Here, then, we seem to have the adaptation to a love-quest of the motif from the Encounter at the Narrow Passage, when the hero comes to the entry of the lady's domain, with which one should compare *Durmart*'s arrival in Ireland to seek the Queen. We have already seen how features of the night on which take place the Rescue from Two Giants (**II**) and the Attack by Three Avengers (**III**) appear in the rendering of the Sparrow-hawk Contest (**V**) by *Durmart*, so that it is not strange that one from the Encounter at the Narrow Passage (**VIIa**) should occur in that of the Encounter with a Huntsman (**IV**). Thus I conclude that *conte d'aventure* X is indicated as the version drawn on by *Durmart*.

Neither the insertion of motifs from later on in this source, nor the postponement of matter from the Ile d'Or Episode (**VI**),[43] can prevent recognition of the series reflected in *Durmart*, with an order that is seen to have the complex of the Encounter at the Perilous Bridge (**I**) and the Attack by Three Avengers

---

40 *Durmart*, 2314-38; *Wigalois*, 2636-56; *Papegau*, 6/31-7; contrast *Descouneus*, 1656-97; *Lybeaus*, 796-852; *Erec*, 747-75.

41 Brugger, *op. cit.*, ZrP LXIII, 169.

42 *Durmart*, 1604-44; *Wigalois*, 3342-3418; *Papegau*, 57/14-58/5.

43 For other possible material from the Fair Unknown type of story to be found elsewhere in *Durmart*, see pp. 138 n. 26, 168 n. 23 below.

(III) coming later than the group of the Encounter with a Huntsman (IV) and the Sparrowhawk Contest (V), which begin it. I have therefore found support in *Durmart* for assumptions on which my table of descent is based, concerning the original order of episodes, the position of *Carduino*, and the relation of *conte d'aventure* X to the extant versions of the Fair Unknown type.

SIR GARETH OF ORKNEY

A romance which is closely allied to the Fair Unknown type is Malory's tale of Gareth, called Beawmaynes, who departs from Arthur's court in circumstances which correspond to those in that kind of story (p. 86). I have cited *Sir Gareth* as an instance where the tension between the hero and the emissary lasts until a late stage of the journey (p. 106), and so one should expect, according to my table of descent (p. 109 f.), a relation between its account and either the original story of the Fair Unknown type or *conte d'aventure* X.

The Problem of Origin

Since 1940 there have been several studies devoted to the genesis of *Sir Gareth*, and they do not agree in their conclusions.[44] Wilson proposed an origin in which *La Cote Mal Taillie* (as found in the *Prose Tristan*), *Descouneus*, and the lost source of this and *Lybeaus*, all played their part. Brugger took the romance as a derivative of the Fair Unknown type. But Schmidz asserts that *Sir Gareth* mounts to a stage of the tale antecedent to that represented by the versions of what I call the Fair Unknown type; which is like Loomis, who held that the best version and perhaps the closest to the original is Malory's account.[45]

Much discussion has been devoted to the climactic adventure, the combat with Sir Ironsyde, which is an analogue to the Encounter with Mabonagrain. Wilson concluded that Malory's tale very probably draws here on *Erec*. But according to Brugger the siege of the lady by Sir Ironsyde is a rationalizing of the enchantment motif in the Fair Unknown type of story, and has been combined with material from the Ile d'Or Episode. On the other hand, both Loomis and Schmidz hold that *Sir Gareth* preserves an original unity, from the source which accounts for the parallel material in the Encounter with Mabonagrain.[46]

44 R. H. Wilson, "The *Fair Unknown* in Malory", *PMLA* LVIII (1943), 1 ff.; Brugger, *op. cit.*, *ZrP* LXIII, 275-328, LXV, 121-86; C. C. D. Schmidz, *Sir Gareth of Orkeney* (1963). In "The Structure of Malory's *Gareth*", *Studies in Language and Literature in Honour of Margaret Schlauch* (1966), 219 ff., R. S. Loomis merely put together material from various parts of his *Arthurian Tradition and Chrétien de Troyes*. My citations from Loomis are from the latter.

45 Loomis, *op. cit.*, 439-41.

46 Wilson, *art. cit.*, 16-20; Brugger, *op. cit.*, *ZrP* LXV, 126-31, 140 f.; Loomis, *op. cit.*, 180 f.; Schmidz, *op. cit.*, 67-90.

There is however agreement over the last encounter on the ride, that Sir Persaunte of Inde corresponds to the host of the Jousting for Hospitality (p. 99 ff.), because both entertain the hero after having been vanquished by him, provide information about the combat he must undergo to free the lady, and accompany him for part of the way. But he soon turns back, and does not guide the hero anywhere near the gate of the lady's fortress. Then the attempt to identify the fight at a water passage with that at the Perilous Ford in *Descouneus* has to face the objection that the ford here is not authentic (p. 87 f.). And are the repetitive encounters with four brothers, who in succession bar the hero's passage in *Sir Gareth* (the Black Knight, the Green Knight, the Red Knight, and the blue knight, Sir Persaunte of Inde), to be equated with the Attack by Three Avengers? Even if these identifications were correct, several adventures in the Fair Unknown type of tale are missing in *Sir Gareth*. Brugger assumed they have dropped out. They were not originally in this kind of story, according to Schmidz, who bases her view, that *Sir Gareth* descends from an earlier stage of the tale than that represented by the versions of the Fair Unknown type (by my definition), on what is only a hypothesis, that its series of knights barring the hero's passage is an essential element which later became diluted with a variety of adventure met on the way, to produce the pattern that I call the Fair Unknown type.[47]

Because of the claims that have been made for the greater authenticity of *Sir Gareth* in relation to the five versions of the Fair Unknown type that stand against it, and for its bearing on *Erec*, one must take pains to determine the status of Malory's tale. For this the ground has already been prepared in this chapter, for when the Gordian knot is cut, by observing the structure of *Sir Gareth*, it sounds very familiar. It is a story allied to the Fair Unknown type that I have defined, but in which the emissary comes for a champion to save her lady by combat with the tyrant and rejected suitor who besieges her with an army, and there is a series of repetitive encounters on the hero's ride to his destination. Therefore, Malory's tale goes with *Ipomedon* II, and this is where comparison must begin.

The comparison made here in Appendix B in fact establishes that Malory's tale descends from a source close to *Ipomedon* II,[48] which clears up the problem of the relationship between *Sir Gareth* and the Fair Unknown type of story. One must look for the influence of the latter upon the allied narrative structure of the former as the reason for particular resemblances of Malory's tale to the Fair Unknown type. Compare what has happened in the story of Lore de Branlant in *Le Livre d'Artus*, a prose romance of the thirteenth century. Material like that in the *chanson de geste* of *Floovant* (p. 164 n. 14) has been fitted into a framework belonging to the class of *Ipomedon* II and *Sir Gareth* (p. 265), which attracts features from a tale of the Fair Unknown type. Thus we have a reflection of the Rescue from Two Giants (**II**: p. 88): a woman's cry

47 Wilson, *art. cit.*, 12; Brugger, *op. cit.*, Zr*P* LXV, 121, 123, 125; Schmidz, *op. cit.*, 56-9.
48 See p. 264 ff. below.

E

is heard in the forest, the hero leaves his companion to go to the rescue, finds a damsel held by a giant about to rape her, with two others waiting their turn with the girl, and the hero attacks first the giant holding the maiden; after his victory he returns, and then sets off to take the damsel home to her father's fortress.[49] Later, there are equivalents of the Encounter at the Perilous Bridge (I) and the Attack by Three Avengers (III), as we shall see (p. 137 f.). For the destination, where the hero is to fight the besieger who wants to have the lady by force, matter is drawn from the Sparrowhawk Contest (V).[50] Similarly, one must analyse the duel with Sir Ironsyde in Malory as a battle where traits of the Fair Unknown type have been added to those of the combat with the lady's besieger and rejected suitor for which the hero has been fetched as her champion.

The Horn to be Blown as Challenge

When Gareth arrives with the emissary and the dwarf before the castle of Dame Lyonesse, he sees many dead knights hanging from trees, and is told that the same fate awaits him if he is vanquished. A huge ivory horn is suspended from a sycamore tree, for the purpose of being sounded by any knight errant to summon Sir Ironsyde, who will arm himself and make his appearance to do battle. Gareth blows the horn so mightily that all the siege and the castle ring with the sound, and Sir Ironsyde arrives and warns him to beware, indicating the bodies hanging on the trees.[51]

The first feature corresponds to one found in the tale of the Fair Unknown, in the impaling of heads on stakes by the adversary at the Ile d'Or in *Descouneus*,[52] which also happens in the magic garden of *Erec*. The Ile d'Or Episode (VI: p. 98 f.) has some ground in common with the Ironsyde adventure, in that the opponent is the besieger (devastator) or the suitor of the lady. The second feature cited from *Sir Gareth* is however absent from the versions of the Fair Unknown type, and differs from that in *Erec*, where the blast horn on a stake is not for the purpose of summoning the adversary. But the complex turns up, in an adventure very like the Ile d'Or Episode, in the early thirteenth-century *Li Chevaliers as Deus Espees*. Here Gawain crosses a deep and wide river to the fortified town of the Port, a name that would suit the description of the city

---

49 *Le Livre d'Artus*, ed. Sommer, vii, 84-8; cf. *Descouneus*, 631-900, and *Lybeaus*, 568-705. There are three abductors in *Le Livre d'Artus* instead of two, owing to the amalgamation with material corresponding to that in *Floovant*. On the criterion of which giant is attacked first, see p. 109 n. 11 above. The taking of the rescued maiden home to her father is carried out by the hero in *Lybeaus* (p. 89).

50 Chrétien's description of the arrival at Laluth provides a close parallel (p. 162). For elements at Branlant from the Sparrowhawk Contest which are not found at Laluth, see pp. 180-82 below. Later, the story may contain a reflection of the Ile d'Or Episode (VI), see p. 267 below.

51 Malory, VII, c. 15 f.

52 The feature is used for the Sparrowhawk Contest in *Lybeaus*, 732-8, with the heads impaled on spears on the battlements.

at the Ile d'Or in *Descouneus*, which an arm of the sea encloses (*Uns bras de mer entor coroit*), and at whose foot, on the other side, beats the high sea across which merchants bring their rich merchandise to the town. To the situation of this city corresponds that of Dame Lyonesse's castle, for *the see bete uppon that one syde of the wallys where were many shyppis and marynars noyse with hale and how*.[53]

The lord of the Port has had his lands devastated by Gernemant of Northumberland, his beautiful daughter's rejected suitor, who has given the respite of a year within which he will fight any knight who wants to champion her cause, on condition that if defeated he will make restitution, but that if no-one can be found to conquer him the damsel and the city will be at his mercy.[54] The term of respite is now near its end, and no-one has yet managed to defeat Gernemant. Gawain undertakes the combat, and is informed that the opponent waits in a stronghold he has raised close to the Port. The hero must go to a meadow which is on the way to it just outside the city, and there he will find a pillar of marble under a beautiful tree and on the pillar an ivory horn hanging on a silver chain, which he is to sound to summon Gernemant. Gawain goes and blows the horn until the whole place resounds and the fortress trembles, and Gernemant arms himself, arrives, and threatens to treat the hero as he already has done the knights whose heads impaled on stakes he indicates, all of which is like Sir Ironsyde. Gawain and Gernemant fight till the hour of *none* has passed, and then the hero smites his opponent to the ground, leaps on him and unlaces his helmet to slay him, as Gareth does, but Gawain cuts off the adversary's head and fixes it on a stake to complete the exhibition of heads.[55]

In *Descouneus*, the place where Malgiers waits for challengers is a tent between the bridge and the city, and before it stands the row of sharpened stakes with helmeted heads upon them.[56] After the slaying of the opponent, the events follow a similar course in both *Descouneus* and *Li Chevaliers as Deus Espees*. The combat has been in the sight of the people and the maiden, and there is a tremendous joy at the hero's victory, which we also find in *Papegau*; adding *Lybeaus* as well, in all these accounts the people come to receive the hero (in *Descouneus* they are already present, watching the battle), accompany him in procession as he enters the city, and welcome him in gratitude.[57] I shall examine later the parallels that continue, including the night when the hero's desire is frustrated by the lady (p. 132 f.).

---

53 *Descouneus*, 1879-82, 1921-8. The resemblance between the situations of Dame Lyonesse's castle and the city of the Ile d'Or was seen by Wilson, *art. cit.*, 13, and Brugger, *op. cit.*, ZrP LXV, 129.

54 This motif is also found in the story of the Dame de Roestoc (p. 264).

55 *Li Chevaliers as Deus Espees*, 4193-4738.

56 *Descouneus*, 1949-70.

57 *Descouneus*, 2187-2214; *Lybeaus*, 1396-8; *Papegau*, 18/7-19/35; *Li Chevaliers as Deus Espees*, 4739-71. In *Meraugis*, 2739 ff., where the hero rides with Lidoine to the Cité sans Nom, which is a rich seaport, the citizens come out to receive him with great joy, and accompany him into the city (p. 217).

The analogy of the adventure at the Port to the whole course of the Ile d'Or Episode, from the combat to the departure after the frustrating night, is a guarantee of its origin. This allows me to attribute descent from the Ile d'Or Episode also to an adventure in the *Vulgate Lancelot*, where Marigart le Rous fights all challengers. Outside the castle there is a fine garden, and in its centre an open space enclosed by sharpened stakes, and the ivory horn which is to be sounded to summon Marigart hangs on a pine. Hector blows the horn, and Marigart, the cruellest knight in the world and looking very wicked, comes to fight in red arms. The combat ends with the hero removing his opponent's helmet and cutting off his head. Here the adversary does not impale the heads of vanquished challengers on the stakes, but has their naked bodies dragged through the streets. After he has been slain, the lady of the castle is delivered, the people of the city make the greatest joy and express their gratitude to Hector, and it is explained that Marigart was the lady's rejected suitor.[58] Then there is the analogue to the Ile d'Or Episode which is to be counted among the material from a tale of the Fair Unknown type in *Durmart*, the combat with Brun de Morois to release Guinevere, where the trophies exposed are battered shields hung on the battlements of his castle, and Durmart is warned that his shield will join the others, and the head of Yder will be impaled on a spear (p. 116 f.). Again we find familiar features. Durmart crosses a bridge, goes through into a beautiful garden, and in an open space he finds a lofty tree from which hangs an ivory horn on a silver chain. This time the adversary is discovered there, who blows the horn himself, whereupon he is asked what this is for, and Brun de Morois answers that he is calling for his arms. When these arrive they are red, his steed being covered with vermilion cloth and his shield of *vermel sinople*, like the arms of Malgiers in *Descouneus*, whose horse is also covered in vermilion and his shield coloured *sinople*,[59] even as Marigart comes to fight in red arms, and Sir Ironsyde's arms are all bloodred. The combat ends when Durmart smites his opponent to the ground, leaps upon him, sits on his chest, tears off his helmet and prepares to cut off his head, just like Gawain with Gernemant and Gareth with Sir Ironsyde.[60]

Lastly, one should compare an element in the non-Arthurian romance of *Floire et Blancheflor* (before 1170) which is derived from the Ile d'Or Episode. Features related to the Fair Unknown type of tale set in clearly from the arrival of Floire before Monfelix. He has to cross to it over an arm of the sea (*un braȝ de mer*), as at the Ile d'Or, and the identification is confirmed by this trait:

> a la rive un cor avoit
> Qui a un pel penduz estoit;
> Li venant a celui cornoient.
>
> (*Floire et Blancheflor*, 1325 ff.)

58 *Vulgate Lancelot*, ed. Sommer, iv, 350-53.
59 *Descouneus*, 2054-62.
60 *Durmart*, 4525-4788.

When this horn hanging on a stake is blown, a man arrives as fast as he can, but in *Floire* he is the boatman who serves the crossing and becomes the hero's host.[61]

I have proved that Brugger was right in assuming the influence of the Ile d'Or Episode on the combat with Sir Ironsyde.[62]

The Source of the Fair Unknown Type

From Sir Persaunte of Inde, I can establish the version of the Fair Unknown type which was used. In Malory's tale, it is the last of the perilous passages when Gareth and the emissary approach a city and see before them a fair meadow, in which it is the custom of Sir Persaunte, lord of the city, to camp in order to joust and to tourney. He is in a tent when they ride up, spies their arrival and sends a messenger to inquire whether the hero comes in war or in peace. On receiving the reply that it is up to him, he comes forth to fight. Gareth is the victor, and Sir Persaunte takes him to his tent and gives him good hospitality. Compare this with the encounter with Schaffilun in *Wigalois*, when the hero and the emissary enter the marches of the lady's domain and see before them a tent surrounded by spears in a field. As they go towards it, Schaffilun spies their arrival, comes out to meet them, and inquires of Wigalois where he is bound. On being informed of his mission, he challenges Wigalois to a jousting to settle whether he can continue on his quest, and the hero is given good hospitality in his tent. The jousting is here next morning, but it is in its correct location in the equivalent episode of *Papegau*. In this version, they come to a pass in the marches with a castle at the end, which is the entry to the lady's domain. It is guarded by the Chevalier du Passage, who halts the hero, imposes a jousting condition when he is informed of his mission, and gives him good hospitality for the night after the hero's victory. The Reconciliation Scene, which in *Wigalois* follows the Schaffilun adventure, is in its turn displaced in Malory's tale, being found almost at the corresponding point, but as they come up to Sir Persaunte, and with an abrupt change in the emissary's manner— from *mesdisance* to appreciation of the hero's qualities—right in the middle of a conversation.[63]

The borrowing by *Sir Gareth* of the Encounter at the Narrow Passage, which adds an adventure to a basic pattern corresponding to that in *Ipomedon* II, is betrayed by evidence of its intrusion in spite of the assimilation between Sir Persaunte and the preceding antagonists. A series of three repetitive encounters, each followed by a night-lodging, the last of which is at a hermitage, has been so disturbed by the insertion of Sir Persaunte, before the stay at the hermitage,

---

61 *Floire*, 1317-30. There is in *Floire* further material adapted from the Ile d'Or Episode (p. 183 n. 54). On the connections between *Floire* and the Fair Unknown type of tale, see p. 201 below.

62 For further consideration of this influence on the combat with Sir Ironsyde, see pp. 211-16 below.

63 Malory, VII, c. 11 f.; *Wigalois*, 3297-3606; *Papegau*, 57/1-58/34.

that preceding the fight with Sir Ironsyde we have two nights without an encounter intervening, and without any progress towards Dame Lyonesse's
castle, for in the meantime the dwarf goes to and fro between both of Gareth's
last lodgings and her fortress.

The appearance of matter from the Encounter at the Narrow Passage (**VIIa**) in
Sir Gareth directs one to compare the next combat with the Encounter before
La Roche (**VIIb**), which follows in *Wigalois* and *Papegau*. There is similarity
in the situation of a duel before the lady's castle, and some specific resemblance.
When Sir Ironsyde arrives to fight with the hero, he rides into a little vale
under the castle, so that all who are in the fortress and at the siege might
behold the battle. Dame Lyonesse is at a window, Gareth looks up at her, and
during the fight he receives signs of encouragement from the lady which rejoice
him. He thereupon bids Sir Ironsyde to make ready, "*and lette us do oure batayle
to the utteraunce*". In *Papegau*, as they approach La Roche sans Paour, the
emissary points out before them a knight advancing whom she says is the best
in the world; the formidable opponent in *Wigalois* is the lady's steward. The
adversary leads the Chevalier du Papegau to a lovely meadow before the gate
of the castle, below the crag on which it stands, in order that the hero should
be seen by the lady, and that she should judge who jousts the better. They put
forth their best efforts because of Flor de Mont, the young lady of the castle,
who leans out of a window watching the combat along with her maidens.[64]
Thus in the Ironsyde adventure there can also be traced a blending with the
Encounter before La Roche, which has to do with the drawing on the Encounter
at the Narrow Passage for a fight to precede that with Sir Ironsyde.

The version of the Fair Unknown type used in Malory's tale contained
matter corresponding to that part of *Wigalois* and *Papegau* which I derive from
conte d'aventure X. That it was *conte d'aventure* X would explain why the
Ironsyde adventure does not agree with the Ile d'Or Episode in *Descouneus*
and *Lybeaus*—there we have no horn to be sounded, the opponent simply
barring the passage—but with the combat at the castle of Brun de Morois in
Durmart, in which the material of the Fair Unknown type came from a source
that must have been *conte d'aventure* X (p. 119).[65]

I have collected matter from various romances which is independent of the
Descouneus/*Lybeaus* tale and supports my table of descent. In the next chapter,
I shall substantiate my assumptions about the early narrative lines of the Fair
Unknown type of story from a work by Chrétien himself.

64 Malory, VII, c. 15 to c. 17; *Wigalois*, 3885-3948; *Papegau*, 58/34-60/34.
65 Also note how *Sir Gareth* goes with *Wigalois* and *Durmart* in having the hero
knighted, not on arrival at court, but at some later feast-day. The derivation from a version
independent of the tale of the Fair Unknown (Y) could explain why *Sir Gareth* agrees with
Carduino in having the emissary announce at Arthur's court that she is the sister of the lady
in distress, which is not the case in other versions of the Fair Unknown type.
On the use of *Erec et Enide* by *Sir Gareth*, and for a summing up of the synthetic nature
of Malory's tale, see pp. 211-16 below.

8

Gawain's Journey to the Castle of Ladies

The story of Chrétien's *Perceval* may be divided into two parts, I and II (not to be confused with the First and Second Continuations of *Perceval*, by followers of Chrétien), and their heroes are respectively Perceval and Gawain. There is a maiden like the Damoisele Mesdisant in *Perceval* II who persists in humiliating Gawain as she accompanies him on his ride, and the hero arrives at a region where he has a host who takes him to an adventure at an enchanted palace, as in the tale of the Fair Unknown. Since the lady's scornful behaviour lasts till a late stage, what one should look for is whether the Fair Unknown type of story, either in its original form or as in *conte d'aventure* X, lies behind Gawain's ride. Though the hero does not meet his lady companion until a later episode of the ride, I start my examination of it from the beginning.

DEPARTURE FROM ARTHUR'S COURT[1]

Gawain sets out from Arthur's court on a quest initiated by the arrival of Guigambresil, who accuses him of slaying his lord, the old King of Escavalon. The hero, who denies this, has engaged in a tryst to defend his honour before the new King. This is quite unlike the Fair Unknown type of material.

TOURNEY AT TINTAGEL[2]

Gawain sees some knights crossing a glade, asks a squire about them, and learns it is Meliant de Lis on his way to Tintagel. The squire informs him that a tournament is about to be held before Tintagel between its lord, Tiebaut, and Meliant de Lis, who has challenged Tiebaut to the tourney as demanded by his *amie*, Tiebaut's elder daughter, to demonstrate his prowess before her. Gawain continues on his way, comes to the fortress and spends the day outside, while the tournament takes place before it. Looking on, the elder daughter of Tiebaut sees Meliant de Lis, declares that no knight pleases her better, and that it is a delight to see such a *bel chevalier*. The Maid of the elegant Little Sleeves, her little sister, contradicts her, saying that there is a better-looking knight present, meaning Gawain. Her incensed elder sister is about to strike her, but

1 *Perceval*, 4749-4815.   2 *Ibid.*, 4816-5655.

the ladies hold her back. Meliant de Lis performs admirably, and his *amie* boasts that he is better looking than all at the tournament, but her sister still maintains there is a *plus bel*. Whereupon the other, enraged, is roused to high words and strikes her. Meliant carries all before him on the first day of the tournament, but Gawain earns scorn for not taking part in the sport, which he avoids in order to reserve himself for his tryst. In the evening he goes to enter the fortress and meets Garin, an old vavasor, with much land and of high lineage, who is before a gate and addresses Gawain, offering him hospitality, and takes him into his home. The Maid of the Little Sleeves goes to Garin's house and appeals to Gawain to enter the tourney next day as her knight, to put right the wrong inflicted on her by her sister. Her father, who is paying a visit to see Gawain, tells him not to pay any attention to the silly child, but she wins Gawain over to do what she asks. We now have a vignette of the girl departing held by her father before him on his horse, explaining the circumstances to him and how she has in mind that her knight's defeat of Meliant de Lis would fling her sister's words in her teeth, and remarking that her sleeves are too small to send as a love-token. At daybreak the little maid comes to bring a sleeve run up for Gawain to have at the tournament, but she finds him out at mass, and waits for his return to present the love-token to him. The armed knights assemble for the second day of the tourney, and Gawain immediately bears Meliant to the ground, sending his horse to the Maid of the Little Sleeves. By noon Gawain is the victor of the tournament, he returns to his lodgings, where the maid thanks him for what he has done, and Tiebaut twice invites him to stay the night. But Gawain refuses to remain, there is a moving little scene of leave-taking between him and the fond child, and he continues on his way.

In the Fair Unknown type of tale, this episode finds its parallel in the Sparrowhawk Contest (**V**: p. 92 ff.). First of all, in *Perceval* II the hero hears of a martial event by meeting someone on the approach to the city who informs him about it. This is not a maid, however, but he does come across one— though not outside the city—who complains of what has happened to her that day in connection with the occasion, and whose champion he becomes to set right a wrong, by defeating a knight who has already won the event on the first day, and against whose *amie* contends the damsel for whom the hero is to fight. As in *Wigalois*, *Papegau*, *Durmart*, and also *Erec*, the event is a special occasion for which there is a large assembly of knights and ladies who have come to the town; but unlike *Erec* it is held before the city, which was the picture in *conte d'aventure* X, as we see from the other texts (p. 119). The opponent is responsible for the holding of the event for the love of his *amie*, as in *Lybeaus*, but the fullest parallel is with *Durmart*, where Cardroain li Ros institutes the contest before Landoc for the sake of Ydain de Landoc,[3] even as Meliant de Lis arranges the tournament before Tintagel for love of its lord's daughter.

3 *Lybeaus*, 724-9; *Durmart*, 2011-14.

We then have one damsel declaring that her *ami* is the best-looking knight at the tourney, and the other maintaining that there is a better-looking one, whereupon the former, incensed, is roused to high words and strikes the latter. In this fashion the ritual of the contest about beauty is preserved, but in mockery, with reversal of sex. The disagreement between the sisters, leading to a blow, corresponds to the procedure of the Sparrowhawk Contest, especially in *Erec* and *Descouneus*, where one knight asserts the claim of his *amie* to be the most beautiful, the other maintains the beauty of his own lady surpasses that of his antagonist's, and there follow words of defiance and the combat. Instead of the enraged opponent we see in *Erec* and *Durmart*, we have the infuriated elder sister. Thus in *Perceval* II is transformed the first day's contest for the sparrow-hawk, which brings about the entry of the hero next day as the champion of the damsel, in Chrétien's treatment here a little girl, the most innocent *amie* that Gawain ever has, who takes part in some engaging scenes which strike a different note from that sounded by the burlesque of what was originally a martial ritual.

We can also see the resemblance to the Sparrowhawk Contest when on the evening of the first day Gawain enters the town, takes up lodgings, and as in *Erec* goes to mass early next morning before returning to arm for the jousting,[4] the early morning mass also being a feature of the event in *Descouneus* and *Wigalois* (p. 96). The tournament is won just before noon, even as *Wigalois* leaves some time after midday;[5] and, as in the Fair Unknown type of tale, when victory has been accomplished the hero goes on his way, the damsel showing her gratitude for what he has done for her. But in *Perceval* II she belongs to the city, where she remains, and it is here that we have the moving scene of leave-taking, instead of the emotional one when they have left the place together, as in *Wigalois*, where the maid is overcome at the parting, which she also is in varied circumstances in other versions (p. 116).

In some respects the narrative in *Perceval* II is a closer analogue to the episode in *Erec* than any account of the Sparrowhawk Contest. For here is the old vavasor—though not poor—that the hero meets outside an entrance, who addresses him first and offers lodgings. And here is the lord of the town who goes to the lodgings after the jousting and twice asks the hero to stay with him, and whose invitation is twice refused.[6]

VISIT TO ESCAVALON[7]

Suddenly Gawain takes to his lance and starts chasing a white hind in the forest. He fails to catch it because his horse casts a shoe; and then he meets the King of Escavalon, a young and handsome man leading a hunting party with hounds,

4 *Erec*, 697-726.   5 *Wigalois*, 3140.
6 *Erec*, 373-96, 1250-81. On the invitation and refusal, see p. 182 below.
7 *Perceval*, 5656-6211.

who insists on sending Gawain to his castle, accompanied by a messenger to charge his sister to love and cherish the guest until he himself returns from the chase. In so far as this is a meeting with a huntsman, we have a parallel to hand in the Encounter with a Huntsman (**IV**: p. 91 f.), and indeed in *Lybeaus* the hero is taken by Otes de Lyle to his castle.[8] But in *Perceval* II there is no dog that comes by, no altercation and no combat. However, in chasing a deer, riding after it with a spear, Gawain is given the part of the adversary in the Encounter with a Huntsman, who appears on the scene thus in *Descouneus* and the equivalent episode in the Second Continuation of *Perceval* (p. 115).[9]

The fortress of Escavalon is situated on an arm of the sea (*sor un bras de mer seoit*), and is busy with merchandise. Gawain arrives at the castle, and the knight who accompanies him there leads him by the hand into the presence of the damsel, who is very ready to comply with her brother's request. Gawain offers to be her knight all his life, asks for her love, and she willingly grants it. They quickly take to kissing and are busy thus enjoying themselves, when they are caught in the act by a vavasor who recognizes Gawain as the slayer of the old King of Escavalon, and forcefully decries the lady's shameful behaviour with her father's killer. At this, down she falls in a dead faint, and comes to when Gawain, taken aback at her distress, has raised her from the floor. She laments that she has to die because of him and he for her, when the citizens hear the news, and she hurries to give him armour. But as he puts it on Gawain discovers that no shield has been provided. So, picking up a chessboard and throwing the pieces to the floor, he cries, theatrically, "Sweetheart, you need not find me another shield!" Meanwhile, the vavasor has gone out to the citizens and called them to arms, to capture the traitor who has killed his lord (*qui mon seignor ocist*), and a crowd of men armed with axes and guisarms come to attack the hero, who defends the narrow doorway of the tower against them. The lady and he take to pelting them from the tower with the enormous chess-pieces, which wreak some damage, and there is a scene of great commotion in the middle of which Guigambresil, the knight responsible for Gawain's departure from Arthur's court, happens to arrive, astonished at the din. When he learns what it is all about, he goes to meet the King returning from the chase, tells him what is going on and that here is the man who has slain the old King, but since he has given Gawain hospitality the King disperses the crowd. Gawain is offered a truce on condition that he engages in a tryst to fight Guigambresil in a year's time and in the meantime to go in quest of the bleeding lance, on which mission he departs.

It is sad to see the poor lady receive an awful shock at the discovery that she has committed such a dreadful act as to make love with the supposed slayer of her father, but the tragedy is very much relieved by the tone of burlesque. This note in the scene means that we should be ready to find Chrétien has drastically transformed a source. Loomis pointed to this as represented by the

8 *Lybeaus*, 1204-18, L 1245-56.
9 *Descouneus*, 1308; *Perceval*, Second Continuation, 24862 f.

Avylyon episode in *Sir Gareth*,[10] where in addition to other resemblances we have the encouragement by the brother to enjoy the company of his sister, and the interruption of love-making by a man with a guisarm, who departs when the brother arrives, but in contrast the scene is one of those where the lady comes to the hero's bed.

Gareth goes to the isle of Avylyon, where he finds Dame Lyonesse, who is staying with her brother Sir Gryngamour. He leads Gareth by the hand into the hall of the castle, Dame Lyonesse comes forth to welcome him, and there take place games and plays, dancing and singing, and Gareth always looks at the lady and falls violently in love. They go to supper, and his love burns hot within him. Sir Gryngamour realizes this, calls his sister aside, encourages her to make Gareth stay there, and also urges the hero to enjoy himself, for his sister is to be his at all times, saving her honour. Gareth is delighted, and goes to Dame Lyonesse and kisses her many times, they greatly enjoy each other's company, she promises him her love for life, and they burn hot in love for each other.

After supper they retire, and a bed is made up for Gareth in the hall. Then, as previously arranged between them, within a while Dame Lyonesse comes to him in a mantle and lies down by his side. He begins to embrace and kiss her, but they are interrupted by an armed knight who suddenly appears and threatens him with a guisarm. Gareth leaps out of bed and cuts his opponent's head off, though not before he himself has been wounded. Sir Gryngamour comes in, attracted by Dame Lyonesse's screaming, and Lynet also arrives, whereupon the strange knight's head is replaced through her magic power, and he departs. Some nights later the same phenomenon is repeated, when Dame Lyonesse again comes to the hero's bed, and the knight with a weapon is this time accompanied by a great light as if there were twenty torches. This frustration of love-making is explained as due to the exercise of Lynet's subtle arts to preserve her sister Dame Lyonesse's honour.[11]

If the Visit to Escavalon derives from such matter,[12] then it has been assimilated to the visit of Alexander to Candace in the *Roman d'Alexandre*. They are lovers from afar meeting for the first time, Alexander has come incognito, and while they are together in private a son of the Queen enters the chamber, recognizes Alexander, and urges upon the Queen that they should kill him in revenge, because *Il m'ocist mon segnor par grant mesaventure*, which is in the version of Alexandre de Paris (III, 4798). Candace protects the unarmed Alexander from the attack he threatens with a weapon, makes her son withdraw, and after love-making Alexander departs. For other elements of the scene at Escavalon there is an analogue in the Havelok story. Havelok and his wife take refuge in a church tower, where they come under siege from men of the

---

10 R. S. Loomis, *Arthurian Tradition and Chrétien de Troyes* (1949), 418.

11 Malory, VII, c. 21 to c. 23.

12 From it Loomis, *op. cit.*, 229 f., also derives another episode in Chrétien, in *Le Chevalier de la Charrete*.

city, on whom the strong hero casts stones from the structure, until the noble Sigar Estalre arrives, calls an end to the assault and arranges a truce with Havelok.[13]

When one compares the situations at Escavalon and Avylyon with the Fair Unknown type of material, the parallels are found to lie there in the Ile d'Or Episode (**VI**: p. 98 f.), the matter of which is reflected, with Gawain as the hero, at the castle of the Port in *Li Chevaliers as Deus Espees*. The fortress of the Ile d'Or in *Descouneus*, like that of Escavalon in *Perceval* II, lies on an arm of the sea and is busy with merchandise, and we have a port in the corresponding material of *Li Chevaliers as Deus Espees* and *Sir Gareth* (The Horn to be Blown as Challenge, p. 122 f.). Both in the versions of the Fair Unknown type and in *Li Chevaliers as Deus Espees* we see the hero arriving and being made welcome, disarmed at the palace, and (except in *Descouneus*) provided by the damsel with rich dress. With the hero's looks thus set off, Giglan seems to be one of the handsomest knights in the world, and they have never seen anything handsomer than Gawain at the Port, which is to be compared with the way the lady feeds her admiring eyes on the hero in *Papegau*. The damsel offers her domain and herself to Descouneus or Lybeaus, while at the Port the hero is accepted as her *ami*. Supper is laid in the evening, and both Descouneus and Gawain sit pleasurably at table. At this meal, Giglan gazes at the fay continuously and falls in love, and Gawain is unable to take his eyes off the damsel of the Port, he so wants to kiss her; Descouneus has already been stunned by the fay's beauty, Lybeaus falls in love with her when she offers him herself, and the Chevalier du Papegau becomes engrossed in an affair with her. After supper, Gawain and the maiden kiss and embrace until it is bedtime. A bed is made up for the hero, and all leave him to lie down both in *Descouneus* and in *Li Chevaliers as Deus Espees*, but he will have little rest.[14]

The Night Scenes at the Ile d'Or

It is not long before the fay comes through her door to Descouneus, wearing only a chemise under her mantle. She asks whether he is asleep, Descouneus answers that he is awake, and she comes and lies down with him. At the Port, the damsel in the same dress is brought to Gawain's bed by her mother, and left there to his love-making. Descouneus does not manage to get any further than embracing the fay, for when he is about to kiss her she draws back, says it will lead to lechery, and departs. Whereas at the Port the love-making is ardent, but also brought to an end by the maiden before it goes as far as the hero wishes. When Gawain can restrain himself no longer, and is on the point of consummation, the damsel bursts into tears and tells him that she has dedicated her virginity to Gawain, of whom she has heard so much. It is no use the hero revealing that he himself is Gawain, she does not believe him, and she leaves.

---

13 Gaimar, *Estoire des Engleis*, 545 ff.

14 *Descouneus*, 2187-2390; *Giglan*, n ii *verso*; *Lybeaus*, 1396-1413; *Papegau*, 18/7-23/10; *Li Chevaliers as Deus Espees*, 4739-4879.

Both heroes are left in a state of anguish at the frustration of desire. Distracted with love, Descouneus dreams all night that he holds the fay in his arms, until he awakes at dawn; he escapes from the Ile d'Or at sunrise. Gawain also has a disturbed night, and at dawn gets up, dresses, and departs from the Port.[15] *Alas she hadde be chaaste!*, exclaims *Lybeaus* at what must be some such treatment suffered by its hero at the hands of the fay.[16]

On a second visit to the fay of the Ile d'Or, Descouneus has an even more eventful night. As before, his bed is made up, they retire, and this time the fay leaves her door open and warns him not to enter her chamber. But during the night after agonies of hesitation he succumbs to temptation and goes to her door, whereupon it appears that he is suspended by the arms over a tempestuous stream. He screams out that he is going to drown, men rise and find him hanging from a sparrowhawk perch, and as soon as they arrive the spell breaks. Later the same night he attempts once more to reach the fay's door, and this time he seems to be holding up the whole roof of the hall. He screams out that he is going to be mortally injured, and again men come, to find that it is only a pillow on his neck. He now gives up trying to enter the fay's chamber, and then a damsel comes through the door to his bed, asks whether he is asleep, and he answers that he is awake. This is just what happened on his first visit to the Ile d'Or, but this time it is one of the lady's maidens, sent to fetch him to her mistress's room. Yet at first he fears that he dreams, but the maiden assures him that this dream will be realized, and he goes with her to the fay's chamber, which is wonderfully perfumed and decorated with fantastic splendour, so that it seems to him like a paradise. The fay is lying in her bed, she takes him by the hand, lays him down beside her, and they give themselves up to each other. She was responsible for the spells, and explains that she has so caused him pain for putting her to shame by leaving her when he first visited the Ile d'Or.[17]

Before drawing comparisons with the Avylyon episode, I should clear up some problems with these night scenes in *Descouneus*, and I also need to do so in order to have the material correctly arranged in readiness for the unravelling of the *conjointure* in *Erec et Enide*. First of all there is the existence of two visits to the Ile d'Or in *Descouneus*, and also to the Amoureuse Cité in *Papegau*, but only one to the fay's domain in *Lybeaus* and the equivalent place in *Carduino*. The second stay in *Papegau*, however, does not support the pattern in *Descouneus*, because it is a perfunctory one on the way back to court, whereas the second visit in *Descouneus*, together with the description of a tournament whose proclamation lures the hero back to Arthur, is a long interruption between the Accomplishment of the Mission and the Wedding to a Queen. Furthermore, the first stay in *Papegau* has three bedroom scenes of which the last has the hero coming to the fay's chamber and finding it wonderfully

---

15 *Descouneus*, 2391-2486; *Li Chevaliers as Deus Espees*, 4879-5135.
16 *Lybeaus*, L 1476.
17 *Descouneus*, 4474-4929.

perfumed—it has already been described as decorated with fantastic splendour. He enters the room, feeling that he is going into paradise, and they give themselves up to each other until just before daybreak.[18] To this corresponds the final scene of the second visit in *Descouneus*. Again, the first illusion of the second stay in *Descouneus* is equivalent to the only one in *Carduino*, where the hero also finds himself suspended over water when he tries to enter the lady's chamber during the night.[19] From all this, it is evident that Renaut has redistributed the scenes of one original occasion between two visits in *Descouneus*, the second stay forming part of an end-pattern which he has taken from elsewhere: the hero disappears after his victory in the climactic encounter, the lady he has saved departs to Arthur's court, and the King proclaims a tournament to lure the hero out of hiding into marriage with her.[20]

Betraying the original order of the scenes, the situation of a damsel coming through the door to the hero's bed in *Descouneus* is repeated in the second stay. The coincidence means that the frustrating experience which Descouneus has on the first visit once followed those that in this text are allocated to the second. And the final position of the voluptuous scene in *Descouneus* and *Papegau* shows that this should be put last of all. Thus, Descouneus stays one night at the Ile d'Or and has Frustration 3, and then the second time he experiences Frustrations 1 and 2 and the Consummation, again on one night. Carduino also departs after one night's stay, when he has Frustration 1. The conclusion is that the original form of the story had a single night at the Ile d'Or, with:

Frustration 1:   the entry into the fay's chamber is prevented by the illusion of being suspended over water.

Frustration 2:   the entry into the fay's chamber is prevented by the illusion of the roof pressing on the neck.

Frustration 3:   the fay comes to the hero's bed, but then withdraws.

Consummation: the entry into the fay's chamber is finally made.

This leaves one with a further difficulty, for in *Lybeaus* and *Carduino* there is no consummation at all, only frustration. Like Descouneus on his first visit, Carduino leaves in the morning after having been defeated by the lady during the night. A succession of frustrating experiences is hinted at in *Lybeaus*, which exclaims how unfortunate it is that the fay should be chaste, for always in the end she causes the hero torment; and it relates that she deceives him with illusion and magic. But it also says that when Lybeaus sees her face it seems to him he is in paradise,[21] and this may be an echo of the scene in the fay's chamber. Certainly, if in the original form of the story I could reconcile consummation with frustration that is in fact never mastered, I would be able to explain all the versions.

18 *Papegau*, 27/29-28/16, 42/12-43/10.   19 *Carduino*, ii, 14/7-17/6.
20 See p. 267 f. below. There also is to be found the affair with a lady at the hero's place of resort after his victory.
21 *Lybeaus*, 1429-33, L 1476-8.

Let us pay attention to what happens in *Descouneus* at the point in the second visit when the damsel comes through the door. It looks as if the experience of Frustration 3 is about to be repeated. But this damsel turns out not to be the fay, and she tells Descouneus she has been sent to fetch him to her mistress's chamber. At first he fears that he dreams, but she assures him that *this* dream will be realized. What Renaut has done is to realize a dream in his original by relating it as fact, the dream that is referred to in *Descouneus* as occurring after Frustration 3 on the first visit, when the hero, distracted with love, dreams all night that he holds the fay in his arms, until he wakes up at dawn. We can see in *Papegau* a trace of the dream condition, in the hero going back to his own bed before daybreak. The realization of the dream, like the return to the fay, is a modification carried out independently in the two texts. Both features in *Descouneus* are attributable to the way the author makes the fay stand for his lady-love, the hero's return to the Ile d'Or being accounted for by his love for the fay, which drives him back to her, and the consummation being an occasion for comment relating the episode to the poet's own affair.[22] In *Papegau*, one feature has to do with the dropping of illusions altogether, and the other with a concentration of the love-interest upon the relations between the hero and the fay, but this time because as King Arthur he is not to marry the lady he delivers by his victory in the climactic encounter.

There was thus originally only a single visit to the Ile d'Or, and in the night spent there two scenes with nightmarish illusions, when the fay leaves her door open and the hero tries and fails to enter her chamber, and a third in which the fay comes to the hero's bed but again frustrates him. Then there is another that is nothing but a dream, when the hero fancies he has been in the end invited to the fay's chamber, finds it like a paradise, worthy of such a pleasurable dream experience, she welcomes him to her bed with open arms, they give themselves up to each other all night, and he awakes from the dream at dawn.

The common ground between all this and the Avylyon episode is as follows. The hero arrives and is made welcome by the lady of the castle, enjoys the pleasure of her loving company, and kissing is indulged in at the Port as well as at Avylyon. When they retire a bed is made up for the hero, there is the coming of the lady to his bed (Frustration 3 in the Fair Unknown type of tale), the nightmare illusions (Frustrations 1 and 2 in that same story), coupled in one account with her presence in his bed but in the other occurring separately when he is going to her chamber, and frustration on every such promising occasion. In addition, the single day at Escavalon is to be compared to the single night at the Ile d'Or.

However, in spite of the likenesses there are some critical distinctions between the situations in Escavalon and Avylyon on the one hand and the Ile d'Or on the other. In the Fair Unknown type of tale the frustrating is exercized by

---

22 *Descouneus*, 4828-61.

the lady herself, whereas it occurs in spite of her in *Perceval* II and *Sir Gareth*, and the frustrations themselves differ. And while at Escavalon and Avylyon there is a welcoming brother, in the Ile d'Or Episode we have a suitor or gigantic besieger (devastator) to be conquered by the hero.

MEETING WITH GREOREAS[23]

As he rides, on a hill before him Gawain sees a shield on an oak-tree, with a lance beside it and a palfrey, which puzzles him, because arms and a palfrey do not go together. When he is nearer, he perceives a damsel who is lamenting the condition of a severely-wounded knight, with streams of blood pouring on both sides *parmi les flans*, who has often fainted with the pain and now lies resting. Such a wound would have been inflicted by a lance piercing right through and protruding on the other side.[24] As Gawain approaches, he is not sure whether the knight is alive or dead, and the damsel tells him that he is in great peril of death from his wounds. She refuses to rouse the knight to answer Gawain's request for news of the region, but the hero gently stirs him up with the butt of his lance. The knight warns him not to proceed further and descend the hill, because here are the marches of Galloway, which if knights pass they never can return. Only he has done so, and he is laid out thus, in such a dire condition that he cannot live till nightfall, because he encountered a knight of greater prowess than he ever met before. But Gawain insists on pursuing his way, and the knight begs him to carry out this request, that if the hero is successful he should return and find out how he is, and if he has died to see to his damsel. Granting this, Gawain moves on.

He comes to the next adventure, the Taking of Orguelleuse from a Garden, and in company with this maiden he returns to the knight, who is in great need of a physician for his wounds. Gawain picks a herb which is very good for relieving the pain and goes to the knight, who seems dead, but his pulse is found to be beating and his face not yet cold. Using the herb, and strips torn from the wimple of the knight's damsel as bandages, Gawain binds his wounds, whereupon the knight recovers his senses and is anxious to arrange for confession nearby before he dies. And so he wants Gawain to give him the *roncin*, or inferior kind of horse, ridden by a hideous and deformed squire who is now coming up at a trot. But when Gawain addresses the squire the latter is insolent, and gets knocked out of his saddle for his pains. There is then a rude exchange between Gawain and the squire, who is infuriated. The knight interrupts to ask Gawain not to heed the squire, but to bring him his *roncin*, and when he does so the knight, who is fast recovering, now sees Gawain clearly for the first time and recognizes him as his enemy. As soon as Gawain goes to help the damsel mount her palfrey to accompany the knight, the latter maliciously rides off on Gawain's own steed and leaves him with the *roncin* instead. Gawain finds this very amusing, and asks for his steed back, but is brought to realize

23 *Perceval*, 6519-6656, 6904-7223.   24 Cf. *Erec*, 3021-4.

how serious the matter is when the knight reminds him, before he departs with the damsel, that Gawain once forced a man to eat with dogs for a month with his hands bound behind his back, upon which Gawain recognizes him as Greoreas, whom he did so punish for rape. And Gawain, with scornful Orguelleuse riding after him, therefore has to continue his quest on the *roncin*, which is a wretched mount indeed.

With mocking Orguelleuse, whom Gawain tells that it does not befit a damsel to be *mesdisant*, and who rides apart from the hero, we are in the presence of the figure corresponding to the emissary in the Fair Unknown type of tale— the lady rides before the hero there, however (p. 106). After the Ile d'Or Episode (**VI**), in the series reflected by *Carduino* and *Erec* we have the Encounter at the Perilous Bridge (**I**: p. 87 f.), and there at the end of the combat the hero's opponent is in a condition similar to that of Greoreas. The battle opens with Descouneus or Lybeaus smiting the adversary fiercely with the lance—low and deep (*Descouneus*) or in his side (*Lybeaus*)—so that he falls off his horse, and a fight on foot ensues. When Wylleam Selebraunche rides off to report to King Arthur, as required by the hero, on the way he meets his three nephews, who make a great outcry at seeing his blood flow and ask who caused him to bleed so profusely. Compare *Wigalois*, where the lord's servants follow him past the ditches when he issues out upon the hero, who immediately thrusts his lance through him, and it protrudes on the other side. The opponent falls off his horse, and bitter lamentation is raised at his fate. But it is the picture in *Descouneus* that we should concentrate on. Here Blioblieris loses much blood from his wound (in *Giglan*, it is made clear that this is the one inflicted by the lance),[25] and is utterly done for:

> Va Bliobl̈ieris lassant
> Por le sanc qu'il aloit perdant
> De la plaie qu'il avoit prisse:
> Ne puet mains faire en nule guisse.
> (*Li Biaus Descouneus*, 465 ff.)

Robert (who doubles the part of the dwarf in this version) takes the steed of Blioblieris and brings it to Descouneus, who mounts it, his own horse having been killed in the fight. Then the hero, the emissary, and the dwarf (along with Robert) depart, leaving Blioblieris greatly lamenting his wound. After his attendants have taken him to his abode, they disarm him and lay him on a bed, where he lies faint and afflicted with pain, waiting anxiously for his three companions—they are due to return in the evening—in order to ask them to pursue Descouneus and obtain revenge. When they arrive, great lamentation is made over their lord's condition. There is similar material to be found in the story of Lore de Branlant in *Le Livre d'Artus*, which makes use of a tale of the Fair Unknown type (p. 121 f.). Coming from a fortress, Guinganbresil demands the hero's horse, or otherwise he will have to fight him. The hero

25 *Giglan*, l iii *recto*.

objects this is *por rober*, just as Blioblieris is accused by Descouneus of practising *roberie* (427); cf. the threat of dispossession in *Lybeaus* and *Carduino* (p. 87).[26] Guinganbresil is struck immediately to the ground by the lance, which pierces right through and causes a stream of blood to gush forth from his side (*parmi le coste li enuoia tout outre · si que li sans en saut a grant ruissel*). The hero's squire takes Guinganbresil's horse away, the hero remarks that his adversary's wound has great need of healing, and they depart. When Guinganbresil revives from his faint, he greatly laments his wound (*se plaint molt durement*), is asked how he is, opens his eyes, and says that they should bind his wound and carry him away; they take him back to the fortress and lay him on a couch. Before they do so, knights arrive and ask who has been responsible when they see the condition of Guinganbresil, set out after the hero in revenge, and a battle ensues that is thus equivalent to the Attack by Three Avengers (p. 90 f.).[27]

In *Durmart*, what corresponds to the Encounter at the Perilous Bridge, as precipitating an attempt to take vengeance upon the hero, is his defeat of Cardroain (p. 117). Here it is the hero, with his opponent lying dead, who has the low lance-wound streaming with blood, and as with Greoreas there is a bandaging—when Durmart binds himself with a pennon—a need expressed for a physician to cure the wound, the pain and the debilitating effect of the great loss of blood is brought out, and the severely-wounded man remains in his dire state with an anxious hope. But in the case of Durmart he is continuing his journey hoping to find a physician to heal the wound.[28] The situation in *Erec*, where the episode corresponding to the Encounter at the Perilous Bridge is the First Encounter with Guivret, takes up an intermediate position. After the battle Guivret says that they *both* have need of a physician, and Erec and he cut off strips from the bottom of their shirts and bind up each other's wounds, a mutual bandaging instead of the single one of Gawain tying up the wounds of Greoreas with strips from the damsel's wimple, or Durmart binding himself with the pennon from a lance. We have seen that in *Erec* the antagonists inflict on each other the same blows and injuries that the Fair Unknown does on his opponent. As a result, we have the wounded hero departing in dire need of treatment also in *Erec*.[29] That the motif of the wound streaming with blood belongs originally to the opponent can be seen not only from *Descouneus*, *Lybeaus*, and the story of Lore de Branlant, as well as *Perceval* II, but also from

26 In *Durmart*, after the analogue to the Ile d'Or Episode, which is the battle with Brun de Morois (pp. 116 f., 124), the hero fights the robber-lord Creoreas and his knights, who from the castle of Roche Brune prey on travellers on the road. In *Descouneus*, the companions of Blioblieris are called *li robeor* (1003). Chrétien thus seems to have taken the name of Greoreas from his source.

27 *Descouneus*, 441-591; *Lybeaus*, 316-441; *Wigalois*, 1983-2007; *Le Livre d'Artus*, ed. Sommer, vii, 91-4.

28 *Durmart*, 2574-3038. Cf. Marie de France, *Guigemar*, 123 ff., where the hero uses his shirt for a bandage with a grievous wound, and sets out he knows not where in the hope of finding the only person who can heal it.

29 *Erec*, 3878-3913.

the existence of the battle in the Attack by Three Avengers, which cannot follow an appeal on the ground of the hero's wounded condition, as this stops an assault, but only an appeal based on his unarmed state, when he is given the opportunity to arm himself (cf. p. 117).

The relation between the Meeting with Greoreas and the Encounter at the Perilous Bridge is such that in both we have the hero, the damsel who accompanies and scorns him, a squire on a *roncin*,[30] and a severely-wounded and horseless knight lying with blood streaming from a wound that has been inflicted by the lance piercing right through his side. In *Perceval* II the combat has already occurred, mysteriously and threateningly, before the arrival of the hero, and the lamentation for the lord is being made by a damsel. The lying faint and afflicted with pain, anxiously waiting for nightfall, is here the earlier picture, and in the open under a tree, while the binding of the wound is instead reflected later. Furthermore, Greoreas has taken a role that belonged to the emissary, who observes, with Blioblieris wounded, that if Descouneus pushes on he will never return, and it is to her that the hero replies he will not turn back on any account.[31] The business with the horses still means that the hero loses his steed, and is supplied with another mount by the squire (originally the dwarf, in the Fair Unknown type of tale), but the way it is done in *Perceval* II achieves a strikingly different effect. The squire there is very different from the admirable dwarf of the Fair Unknown type, since he is hideous, deformed, and insolent to the hero; we also find this transformation in *Durmart* (p. 118). Out of the straightforward material in the Fair Unknown type of story, in the Meeting with Greoreas there has been produced an episode turning from mystery and pathos into burlesque, in which no small part is played by the surprisingly rapid recovery of Greoreas from his dire condition, at the hands of Gawain as the amazingly successful physician.

I have made use of *Descouneus*, *Lybeaus*, the story of Lore de Branlant, *Durmart*, and *Erec* to throw light on the source material from which has been formed the Meeting with Greoreas. I can also have recourse to *Carduino*, for a different aspect. The Encounter at the Perilous Bridge is represented here by a combat with a knight who comes to oppose the hero and is killed by him. Then the dwarf in great alarm informs Carduino that the knight is Agueriesse (Gaheriet), the nephew of King Arthur, and the slayer of Dondinello. As Dondinello is Carduino's murdered father, the hero now realizes that he has fought his enemy.[32] Gaheriet has three brothers, Gawain being one of them, who could deliver the Attack by Three Avengers, but this episode is lacking here. In being the unwitting enemy of Gawain and his brothers because of his slain father, Carduino is in the same situation as Perceval in the *Prose Tristan*, so that his encounter is to be compared with that between Perceval and Gaheriet there, which is an analogue of the Encounter at the Perilous Bridge. Gaheriet inhabits a castle on an island, whose knights joust with all who pass,

30 Cf. *Ipomedon*, 8311; *Durmart*, 1777.
31 *Descouneus*, 500-8.   32 *Carduino*, ii, 20/5-25/8.

opposes Perceval when he arrives, guided by a damsel, and is defeated by the hero.[33] Now this motif in *Carduino*, the unwitting encounter of enemies, ending in recognition, is also present in the Meeting with Greoreas.

TAKING OF ORGUELLEUSE FROM A GARDEN[34]

Gawain has brought Orguelleuse de Nogres back from the next episode, in which he comes to a strong fortress by the sea, crosses into it by a bridge, goes towards the high ground and finds there a damsel under a tree in a garden, admiring herself in a looking-glass. As soon as he sees her, Gawain spurs his horse towards the maiden, and she says "Steady, steady, do not rush". He asks her what she means, and she observes that she knows well what he has in mind, to seize her and carry her away, and he agrees this is true. She refuses to be carried away, she tells him, she is not one of those foolish women that some knights amuse themselves with by taking on their horses along with them, but he can have her company if he brings her palfrey. He goes to fetch it, and meets people who warn him not to touch the horse, for the damsel has been the cause of many a man's death. Gawain pays no attention and comes to the palfrey, where a tall knight sitting under a tree gives him serious warning that he will lose his head if he takes the horse. But Gawain will not desist, and returns with it to find the damsel still looking at herself in the mirror, having removed her wimple and mantle in order to see her face and body properly. She mounts the palfrey, scornfully rejecting his courteous attempt to help her up, because she will not let him touch her, and goes along with him in whatever direction he decides to take, which is back to Greoreas.

In the warnings one can recognize deterrent effects deriving from the emissary's role in the Fair Unknown type of tale, and it is her attitude that we see in the scornful behaviour from now on of the lady who has become Gawain's companion, but this adventure does not sound at all promising as an equivalent of the Rescue from Two Giants (**II**: p. 88), which is what the location of the episode within the series leads one to expect. However, put the key in the lock and turn it, and, lo and behold, the door opens again.

After the Rescue from Two Giants, the maiden relates how she was kidnapped. She was amusing herself in a garden, one of the giants found the door open and came in (*Descouneus*), sprang on her out of the bushes (*Lybeaus*), and took her back to his companion.[35] Like the giant, as soon as Gawain sees the damsel he has an impulse to carry her off and rushes at her, and then he takes her back

---

33 E. Löseth, *Le roman en prose de Tristan* (1891), § 288a. Cf. W. Schofield, *Studies on the Libeaus Desconus* (1895), 187; Loomis, *op. cit.*, 400 f.

34 *Perceval*, 6657-6909.

35 *Descouneus*, 892-8; *Lybeaus*, 664-9, L 698. In *Durmart*, 3055-96, where the hero comes across the damsel of the Red Tent, she is found combing her hair before a mirror held for her. The location of this episode corresponds to that of the arrival at the home of the maiden saved in the Rescue from Two Giants; compare p. 117 above with p. 164 below.

to where he left the person he has just been with. Orguelleuse is thus an amalgamation of the emissary with the maiden taken from the garden by the giant. This is no mere replacement of the giant by Gawain, but a calculated parallelism, with a conscious rendering of the movements in the source, and the delicate and impish playing of a counterpoint against the well-known tale. How impish can be seen when the damsel's denial that she is a wanton is measured against the suggestiveness of her pose, as she sits and looks at herself in a mirror that she holds, like one who is waiting for a lover. This is the picture given for the Great Whore of the Apocalypse in medieval art, and also serves to represent Luxuria.[36]

ATTACK BY GREOREAS'S NEPHEW[37]

Gawain is overtaken, after he has reverted to the course of his ride and reached a river, by Greoreas's nephew, spurring on the hero's own steed. He has been sent in pursuit by Greoreas to bring back Gawain's head. The hero turns round to meet him, in spite of his companion's urgings that he should flee, and tries but fails to get his wretched horse to budge, while his opponent comes steadily charging on. The surprising result of this unequal clash is that the adversary is hurled to the ground, and Gawain recaptures his steed, vaulting from the *roncin* on to its back.

The relationship with the Attack by Three Avengers (**III**: p. 90 f.) stands out. Here is a nephew of Greoreas, as in *Lybeaus* there are nephews of the knight defeated at the Perilous Bridge who come in pursuit; and the avengers sent by him in *Descouneus* to deal with the hero arrive at a gallop. And also in *Lybeaus* the hero hurls the first attacker at once from his steed to the ground; and then the dwarf comes forward to take the horse, leaping on to its back just as Gawain does. Similarly, the dwarf at the corresponding point in *Ipomedon* II, where the hero also immediately strikes the first adversary off his horse, comes forward and exchanges his *roncin* for the opponent's steed (p. 113).[38] The loss of the hero's horse in one episode, and its replacement there by a mount which the dwarf or squire provides, is thus in *Perceval* II neatly twined together in the later episode with the capture of the attacker's steed, which is vaulted on in exchange for a *roncin*; and the note of burlesque continues to be maintained.

OVERNIGHT STAY WITH THE BOATMAN[39]

The river that Gawain has come to is deep and broad, and opposite he sees an imposing stronghold on the cliff, with a very large palace of marble standing

36 Cf. Rigmel waiting for the hero in Thomas, *Horn*, 788 f., 1025 f. On the iconographical tradition of the Great Whore, see L. Réau, *Iconographie de l'art chrétien*, ii. 2 (1957), 715 f. For Luxuria, see E. Mâle, *L'art religieux du XIIIe siècle en France* (9th edn., 1958), 120 f. and fig. 59.

37 *Perceval*, 7224-7370.   38 *Lybeaus*, 472-86; *Ipomedon*, 8285-8334.

39 *Perceval*, 7371-7493.

on a crag (*roche naïve*), its five hundred windows filled with ladies and maidens.[40] This he will enter next day. Coming up to the Jousting for Hospitality (**VII:** p. 99 ff.), Descouneus is in sight of the fine stronghold of Galigan (as Lybeaus is of Synadoun), with towers and high walls and a bridge over a stream; it is at Senaudon, the Cité Gaste, splendidly built with towers and strong walls, and with a bridge over a stream, that he enters a very large palace of marble with a thousand (*Giglan:* five hundred)[41] windows. The enchanted city in *Carduino* has a palace of shining marble, and the hero in *Wigalois* and *Papegau*, coming up to the Encounter at the Gateway of the Magician's Castle (**VIIc**), reaches a bridge over a stream with a splendid stronghold on the other side, where he will enter a large and very beautiful palace in *Wigalois*.[42]

While Gawain was dealing with the nephew of Greoreas, Orguelleuse made off in a boat and abandoned him, but now the ferryman who serves the stronghold arrives. He demands his toll from Gawain, which is the steed of the knight he has seen the hero conquer, for—as he explains—no knight can be vanquished at this crossing without his receiving the horse. Gawain objects to giving it up, because this would result in the painful experience of having to depart on foot. He gives him instead the nephew of Greoreas, who has put himself at Gawain's mercy. Then the ferryman tells the hero not to worry over the disappearance of the damsel, for she has caused many a knight to suffer decapitation at this place, and he ferries Gawain across the river. There, in his house by the waterside, which is fit to receive the visit of a count, he gives him hospitality and an evening meal which excel.

In the Jousting for Hospitality, the penalty for being conquered is the loss of one's steed and a shameful departure on foot. Thus the boatman, exacting his toll for the defeat of a knight, is playing a role comparable with that of Lanpart. At the same time, Gawain obtains what is the hero's reward for victory in the Jousting for Hospitality, because the ferryman becomes his host and provides excellent lodging. A crossing by boat has thus been introduced, taking the place of the bridge over the river, and a ferryman instead of the steward. Compare the introduction in *Floire et Blancheflor* (before 1170) of a ferryman-host and a crossing by boat in matter from the Ile d'Or Episode (p. 124 f.). Daire in *Floire*, who corresponds to the host of the Jousting for Hospitality, and is a *pontonier*, a bridge-keeper,[43] is particularly related to the boatman in *Perceval* II because toll has to be paid to him (p. 148).

The mutually exclusive motifs, of penalty exacted for defeat and hospitality with honour given after victory, are illustrated side by side, though in fact the reception accorded to the hero has not been gained by his triumph over the nephew of Greoreas. Encounters in two episodes are resolved by one in Chrétien, and the business of the horse is so contrived that the same steed is

---

40 *Perceval*, 7224-57.   41 *Giglan*, n iv *verso*.

42 *Descouneus*, 2493-2508, 2773-2872; *Lybeaus*, 1462-7; *Carduino*, ii, 56/3; *Wigalois*, 6767-79, 7059-7311; *Papegau*, 72/20-33.

43 In *Floire*, A 1328, the ferryman is also called a *pontonier*.

the subject of three adventures where there are distinct mounts in the original. Comparison with the tale of the Fair Unknown brings out the ingenuity of the design in *Perceval* II.

FIRST ARRIVAL AT LA ROCHE DE SANGUIN[44]

The next morning, Gawain looks out from a tower and sees the stronghold on the cliff (La Roche de Sanguin), inquires about it, and the host instructs him about the circumstances there. Similarly, in the Arrival at the Lady's Stronghold, Wigalois looks out and sees the castle of Korntin, inquires about it, and is given information. This is on the previous evening, and it is then too, in the Jousting for Hospitality episode, that Lybeaus is instructed about the circumstances in Synadoun (p. 100 f.).

However, unlike the steward in the Fair Unknown type of tale, the boatman who serves the fortress is mysteriously ignorant whose it is. But at any rate he is able to inform Gawain that the stronghold belongs to a Queen, and the hall is well guarded by magic, for she brought a magician to the palace and he has made a marvel, such that no knight enters the place with any vice and can remain and live. It is inhabited by two Queens and the second Queen's daughter, and frequented by old ladies who have lost husbands and lands, by damsels who are orphans, and squires who have come from many countries. All await the arrival of a hero who will dispel the enchantments, and as the lord of the stronghold maintain them, restore their lands to the ladies, marry the damsels off and make knights of the squires.

Like Lybeaus and Wigalois, Gawain is eager to undertake the adventure. The host tries to dissuade him, but fails, and then he rides with Gawain to conduct him to the enchanted location, as the steward does in the Accomplishment of the Mission (**VIII**: p. 102 f.), the place being nearby, as in *Lybeaus*. Not a word is said by Chrétien about entering the stronghold and riding through it. They reach the palace, which has glass windows so clear that one can see all those who enter as soon as they pass the entrance, and in the middle there is a bed all of gold and stretched with cords of silver, where in *Descouneus* we find a table by which the hero waits on horseback for the adventure, leaning on his lance. As in *Lybeaus*, the hero in *Perceval* II walks here and there and looks about a deserted, marvellous and richly-painted place.[45] Then the host gives Gawain particulars about the adventure, the equivalent happening outside the enchanted city in *Descouneus* and *Carduino*. Gawain is warned not to sit on the *Lit de la Merveille*, for no one has ever issued alive who attempted the danger, and the hero would die the worst death that has ever overtaken a

---

44 *Perceval*, 7494-8262. The episode is discussed by E. Brugger, *ZrP* LXV (1949), 145, in his series entitled "Der Schöne Feigling in der arthurischen Literatur". He supposed that it was part of a version of the Fair Unknown type that was incorporated into *Perceval* without its earlier section; see *ZrP* LXIII, 320.

45 *Lybeaus*, 1789-1800.

knight. But Gawain cannot be deterred from the task, and the host soon departs and leaves the hero to face the adventure alone, even as he has to penetrate the enchanted city by himself in the Fair Unknown type of tale.

Eventually the hero sits down, Gawain on the bed, like Lybeaus at the high table, whereupon there is an upheaval. In *Perceval* II the cords of the bed resound, bells on them ring, the windows fly open and arrows and bolts come crashing from unseen shooters. Then the windows close, and Gawain extracts the missiles from his shield and his flesh. The doors and windows in *Lybeaus* rattle like thunder, stones fall from the wall, the dais quakes, the earth shakes, and the roof and vaulting come apart.[46] But in *Perceval* II there follows no combat, except with a lion which is loosed at Gawain by a churl who opens a door; it brings the hero to his knees, with its claws plunged into his shield, but he cuts off the paws and its head. Now Gawain has a shield bearing two lion's paws.

In this, we find the Perilous Bed instead of the table which is in the hall in the tale of the Fair Unknown. But *Lybeaus* shares with *Perceval* II an upheaval on sitting down, its phenomena being similar to some of those that take place with the bed at Corbenic in the *Vulgate Lancelot*.[47] And here Bohort is attacked by an armed knight who issues (on foot) from a room, and then retires to the chamber, where he renews his strength and comes out again with more energy than before. This is like *Carduino*, whose magician-knight rushes (on horseback) upon the hero from a door, is repulsed and withdraws, and then comes charging out again. Also *Descouneus*, where a similar sequence of assaults occurs with two magicians. Evrain attacks from a room, both he and Descouneus are unhorsed, fight with the sword, and the adversary is forced to retire to the chamber. After the hero has remounted, an even more redoubtable opponent, Mabon, charges from the room, and again both are unhorsed and fight with the sword.[48]

But since the sitting on the Perilous Bed results in the ensuing combat being on foot from the beginning, whereas it is on horseback in *Descouneus*, *Lybeaus*, and *Carduino*, one must exclude the Perilous Bed from their common source. The experiences at Corbenic are an assemblage that has at its core the Perilous Bed with its fiery lance, and goes so far as to include a palpable imitation of the adventure in *Perceval* II, with its shower of wounding arrows and bolts,[49] followed by the assault of a lion which catches the hero's shield, so that to the mixture there could well have been stirred in an attack on the pattern we have in *Carduino* and *Descouneus*. As for *Lybeaus*, we clearly have unauthentic material in one of the magicians coming in from out-of-doors to challenge the hero, who mounts and rides out of the hall to fight both antagonists in the

---

46 *Lybeaus*, 1801-18. The rattling is after the battle in *Descouneus*, 3074-3100.

47 *Vulgate Lancelot*, ed. Sommer, iv, 344-6, v, 298 f.

48 *Descouneus*, 2926-3060; *Carduino*, ii, 56/3-58/8.

49 In the Fair Unknown type of story, the wounding by a shower of arrows and bolts occurs during the attack on the hero by the army brought back by the opponent of the Encounter with a Huntsman (pp. 184, 189, 194); this is the *Lybeaus*, 1120-22.

open.[50] All goes to show that in *Perceval* II a Perilous Bed situation has been substituted for the kind of combat that is found in *Descouneus* and *Carduino*, whose agreement, according to my table of descent (p. 110), indicates what there was in the original account of the Fair Unknown type.

As soon as Gawain has accomplished the adventure, the boatman returns with joy, as in *Descouneus* the host enters joyfully with the emissary and the dwarf, who also hasten into the city in *Carduino* when they realize the hero has been successful. He informs Gawain that he has achieved the end of the enchantments and all will serve and honour him. The scene that follows is in agreement with the Fair Unknown type of tale in having the motif of the hero who, because he brings an end to the enchantments, gives joy to the inhabitants and is offered the lordship of the land. However, there has been no mission to destroy a magician-knight, the enchantments being a moral test alone, which suits a Perilous Bed adventure. And unlike *Descouneus*, *Lybeaus*, and *Carduino*, we have no lady delivered from imprisonment and transformed by a serpent-kiss.

Squires come and disarm Gawain, damsels enter, with an attendant carrying rich clothing, and kneel and honour him, which gives the hero great joy. Their leader, wearing a circlet of gold—she is the second Queen's beautiful daughter, Clarissant—announces that they are joyful to see him, the best of all worthy men, and that the Queen sends him salutations, commands they should take him as their true lord, and offers him the rich dress to wear. Now we know why there is no imprisoned lady to be transformed by a serpent-kiss. It is in *Wigalois* and *Papegau*, where this motif is lacking, that we have not only the Queen but also her beautiful daughter, and the connection with this version is confirmed by the sequel in *Perceval* II.

Clarissant returns to the Queen, leaving Gawain in the meantime to put on the clothes, and the boatman takes him to the top of the castle to view the wondrously beautiful country. Gawain declares that he wants to hunt in the forest that lies before them, but the boatman says he will not be able to obtain permission to leave the place; which annoys the hero, who goes back to the palace in a huff. Clarissant arrives with the message that the Queen will come to see him and the meal is ready, but Gawain says he will not enjoy a meal until he has heard the news that will give him joy—which refers to permission to leave the castle. The princess returns to the Queen and reports Gawain's ill humour, whereupon the Queen remarks he will cheer up when he sees her, and she sets out accompanied by two hundred and fifty damsels. An aged lady, she converses at length with Gawain, asking for news of King Loth's sons (of whom Gawain is one) and others at Arthur's court. When Gawain so praises Guinevere that he asserts no-one can leave her without sorrow or part from her in anger, the Queen observes that he will not do so from herself. Gawain answers that he well believes it, since before he saw her he did not care what he did, he was so vexed, but now he could not be more joyful. She rejoins that his

50 *Lybeaus*, 1819-1962.

joy will double, continually increase, and never fail. With this, the striking digression comes to an end as Gawain, attended by two hundred and fifty damsels, eats a hearty meal at which he is served with whatever he wishes, and conversation, songs, and dances follow, until he goes to rest at night on the *Lit de la Merveille*.

In the Arrival at the Lady's Stronghold (p. 85), which is Roimunt in *Wigalois* and La Roche sans Paour in *Papegau*, the hero meets the beautiful princess and her mother the widowed Queen. It is this situation which is developed by Chrétien, in such a way that we have two widowed Queens at La Roche de Sanguin and not just one, with the second Queen's daughter Clarissant corresponding to the princess Larie (*Wigalois*) or Flor de Mont (*Papegau*), and La Roche de Sanguin (in which Roche means a fortress built on a crag) to Roimunt or La Roche sans Paour, a stronghold described in *Papegau* as *une roche qui est moult fort et moult belle* (26/3). The boatman in *Perceval* II plays a part similar to that of the steward in *Wigalois*, and the function of Clarissant as messenger gives her a role which is that of the emissary at Roimunt. On arrival there, Nereja leaves the hero and goes to report to the Queen, while Wigalois is looked after by the steward and disarms. The emissary returns to convey to Wigalois a gift of rich dress, which he puts on. Gawain's desire to enter the forest he sees below is paralleled when Wigalois (at bedtime) looks down upon the country, sees the castle of Korntin and asks the steward for the way there through the forest, but is told that alas he will not be able to find any such way. One can only reach Korntin by following a strange animal guide when it appears before Roimunt.[51]

Very interesting is the relation between, on the one hand, Gawain's annoyance and his change to joy in Chrétien and, on the other, what there is in *Wigalois*, where we find it is not the sight of the widowed Queen but that of the beautiful princess which converts the hero from ill humour at not being able to leave the castle for the forest. The emissary takes Wigalois to see the Queen, and she confirms that if he accomplishes the mission he will gain both the kingdom and the princess. Then Wigalois becomes impatient for permission to depart, and is irked by the delay. Now Larie speaks with him and his mood changes to joy, because it gladdens him to look upon the beautiful damsel. Whereas in Chrétien we have the lengthy conversation with the Queen, in *Wigalois* there is the important scene between the hero and the princess, in which he declares his love and it becomes apparent that she returns it. It is in fact true of this hero that his joy will double, continually increase, and never fail, because Wigalois will succeed in his mission, gain the princess in marriage, and reign with her over the land. A very pleasant evening meal follows the love scene, after which they sit, till Wigalois goes to bed in a beautiful hall.[52] Roimunt is full of lovely ladies, while La Roche sans Paour is crowded with damsels, and at La Roche de Sanguin such company is used amusingly by

---

51 *Wigalois*, 3851-83, 4297-4342; *Papegau*, 63/8-10.
52 *Wigalois*, 4008-4296; *Papegau*, 61/10-62/35.

Chrétien to bring out the delight of the susceptible Gawain at the attention they lavish upon him.

This episode in *Perceval* II is thus a blend in which not only has a Perilous Bed situation been placed in the context of matter from the Fair Unknown type of tale, but the enchanted location to which the host conducts the hero, in one form of that story, has been made to coincide with the place where the princess and the widowed Queen live in another version. Such double derivation of the framework has been exploited for the sake of mystery. From the conjunction of *Descouneus* with *Carduino*, we know that the original story had a Cité Gaste, and correspondingly we are given no sign of inhabitants when Gawain enters La Roche de Sanguin, apart from the bed—which belongs to an element from outside the Fair Unknown type of tale—and a solitary figure that I shall shortly consider. The inhabitants only appear when the hero has surmounted the enchantments, and yet on the approach to the stronghold Gawain has seen ladies looking out of the windows, as when the Chevalier du Papegau is *devant la roche du chastel*[53]

The Rich Man at the Foot of the Castle

There still remains the greatest mystery of all. When the boatman accompanies Gawain to the palace, we have a pause while they contemplate an *eschacier*, in other words a man with an artificial leg (*eschace*). It is richly decorated with silver and bands of gold and jewels, he sits on a bundle of rushes on a step at the foot of the palace, whittling an ash stick with a knife, saying not a word to them, and they in turn do not address him. The host asks Gawain what he thinks of this man, and the hero remarks that what he sees on the artificial leg is very beautiful, whereupon he is informed that the man is rich. Then the host and Gawain come to the entrance, which has two gates, and Chrétien appeals to the authority of his source as he describes their richness.

While staying within the field whose bearing on *Perceval* II has been shown, the *Wigalois/Papegau* account, we find a man whom the hero comes across sitting on a step before the entrance of a splendid castle with two wide, pillared gates, and who is left still sitting there while the hero carries out the Accomplishment of the Mission within. In *Wigalois*, the Encounter at the Gateway of the Magician's Castle (**VIIc**) takes place with two gate-keepers found sitting on a step before the imposing and double-gated entrance of Glois. These are grey-haired knights, over a hundred years old, with long, thick, broad beards, and hair braided, curled, and dressed with bands, who are armed but with their shields hung up. Under a linden-tree, they guard the entrance day and night. One of them is soon killed by Wigalois, but the other, Count Adan von Alarie, plays an important part in the narrative. On his defeat, he supports Wigalois on his mission, shows him how to enter the castle but himself remains outside, eventually hastening to him in the palace when Wigalois has achieved the destruction of the magician (in **VIIIa**).[54] The hero then commits to Adan the charge of Glois and its great treasures. Adan von Alarie is another reflection of the steward in the original tale of the Fair Unknown type, and indeed Lanpart is a grey-haired knight who is found sitting down before a castle. I then turn to him, remembering that Chrétien's model for the sitting figure has a common source with the steward in *Descouneus*. Lanpart is unarmed and dressed in a *robe d'eskerlate* with a rich belt, ornamented like the *eschace* by bands, with fine silverwork. He has been playing a game of chess with another knight and just checkmated him, and so as in *Wigalois* there are two sitting figures.[55]

Of particular interest because of their early date are two derivatives of the Jousting for Hospitality to be found in *Floire et Blancheflor* (before 1170). At the entry to Babiloine there is a very deep and wide water passage, and the *pontonier*, the bridge-keeper, who is rich and has a large tower and house, sits on the bridge on a marble slab at the end of it and under a white poplar. He is fine-looking and well-dressed, and seems a worthy man. Toll has to be paid to him, for one's horse as well, and from him Floire obtains lodgings in his tower, joyfully given and with splendid hospitality.[56] This host, called Daire, helps Floire to enter the Emir's castle in the middle of Babiloine, sending him on to its gate-keeper, whom he describes as a dangerous man who beats and robs those comers he suspects, but who, if his suspicions are calmed, will play chess with one. When Floire arrives at the foot of the Emir's castle, the gate-keeper's suspicions are duly calmed and he desires to play chess. Instead of the three courses of jousting, with turns at the end of each course (p. 214), we have Floire winning the first game of chess, returning to gain the second, and returning once more to win the third—with sitting spectators present and out of doors before the castle—whereupon the gate-keeper takes him indoors for dinner and greatly honours him.[57]

There is another bearing available from Gornemant de Gorhaut in *Perceval* I, who evidently descends from the steward in the Fair Unknown type of tale. Perceval comes to a castle, asks lodgings for the night of Gornemant, and the

54 *Wigalois*, 7059-7272, 7839-8010; *Papegau*, 73/18-74/3, also has an encounter with two men at the entrance to the castle.

55 *Descouneus*, 2584-94. There seems to be an echo in the similar situation of 325-35, where Blioblieris, by the unauthentic defended ford, is sitting unarmed, with his shield hung up before the entrance to his shelter, and diverting himself by playing a game of chess with two attendants.

56 *Floire*, 1371-1508. On the relation between this *pontonier* and the boatman in *Perceval* II, see p. 142 above.

57 *Floire*, 1707-25, 1883-2025. One can see a general resemblance to the Fair Unknown type of tale when the gate-keeper helps Floire to enter the Emir's castle in order to accomplish his quest, and as a result Blancheflor is delivered from the magician who holds her and intends to marry her. There is then a wedding between Floire and Blancheflor (at the hands of the Emir, who also offers to crown them), which is an occasion of the greatest festivity, and the couple return to Floire's country to reign there. On the connections between *Floire* and the Fair Unknown type of tale, see p. 201 below.

latter grants it, but first arms himself and mounts his horse, and gives the hero a practical lesson in jousting.[58] Gornemant is a courteous and worthy man, wears a *robe porprine*, informs the hero that he will give him hospitality willingly but on a condition—instead of requiring the jousting custom he takes the hero through a jousting lesson—and provides good lodgings and an evening meal. The resemblance to Lanpart is thus striking, and we are told that Gornemant keeps rich house, even as the habitation of the boatman in *Perceval* II is fit for a count to visit, and the *pontonier* in *Floire* is rich and has a large tower and house. Now when Gornemant is met we are given this scene. He is on the bridge before the castle whiling away the time pleasantly, accompanied by two retainers, and as Perceval heads towards the bridge Gornemant waits for him, carrying a staff in his hand *par contenance*, that is, by way of customary conduct for a man of rank.[59]

The steward Lanpart, the boatman, the *pontonier*, and Gornemant all show marks of wealth, are all met in the open before a castle, and two of them are diverting themselves as they wait, Gornemant bearing a staff, which a steward does in sign of his office,[60] and Lanpart playing chess, even as the Emir's gate-keeper has a penchant for the game at the foot of the castle. Adan von Alarie sits on a step under a tree before the castle gateway, where Wigalois finds him on crossing a bridge, and the *pontonier* is found at the end of a bridge, where he sits before his tower on a marble slab under a tree. If I equate the *eschacier* with Adan von Alarie, this will complete the tally of personages in *Perceval* II (the others being Orguelleus del Passage and Guiromelant, as we shall see) representing three different reflections in the source (in **VIIa**, **VIIb**, **VIIc**, all derived from **VII**)[61] of the steward in the original form of the story, while we also have the representative of the latter himself. In *Perceval* II the introducer to the enchanted location, and the supporter who hastens within when the hero has been successful, is already the boatman, corresponding to the host-guide (Lanpart), and his *alter ego* sits silent and is inspected, as an image derived from the other account. There he was a gate-keeper, and how the romancer's mind worked to produce an *eschacier* out of this can be gathered from a grim jest spoken by Raoul in the *chanson de geste* of *Raoul de Cambrai*, which reveals that a gate-keeper in real life was often a man with an artificial leg. Ernaut, who has lost a hand, can become a watchman, and Rocoul, whose leg has been cut off below the knee, can take up the profession of gate-keeper:

> "Or vos donrai .j. mervillous mestier:
> E. ert mans, et vos voi eschacier;
> Li uns iert gaite, de l'autre fas portier."
> (*Raoul de Cambrai*, 2928 ff.)

58 See D. D. R. Owen, *The Evolution of the Grail Legend* (1968), 137-9.
59 *Perceval*, 1305-1596.
60 Arthur's steward bears a staff of office in *Perceval*, 2795.
61 On the derivation of the Encounter at the Narrow Passage (**VIIa**), the Encounter before La Roche (**VIIb**), and the Encounter at the Gateway of the Magician's Castle (**VIIc**), see p. 204 f. below.

In Chrétien the figure's transformed condition, of a rich man holding a staff which he whittles and wearing the splendid ornamentation in bands, with silverwork, on an artificial leg, is more intriguing than that of a wealthy ferryman.

Thus I trace in this episode the blending at La Roche de Sanguin of the original Cité Gaste (to which the hero is led by the host in **VIII**) with two corresponding castles in the source of the account in *Wigalois* and *Papegau*, one being the stronghold where the hero meets the widowed Queen and her beautiful daughter (and is looked after by the steward, in **ALS**), and the other the magician's fortress (before whose gateway, in **VIIc**, sits the impressive figure on a step), which is occupied by ladies who in *Papegau* go to the hero in the hall joyfully when he has accomplished the mission (in **VIIIa**). The features in the First Arrival at La Roche de Sanguin that derive from this other version mean that a Wedding to a Queen would be to the Queen's daughter, as in *Wigalois*, but Gawain is not offered the lordship of the land by the Queen through marriage with Clarissant. However, the wedding motif does make its appearance later.

ENCOUNTER WITH ORGUELLEUS DEL PASSAGE[62]

Next morning, Gawain looks out of a tower, and sees a damsel with a knight passing on the other side of the river, even as Wigalois, who also stays a night, perceives that the animal guide has arrived before the lady's castle. In both cases the sight causes the hero to leave immediately. Gawain inquires who the lady is, and learns it is the damsel who accompanied him the previous day, who should be avoided for her nastiness. He is not to bother either with the redoubtable knight, who has put many to death at this crossing. Compare how Wigalois was previously warned by the emissary that the animal guide has led many brave knights to their death. Gawain, taken over by the boatman, recrosses the river and rides towards the damsel and the knight, just as Wigalois leaves Roimunt and goes to meet the animal.[63] The departure of the hero from the lady's stronghold, in the source, is to carry out his mission to destroy the magician; but it takes Gawain back to the course of his approach to La Roche de Sanguin, and precipitates a new series of adventures leading up to his second arrival there.

The knight, who is Orguelleus del Passage a l'Estroite Voie, catches sight of Gawain and feels relieved, because he was afraid the hero had escaped him, his duty being to be on the look-out for any knight who comes to cross to La Roche de Sanguin and to oppose his passage. They clash, Gawain is the victor and hands the knight over to the ferryman, just as he did the nephew of Greoreas, also defeated at this crossing (p. 141 f.).

62 *Perceval*, 8263-8413, 8644-8.
63 *Wigalois*, 3873 f., 4480-94; *Papegau*, 62/35-64/10.

The adventure is to be compared with the Encounter at the Narrow Passage (**VIIa**), which supplies the reason for the knight's appellation. In *Papegau,* the hero comes to a pass in the marches so restricted that no-one can enter the lady's domain except by a castle at the end of the pass:

> Et ont tant chevauché qu'ilz vindrent au pié d'une montaigne qui estoit si serree que nul ne pouoit yssir de celle marche ne entrer en la terre de madame Flor de Mont, se par ung chastel non qui estoit houtre la montaigne a l'entree de l'Ile Fort.
>
> *(Le Chevalier du Papegau,* 57/5 ff.)

This entry is guarded by a redoubtable knight, the Chevalier du Passage, who halts the hero and imposes a jousting condition for his passage in which the Chevalier de Papegau would be completely at his mercy if defeated, *sans plus riens faire du destrier.* But the hero is the victor and is given good hospitality for the night. The equivalent in *Wigalois* is the encounter with Schaffilun, who is found in a tent surrounded by spears, in a field in the marches as they approach Roimunt. Schaffilun also proposes a combat to settle whether the hero is to ride on to accomplish his mission, and gives him good hospitality for the night.[64] I have compared to this episode Gareth's encounter with Sir Persaunte, whose tent is found in a fair meadow as the hero approaches Dame Lyonesse's castle, and who comes forth to oppose him, but on defeat again becomes the good host; also Durmart's adventure on entering Ireland, when his adversary declares the hero must either give up his intention of seeking the Queen or otherwise have to fight him (pp. 119, 125).

In *Perceval* II we thus have a sportive variation of the Encounter at the Narrow Passage. Naturally the knight was not around to dispute the crossing with Gawain the previous day, because the hero entered the domain in an episode corresponding to the Jousting for Hospitality (**VII**); the Encounter at the Narrow Passage belongs to a different version of the story. One can also see under what principle Orguelleuse de Nogres has been made to disappear from the former of these adventures and to reappear in the latter. From the entry to the land onwards, she does not belong to a sequence derived from the original story of the Fair Unknown type. She has proceeded, so to speak, to the stations on the branch line.

CROSSING OF THE PERILOUS FORD[65]

After his conquest of Orguelleus del Passage, Gawain is still treated with contempt by the *male pucele,* who refuses to accept this evidence of his prowess, remarking that often *li febles abat le fort,* just as the emissary in *Ipomedon* II discounts the hero's victory because it has been achieved *plus par sa folie ke par*

---

64 *Wigalois,* 3297-3611; *Papegau,* 57/1-58/34.
65 *Perceval,* 8414-8534, 8902-16.

sa grant chevalerie, or in *Sir Gareth* by mishap.[66] The damsel now dares Gawain to accomplish what she says her *ami* the defeated knight used to do for her, to cross the Perilous Ford, to which she leads him. Gawain remembers having heard that he who is able to pass the Perilous Ford would have the greatest honour in the world. The danger is emphasized by the ladies of the palace, who are looking on, tearing their hair at the fate to which the *male pucele* is leading Gawain. But when it comes to the point he makes his horse simply jump across, though it does land in the water. On the other side takes place the meeting with Guiromelant, and then Gawain recrosses, with a better jump, back to the damsel.

In the Fair Unknown type of story, there is nothing equivalent at the corresponding point, and the Perilous Ford in *Descouneus* is not authentic (p. 87 f.). This *Gué Perilleus* in *Perceval* II is hardly treated seriously, for it is jumped across instead of being the site of a combat with someone posted there.

MEETING WITH GUIROMELANT[67]

On the other side of the Perilous Ford, Gawain converses with Guiromelant, whom he finds hunting with a hawk and bird-hounds in a garden. He congratulates Gawain for having achieved the greatest honour by accomplishing what no-one has ever done before, the crossing of the Perilous Ford. With this, Gawain realizes that the damsel lied to him when she said that her *ami* used to do it for her. Then Guiromelant explains many things, and first of all he tells Gawain the same story about his affair with the *male pucele* that she will relate to Gawain to account for her behaviour. It is from Guiromelant that Gawain learns the name of the damsel, of her *ami* whom he has conquered, and of the fortress, though Guiromelant at first refuses to say what it is called, until persuaded to do so by proof that Gawain has overcome its enchantments. He tells the hero that one Queen there is Ygerne, the mother of King Arthur, and the other is Gawain's mother; which are astonishing facts, as Gawain supposes they are both dead, and Clarissant thus turns out to be his sister. Asking Gawain to take her a ring from him, Guiromelant says that she is his love, while at the same time expressing hatred for her brother Gawain as his enemy in a family feud. When Gawain reveals his identity Guiromelant challenges him to a duel, to take place either immediately, after he has gone back to his own city (which is within sight) in order to arm himself and then return for the fight, or alternatively a week later, as a battle to be watched by ladies and knights both from Arthur's court and Guiromelant's realm at that very place, later defined as in the meadowland below the citadel of La Roche de Sanguin.[68] Gawain accepts the second alternative, and recrosses the Perilous Ford.

Here, in the return of a huntsman to his castle to arm himself and come back to fight the hero, Chrétien has set down a motif from the Encounter with a

66 *Ipomedon*, 8353 f.; Malory, VII, c. 5 to c. 8.
67 *Perceval*, 8535-8916.   68 *Ibid.*, 9116 f.

Huntsman (**IV**: p. 91 f.), but otherwise one should refer to the Encounter before La Roche (**VIIb**). The hero and the emissary in *Papegau* are approaching La Roche sans Paour when she begins to weep, saying that it is because he now has to fight the best knight in the world, whom she points out before them. He has seen them coming, and the hero does not flinch from jousting with the opponent, who leads him into the most beautiful meadow (*prael*) in the world, *devant la roche du chastel* and before its gate. This site has been chosen for the combat in order that the lady of the castle should judge who jousts the better, and they put forth their best efforts because of Flor de Mont, who leans out of a window watching the battle, along with other damsels. The ladies admire the achievement of the champion sent by Arthur, and the hero sees this and is inspired to give such a stroke that the fight is ended. The equivalent in *Wigalois* is when the hero arrives before Roimunt, the stronghold on the *berg*, and sees a knight in readiness to fight advancing towards him. The emissary warns Wigalois not to oppose this redoubtable opponent, who is the steward there, but he will not desist and they joust.[69] We have seen that there is some correspondence to this episode when Gareth arrives before Dame Lyonesse's castle, has a duel with Sir Ironsyde where the adversary rides for it to be held, in a little vale under the fortress, so that all its inhabitants (and those at the siege) can watch the battle, and Dame Lyonesse is at a window giving the hero encouragement (p. 126).

Thus Guiromelant is to be equated with the last antagonist fought by the hero before he arrives at the lady's stronghold in Chrétien's second source of the Fair Unknown type, in a watched combat at a site selected by the opponent, and which is a lovely meadow before the rocky height on which the castle stands.[70] The motif from the Encounter with a Huntsman has been employed to postpone this battle, not for later the same day but for a week. In this free variation on the Encounter before La Roche, the conversation between the hero and his adversary is an invention, and the poet's imagination has provided the relationships between the various persons. Guiromelant has been used to tie things up neatly, and a web of love and family connections is established between the figures who in the source were the emissary and the last two antagonists before the arrival at the lady's castle, the second of these adversaries and the princess, and the royal ladies of the stronghold and the hero, while the combat with the last opponent comes to be motivated by a family feud.

RECONCILIATION SCENE[71]

At last Orguelleuse admits Gawain's prowess, and begs his mercy for her fault in making him endure such torment. Now she explains the cause of her behaviour.

---

69 *Wigalois*, 3885-3948; *Papegau*, 58/34-60/34.

70 In the Jousting for Hospitality (from which the Encounter before La Roche is derived) there evidently was a watched combat (p. 214).

71 *Perceval*, 8917-67.

F

Guiromelant was a suitor that she hated, who killed her *ami* and thought to gain her love. But he wasted his time, for as soon as she could she dispensed with him and took Orguelleus del Passage as her *ami*, though in fact he means nothing to her. It was the killing of her first love which had turned her into such a nasty person, not caring whom she ill-treated.

The begging for forgiveness corresponds to that of the emissary (pp. 89, 111), but because Orguelleuse is not such a person, accompanying the hero on a mission for which she doubts his fitness, a different cause for her misbehaviour has been invented. She is not just a Damoisele Mesdisant, therefore, but a Damoisele Felenesse (8911) who now comes to her senses. She is a danger to knights, but she preserves enough, from the role of the lady who tries to deter the hero from the dangerous mission, to urge Gawain to flee from the attack by Greoreas's nephew, while on the contrary she dares him to cross the Perilous Ford.

We have now apparently produced a sequence **VIIa VIIb RS**, whereas it is **VIIa RS VIIb** that is found in *Wigalois*. However, compare this motion: Gawain rides from Greoreas to Orguelleuse, back again to Greoreas, and then reverts to the course of his ride. Similarly, after the Encounter with Orguelleus del Passage, Gawain crosses the Perilous Ford and meets Guiromelant, then recrosses to the damsel, and after their reconciliation they ride to the river to be taken across to La Roche de Sanguin. This makes the Reconciliation Scene bear the same relation to the Encounter with Orguelleus del Passage as the second part of the Meeting with Greoreas does to the first. In other words, in the same manner as the sequence **I/1 II I/2** renders **I II**, the series **VIIa VIIb RS** will reflect an original **VIIa RS VIIb**.

SECOND ARRIVAL AT LA ROCHE DE SANGUIN[72]

Gawain and Orguelleuse, after their reconcilement, ride to the boatman and are ferried over. The Queen is seated before the palace, and the maidens are dancing and singing in great joy. The two Queens embrace the hero, he is disarmed and brought joyfully into the palace, where he sits with Clarissant, and hands her the ring with the message that she is Guiromelant's love. But Clarissant denies that she loves him. She is only his love from afar, for they have never seen each other, and though he bestowed his love upon her a long time ago he has never come. His messengers have so implored her that she has granted him her love, but *de plus ne sui encor s'amie.* The two Queens, who are not aware that Gawain and Clarissant are brother and sister, look on approvingly and speak of him taking her to wife.

In the Arrival at the Lady's Stronghold, the Chevalier du Papegau is received at La Roche sans Paour with great joy, at the palace the maidens disarm him, laughing, singing, and playing, and he meets the Queen. Wigalois is received

72 *Perceval*, 8968-9073.

with joy at Roimunt, too, and meets the Queen, with whom is Larie. The Queen confirms that he will have Larie's hand if he accomplishes the mission, and when the princess speaks to him he declares his love, committing himself to her and expressing joy at undertaking a danger whereby she is to be won. Her only reply is to wish him well, but she shows him with her eyes, secretly in her mother's presence, that she returns his love. In effect, *de plus ne sui encor s'amie.* With eyes they speak together in sweet pastime until the call to supper comes.[73]

A love theme has not been excluded in *Perceval* II by making Clarissant the hero's sister, for to the Queens a marriage between them seems desirable, and Gawain gives Clarissant a declaration of love, though not a love between them. It appears that Chrétien has taken an affecting scene in which love is made with the eyes, and turned it into a skit on *amor de lonh.*

In setting out below the series in *Perceval* II, I indicate that La Roche de Sanguin is related to the Cité Gaste (**VIII**), the lady's stronghold (**ALS**), and the magician's castle (**VIIc VIIIa**), italicize episodes that are not (or not essentially) derivable from the Fair Unknown type of story—my labels showing the common ground—make it clear that the Visit to Escavalon is a unity (*IV-VI*), and convey the movement to and fro between "stations": from one part of **I** the hero rides to **II**, back to the other part of **I**, and then straight to **III**; from La Roche de Sanguin he recrosses the river, back to **VIIa**; he crosses the Perilous Ford (*PF*) to **VIIb**, recrosses it, back to **RS**, and then, crossing the river again to La Roche de Sanguin, goes straight to **ALS**, which is thus represented in both arrivals. The sequence **VIIa RS** *PF* **VIIb** then takes up the same location as **VII**:

Perceval II: *DA* **V** *IV-VI* **I/1 II**

        I/2 —— **III VII**

                            VIII

                         VIIc VIIIa

             ALS

            VIIa *PF* **VIIb**

            RS ———— **ALS**

This series is clearly related to those in the versions of the Fair Unknown type, but the extraneous sequence *DA IV-VI PF* within it forms a series which resembles the pattern of the fourteenth-century English romance of *Sir Gawain and the Green Knight.* Here, the Green Knight arrives at Arthur's court and proposes a Beheading Match. Accepting this, Gawain cuts off the Green Knight's head, and its owner picks it up and departs, having engaged the hero in a tryst to meet him for the return blow in a year's time. Gawain sets out from

---

73 *Wigalois*, 3973-4286; *Papegau*, 60/35-62/29.

Arthur's court to keep the tryst, and arrives at the castle of Sir Bertilak (identical with the Green Knight, who is his transformation). The situation here resembles that of the Avylyon episode in *Sir Gareth* (p. 131),[74] except that the frustration of love-making with the lady (Bertilak's wife) in Gawain's bedroom is due to the hero's virtue and not interruption by a strange knight with an axe who is decapitated and his head replaced, and the bed scenes are played while the lord of the castle is out hunting, like the love scene at Escavalon in *Perceval* II. Gawain keeps his tryst by a stream where the Green Knight comes to meet him from the other side by crossing a ford. For convenience, the pattern shared by *Perceval* II with *Sir Gawain* will be called "the tale of a tryst".[75]

It is also clear that for *Perceval* II two versions of the Fair Unknown type have been used, one whose series is comparable with those in *Carduino* and *Erec* (p. 109), and the other in agreement with those in *Wigalois* and *Papegau* in that part of their story which is devoted to the domain that is the destination of the ride, for after Gawain's recrossing of the river from La Roche de Sanguin we see the reflection of the sequence **VIIa RS VIIb ALS** (p. 85). One version must be the original story, and the other *conte d'aventure* X, whose series of adventures would first run parallel to that of the former.[76] The employment of two versions of the tale means, as with the *Wigalois/Papegau* account (p. 109), that there would be available two variants of the material in common, and two **RS** locations to choose from, of which the later one, that in *conte d'aventure* X, has been retained.

As the initiator of the ride, one type of story had the figure represented in *Perceval* II by Guigambresil, and the other that whose reflex is Orguelleuse de Nogres. The former remains for the departure from Arthur's court, and the latter is left over, deprived of her original function, to be met with in the course of the ride, where she takes the place of a damsel who was the subject of an adventure. Then the Visit to Escavalon is a unified whole, whereas the equivalent in the Fair Unknown type of tale is two episodes, the Encounter with a Huntsman and the Ile d'Or Episode, which have nothing to do with each other, even when in *Lybeaus* they are juxtaposed. In *Perceval* II, therefore, the interlacing of material from the tale of a tryst with that of the Fair Unknown type has been so carried out that two episodes of the latter, **IV** and **VI**, have been replaced by one, largely based on matter similar to theirs which in the tale of a tryst constituted a unity. This accounts for the representatives of **IV V VI** turning up in an order coinciding with that in *Lybeaus*.

With the disentanglement from each other of the three strands interlaced into *Perceval* II, it can now be accepted with confidence from one of them that the

74 Loomis, *op. cit.*, 418.

75 The Perilous Ford in *Perceval* II supplies the missing feature which completes the comparison with *Sir Gawain* and *Diu Krône* made by R. S. Loomis, *JEGP* XLII (1943), 170.

76 There is evidence of this from *Durmart* (pp. 117, 119 f.).

original story of the Fair Unknown type had the shape which comparison of the various versions with *Erec* was found to indicate:

E Enfances
AA Arrival at Arthur's Court
DA Departure from Arthur's Court
1 Encounter with a Huntsman (**IV**)
2 Sparrowhawk Contest (**V**)
3 Ile d'Or Episode (**VI**)
4 Encounter at the Perilous Bridge (**I**)
5 Rescue from Two Giants (**II**)
RS Reconciliation Scene
6 Attack by Three Avengers (**III**)
7 Jousting for Hospitality (**VII**)
8 Accomplishment of the Mission (**VIII**)
WQ Wedding to a Queen

In addition, since it is after (6), there is an episode to be recognized now as occurring just before (7). It has been between **III** and **IV**, and is where the hero escorts the maiden saved from the giants back to her father's castle, the Return of the Rescued Damsel (**RRD**), which is preserved in *Lybeaus* and reflected in the story of Lore de Branlant, as well as partially represented in Carduino's departure with the maiden in the morning (pp. 89, 122).

The Catalan poet Guiraut de Cabreira alludes to Erec in his *Ensenhamen*, a catalogue of stories that ought to be in his minstrel's repertoire:

Ni sabs d'Erec
com conquistec
l'esparvier for de sa reion.

(*Ensenhamen*, 73 ff.)

That Erec takes part in the Sparrowhawk Contest as a stranger to the land is a point also brought out in Chrétien, where the hero announces to his opponent that he is a knight *d'autre terre*.[77] But, with *Erec et Enide* composed 1184-86, as I have shown, and the troubadour dying between 1168 and 1170,[78] he will be speaking of the *conte Erec*, which means that its mark was the Sparrowhawk Contest, and it is to be dated before 1170. One can identify it with the original story of the Fair Unknown type, and from the *conte Erec* are then descended *conte d'aventure* X, whose date is fixed by that of *Perceval* II, as no later than 1190; the *Descouneus/Lybeaus* narrative (Y) or the tale of Gawain's son Guinglain, which is referred to when he is mentioned as the Fair Unknown in the Second Continuation of *Perceval* (held to have been written before 1200), whereas in the First Continuation the son of Gawain known by a different appellation from

77 *Erec*, 843.
78 M. de Riquer, *Les chansons de geste françaises* (1957), 335-9.

his real name is Lieoniax, who is begotten on the Damoisele de Lis;[79] and as the next step the *Wigalois/Papegau* account (Z), basically a combination of the X and Y versions made before c. 1210, when *Wigalois* was composed.

We do not have the *conte Erec*, but, just as astronomers can predict from the course of visible planets much concerning another as yet unseen, so we may gain our conception of this lost Arthurian story of adventure from the conjunction of texts whose interrelationship is understood. As for its manner of existence, we can gather this from the comparable remarks made by Chrétien and Thomas, composer of a *Tristan*. Like the *conte Tristan* it would be a tale with variations in the telling:

> d'Erec, le fil Lac, est li contes,
> que devant rois et devant contes
> depecier et corronpre suelent
> cil qui de conter vivre vuelent.
>
> *(Erec et Enide,* 19 ff.)
>
> Entre ceus qui solent cunter
> E del cunte Tristan parler,
> Il en cuntent diversement:
> Oï en ai de plusur gent.
>
> *(Tristan,* D 841 ff.)

And yet, since in spite of variations the several versions of the Tristan story that we possess are fairly consistent, and as it is evident that even the derivative X, Y, and Z forms of the Fair Unknown type still looked like each other to quite an extent, the retellings of the *conte Erec* must have remained basically similar.

---

79 *Perceval,* First Continuation, 1570-1733, 6569-6676, 7796-8269; Second Continuation, 22387-9, 31070-72. We find the Fair Unknown mentioned in the romance of *Jaufré,* 108, which is claimed to be composed about 1180, but it refers to *Cligès.* There is a reference to the Fair Unknown in *Flamenca,* 680, another work for which a twelfth-century date has been claimed, but in this text we also find Chrétien's romances mentioned. On the dates of these two works, see *Arthurian Literature in the Middle Ages,* ed. R. S. Loomis (1959), 398 n. 1, 402 f., where the dedication of *Jaufré* is tentatively placed in 1205 or shortly after; it is dated later than 1200 by M. de Riquer, *BBSIA* VI (1954), 111.

9
The Conjointure—I

In setting out to find how *Erec et Enide* fits against the impression of the *conte Erec* that has been gained, I can proceed under the guidance of the grid that has been plotted over the lineaments of Chrétien's romance, when I located strategic features of the relations between it and the Fair Unknown type of tale. The place in the parallel course will be kept before us at the head of each episode by use of the labels for the sequence in the *conte Erec* (p. 157).

HUNT OF THE WHITE STAG[1] (DA)

The story does not begin like the Fair Unknown type of tale at all. Instead, it Arthurianizes the opening of *Anticlaudianus*, with the project announced by the head of the court now being to hunt the white stag[2] in order to renew a custom. When the most important member of the court observes that the project requires the carrying out of a certain act, in Chrétien this is a kiss that shall be given to the most beautiful damsel at court by the hunter who kills the stag.

Here we have the first element from the avowed source, the *conte Erec*, but not from its opening. In the Ile d'Or Episode, the fay in *Papegau* proclaims a tournament, and the victor wins the right to give a kiss to her before all the court:

> la dame fait crïer ung tournoyement l'uitiesme jour, en telle maniere que celluy qui avra le pris du tournoyement la baisera par amours une foys devant toute la baronnie, et si le tiendra ung an pour son amy.
>
> (*Le Chevalier du Papegau*, 27/2 ff.)

The motif also turns up in *Meraugis*, 162-72, where a tournament is proclaimed by the Pucele de Landemore in which the prize for the victor is to give her a kiss. On the same occasion, the loveliest damsel is to be awarded a sparrowhawk, and a knight declares that for the sake of the heroine he would dare to prove that she is the most beautiful in the world (p. 95). Here this prize, derived from the Sparrowhawk Contest, confirms that the other is taken from the Ile d'Or Episode of the same story.[3] Thus, when in *Erec et Enide* the winner of the hunt

---

1 *Erec*, 27-114, 277-341.
2 Cf. the chasing of a white hind in the Visit to Escavalon in *Perceval* II, which I have compared (p. 129 f.) to what happens in the Encounter with a Huntsman.
3 For other material of the Fair Unknown type in *Meraugis*, see pp. 118 n. 39, 123 n. 57 above and p. 217 below.

is to give a kiss to the loveliest lady at court, this custom, which is otherwise unknown, has been transformed from a tournament. In this way the romance starts rolling forward in fulfilment both of the model in *Anticlaudianus* and of the level that the work has as a story based on material from the *conte Erec*. As a result of the amalgamation, when in Chrétien the most important member of the court points to the difficulty of achieving the project, it is because each damsel would have her claim to be the most beautiful sustained by her own *ami*. This means that the kiss takes on the dimensions of a prize like the sparrowhawk, to which the loveliest lady is entitled and which has to be fought for by her champion.

Arthur answers Gawain's objection by insisting that the hunt must take place, because a king cannot go back on his word, which connects the hunt with a motif in the Departure from Arthur's Court (p. 85 ff.) in the source. The original hero makes such an assertion about a king, as he insists on being given the mission as the promised boon: *Rois es, si ne dois pas mentir (Descouneus,* 221), *reis ne deit mentir pur ren (Ipomedon,* 8058).[4] The use of matter from this episode in the source continues with its application to the hunt in the forest next day. Arthur and his companions are followed by Guinevere with one of her damsels, and after them comes swiftly the young and handsome knight Erec, who gallops down the road, catches up with the Queen and asks if he may accompany her.[5] Guinevere plays the part of the beautiful lady, her maiden that of the attendant, and Erec is the hero who catches up with them after they have left the court. But in the original the attendant is a dwarf, and the lady is *mesdisant* and refuses the hero's company, whereas Guinevere is gracious and says she could not have better company than Erec. And instead of the youth who has yet to prove his prowess and is fully armed as he sets out on his mission, we are given a knight of the Round Table who has achieved a great reputation at the court and who is now without armour.

ENCOUNTER WITH YDER[6]   (1 = **IV**)

We have seen that the confrontation with Yder in the forest corresponds to the Encounter with a Huntsman (p. 91 f.), with Erec, unarmed, as the huntsman, and the original hero, who is accompanied by a damsel and a dwarf, represented by Yder with such company. The dwarf, like the equivalent figure in *Ipomedon* II and *Durmart,* and the hideous squire in the Meeting with Greoreas (p. 139), is on a *roncin* or inferior kind of horse. Erec's request is rudely rejected, and as

---

4 The King asserts that *"Rois sui, si ne doi pas mentir"* in his turn to the emissary, in *Descouneus,* 245. The same assertion is made by him in *Erec,* 1749, when he is about to bestow the kiss in completion of the custom.

5 Note how the situation has raised the question posed by R. R. Bezzola, *Le sens de l'aventure et de l'amour* (1947), 96: *"pourquoi donc Erec, le protagoniste du roman, n'est-il pas parti avec le roi et les autres chevaliers?"*

6 *Erec,* 115-276.

he leaves in search of arms to obtain revenge he continues to fulfil the role of the original huntsman. But the situation has been developed within a new context, a meeting of parties in the forest and the Queen's desire to know the identity of the unknown knight and his damsel, while the dwarf has been made malevolent and responsible for the infliction of the injury that requires revenge (cf. pp. 118, 139).

Various features of the adventure are derivable from an account, represented in *Durmart*, which Loomis indicated as the source of the Encounter with Yder. Arthur and his knights engage in a hunt, and the Queen, a damsel, and an unarmed escort, Yder, are left behind. Suddenly an armed knight rides up and abducts Guinevere, striking Yder down when he seizes his bridle, and Yder, being unarmed, can only follow after until he reaches the abductor's castle, hoping to obtain arms with which to seek battle with him to rescue the Queen. In Chrétien, Erec has replaced Yder, whose name is given instead to his opponent.[7] The group of Guinevere, a damsel, and an unarmed escort has been used for that which leaves Arthur's court in the Fair Unknown type of tale, and the escort, as the huntsman, is now integrated into what corresponds to the Encounter with a Huntsman, resulting in two parties of three, which are doublets in relation to the *conte Erec*. Instead of the chase moving towards the place of the encounter, as there, it can now go away, while the injury to be revenged becomes a blow, which are replacements that suit the exchange of roles between the hero and the huntsman of the original story. Furthermore, the amalgamation enables this adventure and the next, the Sparrowhawk Contest, to be resolved by a single act of fighting, as Erec departs in search of arms, not back to the city he had left, but in pursuit of Yder to Laluth.[8]

Having chosen the proclamation to be of a hunt, and not a tournament—in order to incorporate the matter from the Encounter with a Huntsman—for the hunting scene itself the author therefore turned to a *conte* of Guinevere's abduction which could be adapted and dovetailed with his other material to launch Erec towards the Sparrowhawk Contest. Having achieved this result, the author brings the hunt to an end, with Arthur as the killer of the white stag, returns all to the court, and sets the scene equivalent to that of Nature's assembly after its head announces the project and the principal member raises the problem about its accomplishment, which means that the hunt, along with the encounter that it contains, is an insertion in relation to the structure of *Anticlaudianus*. In Chrétien it is thus after the member of the court has set off on the quest that it is in a great murmur over the carrying out of the project. And when the council deliberates over the difficulty, until it accepts a proposal by Guinevere that the

---

7 *Durmart*, 4185-4372. See R. S. Loomis, *Arthurian Tradition and Chrétien de Troyes* (1949), 77-9, and cf. *Lanʒelet*, 6696 ff., where there is a hunt of the white stag (with some influence from Chrétien via Hartmann von Aue), in which Guinevere is abducted by King Valerin.

8 M. Mills, "The Huntsman and the Dwarf in *Erec* and *Libeaus Desconus*", *Romania* LXXXVII (1966), 37, 50.

project be postponed until Erec returns, the suggestion does not follow logically from the circumstances, for the hero has departed to seek revenge, and not a lady whose beauty would silence opposition. This leads to mystification of the author's audience, which the Welsh redactor and Hartmann avoid by relating the Sparrowhawk Contest before the scene of Guinevere making her proposal, so that one already knows that the hero will return with Enide. This does not however remove the internal illogicality, but only the mystifying effect. It is also an alteration of the order that *Erec et Enide* derives from the model in *Anti-claudianus*. Apart from having the straightforward part of the project, the hunt of the white stag, carried out immediately and used, in the Encounter with Yder, to give occasion for Erec's departure, the sequence of narration in Chrétien agrees with that of Alain, in whose poem the assembly accepts the suggestion of Racio and then the journey of Prudencia on her mission takes place. Thus the account does not follow the hero when he leaves the Queen (as it does in Hartmann and *Gereint*), but we are brought back to the court, and it is after the council has adopted Guinevere's proposal that we go with Erec to Laluth for the Sparrowhawk Contest.

SPARROWHAWK CONTEST[9]   (2 = V)

Yder continues to correspond to the hero of the Fair Unknown type, as with the damsel and the dwarf he arrives in azure arms and takes up lodgings in the town for the Sparrowhawk Contest next day (p. 92 ff.). Erec, though alone, provides another image of that hero, finding hospitality in circumstances similar to those of Gawain in the Tourney at Tintagel (p. 127 ff.), which in *Perceval* II is the equivalent of the Sparrowhawk Contest. Laluth is crowded for the event —lodgings there are full—and when Erec enters the town he passes through it until he sees a vavasor sitting by himself on a step outside his home, thinks him a *preudom*, goes to ask him for hospitality, and the lady of the house is called out to receive the guest. The story of Lore de Branlant in *Le Livre d'Artus* draws on a tale of the Fair Unknown type (p. 121 f.), and the hero's entrance into Branlant throws light on what there was in Chrétien's original. Branlant is so full of people that the hero cannot find lodgings, he turns into a narrow street and sees a man *qui bien sembloit preudome seoir sus les degrez de sa maison*, goes to ask him for hospitality, and the lady of the house comes forward and looks after the guests.[10]

9 *Erec*, 342-1458.
10 *Le Livre d'Artus*, ed. Sommer, vii, 94 (the man is a *bouchier* and rude to the hero). Here the stabling, in Chrétien carried out by Enide, is done along with other service by the squire, i.e. the dwarf in the original, whose service at lodgings is seen in *Ipomedon*, 8370 f., 8630-32. As in *Erec et Enide*, we find that the hero goes to mass next morning, returns to his lodgings, arms (p. 129), and on his way to battle the inhabitants admire him as he passes through the city (p. 204): see Sommer, vii, 96 f. For matter at Branlant from the Sparrow-hawk Contest which is not at Laluth, and therefore proves independence of Chrétien, see pp. 180-82 below.

As in *Perceval* II, when the hero of *Erec et Enide* comes across a maiden at this point of the narrative for whom he jousts, it is not on the approach to the city, but at his lodgings. This time however she is the host's daughter; and also her father, and not anyone met on the way, informs the hero about the martial occasion. Attention is thus focused on the household, where we have an old vavasor as in the Tourney at Tintagel, but there he is well-off, whereas Erec's host is poor. And Enide's old and worn-out *chainse* is so different from the same white garment, attractive and made of perfectly new and rich material, a silk adorned with a pattern in sparkling gold, which is worn by the damsel whom Durmart sees riding alone towards him in the forest and on whose behalf he fights next day for the sparrowhawk.[11]

Then Erec proposes to enter the contest with Enide, and he is led to arrange with his host to make such use of his daughter in order to avenge the insult to Guinevere. Now since Descouneus takes part in the contest to obtain vengeance for the damsel he has met, and Wigalois similarly puts right a wrong for her, as also does Gawain in the Tourney at Tintagel, therefore Erec's meeting with Yder in the forest, in relation to the Fair Unknown type of tale, is not simply equivalent to the clash with the hero in the Encounter with a Huntsman. It also creates a cause for Erec's entry into the contest against Yder which is comparable with that provided in the source by the opponent's defeat of the damsel's *ami* on the previous day. Indeed Guinevere, like her, has reason for grievance in the treatment meted out to the escort who was acting on her behalf. However, instead of the Queen complaining and the hero then offering to set the matter right, we have Erec undertaking revenge on his own account as well as hers, which blends with the matter from the Encounter with a Huntsman. It imparts to Erec a responsibility for the sparrowhawk contest that the author brings out again when he divests the beautiful maiden of all accountability for the combat. Enide does not provide the cause for it, and she is not even asked to take part in the contest, when the terms on which it was fought in the original are so altered that it is not the lady who engages an *ami* to support her claim to the prize, but the knight who wishes to win it brings a lovely *amie* whom he puts in for the sparrowhawk. This clinches a rearrangement of material, to make the vengeance sought by the unarmed huntsman become that deliberately exacted by victory in the contest, in which the event is not on its second day—the Encounter with Yder holds the place of the first day's combat —and where the functions of the damsel for whom the sparrowhawk was conquered in the source are discharged by two figures, Enide, the beauty contestant, and Guinevere, the lady who suffers wrong.

When we come to the contest, Yder is still like the hero of the Fair Unknown type, advancing with his *amie* to claim the prize for her, while Erec, hurrying up to challenge with his damsel, corresponds to the original adversary, as he does in the Encounter with Yder. But the author sees to it that Yder, though he

11 *Durmart*, 1897-9.

is not the defender of the bird, has achieved a domination over other knights at this annual event, and that Erec should pass from challenger to supporter of a claim, as he tells Enide to take the sparrowhawk, which puts the contest back on the required rails. It is now that Erec, replying to the provoked antagonist, declares he has come to seek the hawk and that it is right, no matter who objects, that the damsel should have it. A combat ensues whose course is apparently based on that of the fight in the *conte Erec*, ending with the defeat of the opponent, who is made to give his word to go as prisoner to Arthur's court.

In the source, there is a leave-taking from the damsel with whom the hero enters the contest, but instead he remains with her in Chrétien. He was so very struck by her that he had made her father an offer to marry the maiden. This scene, along with much of what takes place at the host's house, including the demonstration of the damsel's modest and humble behaviour, is unparalleled in the Fair Unknown type of tale, except in the manner I shall indicate.[12]

Erec borrows arms and armour—he refuses the loan of a sword and steed— from his old, white-haired host at Laluth, and he also asks for his daughter, who is then bestowed on him. There is some parallel here with matter in *Lybeaus*.[13] In this text the maiden who is saved in the Rescue from Two Giants is taken home to her father by the hero, an episode which, if the disorder in *Lybeaus* is righted, can be seen to come after the Attack by Three Avengers (p. 89); in *Le Livre d'Artus*, where the story of Lore de Branlant draws on a tale of the Fair Unknown type, there is an equivalent episode in which the rescued Floree is taken back to her father's fortress (p. 121 f.).[14] The father is the old, grey-haired Earl Antore in *Lybeaus*, who offers his daughter to the hero in marriage. Lybeaus refuses, on the ground that he must continue on his mission, but he accepts the gift of arms, armour, and a steed, and wears Earl Antore's armour in the Sparrowhawk Contest, which follows immediately,[15] owing to the dislocation in this version. Now, in the original story the father of the maiden saved in the Rescue from Two Giants (5 = II) could not have provided arms that were used in the Sparrowhawk Contest (2 = V), for this had already been held. If account is taken of the shift of episodes to the beginning of the ride in the source of *Lybeaus* and *Descouneus*, it will be seen

12 For the parallel in the stabling of the hero's horse, see p. 162 n. 10 above.

13 Loomis, *op. cit.*, 81.

14 *Lybeaus*, 676-705; *Le Livre d'Artus*, ed. Sommer, vii, 86. Loomis, *op. cit.*, 82-4, assumed a common source here for *Lybeaus* and *Le Livre d'Artus* as well as for the rescue of a maiden from Saracens in the *chanson de geste* of *Floovant* (towards the end of the twelfth century), but he was clearly wrong in attributing to it the features which are only shared by the last two texts. The resemblance between *Lybeaus* and *Floovant* is slight compared with the manner in which the account in this section of *Le Livre d'Artus* has points of contact on the one hand with *Floovant* and on the other with the Fair Unknown type of tale. Loomis's arguments against derivation of material in *Le Livre d'Artus* from *Floovant* are of no value.

15 *Lybeaus*, 766-8.

that the Return of the Rescued Damsel was originally located just before the Jousting for Hospitality (p. 157); at the corresponding point in *Erec et Enide* there is a similar bestowal by the owner of a castle (p. 195). We therefore have a coincidence when in both *Lybeaus* and *Erec et Enide* the hero wears arms in the Sparrowhawk Contest which have been provided by a man of rank. In one text he does so because the episode there happens to follow immediately on the bestowal, and in the other Chrétien has found use for material from later on in the source. When Erec receives arms and armour from his old, white-haired host which he wears for the contest, the motif of the departure to seek arms with which to obtain revenge, from the Encounter with a Huntsman, is merged with that of the bestowal of arms on the hero by the old, grey-haired father of a daughter.

To illustrate the integration of the fresh matter with the material from the source, I shall take the context for the offer of marriage. The dialogue between Erec and his host after supper on the evening of the hero's arrival is first about this maiden who is new to the adventure, as Erec asks why she is so poorly dressed, the host explains it is due to the poverty resulting from the loss of all his lands, and launches into a panegyric on his daughter. Then Erec's inquiry why the town is so full of knights shifts the central part of this conversation into another gear, comparable with that of the dialogue between the hero and the damsel outside the city in the original. Information on the annual occasion held at Laluth is given by the host, and Erec's question, as to the identity of the knight who has arrived there with a damsel and a dwarf, provides the opportunity for the author to cast on Yder the mantle of the dreaded opponent at the Sparrowhawk Contest. This identification supplies the stimulus for the hero's decision to take part in the contest in order to obtain vengeance for a lady. With the request that Erec makes for the loan of arms and for Enide, we leave the matter which originally belonged to the dialogue between the hero and the damsel whose champion he becomes, and pass to an element of this conversation in Chrétien that is related to another part of the source, where an old man of rank offered the hero his daughter and bestowed on him arms and armour. When Erec asks to have his host's daughter for the contest, he promises to marry her if he wins, and her father bestows Enide upon him. From the new maiden as the point of departure we have thus come full circle, through information about the contest to other material adapted from the source, which leads us back to her to find that the beauty contestant is to be this damsel, and that the episode sets us upon a theme of marriage which in the original existed only in an offer made to the hero that he rejected.

One can see this theme bringing about the accomplishment of Arthur's project, when the defeated opponent is ordered not only to put himself in the hands of Guinevere, which conforms to the adapted motif of revenge, but also, in continuation of the fresh matter that has been introduced, to announce that Erec will come next day with a maiden who has no match. A description is then supplied of Yder's arrival at Arthur's court, along with his damsel and dwarf, and people there, seeing him come, comment on the proof of combat to be seen in the battered condition of his armour, which is like the arrival of Descouneus, along with the emissary and dwarf, at the city of the Sparrowhawk Contest.[16],

Returning to Laluth, the narrative is taken up with the Count's offer of hospitality to Erec and the hero's refusal of this, and with talk about Enide, the wedding, and the journey of the couple to Arthur's court, including Erec's insistence that the maiden is to come just as she is. One recognizes here some material from the original Sparrowhawk Contest in the return after the battle to the hero's lodgings, where the lord of the city invites the hero twice to stay with him and is twice refused, as in the Tourney at Tintagel;[17] and when *grant joie orent fet cele nuit*, the resorting to the hero's lodgings parallels what took place in the source on the evening before the battle (p. 181 f.).

Next morning, the hero and the heroine ride out of Laluth, Enide carrying the sparrowhawk, like the damsel for whom it was won in the source, but utterly different in dress and personality. Again, when Chrétien dwells at length on the weeping of Enide and her parents at their parting—after they have accompanied the hero and heroine for some way to see them off—one should compare the flow of tears at the corresponding point in the original; but there the maiden would have been in this state of distress at her parting from the hero (p. 116).

ARRIVAL AT ARTHUR'S COURT[18]   (3 = **VI**)

When a hero of the Fair Unknown type arrives at Arthur's court, it is typical for his name not to be known and for a descriptive appellation to be used instead. This is so of Enide, *la pucele au blanc chainse*, which invites comparison with *cil a la cote mal taillie*, of a hero who is also called after his dress. The garment worn by Carduino and Perceval is made of skins, but La Cote Mal Taillie, according to the *Prose Tristan*, wears fine clothing which has holes, though unlike Enide's *chainse* these are not due to age, but the slashes received by his father when he was murdered while wearing the overgarment. In the fragment of *La Cote Mal Taillie*, the youth offers the King his service (which if accepted should mean that he would have to be provided with the best of raiment) and Arthur laughs at his presumption and thinks him a fool, but Gawain urges that the King should not reject the well-behaved young man because of his dress, for prowess does not lie in clothes. Compare Perceval, who wears a *roube sote*, a ridiculous attire, which includes *la cote de cerf mal faite et mal taillie*,[19] when he comes to ask the King to make him a knight, and is defended from Kay's mockery by Arthur himself, with the argument that the youth, though foolish, may have prowess in him.[20] His poor clothing is replaced by fine raiment when he is knighted by Gornemant de Gorhaut.

16 *Descouneus*, 1665-72.   17 *Perceval*, 5590-5637.
18 *Erec*, 1459-1796.   19 *Perceval*, 1423-5; see also 499-504.
20 *Ibid.*, 1008 ff.

Again, we have ridiculous dress with Ipomedon, when he arrives at Meleager's court disguised as a fool, asks to be accepted as one of his retinue and is laughed at, in another account allied to that of the Fair Unknown type.[21] In *Erec et Enide*, a similar point to that in *La Cote Mal Taillie* is made when Erec tells Guinevere that the maiden wears poor dress, but on grounds of neither beauty nor birth does he have the right to refuse the damsel marriage. He then suggests that the Queen should provide her with attractive clothes, and she immediately does so.

The poor state of the maiden's own attire is explained by an upbringing that one should compare with the Enfances of a hero who is of noble birth but raised (by his widowed mother) in a simple rural life. This happens to Carduino and Perceval, of whom the latter's father, like Enide's, had fallen into poverty. Thus the insistence of Erec that Enide should go to Arthur's court in her own poor garments leads to the fulfilment of a motif requiring that there should be an arrival in dress which expresses such Enfances and consorts ill with courtly surroundings, like a hero of the Fair Unknown type who, as pointed out by his defender, ought not to be rejected because of that. But in Chrétien the lesson is harnessed to the theme of marriage, and sharp notes are replaced by idealism, as there is neither presumption—Erec brings the maiden and makes the claim for her—nor mockery, the heroine's qualities being recognized on sight and the finest raiment instantly provided. Then there immediately follows Arthur's bestowal of the kiss on Enide, a ritual that is to be compared with the knighting of the Fair Unknown type of hero, but again Enide has not come to claim it— the King and Queen judge that Enide must have the kiss.

The Arrival at Arthur's Court does not hold the same position in *Erec et Enide* as in the source, but we find that Chrétien's story is at the same time still running parallel to the original. For the arrivals at the Ile d'Or (p. 132) and at Arthur's court in Chrétien have features in common.[22] However, the tension between the emissary and the hero contrasts with the silent admiration that Erec and Enide have for one another as they ride along; and the couple in the Fair Unknown type of tale go towards the Ile d'Or, as the hero continues on his mission, whereas the master-plan inspired by *Anticlaudianus* requires the return of Erec to Arthur's court with the ideal maiden.

Enide has her garments removed at the court, and is presented by the Queen with splendid raiment, which enhances her beauty. Then she enters a hall full of knights, Guinevere comes to meet her and takes her by the hand to the King, who also takes her hand as he sets Enide by his right side, Guinevere sits down on his left, and then Queen, King, and all agree that the maiden is beautiful beyond compare. In the Ile d'Or Episode, we have the disarming of the hero and the presentation of rich apparel by the lady. With his looks thus set off,

21 *Ipomedon*, 7759 ff.
22 When Enide travels with the hawk, one may compare the emissary in *Wigalois*, who is presented with the bird won by the hero for the beautiful damsel (because she gives it up in her distress at the parting with him): see p. 196 n. 22 below.

they have never seen anyone handsomer at the Port, and Giglan seems to be one of the handsomest knights in the world. Descouneus enters the hall, which is full of knights, the fay comes to greet him, takes him by the hand to sit beside her on a silk cloth, and she immediately falls in love with the very handsome youth. Thus there is some correspondence here between Enide and the hero of the Fair Unknown type, but on the other hand Guinevere speaks of Erec having conquered such a beautiful lady, even as in *Descouneus* the lovely fay declares that the hero has conquered her.[23]

In the equivalent scene of *Papegau*, the fay looks in silent admiration at the hero sitting with her on the silk cloth:

> La dame regarde si vivement le Chevalier du Papegau, toute sa façon, les yeulx, la bouche, le front et le menton et toute la personne, si qu'elle ne se puet saouler de le regarder.
>
> (*Le Chevalier du Papegau*, 22/1 ff.)

So in fact did Erec gaze admiringly at all parts of Enide's person, as they rode side by side on their way to Arthur's court, and he too could not surfeit himself with looking:

> De l'esgarder ne puet preu faire:
> quant plus l'esgarde et plus li plest,
> ne puet müer qu'il ne la best;
> volantiers pres de li se tret,
> an li esgarder se refet;
> molt remire son chief le blont,
> ses ialz rianz et son cler front,
> le nes et la face et la boche,
> don granz dolçors au cuer li toche.
> Tot remire jusqu'a la hanche,
> le manton et la gorge blanche,
> flans et costez et braz et mains.
>
> (*Erec et Enide*, 1466 ff.)

The beauty of Enide having been recognized as peerless, there takes place the bestowal of the kiss before the whole court, as Arthur addresses her as his sweet *amie*, to whom he gives his love: and in the Fair Unknown type of tale the fay tells the hero about such an occasion. As they are sitting on the silk cloth side by side, according to *Descouneus* she informs him she will proclaim that there should be an assembly in eight days' time, when she will take a husband;[24] the event for the eighth day that we find her announcing in *Papegau* is a tournament for which the prize is to be a kiss given to her by the victor before all the court, and then she will have him as her *ami* for a year (p. 159).

---

23 *Descouneus*, 2215-87; cf. *Durmart*, 14772 ff., where the lady who has been delivered from her besieger similarly bestows herself hastily upon the hero as a *don* he has conquered.

24 *Descouneus*, 2291-8.

Thus in Chrétien an equivalent proclamation has been used for the beginning of the romance, and at the point corresponding to that of the announcement in the source the kiss is given before the assembled court. But there is a difference in the kiss of love, which in Chrétien is given *sanz vilenie, sanz malvestié et sanz folage*, and so with a courtly love which is platonic, bearing some relation to that imposed on their *amis* by Gaite and Cardiones in the later version of *Athis et Prophilias*, or demanded by Ipomedon when he asks to be accepted as the lover who kisses the Queen (p. 40).

WEDDING OF EREC AND ENIDE[25] (3 = VI)

Chrétien explains that now it is necessary for her real name (*droit non*) to be known, for without it a woman cannot be married, and so for this event it becomes known for the first time that Enide is her baptismal name: *Enyde ot non au baptestire.*[26] He does not say why it was not known before, and we have none of the motifs that account for the ignorance of the hero's name in tales of the Fair Unknown type or those allied to it. Some mystery then arises, and under the guise of explanation Chrétien's comment only succeeds in drawing attention to the unexplained. Furthermore, he seems to imply that up till now Enide has been known to Arthur's court as *la pucele au blanc chainse*, but in fact he only gives this appellation to her himself. It can be seen that the mystifying effect created results from juxtaposing material from two occasions far apart in the source. The hero's name is not known there until it is revealed to him when he has accomplished his mission: "*Guinglains as non en batestire*" (*Descouneus*, 3233). King Arthur is then informed: "*Par droit non l'apielent Guinglain*" (*Descouneus*, 5201). As the Wedding to a Queen followed upon the Accomplishment of the Mission in Chrétien's original, it is true to say that the hero's real name becomes known there for the wedding at Arthur's court. But in *Erec et Enide* the passage from ignorance to knowledge of the heroine's name occurs in one and the same stay with the King, as we are taken from an Arrival at Arthur's Court to a marriage that fits into a pattern of correspondence with the Wedding to a Queen. The hero there, who was once a youth in lowly circumstances, goes with a Queen to Arthur's court and is raised to royal rank by taking her to wife, and then travels with her to her domain. The poor heroine Enide, who has gone to Arthur's court with Erec, is similarly elevated by marrying the prince, and accompanies him home in the Return to Estregales.

Before the wedding, Enide's poor parents are looked after by being sent from Laluth direct to Erec's country Estregales, and so, bypassing Arthur's court, they are not present at this ceremony; but they are sent for to attend a later one, the coronation of Erec and Enide, which also takes place at Arthur's court. Since both events are together equivalent to one in the Fair Unknown type of

25 *Erec*, 1797-2214.
26 Presumably her baptismal name is asked for at the wedding ceremony and given by Enide herself, even as Gawain in *Perceval*, when asked for his name, answers: "*j'ai a non en baptestire Gavains*" (4485 f.).

tale—it is the crowning at the end of the romance that corresponds in position to the Wedding to a Queen with its coronation—the result is that the two separate arrangements with regard to the heroine's parents can be compared to the single situation in *Carduino*. There the hero's widowed mother is sent for to Arthur's court, where she attends the wedding and coronation, and then goes with the newly-married couple to the city ruled by the princess.[27]

Though the Wedding of Erec and Enide does not hold the same position in Chrétien as the Wedding to a Queen in the source, we find that his story is at the same time still running parallel to the original. For the bestowal of the kiss is followed by the wedding in Chrétien, even as in the source a union would ensue. But in Chrétien the two formal occasions are only linked in the person of Enide, who reflects aspects of the fay in receiving the kiss (from Arthur) and partaking in the union (with Erec). In the fay's announcement thus lies compact the seed from which springs in Chrétien the whole Arthurian complex that holds a place in the structure equivalent to that of the proclamation and carrying out of Nature's project in *Anticlaudianus*. Instead of the tournament, a hunt of the white stag; the bestowal of the kiss, in which the King who announces the competitive event also becomes its winner, and the part of the kissed is passed on to Enide; and then the union, with the role of the partner taken from the kisser and given to Erec. And so, with the author redistributing the functions of the two figures in the original among three in his own story, we come eventually to the hero.

Then the hot love-making of the bridal night in *Erec et Enide* reminds one that such a torrid bedroom scene takes place that night at the Ile d'Or in the pleasurable dream of consummation, when the hero fancies he and the fay are giving themselves up to each other and she is lying in his arms all night (The Night Scenes at the Ile d'Or, p. 132 ff.). Indeed, as we see from *Descouneus*, this occasion lends itself to treatment similar to that of the bridal night in Chrétien.[28]

After the wedding it is agreed to hold a tournament below Tenebroc; they assemble in due course, and the winner is Erec. In the source, the tournament (along with the kiss and the union associated with it) could only have existed in the declaration by the fay, as the hero flees from the Ile d'Or at dawn next morning. Nor does the consummation really happen there in the original form of the story. But in *Papegau*, with the original stay of one night sufficiently prolonged, the tourney with the hero as victor, the bestowal of the kiss, and the consummation scene, used to express the union, all become fact.[29] In relation to the Ile d'Or Episode, *Erec et Enide* realizes the same features as *Papegau*, but matters are so arranged that what was originally a complex falls into three separate elements: the union is independent of the kiss, and the tourney leads to neither. Here, having lost one function, the competition to give the kiss, to the Hunt of the White Stag, and another, the gaining of the most beautiful

27 *Carduino*, ii, 69/7 f., 71/7.   28 *Descouneus*, 4792-4820.
29 *Papegau*, 27/9-43/19.

damsel, to the Sparrowhawk Contest, the tournament can only retain the third, the demonstration of the hero's fitness above all others to be her spouse. It has become a coda to the wedding, even as the picture of admiration finds a place in *Erec et Enide* as the prelude to the Arrival at Arthur's Court.

RETURN TO ESTREGALES[30] (3 = VI)

As the coronation of the Wedding to a Queen is omitted from the Wedding of Erec and Enide, being kept for the end of the romance, this makes it necessary for the hero's father to be still alive and ruling in Estregales when Erec takes Enide there. But the scenes of welcome and joy at the arrival would find a natural place in the original when the Queen returns with a new King, even as the prince Erec brings home his bride. Such comparable matter appears in *Descouneus*.[31]

The phenomenon already observed occurs yet again, since the Return to Estregales does not hold the same position in Chrétien as the journey back to the Queen's domain in the source, and yet we find that his story is at the same time still running parallel to the original. There we have not yet left the scene in the fay's hall, for in Chrétien we now come to the splendid picture of Enide on a silk cloth, sitting among her ladies: the fay sits with the hero in *Descouneus* and *Papegau* on a silk cloth, surrounded by the members of her court. At this point there are similar passages in *Descouneus* and *Erec et Enide*:

> La dame par le main l'en guie;
> Sor une kiute de brun pale,
> Qu'aportee fu de Tesale,
> Iluec se sont andoi asis.
> Molt i ot chevaliers de pris
> En la sale de totes pars.
>> (*Li Biaus Descouneus*, 2278 ff.)[32]
> An une chanbre fu assise
> Dessor une coute de paile
> Qu'aportee fu de Tessaile.
> Antor li avoit mainte dame.
>> (*Erec et Enide*, ed. Foerster, 2406 ff.)

LAPSE INTO AMOROUS INDOLENCE[33] (3 = VI)

We have seen how Enide's rebuke, that Erec was neglecting his duty to exhibit prowess, corresponds to the point of the Ile d'Or Episode where the emissary takes Descouneus aside and tells him he must not accept the fay's love and remain, for that would be to commit the shameful act of forgetting his mission

30 *Erec*, 2215-2429. 31 *Descouneus*, 6209-36.
32 Cf. *Papegau*, 21/26-36. 33 *Erec*, 2430-2790.

(p. 99). Erec's lapse reflects the succumbing to the fascination of the beautiful fay in the original (p. 132), with a realization comparable with that which has taken place in *Lybeaus* and *Papegau*, where the hero forgets his mission until one day he receives the rebuke from the emissary.

At the same time, we have in Chrétien equivalence with the Departure from Arthur's Court (p. 86) in the source, so that once more there is a combination of material, drawn both from a correct sequence and from somewhere else in the original. For what Enide does also corresponds to the emissary's act at Arthur's court, when she slights the hero's valour, and in both stories this makes him determined to prove his prowess by carrying out the ride. In a switch of roles Erec is also the Chevalier Mesdisant who has been angered and is humiliating his companion (p. 106 f.). A beautiful lady in rich dress and with splendid harness accompanies the hero in both stories, but in the tale of the Fair Unknown type the emissary arrives in this condition at Arthur's court,[34] whereas Chrétien equips the heroine in this manner by making Erec order his wife to wear her most beautiful dress and to saddle her best palfrey, of whose splendid harness we become aware in the next episode.

But otherwise, apart from the arming of the hero before he departs, there is nothing in common between this episode in Chrétien and the Fair Unknown type of story. The new matter makes it the unforgettable domestic tragedy of Erec and Enide.

ENCOUNTERS WITH MARAUDERS[35]   (3 = VI)

The marauders intend to rob the hero, initially of Enide and her horse with its equipment. They are encountered in two bands, of three and five knights respectively, and they do not attack in force but one at a time, for which Chrétien provides an explanation: in those days, it was not the custom for two knights to join in an assault against one. In contrast, the two antagonists who assail Lybeaus together in the Attack by Three Avengers (p. 90 f.) lack this moral streak that in Chrétien is found in robbers. But otherwise there are resemblances between this fight in *Lybeaus* and the battle with the first band of marauders in *Erec et Enide*, over and above the agreement in the number of opponents. Such similarity between Chrétien and the Attack by Three Avengers in the original must be why in *Descouneus* the material of this episode has been assimilated to that of the assault by the band of three robbers in *Erec et Enide*. Because of this, care must be exercised when using *Descouneus* as a representative of the original here, but it appears that Renaut preserves an authentic feature when he refers to the avengers as robbers (p. 137 f.).

Enide observes, when she sees the robbers, that the contest is not fair between one knight and three. Similarly, in her appeal to the avengers, the emissary says that Descouneus has no strength against the three of them. There must have

34 *Descouneus*, 135-56; *Lybeaus*, 109-20; *Ipomedon*, 7940-69.
35 *Erec*, 2791-3079.

been something of the kind in the original, because in *Lybeaus*, when the hero is attacked simultaneously by two of the avengers, he remarks that it is not at all pleasant for one man to fight against two. Then it is striking how Enide arouses Erec from thought, even as Descouneus is awakened from sleep, and her words would find a natural place in the Attack by Three Avengers, where it is Robert (i.e. originally the dwarf) who warns Descouneus (p. 118):

"Ci vienent poignant aprés vos
troi chevalier qui molt vos chacent."

(*Erec et Enide*, 2842 f.)

The first antagonist is immediately thrust to the ground, but he remains alive in *Lybeaus*—cf. *Ipomedon* II (p. 113)—whereas in *Erec* he is killed. In *Lybeaus*— cf. *Ipomedon* II again—his horse is captured, while in Chrétien this happens to each opponent's steed. A second adversary is tumbled off his horse and left injured, in *Descouneus* and *Lybeaus* with his arm broken, and in *Erec* so seriously wounded that he is in a faint. Furthermore, in both *Lybeaus* and *Erec* a third opponent gives up immediately when the hero has dealt with the other two, surrendering at once in *Lybeaus*, but in Chrétien taking to flight.[36] This battle with robbers in *Erec et Enide* may thus be taken as an adaptation of that in the Attack by Three Avengers, in which the effect of Chrétien's explanation, coming as it does after Enide's remark, is to draw attention to a distinction and contradict the situation we see in *Lybeaus*, especially as he puts the custom as that of two knights not delivering a concerted assault, when in fact there is an impending attack by three.

The Attack by Three Avengers is not located at the corresponding point in the Fair Unknown type of tale, and so, in view of the repeated phenomenon that has been observed, one ought to see what in this story holds a position equivalent to that of Chrétien's episode in his. The rebuke delivered by the emissary after supper is followed by The Night Scenes at the Ile d'Or (p. 132 ff.), in which the hero suffers frustrations at the hands of the fay, a series of colourful experiences that must have contributed a good deal to the success of the *conte*. Now, if it were not indicated by the pointer on my cursor, I could never have hit upon this matter as the origin of an episode where the hero has encounters with robbers. Any surprise that may have been felt so far at the handling of the source material in *Erec et Enide* can only be mild compared with the astonishment which is bound to come when the treatment of the original is now exposed. This part of my demonstration obtains results so unexpected, so dependent on the wording of passages and therefore so crucial to the question of authorship— if any uncertainty can remain as to whether it is Chrétien, and not some predecessor, who fabricated the story of Erec and Enide—that it must be laid out at length.

Comparison between the Encounters with Marauders and The Night Scenes at the Ile d'Or leaves no room for doubt that the former is related deliberately

---

36 *Descouneus*, 963-1193; *Lybeaus*, 454-519; cf. *Ipomedon*, 8242-8334.

to the latter. Not only are the situations in the original alluded to by Chrétien in due order, but there are three sets of reflections, which follow upon one another thus:

> Set 1:   Temptation; Frustrations 1, 2, and 3
> Set 2:   Temptation; Frustrations 1, 2, and 3
> Set 3:   Frustrations 1, 2, and 3

This provides a long series of correlatives, so many locks, as it were, ensuring that a key which fits all cannot fail to correspond to that which originally turned them.

The allusion rests chiefly on the following conceptions. First of all, that he who tries to enter a lady's chamber with the intention of possessing her is a robber. For the lady herself, regarded as the object of sexual desire, an equestrian *double entendre* is used, such as occurs in a licentious song by Guillaume de Poitiers, *Companho, farai un vers*, in which the troubadour considers the choice between two horses, both excellent for him to mount, and where the circumstantial detail about them is meant to apply to two ladies. At the same time, the fay as a beautiful woman is represented by Enide, and as having the power of attack or defence she is expressed by Erec. I shall now show in detail how the innuendo works.

The first band has three marauders, as many as the number of frustrating experiences at the Ile d'Or, and the first robber's speech to his fellows alludes to the original hero's attitude at the outset:

> The marauder very much covets the palfrey on which Enide comes riding. "Do you know, sirs, what is in prospect for you?", says he to his two companions. "If we do not make a haul here, we are good-for-nothing cowards, and extraordinarily unlucky. Here comes a very beautiful lady, whether maiden or not I don't know, but she is very richly dressed. Her palfrey, her saddle, her breaststraps, and her lorains are worth at least twenty marks of silver. I want to have the palfrey, and you can have all the rest of the booty. I don't want to have any more for my share. The knight shall not get away with anything of the lady, so help me God. I intend to make such an assault on him, I assure you, that he will pay dearly for it."
>
> (*Erec et Enide*, 2796-2816)

The three "robbers" have but one identity, the original hero, who takes part in all three frustrations, and the passage stands for thoughts of the kind that would run through the mind of one in the situation of Descouneus, who in throes of desire looks at the inviting open door of the fay's chamber, telling himself that she wants him to enter it, and if he does not do so she will hold him a recreant.[37] In this opportunity too good to be missed, there is the prospect of seizing the "palfrey", that is, gratifying sexual desire, and possessing the

---

37 *Descouneus*, 4522-46.

precious "saddle, breast-straps, and lorains", meaning the lovely bodily parts, but the "palfrey" is the primary aim, whether the lady is a virgin or not. The violent assault intended on Erec, which would not let him get away with anything of the lady, is also that which the original hero has in mind to make upon the fay.

First one marauder attacks and is defeated, another comes and is vanquished in his turn, and then the third runs away and is chased by Erec, who conquers him. This gives the same rhythm as the succession of experiences at the Ile d'Or, in which the hero tries to enter the fay's chamber, but is repelled by magic, has a second try and suffers another such repulse, and then, when he does not dare to repeat the attempt for the third time, she comes to his bed but again frustrates him. So much for the general course of the battle in *Erec et Enide*, and now let us look at each individual fight with one of the robbers. The first marauder delivers his assault:

> Both the robber and Erec give spur and clash together holding their lances at full extent. But the robber misses Erec, whereas Erec uses him hard, for he knows well how to attack straight at the target. . . . Erec thrusts a foot and a half of his lance into his body. In withdrawing it he turns his weapon, and the marauder falls. He cannot escape death, for the point has pierced to the heart.
>
> (*Erec et Enide*, 2857-70)

The "attack" on the fay misses its aim, because the hero fails to get into her chamber, whereas with the "lance" of a spell she goes straight to the target, being well-skilled in magic. In Frustration 1 the spell gives the hero a great fear that he is about to die.

The second marauder attacks and is vanquished in his turn:

> The knight's lance flies into pieces, while Erec drives a quarter of his lance's length through the other's body. The robber will give Erec no more trouble this day, for Erec tumbles him off his horse in a faint.
>
> (*Erec et Enide*, 2878-83)

His lance flies into pieces, because the original hero's attempt to enter the fay's chamber is thwarted. The use of the equestrian *double entendre*, which has been applied to a horse as prospective booty, is here also extended to one from which the rider has been unseated, for Descouneus can be said to be "tumbled off his horse" in the sense that his designs on the person of the fay are brought to nought. In Frustration 2 the repulse leaves the hero lying very shaken, and he gives the fay no further trouble.[38]

The third marauder makes no attempt to attack Erec, but flees and is chased:

> When the robber sees him coming, he begins to flee. He is afraid and does not dare to face him, and so he hastens to take refuge in the forest. But his

---

38 *Ibid.*, 4659-91.

flight is of no avail. Erec follows him close and cries aloud: "Knight, knight, turn about and prepare to defend yourself, or I shall strike you while you are fleeing. Your flight is of no avail." But the robber has no desire to turn about, and flees as fast as he can. Erec chases and overtakes him, hits him squarely on his painted shield, and tumbles him over on the other side. To those three he gives no further heed. He has killed one, wounded another, and so got rid of the third that he threw him off his horse on to his feet. Erec takes the horses of all three, and ties them together by the bridles. They are all of different colour: the first as white as milk, the second black but not bad looking, and the third all dappled.

(Erec et Enide, 2885-2909)

Here, in another lively scene, the flight to refuge stands for the original hero's lurking in his bed, afraid to try again because after two humiliations he is certain that he will fail a third time.[39] In Frustration 3, the fay "chases" him by coming to his bed, and after her third "victory" over him she pays no further attention to the hero. Her first spell gave him a great fear of losing his life, and her second a terror that he would receive a mortal injury, while he was "got rid of" on the third occasion by her drawing back in repulse, thus "throwing him off his horse on to his feet". The "horse" that the "robber" in each encounter has been "thrown off" is led away, as the fay departs, and in spite of variety they have but one identity, like the "robbers".

This completes the first set of allusions, and we come to another as Erec and Enide, who is in charge of the three captured steeds, approach the second band of marauders, of whom there are five. As before we find introductory remarks, this time sententious comment, again aimed at the situation of the original hero as he contemplates the open door:

> As soon as the robbers see Erec and Enide, they speak of how they will divide their equipment among themselves, just as if it is already in their possession. Covetousness is a bad thing. But they do not find it to their taste that vigorous defence is made. One should not count one's chickens before they are hatched, and there is many a slip betwixt the cup and the lip. So it was with them in this attack.

(Erec et Enide, 2931-40)

One wants to have the lady, another the dappled steed, the third the black, the fourth the white, and the last marauder intends to possess Erec's horse and arms. All the "horses" have the same identity as Enide.

So far it would have been possible to argue that the relationship to the experiences at the Ile d'Or is coincidental, but hereafter the circumstantial detail is such as to make it certain that the episode of the Encounters with Marauders is based on those scenes. The next reference to that material comes this time in Enide's warning to Erec about the robbers:

---

39 *Descouneus*, 4683-91.

"Four of them have remained behind, and the fifth is coming at you as fast as his steed can carry him. At any moment he is going to strike you. The other four have remained behind, but they are not far away at all. In case of need, they will all come to his aid."

(Erec et Enide, 2986-92)

In Frustration 1, Descouneus finds himself dangling by his arms from a plank over a tempestuous stream, but four giants on the bank of a great river are suspending Carduino so that he hangs by his arms and his feet just touch the water.[40] With the sense of humour that has already been evident, Chrétien here alludes to the first nightmarish illusion in his source, which his evidence proves to have been the one we find in the Italian version. This gives a picture of five figures, with four of them on the bank, close to the fifth who is dangling over the water, and Chrétien chooses to interpret this as a group of four who can if necessary draw the one out of danger.

The allusion to Frustration 2 is now provided by the fight with the first of the five marauders:

Erec strikes him with such force that his shield flies from his neck, and thus he breaks his collar-bone. His stirrups break, and he falls. There is no fear that he will rise again, for he is badly bruised and wounded.

(Erec et Enide, 3010-15)

Which conveys very well the original hero's impression that the whole roof is lying on his neck, his bones are being crushed, and he is going to receive a mortal injury.[41]

Another marauder appears, and Erec deals with him thus:

Erec sets his well-forged steel blade right at his throat, underneath the chin. He so severs all his bones and nerves that the point protrudes at the back of the neck. The hot red blood flows on both sides from the wound. The spirit departs, the heart fails.

(Erec et Enide, 3018-25)

This bloody scene of violence, as an example of Chrétien's technique of transference, may best be appreciated by laying these passages side by side:

> En lui joïr a painne mise.
> Les son menton li met sa face.
> *(Li Biaus Descouneus, 2438 f.)*
> Erec li met tot a bandon
> desoz le manton an la gorge
> le fer tranchant de boene forge.
> *(Erec et Enide, 3018 ff.)*

---

40 *Ibid.*, 4551-78; *Carduino*, ii, 16/1-17/6.
41 *Descouneus*, 4634-48.

The weapon that the fay employs in Frustration 3, as she sets out to arouse the hero's desire, is to place her face against him, by his chin. The hot red blood must have flowed as his resistance weakened, and his heart missed a beat.

Thus ends the second set of allusions, and a third ensues, in the fates of the remaining marauders. There is first an encounter in a ford:

> The third robber rushes from his hiding-place on the other side of a ford, and comes straight across it. Erec spurs forward and meets him before he has come out of the water, striking him so hard that he beats down flat both rider and horse. The horse lies on the body, so that the marauder has to drown in the water.
>
> (*Erec et Enide*, 3026-34)

As we have seen, Frustration 1 has the suspension over flowing water, which gives the hero a great fear of drowning. Then the next marauder's fate is so clearly related to Frustration 2 that from Chrétien one can well imagine the original hero feeling a mighty blow on his spine, throwing him forward with an immense weight lying on his neck, crushing his bones, and threatening mortal injury to the upper part of his body:

> Erec strikes one of the robbers on the spine so hard that he throws him forward on to the saddle-bow. He has put all his strength into the blow, breaks his lance upon his back, and makes him fall forward on to his neck. Erec makes him pay dearly for the lance which he has broken upon him, for he soon draws his sword from the scabbard. The other unwisely raises himself, as Erec gives him three such strokes that he slakes his sword's thirst in his blood. He severs his shoulder from the body, so that it falls down on the ground.
>
> (*Erec et Enide*, 3043-55)

We return to the more general allusive manner of the earlier passages, when the last marauder flees, but cannot escape:

> With the sword Erec attacks the robber, who flees precipitately, without company or escort. He does not dare to face Erec, and cannot turn aside. He is forced to abandon his horse, because there is no further hope. He throws down his shield and lance, and slips to the ground. When Erec sees that the robber has let himself fall to the ground, he does not care to pursue his attack any further, but stoops for the lance, not wishing to leave that because of his own which he has broken, and he carries off the lance and goes away. He does not leave the horses behind, but catches all five of them, and leads them off.
>
> (*Erec et Enide*, 3056-71)

Once more the original hero's lurking in his bed, afraid to try again, and the fay's coming to him in Frustration 3, are the "flight" and "chase". He is unable to avoid the humiliation that comes upon him, and which makes him "abandon his horse", because he falls into despair as he lies distracted with love. Having obtained this result, the fay does not need to pursue her "attack" any further. He has now "thrown down his lance", his aiming to possess her this night, and she takes it away irrevocably, by closing her door.[42] And, as before, the "horse" of each "robber" is removed, with the departure of the fay.

Following upon this remarkable instance of Chrétien drawing material from a source, we find another in the same vein.

NIGHT-QUARTERS AND A MEAL IN THE OPEN[43]   (3 = VI)

Erec and Enide ride until nightfall, and then stay until morning under a tree in a clearing. Chrétien here caps the allusive treatment of the frustrations suffered by the original hero with a similar embodying of his dream, thus completing the parallelism with The Night Scenes at the Ile d'Or (p. 132 ff.).[44] When Erec and Enide take up night-quarters in the forest, he sleeps and she keeps watch, not sleeping all night, and holding all the horses tight in her hand until the morning breaks. This confirms the correctness of two assumptions made in my interpretation of the Encounters with Marauders. One is that all the "horses" have but one identity, the fay as the object of sexual desire. The other is that Erec and Enide stand for two aspects of one person, there the fay, but now of the original hero. Erec is this time to be compared with that figure sleeping, and Enide to the same person dreaming all night that he is holding the fay—all the "horses"—until dawn breaks. Enide's state of mind during her night-watch, as she blames and reproaches herself for what she had done, and curses herself for the act that has reduced her to the humiliation she suffers, resembles that of Descouneus as he falls asleep, distracted and greatly humiliated, and cursing his evil fate, that has too grievously gone awry.[45]

Once more, while thus rendering what occurs in his source at the corresponding point, Chrétien reflects another place in the original. The parallel with the encampment in the forest on the night of the Rescue from Two Giants is made clear when Erec and Enide, after leaving the forest next day, towards noon meet an intelligent squire who is accompanied by two servants carrying bread and wine and rich cheeses. When the squire sees them, he realizes that they must have spent the night in the forest. They have neither eaten nor drunk (*n'avoient mangié ne beü*) and so he offers them the food. There then takes place an enjoyable picnic. First the squire helps Enide to alight, gives the horses to his servants to look after, relieves Erec of his helmet and unlaces the chinpiece, and then spreads a cloth on the turf and busies himself attending to them. He passes them cake and wine, and prepares and cuts a cheese, while Erec and Enide

---

42 *Descouneus*, 2457-64.   43 *Erec*, 3080-3172.
44 The dream of sexual intercourse, resulting from enchantment, is a motif which Chrétien uses in his next romance (*Cligès*, 3299 ff.), where he adds it to material corresponding to that in *Orson de Beauvais*, on which see p. 33 above.
45 *Descouneus*, 2459-71.

eat and drink their fill with the squire serving diligently and omitting no attention. Over fifty lines of the romance are occupied with this picture, which mirrors a scene in the source where the hero and the emissary take part in an enjoyable meal during the night (p. 89), and which can be reconstructed by the aid of the relationship I have established between the various texts that can be brought to bear on it (pp. 113, 117 f.). In a forest meadow where they stop for the night, the intelligent dwarf[46] disarms the hero, looks after the horses, spreads cloths on the grass and lays supper. But they neither eat nor drink,[47] for there then takes place the interruption of the adventure with the giants. When the hero returns, the dwarf again disarms him and then busies himself with excellent service, the fare for the hero and his lady companion being (apart from the roast that belonged to the giants) picnic food, as we see from the wine, loaves, and ham in *Descouneus*, and wine and pies in *Durmart*.[48]

ESCAPE FROM THE AMOROUS COUNT[49] (3 = VI)

The intelligent squire also acts as a link with the next adventure, as he is asked to engage suitable quarters for Erec and Enide in the town nearby. He returns and conducts them to lodgings. This entry into the town and the taking up of quarters there reminds one of what happens as the adventure of the Sparrow-hawk Contest opens, and that this association is correct soon appears from the sequel.

The squire goes on his way from Erec's lodgings to the Count's palace, and passes in front of the galleries, where the Count leans out and holds a conversation with him, in the course of which the squire remarks that he has conducted to a citizen's house a very courteous knight and the handsomest man he has ever seen. The Count hastens to go and meet this very handsome knight. It is evening and there are many lighted wax-tapers and candles in large numbers, because, as Chrétien explains, Erec habitually keeps very rich lodgings. When the Count enters, Erec, who has good manners, rises and greets him politely, the Count returns his salutation, and they sit down side by side and chat with each other. The Count offers to refund his expenses, but Erec refuses, saying that he has sufficient means and does not need to accept anything from the Count.

For the parallel I go to the Tourney at Tintagel (p. 127 ff.), which in *Perceval* II is the equivalent of the Sparrowhawk Contest. The squire in *Erec et Enide* is seen to be given some of the original host's role, for Garin in *Perceval* II,

---

46 The dwarf is called *sagio* in *Carduino*, and he is said to be full of accomplishments in *Lybeaus*, 136-40.

47 Cf. *N'ont que mangier a cel souper* (*Descouneus*, 609). In the tale of the Fair Unknown, however, they go to bed without supper. Though the same happens in *Erec et Enide*, to judge from the agreement between *Carduino* and *Ipomedon* II this is not the original situation.

48 *Descouneus*, 594-619, 815-22, 901-51; *Lybeaus*, 445-53; *Carduino*, ii, 26/4-27/7, 37/5-38/4; *Ipomedon*, 8185-8, 8202, 8323-6, 8386 f., 8615 f., 8918, 9016; *Durmart*, 2137-2206.

49 *Erec*, 3173-3652.

after conducting Gawain to lodgings, sets out to see Tiebaut, his lord, but the latter has already left his house and they come across each other in the street. It is evident that the Count in *Erec et Enide* here corresponds to Tiebaut, lord of Tintagel.[50] Garin tells Tiebaut that he will see at his own house the handsomest knight on earth, and escorts Tiebaut to Gawain's lodgings, where the Maid of the Little Sleeves has already resorted. When Tiebaut enters, Gawain, who has good manners, rises and greets him politely, salutations are exchanged, and they sit down side by side to converse with each other. Tiebaut offers to provide Gawain with provisions for his journey, and the hero answers that he does not need them.[51] The resemblance between this section of *Perceval* II and the equivalent part of *Erec et Enide* is particularly close here:

> Quant mesire Gavains le voit,
> Qui molt estoit bien ensaigniez,
> Si se lieve et dist: "Bien veigniez."
> Et il le salüent andui,
> Puis si s'asieent dalez lui.
>
> > (*Perceval*, 5296 ff.)
>
> Erec contre lui leva sus,
> Qui mout estoit bien anseigniez,
> Si li dist: "Sire! bien veigniez!"
> Et li cuens resalua lui.
> Acoté se sont anbedui
> Sor une coute blanche et mole,
> Si s'antracointent de parole.
>
> > (*Erec et Enide*, ed. Foerster, 3270 ff.)
>
> "Vos donrai vitaille a porter
> Et chevax qui le porteront."
> Et mesire Gavains respont
> Que il n'a nul mestier del prendre.
>
> > (*Perceval*, 5322 ff.)
>
> Li cuens li porofre et presante
> et prie que il li consante
> que de lui ses gaiges repraigne.
> Mes Erec baillier ne li daigne,
> einz dit qu'asez a a despandre,
> n'a mestier de son avoir prandre.
>
> > (*Erec et Enide*, 3269 ff.)

In the Fair Unknown type of tale, the most we know about the evening before the contest is in *Wigalois*, where we are told that the hero has the full sympathy of the people there and the time is spent in festivity.[52] But in the

---

50 In *Lybeaus*, 763-83, it is the hero who goes from his lodgings to the palace and encounters the lord coming towards him from it, with whom he converses.
51 *Perceval*, 5168-5331.   52 *Wigalois*, 2930-67.

story of Lore de Branlant in *Le Livre d'Artus*, which makes use of a tale of the Fair Unknown type (p. 121 f.), and draws on the Sparrowhawk Contest for Branlant (p. 162), the hero is expensively installed in his lodgings there with a great blaze of light, just as we have seen with Erec:

> ot si grant luminaire quant ce uint a lanuitier en la meson quil estoit auis que toute fust esprise de feu ardant.

At Branlant the hero is well entertaining those who resort to his lodgings, with much festivity, but he is not visited by the ruler of the city this evening. After the battle next day the house is again ablaze with light, however, when she arrives with her seneschal:

> sembloit que toute la maison arsist de luminaire qui i estoit.

And now the scene is like an amalgam of the two occasions in the Tourney at Tintagel when the lord of the city goes to the lodgings, the one on the evening of the hero's arrival, which I have described, and the other when he returns after the jousting and the lord invites him twice to stay with him and he twice refuses, as also at the Sparrowhawk Contest in *Erec et Enide* (p. 166). At Branlant the hero jumps to his feet, welcomes the visitors and sets them beside him:

> si saut sus & dit que bien ueignanz soient il . si les prent as mains & les assiet deioste luj.

They converse together, and on behalf of the lady the seneschal twice invites the hero to stay with her. Furthermore, he makes the same offer as is made to Erec by the amorous Count, which is also refused:

> ele uielt que uos aiez uos gages de luj . sire fait messires Gauuain la uostre merci & la soe de ce que uos me presentez . mais sachiez que mi gage sont tuit quite en iusque ci.

The events at Branlant,[53] acting as a link between those at Laluth and Tintagel, prove conclusively that the Escape from the Amorous Count draws on the Sparrowhawk Contest.

The identification of the material in the Escape from the Amorous Count means that the common source of *Erec et Enide* and *Perceval* II brought out not only good looks but also good manners in the hero, so that he would be like La Cote Mal Taillie, and not the foolish *vallet salvage*, Perceval (p. 166 f.), who shares with Carduino and Lybeaus a forest upbringing by a widowed mother. Beauty and good manners are also possessed by Enide, who has so often been found to carry out the same role as the hero of the Fair Unknown type.

The Sparrowhawk Contest does not have the same location in the original as the Escape from the Amorous Count in Chrétien, but as the latter episode

---

53 *Le Livre d'Artus*, ed. Sommer, vii, 96, 100 f.

continues we find ourselves back on course with the sequence in the source. While the Count is conversing with Erec, he catches sight of Enide sitting some distance away, is very impressed by her beauty, falls deeply in love and asks Erec for permission to talk with her. He takes his seat beside Enide and privily asks her to become his sweetheart and lady over his domain. We have now been transported back to matter drawn from the Ile d'Or Episode. For there the amorous fay sits side by side with the hero, falls in love with him and offers to make him her lord, in possession of her domain and her love.

Enide refuses, but the Count threatens to kill Erec right away if she does not accept his proposal, and so she devises a ruse. Pretending to fall in with his offer, she suggests a stratagem to the Count which he adopts, that more conveniently for both their reputations he should send his men to seize her by force in the morning when Erec is about to rise, and so have him taken and killed while resisting them. The situation at the Ile d'Or is that when Descouneus thanks the fay for her offer, she is so distracted by love that she descends to force and trickery, but unlike the Count in Chrétien the artifice is her own. Sitting beside the hero, and intent like the Count on obtaining possession of the beautiful person by hook or by crook, she is planning to see to this. She tells Descouneus that before nightfall she will announce to all the princes of her domain that they should assemble in eight days' time, when she will take a husband, and she is informing all in the country; in *Papegau*, the occasion is to be a tournament to decide who is to be her *ami*, and she will take him for one year (p. 168).[54] The fay's wile is perceived by the emissary, who takes Descouneus aside after supper and warns him that the fay has sent for her barons throughout the land because she wants to take him as husband, and if he does not wish to accept her he will be seized. This treacherous plan is reflected in Chrétien as that by which the amorous Count is to send his men in the morning to obtain possession of Enide by force.

Enide's intention is that Erec and she, through her ruse, should manage to escape from the town before the Count's men come. Similarly, the emissary advises Descouneus to get away in the morning by means of a ruse. She will arrange to have the horses ready before dawn at the gate leading to a chapel, and he is to give the gate-keeper the excuse that he wants to go to church. As arranged, at dawn Descouneus quickly rises, is duly let out by the gate-keeper, goes to the chapel, finds the emissary and his horse ready, and they flee from

---

54 In *Floire et Blancheflor* (before 1170), which makes some use of the Ile d'Or Episode, there is an adaptation of this scene. Floire is told that in a month's time all the barons will assemble for a festive occasion when the Emir will take a wife. The mode of selection, with reversal of sex, is naturally not a tournament. It is to be the fall of a flower from a marvellous tree on one of the maidens assembled for the event, and one should note that she will become the Emir's wife and lady of the land for but one year. The Emir, who is as intent on marrying the beautiful Blancheflor as the fay is on having the handsome Descouneus as her husband, will take her to wife. He will ensure by enchantment that the flower falls upon his choice. See *Floire*, 1730-1863.
On the connections between *Floire* and the Fair Unknown type of tale, see p. 201 below.

the Ile d'Or before the sun has risen. In Chrétien, Enide explains the state of affairs to Erec for the first time when she wakes him up as it is nearly dawn, so that he sleeps soundly all night. Erec asks her to have the horses saddled— we have seen that the emissary arranges that these are ready—and they mount and escape from the town before the sun rises, just like the hero and the emissary leaving the Ile d'Or.[55]

While Erec lies asleep all night, Enide keeps vigil in sorrow and anxiety. This second night-watch of hers, beside Erec lying asleep, can be seen to correspond to that part of the source material where the hero dreams all night at the Ile d'Or, which confirms my interpretation of the first occasion as Erec standing for the original hero sleeping, and Enide the same figure dreaming that night. The echo of the forest night-watch in Enide's vigil at the lodgings is another step away from the source, but its connection is still identifiable from the location in the material.

The rest of this episode in Chrétien takes us to matter from yet another part of the original story. The Count, having discovered that the birds have flown, follows their trail, threatening to kill Erec and urging his hundred men on to present him with his head. They go on at top speed, filled with hostility, and make Erec out at the edge of the forest before he is hidden by the trees. Enide hears the clang of arms, sees that the valley is full of the enemy and warns Erec to make good his escape because he is no match for them. But he rejects this advice as showing little esteem for him, turns about to face the enemy, sees the seneschal make a sortie before the others, and drives his sword through him. Then, even though the Count is unarmed apart from shield and lance, this adversary comes on and strikes Erec such a blow that he nearly loses his stirrups, and it splits his shield but fails to get through his hauberk. The Count having broken his lance, Erec runs his own through him, knocking the Count senseless from his steed. Then Erec turns and rides away into the forest, while the Count's retainers pause over their lord, vowing to avenge him. But the Count hears what they say, opens his eyes and orders them to desist. He has done an evil deed, of which he now repents.

M. Mills has shown how this is related to the Encounter with a Huntsman in *Lybeaus*.[56] Here, when the huntsman comes back bent on revenge (p. 91 f.), he returns with a little army. A lively scene is described, as his friends arm themselves for battle, fiercely threaten to deal with the hero, and sight him from a distance, while he observes how the whole region is swarming with them. He advises his companions to withdraw into the woodland, because he is intent on facing the enemy. The course of the battle has Lybeaus striking down man after man, until at last the leader is dealt with, and there are reminiscences of other English romances in the fighting.[57]

It is ridiculous that after such slaughter of his men the adversary should

---

55 *Descouneus*, 2273-2364, 2472-86.
56 Mills, *art. cit.*, 37-9.
57 *Ibid.*, 47; also the notes on the appropriate section of *Lybeaus*.

be reconciled with Lybeaus, take him home to his castle and rejoice with him.[58] But the motif of reconciliation has some parallel, not only in the Count's repentance in Chrétien, but also in the opponent's change from hostility after his defeat in the adventures of *Durmart* and the Second Continuation of *Perceval* that are equivalent to the Encounter with a Huntsman (p. 115).[59] The abrupt end of the fight in *Erec et Enide*, where without delay the hero's antagonist breaks his lance and is struck to the ground, corresponds to what happens in matter from the Encounter with a Huntsman in *Wigalois* and *Durmart*.[60] Lastly, the amorous Count's lack of armour, as he pursues Erec with a lance, is like the condition of the huntsman when he first appears on the scene, unarmed and chasing a stag with a spear (p. 129 f.).[61]

My comparison has shown that the figure of the amorous Count is complex in origin, gathering together the personalities of the lord in whose town the Sparrowhawk Contest is held in the source, the fay of the Ile d'Or, and the opponent of the Encounter with a Huntsman.[62] We end with a new character.

The following tabulation brings out what I have so far established as basic material drawn on for each episode (an asterisk indicates what maintains the sequence in the *conte Erec*, and italics the title given to an assumed *conte*):

HUNT OF THE WHITE STAG
    announcement of a competitive event for which the prize is a kiss to be given to a lady (Ile d'Or Episode)
    head of a court embarks on a project of which one of the two parts is difficult to accomplish (*Anticlaudianus*)
    *Departure from Arthur's Court (**DA**)

ENCOUNTER WITH YDER
    *Encounter with a Huntsman
    Abduction of Guinevere during a Hunt in the Forest
    departure on a quest during which the project is suspended by the head of the court (*Anticlaudianus*)

SPARROWHAWK CONTEST
    *Sparrowhawk Contest
    bestowal of arms on the hero by the old, grey-haired father of a daughter (Return of the Rescued Damsel)

58 *Lybeaus*, 1078-1218.
59 *Durmart*, 1737-48; *Perceval*, Second Continuation, 25042 ff.
60 *Wigalois*, 2304-16; *Durmart*, 1652-92.
61 *Descouneus*, 1305-8. In the episode of the Second Continuation of *Perceval* which corresponds to the Encounter with a Huntsman, the huntsman arrives without a shield and chasing the stag with a lance (24862-5).
62 There is also some resemblance of the amorous Count to the opponent of the Perilous Bridge, because of the deep wounding in the abdomen, his fainting, and being carried back to his castle (p. 137 f.).

G

ARRIVAL AT ARTHUR'S COURT
Arrival at Arthur's Court (**AA**)
*arrival of the admired one at the court where the kiss is to be publicly bestowed on the lady by the winner of the competitive event (Ile d'Or Episode)
return from the quest that makes possible the completion of the project by the head of the court (*Anticlaudianus*)

WEDDING OF EREC AND ENIDE
Wedding to a Queen (**WQ**)
*union that follows on the kiss and is associated with a tournament (Ile d'Or Episode)
a perfect creation is brought into existence (*Anticlaudianus*)

RETURN TO ESTREGALES
return to the domain (Wedding to a Queen)
*the beautiful person sits upon a silk cloth, surrounded by members of the court (Ile d'Or Episode)

LAPSE INTO AMOROUS INDOLENCE
the perfect creation comes under the assault of imperfections (*Anticlaudianus*)
a Paris, subdued by the voluptuousness of carnal love, is subject to the curse of Genius on one who has abused the endowments of Nature (*De planctu Naturae*)
*rebuke to the hero delivered by a lady, that he should not forget his martial duty through the love of a woman (Ile d'Or Episode)
the hero departs on an adventurous ride, accompanied by a lady who disparaged his prowess (Departure from Arthur's Court)

ENCOUNTERS WITH MARAUDERS
Attack by Three Avengers
*frustrations, on succumbing to the temptation of possessing the inviting prospect (Ile d'Or Episode)

NIGHT-QUARTERS AND A MEAL IN THE OPEN
*sleeping, and holding all night until dawn breaks (Ile d'Or Episode)
the hero and his lady companion have a picnic, with an intelligent squire busying himself with excellent service (Reconciliation Scene)

ESCAPE FROM THE AMOROUS COUNT
arrival at a city, taking of lodgings, and visit paid to the hero there by the city's lord (Sparrowhawk Contest)
*the city's ruler offers love and the domain, and intends to possess the beautiful person by hook or by crook, but, through a ruse devised by his lady companion, the hero escapes with her before sunrise (Ile d'Or Episode)

assault by an army led from his castle by a lord in chase of the hero, who promptly strikes him to the ground (Encounter with a Huntsman)

All the way from Enide's journey with Erec from Laluth up to the Escape from the Amorous Count, the events in Chrétien—although partially derived from elsewhere in the original—have been found to reflect those at the Ile d'Or, from the arrival of the hero there to his escape from the fay. But with the next episode in *Erec et Enide* we move on to another bar of the grid that I set up to map Chrétien's romance.

10

The Conjointure—II

So far the adventures of Erec and Enide since they left Estregales, in relation to the sequence of events in the Fair Unknown type of tale, have provided combats although the material in the source had nothing to do with fighting. But from now on Chrétien's story runs parallel to encounters on the original hero's ride.

FIRST ENCOUNTER WITH GUIVRET[1] (4 = I)

We have seen that Erec's clash with Guivret, after passing over a bridge in front of his castle, corresponds to the Encounter at the Perilous Bridge (p. 87 f.), even as to the general course of the battle itself, except that strokes which the Fair Unknown deals to his adversary are in Chrétien delivered by Erec and Guivret upon each other. This results in both of them, as Guivret observes, being in need of a physician, and there ensues a mutual bandaging, with strips cut off from the bottom of their shirts. The Encounter at the Perilous Bridge ends with the adversary utterly done for and with a wound streaming with blood; in the derivative in *Le Livre d'Artus* the hero leaves Guinganbresil in this condition, remarks that his wound is in great need of healing, and it is bound before he is taken away; and Greoreas, in great need of a physician for his wounds, lies fainting with loss of blood until they are bandaged, in the equivalent episode of *Perceval* II, the Meeting with Greoreas (p. 136 ff.). Thus the motif attached in the source to the opponent has been extended to the hero in *Erec et Enide*, who also departs in great need of salve for his wounds.[2]

Guivret's invitation to Erec after the combat, to come with him to a residence of his nearby where they can have their wounds tended, is to be compared with what happens in the Encounter with a Huntsman in *Lybeaus*, at the end of which the opponent takes the hero to his castle and sees to the healing of his wounds.[3] Erec however refuses the invitation, which suspends the healing, his need for treatment being only partly met by the bandaging of his wounds that now takes place.

---

1 *Erec*, 3653-3913.
2 The parallel with Durmart, who, with his wound bandaged, journeys in hope of finding a physician to heal it, is to be explained as due to complete transference of the motif from the opponent to the hero in *Durmart* (p. 138 f.).
3 *Lybeaus*, 1204-18, L 1245-56. See M. Mills, "The Huntsman and the Dwarf in *Erec* and *Libeaus Desconus*", *Romania* LXXXVII (1966), 45.

In the tale of the Fair Unknown, after his defeat the adversary—whether of the Encounter at the Perilous Bridge or the Encounter with a Huntsman—is made to give his word to go to Arthur's court, but this does not happen to Guivret. He is asked to identify himself, which he does as Guivret le Petit, powerful King of that region, who wants to be Erec's friend and offers him full hospitality. When the hero refuses this, the little king promises that he will go to aid him with all the men he can summon, whenever he hears that Erec has need of help, and on these terms they part.

A well-known parallel to Guivret is the fairy king Auberon in *Huon de Bordeaux*, a *chanson de geste* of the early thirteenth century. Auberon has the custom of trying to get into his power those who trespass on his forest domain, and as with Guivret the hero's confrontation with Auberon ends with the offer to him of the dwarf-king's friendship and an invitation to a castle. He is entertained there, and given a promise that Auberon will come to his aid with all his armed men whenever the hero requires his help and calls on Auberon's aid by blowing a magic horn that the fairy king gives him.[4]

A figure like Guivret and Auberon is found in the Dutch *Roman van Lancelot*, of the early fourteenth century, where in a forest Gawain hears the sound of a hunt and finds a pack of tiny white hounds, one of which he picks up in order to take to the Queen. A diminutive knight appears and upbraids him for stealing his hound. He declares that he is King of the region and commands five hundred knights, becomes Gawain's friend and invites him to his castle, where Gawain is entertained. Then the dwarf-king uses magic to help Gawain with his quest.[5] Here we have identification of the fairy king with the personage who is the opponent in the Encounter with a Huntsman, but the latter is not a dwarf in the versions of the Fair Unknown type, though his hound is small (p. 91 f.).[6]

Chrétien has introduced the dwarf-king (though he refrains from calling him a dwarf, he speaks of his small size) to the role of the adversary at the Perilous Bridge, and this is sufficient to account for the invitation to his castle. But the Dutch *Lancelot*, as well as *Lybeaus*, where the huntsman-lord comes with an army (p. 184), like the dwarf-king (p. 195), show how likely it is that such an element did belong authentically to the Encounter with a Huntsman. If so, its specific form, to do with healing, was drawn on to go with the little king in *Erec et Enide*.

4 *Huon de Bordeaux*, 3170-3774.
5 *Roman van Lancelot*, iii, 12635-13045.
6 On Guivret, Auberon, and the dwarf-king in the Dutch *Lancelot*, see V. J. Harward, *The Dwarfs of Arthurian Romance and Celtic Tradition* (1958), c. viii and c. x. R. S. Loomis, *Arthurian Tradition and Chrétien de Troyes* (1949), 139-45, treats of the first two, and the relationship of the last figure to both Guivret and the huntsman in *Lybeaus* is discussed by Mills, *art. cit.*, 51-4. For destructive criticism of the derivation of dwarfs from Celtic myth, see A. J. Bliss, "Celtic Myth and Arthurian Romance", *Medium Aevum* XXX (1961), 19 ff.

MEETING WITH ARTHUR AND HIS COMPANY[7]   (4 = I)

Arthur and his company have arrived that day and are encamped in the forest, and Kay is riding about and comes across Erec and Enide. He does not recognize them, and by his presumptuous treatment of the hero, in trying to make him come to the King and Queen, brings about a clash in which Kay is immediately struck to the ground, and his horse taken and handed to Enide for leading away. Kay returns to the King, tells him what has happened, and Gawain is sent to persuade the unknown knight to come to Arthur. Gawain does not recognize Erec either, but in the end the hero reveals who he is.

From the same pattern is constructed an episode in a later romance by Chrétien,[8] but there was no such adventure in the source of *Erec et Enide*. However, the meeting with Kay and Gawain is to be compared with the unwitting encounter (of enemies) that ends in recognition, to be found in *Carduino* in the episode which represents the Encounter at the Perilous Bridge, and in the equivalent adventure of *Perceval* II, the Meeting with Greoreas (p. 136 ff.). Chrétien has thus peeled off a motif, and produced an encounter to express it, from the original adventure that he has just fashioned into the First Encounter with Guivret, and which had the opponent immediately struck to the ground and his horse taken and led away.

Erec is finally persuaded to stay with Arthur by the stratagem of moving the camp into the path of the ride, a scene which has no parallel in the Fair Unknown type of tale. But the theme of severe wounds in dire need of treatment, whose origin lies in the Encounter at the Perilous Bridge, is continued when Kay urges Erec to come and stay because he can see how wounded he is, in Erec's remark that despite his wounds he will not turn aside, Enide's distress at her husband having hardly a limb without a wound, and the joy in the camp that turns to sadness when Erec's wounds are revealed as his armour is taken off.

Erec is treated with an ointment that has been made by Morgain, of such virtue that no wound can fail to be cured by its daily application for a week, and Arthur declares that out of love for Erec he intends to remain in the forest a full fortnight, until Erec is completely healed and restored to health. Again one must compare the hospitality afforded by the huntsman to Lybeaus and the emissary, which results in Lybeaus's wounds being healed by the end of a fortnight.[9] Erec however insists on leaving Arthur after only one night, so that the healing of his wounds is still suspended.

RESCUE FROM TWO GIANTS[10]   (5 = II)

In this episode, Chrétien varies from his original, apart from the adventure occurring in the daytime instead of at night, particularly in having a knight

---

7 *Erec*, 3914-4279.   8 *Perceval*, 4144-4492.
9 *Lybeaus*, 1249-56.   10 *Erec*, 4280-4551.

saved who was being ill-treated by the giants, and not the maiden who cries for help (p. 88).[11] With this alteration, the damsel has her own knight available to escort her, and she can be got rid of without having to return with the hero to his companion and then be taken back to her father (pp. 89, 122), so that Erec is alone as he returns to Enide. The knight is asked to report to Arthur, like defeated opponents in the source.

REFUSAL TO EAT AT LIMORS[12] (RS)

As Erec makes all haste to return to Enide, his wounds break open and the bandages burst. The wounds never stop bleeding, and he reaches Enide with his body bathed in blood, loses his stirrups and falls in a faint, apparently lifeless. Enide laments her grief so loudly that the passing Count of Limors hears her and comes to see what is the matter. His men make a litter, lay Erec on it, and he is carried to the castle of Limors, with Enide continuing in her state of grief. There they stretch out the body on a table in the hall, and everyone asks why this mourning and this mystery. Erec lies thus until well on into the evening.

The scene is quite familiar, because it is like that in the Encounter at the Perilous Bridge, where Blioblieris ends on the ground with a wound flowing with blood, utterly done for. He has to be taken away by his attendants to his shelter, where they lay him on a bed, and there he lies faint and afflicted with pain, waiting for his companions to arrive that night. In *Wigalois*, the lord's attendants follow him past the castle ditches and at the end of the combat bitter lamentation is raised at his fate. Comparably, in *Lybeaus* a great outcry is made at the condition of Wylleam Selebraunche, who is bleeding profusely. The corresponding episode of *Perceval* II has a damsel lamenting the state of Greoreas, who lies with streams of blood pouring from a wound, often fainting with the pain, and in such peril of death from his wounds that he may not be able to live till nightfall (p. 136 ff.). In *Erec et Enide*, the theme of those severe wounds, taken from the Encounter at the Perilous Bridge and extended to the hero, has now come to a climax in their flowing with blood, with the hero in a condition similar to that of the opponent after his defeat in that episode of the source. The adaptation has the bitter lamentation made by Enide at her husband's fate, and introduces a new figure, the Count of Limors, whose servants carry Erec to their lord's castle like those who take Blioblieris away, to what was a castle in the original story, *Descouneus* having altered the location to a defended ford (p. 87 f.). This taking back of the severely-wounded and fainting adversary

---

[11] M. Pelan, *L'influence du "Brut" de Wace sur les romanciers français de son temps* (1931), 38 f., claims the influence of Wace on the episode. In the adventure with the giant of Mont Saint-Michel, the only parallel with Chrétien that deserves any consideration is the meeting with a lamenting (old) lady with rent raiment who is asked to explain why she weeps, and tells of the abduction and ill-treatment of another person (a maiden).

[12] *Erec*, 4552-4878.

to the fortress is to be seen in an episode of *Le Livre d'Artus* that draws on the Encounter at the Perilous Bridge (p. 137 f.). The latter does not hold a position in the Fair Unknown type of story which corresponds to that of this section in *Erec et Enide*, but Chrétien still manages to run parallel to the sequence in the original, as will be evident when I consider what happens at Limors.

Having been struck by the heroine's beauty and greatly desiring her, the Count forcibly marries Enide, and then has tables set up and food prepared for the evening meal. They make Enide sit down and place a table before her. The Count, sitting opposite Enide at the table, begins to be angry at his failure to console her, urges Enide to forget her grief, assuring her that mourning never revives the dead, and tells her to rejoice at the marriage, which has drawn her out of poverty and raised her to riches. Warning Enide not to anger him, he issues his invitation to the meal: "Eat, now that I invite you to do so." But Enide refuses, saying that she will never eat or drink until Erec eats first, whose body is lying there in the hall. The Count declares this is impossible and threatens Enide, but she remains adamant. Then he loses his temper and hits her in the face, she shrieks, and the Count's men protest that their lord should be ashamed of having struck her because she will not eat.

This is a very interesting example of Chrétien's treatment of his source, for he has taken a scene there at the corresponding location and turned it on its head. We have already found it represented, in so far as it concerns eating, in the pleasant meal in the open while the intelligent squire busies himself with service (p. 179 f.). Following the Rescue from Two Giants in the original, when the hero has returned to the emissary after his victory, they sit together happily and reconciled at a supper laid on the grass and have a meal in which they find much enjoyment (p. 89), no doubt all the more in that the giants are stretched out dead, gone beyond recall. Whereas Enide, sitting with the Count at a table set for supper, in her grief refuses to enjoy the meal because Erec is lying there apparently dead. An invitation to the meal that has been laid occurs at the point in *Ipomedon* II which corresponds, when the emissary invites the hero to eat the meal with her after his victory over the gigantic abductor Creon (p. 113). Now, whereas the Count's anger grows, in the source the emissary's anger has gone.

What with the clamour that is going on, Erec revives, rises up and strikes the Count dead with his sword. Confusion arises as all give way before him, crying: "Flee, flee, here comes the dead man!" Erec and Enide make their way to the court-yard and find a stable-boy leading Erec's steed to water, all equipped with bridle and saddle. Thus, in a manner somewhat reminiscent of the escape from the amorous Count (p. 183 f.), and so that from the Ile d'Or, Erec and Enide get away.

The emissary's invitation to the hero, signifying her desire for reconciliation, does not impose acceptance on the hero. But the Count enforces union upon Enide and tries to compel her to accept the position. This is the fulfilment of what nearly came to pass in the Escape from the Amorous Count, so that the mistress of the Ile d'Or, in her intention to gain possession of the beautiful person she has fallen in love with at first sight, is reflected once more, with the enforcement this time actually exercised. The echoing at Limors of the escape in the adventure with the amorous Count may then be compared with that of the forest night-watch in Enide's vigil at the lodgings: an experience in the original has two renderings, with the second another step away, though its connection is still identifiable from its context (p. 184). Thus the Refusal to Eat at Limors, like the Escape from the Amorous Count, is compounded with elements from three places in the source, with the core situation related to an occurrence at the corresponding location there.

As in the case of the amorous Count, I have found for the Count of Limors a complex origin in relation to the Fair Unknown type of tale. A fresh figure who is brought on to a scene derived from the Encounter at the Perilous Bridge, he also corresponds to the emissary inviting the hero to the meal which has been set, as well as to the mistress of the Ile d'Or with her compulsive desire to have him under her control. And once more the combination produces a new character, but even more obviously than before, as the author handles his source material with even greater freedom. We have no parallel there—it is to be found instead in *Orson de Beauvais*—for the marriage enforced on a presumed widow, who cannot be made to eat the meal after the wedding, and whose original husband returns from supposed death to strike the villain down at mealtime and to repossess his wife (p. 33). The new matter includes such scenes as the Count coming upon Enide in her sad situation and trying to console her, his attempt to force her to eat and be merry, as he hits her and insists that now they are married he can do with her as he pleases, and Enide refusing to be consoled by the Count and exclaiming that she will not eat until her apparently dead husband eats first. Dramatic irony is introduced when the Count says this is impossible, whereupon the corpse rises and smites him, and excitement, as all take to flight in terror at the dead man who has come to life, and Erec leaps upon his horse and goes off holding Enide before him.

RECONCILIATION SCENE[13] (RS)

As Erec rides away with Enide from Limors, their affectionate reconciliation occurs, when the hero says he has put her fully to the test, is certain she loves him, loves her more than ever before, and pardons her *se vos rien m'avez mesdit*. The reconcilement, which in the source is associated with the meal after the giants have been killed (pp. 89, 111, 113), in Chrétien comes immediately after the episode in which the emissary's invitation to that meal is reflected.

The double relationship it bears to the original is like two sides of a coin: obverse, in that Enide has spoken *mesdisance* of Erec and is now pardoned; reverse, because we have a Chevalier Mesdisant openly acknowledging to a patient and courteous lady that the quality he has doubted in her is now proved

13 *Erec*, 4879-97.

to the hilt. But they are a husband and wife who have progressed from the break-down in their relations to being reunited in love. On this important theme Chrétien has strung the adventures of the ride from Estregales (p. 172), just as those in the original are put upon the corresponding string with the Departure from Arthur's Court.

SECOND ENCOUNTER WITH GUIVRET[14] (6 = III)

Erec and Enide continue to ride away from Limors. Then there takes place on that moonlit night the clash with Guivret which, with the substitution of a mistaken attack by a rescuer for an assault in revenge, corresponds to the Attack by Three Avengers (p. 90 f.), with the hero's companion appealing to the adversary not to assail a man in his condition, as that would be shameful and wrong conduct.

At the same time, we have matter drawn from another episode in the original, the Encounter with a Huntsman (p. 91 f.), whose influence on the Second Encounter with Guivret has been noted by M. Mills.[15] As in *Lybeaus*, fully-armed men are assembled in large numbers by their leader, who takes them threateningly towards their objective, but here Limors and not the hero, for they come to rescue Enide. When Erec espies them, he makes Enide hide behind a hedge and declares he will not fail to resist the assault, which is like Lybeaus at the corresponding point advising his companion to withdraw into the woodland, because he is intent on facing the enemy. When the clash comes, Guivret deals such a blow that he strikes Erec down quite helpless. A stunning stroke is delivered by the huntsman-lord in *Lybeaus*, as Mills observes; but the hero is not struck to the ground. So I compare instead the abrupt end of the clash, not only with the first antagonist in the Attack by Three Avengers in *Lybeaus* and the corresponding combat of *Ipomedon* II, the fight with Malgis (p. 113),[16] but also in the Encounter with a Huntsman in *Wigalois*, the equivalent adventure in *Durmart*, and the Escape from the Amorous Count in Chrétien himself, in a corresponding encounter (p. 184 f.), where in all cases it is the hero who gives his adversary the blow that sends him helpless upon the ground. In the Second Encounter with Guivret we have a change from hostility,[17] as in the Encounter with a Huntsman, where Lybeaus is taken to the huntsman's castle; while Durmart is given a hunting dog to help him find the Queen he seeks, and the amorous Count repents. Thus, more than before, Guivret corresponds to the huntsman-lord.

14 *Erec*, 4898-5073.
15 Mills, *art. cit.*, 39-46.
16 *Lybeaus*, 475-80, L 502-4; *Ipomedon*, 8215-18.
17 Guivret recognizes Erec as his friend, which puts to use the motif of the unwitting encounter that ends in recognition, on which is based the Meeting with Arthur and His Company (p. 190), and that existed in the Encounter at the Perilous Bridge (p. 139 f.), where the unwitting encounter was that of enemies.

But instead of coming with his army in revenge Guivret arrives in rescue, because the dwarf-king has been introduced into the original material. When Huon blows the magic horn, Auberon hears it from his own forest region and right away, by magic, arrives leading a massive army in rescue.[18] Comparably, in the short space of time that has elapsed since the Count of Limors took Erec to his castle and decided to marry Enide, Guivret has heard the news, immediately assembled his army, and marched all this way towards Limors.

A motif whose suspension has lasted since the First Encounter with Guivret (p. 188) is now completed. Erec accepts Guivret's invitation to go with him to a castle of his to have his wounds cared for, like Lybeaus at the huntsman's castle.

STAY AT GUIVRET'S CASTLE[19] (RS RRD)

The clash between Erec and Guivret is followed by a midnight meal, with the little king offering pies and wine to the hero and his lady companion, like the dwarf in a scene on the eventful night in the source (p. 180). It is adapted to a situation where the hero is so weak that he eats like a sick man and has to be given watered wine. The hero is invited to eat the meal by both Enide and Guivret (5123: *andui de mangier le semonent*), as Enide has been by the Count of Limors (4775: *mangiez, quant je vos an semoing*), in matter also related to that same scene (p. 192).

They go to sleep where they are, and leave in the morning for Guivret's castle, even as the original hero, in the Return of the Rescued Damsel (p. 157), departs in the morning for the castle which belongs to the father of the maiden saved in the Rescue from Two Giants. This means that Chrétien preserves the resorting to a castle which in the source took place just before the Jousting for Hospitality (p. 164 f.). By the father of the rescued damsel Lybeaus is presented with *ryche wede, scheld and armes bryght, and also a noble stede* as he leaves,[20] and at the equivalent point Guivret bestows on Enide an excellent palfrey with splendid harness.

It can be seen that the events of one night in the source, together with the associated departure next morning to the castle, have been dealt with as a unit by Chrétien. Compare his handling of the Ile d'Or Episode, drawn on for a series of episodes culminating with the Escape from the Amorous Count, which evidently has the function of reflecting the original episode overall, from the offer of love and the domain to the escape from the city (p. 183 f.). Similarly, we have a series of episodes in Chrétien that begins with a Rescue from Two Giants and ends with one which takes us from a midnight meal in the forest to a castle next day.

At the castle, Guivret's sisters so look after Erec that before the end of a

18 *Huon de Bordeaux*, 3855-71, 4509-29, 6668-84.
19 *Erec*, 5074-5318.
20 *Lybeaus*, 700-5.

fortnight he feels no further pain, even as Lybeaus is healed by the end of a fortnight at the huntsman's castle (cf. p. 190), though this may well be an unauthentic fulfilment of an invitation to the castle to have wounds healed.[21] Compare the Meeting with Greoreas (p. 136 ff.), who is said to be in dire need of a physician to heal his wounds, and recovers through the bandaging treatment by Gawain in *Perceval* II. This is a fulfilment of a formula in the original, to judge by another adaptation of the Encounter at the Perilous Bridge, a combat with Guinganbresil in *Le Livre d'Artus*, in which the hero remarks that his opponent's wound is in great need of healing, and the bandaged man is taken away in dire condition to the fortress (p. 137 f.).

In the original story, the hero departs from the castle with the emissary to continue on his mission, but Erec and Enide leave Guivret's castle to go to Arthur's court. However, Guivret accompanies them on their journey, so that we have a semblance of the cavalcade in the source, which means that the introduction of the dwarf-king into the material was favoured by his fitting into this pattern. Moreover, Enide rides a mount with such resplendent harness that she reminds us of the emissary as she is described when she first appears on the scene, arriving at Arthur's court.[22]

ARRIVAL AT BRANDIGAN[23] (7 = **VII**)

This episode, being equivalent to the Jousting for Hospitality (p. 99 ff.), also corresponds to the Overnight Stay with the Boatman (p. 141 ff.) in *Perceval* II. Like the riders in these, they come in sight of the domain, but in both of Chrétien's romances the region is not the destination to which the hero is being led on a mission, which it is in the Fair Unknown type of tale. The domain comes into view in the course of a ride, in *Erec and Enide* as they are journeying to Arthur's court. From Guivret's warning not to enter Brandigan because of its *molt mal trespas* it could well appear that the adventure there is as unavoidable as *la costume male* in the Jousting for Hospitality, but in fact it is only the hospitality of Evrain that cannot be avoided. And in the source the hero insists on going to ask for lodgings in spite of being warned about the jousting custom, whereas in Chrétien the hero does so without knowing any more about the adventure than its name and its danger, that knights from many lands have come to accomplish it and have not returned. Guivret does not wish to tell

---

21 Cf. *Descouneus*, 1666-72, where the hero, far from having received attention after his encounter with the huntsman, arrives in battered armour at the city of the Sparrowhawk Contest.

22 *Descouneus*, 149 ff.; *Lybeaus*, 118 f.; *Ipomedon*, 7943 ff.

Guivret brings hawks and hunting dogs for Erec and Enide, and in the original a hunting dog is acquired in the Encounter with a Huntsman and taken along on the ride, while the bird won in the Sparrowhawk Contest is found accompanying the cavalcade in *Wigalois* and *Papegau*, having been presented in the former to the emissary, who rejoices in the possession of both gifts (*Wigalois*, 3234-64).

23 *Erec*, 5319-5623.

him what more he knows because it would not fail to spur Erec to undertake the adventure. Thus the mystery is made to begin.

The Island Fortress

In the original, as shown by a comparison of *Descouneus/Lybeaus, Carduino*, and *Perceval* II, there was a Cité Gaste in the domain for the Accomplishment of the Mission (pp. 102 f., 143 ff.), but Chrétien does not provide this striking feature at Brandigan. Nor does the land in *Erec et Enide* have what particularly distinguishes the region in *Wigalois/Papegau*. The fine castle where the Accomplishment of the Mission takes place is a habitation of ladies at Chastel Perilleux (*Papegau*), and we are told that the magician Roaz had only women at Glois (*Wigalois*). As for the lady's stronghold, Roimunt (*Wigalois*) possesses a large number of beautiful, richly-dressed, noble and excellent ladies, while La Roche sans Paour (*Papegau*) is full of maidens. Indeed, in *Papegau* the kingdom is the Royaume aux Damoiselles.[24] *Perceval* II confirms that in *conte d'aventure* X there was a castle inhabited by ladies at the Accomplishment of the Mission and where the Queen and the princess live. We thus have to do here with the City or Fortress of Maidens (Chastel as Puceles), a well-known Arthurian motif, which is not only lacking in *Erec et Enide*, but also in *Descouneus, Lybeaus,* and *Carduino*. However, it will be found that the Fortress of Maidens does bear on Brandigan.

Let us examine the topography of Maidenland as depicted in the Swiss *Lanzelet* by Ulrich von Zatzikhoven, which was based on an Anglo-Norman romance written by 1194. It is a region that is splendidly broad and long, with a beautiful enclosure inhabited by ladies, and it is ruled by a fay-queen. The fine castle, adorned with great art, shining like a star-cluster inside and out with gold, stands on a crystal mountain round like a ball. They fear no foreign enemy nor any king's host, for around the land goes the sea, and a wall so strong that it is insurmountable, while the gateway, the only means of entry, is made of a diamond. There they are without fear (*âne vorhte*).[25] Corresponding to this description, *Papegau* says in general of its Royaume aux Damoiselles that it is very beautiful, almost surrounded by the sea, and its name is Ile Fort.[26] The impregnability of the domain is obviously needed for a realm of women to be safe.

Such a topography is reflected in *Wigalois/Papegau* at the castles inhabited by ladies, and more obviously where the Accomplishment of the Mission takes place. Chastel Perilleux is situated on a round mountain that is not high, but is the most beautiful and the strongest in the world, and the land is surrounded by a deep, wide, and dark stream which can only be crossed by a narrow bridge leading to a gate, and beyond lies the most beautiful and the strongest castle in the world. Glois is high, large, and round, and to reach it one has to cross a great stream by a similar passage, on which there is a gate. The stronghold

24 *Wigalois*, 4101-26, 8040-51; *Papegau*, 25/28 f., 74/7-75/28.
25 *Lanzelet*, 193-225. 26 *Papegau*, 25/26-9.

beyond has a marble wall of red and green variegated with gold, shining like a mirror and sparkling within with gold and precious stones, while inside there is a large and beautiful palace.[27] A less obvious reflection of Maidenland topography can be seen in the land that begins with the entry to the domain and extends to the lady's stronghold. A narrow pass leads to the Royaume aux Damoiselles, and at the end of it, as the only means of entry to the land, there is a castle (p. 151). The lady's fortress itself stands on a mountain, and fittingly preserves the motif of impregnability: it is capable of being easily held against a king's host (*Wigalois*), and in it they are without fear, as shown in *Papegau* by its name, *sans paour* being the same as *âne vorhte* in *Lanzelet*.[28] Evidently, the replacement of the bridge by a narrow pass changed the domain from an island, which the name Ile Fort indicates, into the peninsula described in *Papegau*.

Maidenland is therefore doubly reflected in *Wigalois/Papegau*. On the other hand, the capital of the domain is not shown to be a Castle of Maidens, but an abandoned stronghold inhabited by ghosts, lying in ruins in *Papegau*, while in *Wigalois* sounds of lamentation and distress are heard from it at night (while it burns), and yet it is still (and unburned) during the day. This bears the motif of the Cité Gaste. In the Approach to the Abandoned Castle, Wigalois enters the land of Korntin by a bridge over a terribly deep ditch and passes through a gate. Beyond is the splendid castle, with a marble wall shining like glass and skilfully constructed, within which there stands a rich palace built with great art, of clear crystal so that one can see everything in it,[29] even as in *Perceval* II the palace has such windows of clear glass that one can view all who enter as soon as they pass through the entrance (pp. 141-3).

With the region as a complex in *Wigalois/Papegau*, of three lands containing a Fortress of Maidens as the lady's stronghold, a Cité Gaste, and another Fortress of Maidens where the magician is destroyed, it seems logical to see in each a different reflection of the original single place, which is all at once lady's stronghold, Cité Gaste, and fortress occupied by the magician(s) in *Descouneus*, *Lybeaus*, and *Carduino*. This should mean that Senaudon (Synadoun), whose lady is Queen of Wales in Renaut de Beaujeu, is not the original location, but that in the *Descouneus/Lybeaus* tale (Y) it has replaced the Royaume aux Damoiselles and its enchanted stronghold that is restored by the hero to its former condition as a Castle of Maidens. Compare the transformation, in the Second Continuation of *Perceval*, which causes the hero to be very puzzled at what happens. The place he enters appears to be desolate, but later becomes a Castle of Maidens full of life.

Perceval arrives at a deep and wide river, on the other side of which he sees the most beautiful country and meadowland he has ever beheld, and a very powerful fortified town with a castle and a large hall, and a wall built of coloured

---

27 *Wigalois*, 6767-79, 7059-72, 7273-83, 7307-11; *Papegau*, 70/23-31, 72/20-33, 73/18-20.
28 *Wigalois*, 3630-8; *Papegau*, 26/3-5, 59/32, 76/27 f.
29 *Wigalois*, 4297-4318, 4510-4608; *Papegau*, 65/5-7.

marble blocks, vermilion and yellow. The Cité Gaste in *Descouneus* also has a fine and strong wall constructed with marble blocks of several colours.[30] Perceval crosses the bridge, passes through the gate, and comes to the hall, outside the door of which there is a *table* or gong of brass with a steel hammer hanging from a silver chain.[31] Inside the hall he finds no sign of habitation, though he searches everywhere, and he goes out again and strikes the gong several times with the hammer, which makes the stronghold shake and resound with the clang. He persists, with the sound threatening to bring the hall tumbling down, and it springs to life with maidens. He is disarmed, and in the hall, which is now fully and richly draped, he is given a rich mantle and taken to the lady of the fortress. He finds her in a room full of beautiful damsels who give him such a welcome that he feels his heart thrill. Tables are laid, they have a meal, conversation follows, and the lady tells Perceval that the place is the Fortress of Maidens. That the hall was so *agastie* at first, but now is full of people, is explained as due to the intention to cause cowardly strangers to depart, when they arrive and find the hall *gaste*. Perceval stays the night, but in the morning he wakes up to find himself lying in the open, the fortress having vanished.[32]

The initial desolation of this place supports my identification of the Cité Gaste with the Castle of Maidens. Further evidence for it comes from Chrétien himself. In the episode of Pesme Aventure in *Yvain*, the hero, accompanied by his lion and a damsel who has come to fetch him on a mission, arrives at a fortified town, and as the day is drawing to a close they enter it. This is his very last adventure before he reaches Arthur's court (cf. the Arrival at Brandigan), and the scene is related to the Jousting for Hospitality and the Accomplishment of the Mission. In the Chastel de Pesme Aventure, a lady (like the emissary in the Fair Unknown type of tale) warns him not to spend the night up in the castle, informs him the custom in this city is such that they dare not receive in their houses any gentleman who comes from outside the region, and advises him to turn back. But Yvain answers he does not know where to find a lodging-place this night, and presses on to the castle, where a gate-keeper lets him in. The hero learns that he may expect great shame, and eventually comes to a large hall where he finds no-one to answer him. They pass through the house, and rather mysteriously—for they never hand them over to anyone, as Chrétien emphasizes—their horses are stabled, by those who already consider Yvain's as theirs although its owner is still perfectly hale and hearty. Thus the same penalty for defeat is expected as in the Jousting for Hospitality, the loss of his steed. Yvain reaches a garden, where he discovers a rich man reclining at his ease and whiling away the time by listening to a romance read to him by his daughter, which brings to mind the rich host of the Jousting for Hospitality, who is also met out of doors diverting himself (p. 149). The hero is received joyfully, lodged with great honour and given an excellent evening meal.

30 *Descouneus*, 2859-66.
31 This *table* is set on four small pillars, but in *Yvain*, 212, such a *table* is suspended.
32 *Perceval*, Second Continuation, 24241-728.

The next morning, the master of the house informs him there is established in this city a terrible custom that he has to maintain, and which no knight who lodges there can possibly escape. This corresponds to the Jousting for Hospitality custom, but is attached to the equivalent of the Accomplishment of the Mission (p. 102 f.). The custom at the Chastel de Pesme Aventure turns out to be that of sustaining an attack by two of the lord's men, who are born of a woman and a demon, so that they are a devilish pair of brothers, like the enchanters Mabon and Evrain in *Descouneus*. If Yvain conquers both, he will receive by right the city, all the land, and the lord's beautiful daughter as wife, which corresponds closely enough to what the hero of the Fair Unknown type gains by his defeat of Mabon and Evrain. The strange couple in *Yvain*, who are called giants, appear together, dressed as participants in a judicial combat (*chanpions*), with bodies protected and heads *desarmez*.[33] They insist that the battle must be that of Yvain alone against both of them, which sounds like the familiar pattern, but we do not have the two successive encounters of *Descouneus*. Instead, Yvain finds he has to fight both opponents simultaneously.[34] The hero defeats them with the help of his lion, and one of the two adversaries is killed, as he is in the tale of the Fair Unknown. Then Yvain refuses the reward and departs.[35]

The dressing as *chanpions* is peculiar, when Yvain is not so arrayed and we have two against one. Chrétien has dressed the opponents in this manner in order to bring about the same fate as that which befalls Mabon, as can be seen from the way that Yvain deals with the adversary whom he slays. He has turned away, distracted by the presence of the lion, and at that moment Yvain cuts off his undefended head:

> La teste nue et le col nu
> li a li gloz abandoné,
> et il li a tel cop doné
> que la teste del bu li ret,
> si soavet que mot n'an set.
>
> (*Yvain*, 5648 ff.)

Mabon's helmet is knocked off by Descouneus, leaving *la teste desarmee*, and as Mabon shrinks from him, turning away his head, the hero strikes and kills him:

> La coife ne le pot tenir
> Que le cief n'en fesist partir.
>
> (*Li Biaus Descouneus*, 3057 ff.)

Thus the resemblance of the episode of Pesme Aventure to material of the Fair Unknown type is perfectly recognizable. In relation to it, the motifs in *Yvain* are so arranged as to be made intriguing. There is an apparently-deserted

---

33 Loomis, *op. cit.*, 323-5.
34 The hero in *Lybeaus* fights both opponents together.   35 *Yvain*, 5101-5803.

hall that later turns out to be the well-populated house of the host, who is very hospitable but imposes *une molt fiere deablie* next morning, and who keeps as his retainers the devilish pair to be fought, yet rejoices at their destruction.

In addition, he has in his grounds three hundred maidens, shamefully ill-treated and exploited as if in some dreadful factory, who are kept working there at weaving and embroidery in dire condition and bowed down with woe. These damsels are confined in a meadow (*prael*) that is enclosed with large stakes, and they belong to the Isle of Maidens. It is explained that their King once happened to come to the Chastel de Pesme Aventure and was forced by the demonic brothers to ransom himself with the annual payment of thirty of his maidens, on the condition that he would be relieved from this tribute, and the damsels delivered, when the two villains are conquered in battle. They do not expect ever to be liberated, and what grieves them greatly is often to see young and excellent knights slain, paying dearly for their lodging, as they also expect Yvain to do, losing his renown or buying his life by ransom, all of which is reminiscent of the Jousting for Hospitality. But with Yvain's victory the wretched maidens are released from captivity at last, and they rejoice greatly on leaving their prison.

The presence of these damsels at the Chastel de Pesme Aventure, and the region they belong to, is to do with the Isle of Maidens being the destination of the hero's mission in the original tale of the Fair Unknown type. This I now confirm from a Castle of Maidens in an early non-Arthurian romance. According to Delbouille, Chrétien's description of Brandigan is based on that of Babiloine in *Floire et Blancheflor*[36] (before 1170), and indeed there is a striking resemblance between Brandigan and the city that is the end of Floire's quest for Blancheflor. But it turns out that the author of this *roman idyllique*, the genesis of which has been a problem, adapts to a setting of *turquerie* material from the Ile d'Or Episode, the Jousting for Hospitality, the Accomplishment of the Mission, and the Wedding to a Queen, which establishes Babiloine as corresponding to the region which is their hero's destination.[37]

Babiloine extends for twenty leagues (*Dure vint liues tout d'un sens*), and is thus larger than Senaudon (*Cinc liues duroit la cités*). A high wall encloses Babiloine, so strong that at no point does it fear assault (*De nule part ne crient asaut*). It fears neither king nor Saracen general (*ne doute roi ne aumaçor*), and not even the Emperor of Rome could achieve anything (A 1616 f.). No-one could conquer Babiloine by war. It is not enclosed by water, as Senaudon is by two roaring streams, but we have a very deep and wide water passage, crossed by a bridge at the end of which there is a large tower belonging to the bridge-keeper (p. 148). Senaudon is a magnificent fortress, and so is Babiloine, in the

---

36 M. Delbouille, "A propos de la patrie et de la date de *Floire et Blanchefleur*", *Mélanges de linguistique et de littérature romanes offerts à Mario Roques* (1952), iv, 92 ff.

37 See Index s.v. *Floire* (material of F.U. type). The hero Floris is mentioned by Guiraut de Cabreira in *Ensenhamen*, 170, for the date of which see p. 157 above.

middle of which stands a *tor d'antiquité* all of marble, like the *palais d'antiquité* at Senaudon. Of such a city we apparently have a reflection in the fortress before which occurs the meeting with Gornemant de Gorhaut in *Perceval* I, which is equivalent to the Jousting for Hospitality (p. 148 f.). Here we find a splendid and powerful stronghold, built on a *roche naïve*, and the castle in the middle is large and strong. The sea beats at the foot of the outer wall, which has four smaller towers (cf. the high towers along the wall of Senaudon), and before the *chastelet*, described as round, lies a deep, black torrent rushing towards the sea, and crossed by a bridge which is strongly fortified and has upon it a tower. We do not learn the name of this place, and one naturally assumes that the castle in the middle is occupied by Gornemant when one hears that Perceval stays at the fortress with him. But the castle in the middle of Babiloine is inhabited by a hundred and forty beautiful damsels, from whom it is called *la tour as puceles* (A 1700).[38]

At Brandigan, even as we have neither Cité Gaste nor Castle of Maidens, so the construction of the place is not shown to be magnificent—we only know that it is a fine fortress. Yet we still find much of the topography associated with Maidenland, the Ile Fort, the strongholds inhabited by ladies in *Wigalois* and *Papegau*, and the city with the Castle of Maidens in *Floire et Blancheflor*. In particular, there are verbal agreements with the description of this last. Evrain's kingdom comes into view as a fortress totally enclosed by a wall, and beneath, describing a circle, there runs a very deep stream, roaring and rushing like a storm, and crossed by a bridge that leads to the gate of the city. The place is so strong that it fears neither king nor emperor (*roi n'anpereor ne dote*), and if the royal domain of France, together with the whole kingdom and all who live as far as Liege, were ranged about to lay a siege, they would never take it in their lives. At no point does it fear assault (*de nule part ne crient asaut*), for the island on which the city stands stretches away fifteen leagues or more (*plus dure de quinze lies*), and within the enclosure grows all that a strong fortress needs, supplying it with fruit, wheat, and wine.[39] If it had no wall or tower, but only the stream that surrounds the place, it would still be so secure and strong that it would have no fear of anyone.

38 *Floire*, 1599-1700; *Descouneus*, 2776-84, 2801-18, 2854-70; *Perceval*, 1305-50, 1884-92.
Babiloine also has features of the living city at the Ile d'Or, as described in *Descouneus*, 1875-1930. Both are full of towers held by vassals: *ou estont li baron chasé* (*Floire*); *tot sont casé del castiel* (*Descouneus*). The Emir's castle is sustained by great pillars of white marble like crystal, and above is set a carbuncle which shines at night like the sun, so that merchants and others, by land or sea, are guided by it. The palace at the Ile d'Or, made of what looks like crystal, is supported by twenty towers, a carbuncle above shines at night like the sun, and the city is a port to which merchants come. For matter at Babiloine adapted from the Ile d'Or Episode, see p. 183 n. 54 above. For another element in *Floire* which has come from the same episode, see p. 124 f. above.

39 At Korntin, which contains a reflection of the Cité Gaste, the hero crosses a bridge into a well-cultivated land with vines growing in abundance (*Wigalois*, 4535-8). Babiloine is well supplied with fruit (p. 207).

The Meeting with the Host

The connection with the old spatial relations of the scene is not obvious, not only because there is no Cité Gaste at Brandigan, but owing to the omission of the Jousting for Hospitality in *Carduino*, the alteration to two cities a day's journey apart in *Descouneus*, and the obscurities in *Lybeaus*. I shall seek to determine it as follows.

Lybeaus has to go for the jousting custom into the field outside the castle gate, at first sight the gate of the castle through which he has just come to ask for lodgings, at the entrance to Synadoun. Yet, on his defeat, the people throughout Synadoun would pelt him with refuse. In the same circumstances, Descouneus would have to return under a shower of refuse through Galigan.[40] Such a fate is realized in an adventure experienced by Garahes in the First Continuation of *Perceval*, which gives him the fear that he has brought upon himself the same loss of renown that we see the Fair Unknown being warned about:

> "And thanne to thy lyves ende,
> In whett stede that thow wende,
> For coward werst thou knowe."
>
> (*Lybeaus Desconus*, 1501 ff.)

One day Garahes comes to the most beautiful plain he has ever seen, and a wide and deep river, by which rises the most splendid fortified town in the world, with a magnificent marble wall of variegated colour. He enters through the gate to look for lodgings, but finds the place apparently deserted and passes along to the castle, where he goes with his horse into the hall, then explores the chambers, yet still sees no-one. At last he discovers in a garden a tall wounded knight lying on a couch in a tent, tended by a damsel. But he is forced to joust there with the Petit Chevalier, a handsome dwarf, who vanquishes him and explains the custom laid down in this garden, that all those he conquers are set at the end of a year to the shameful trade of weaving—already a thousand such knights are busy at it. Garahes may depart, but must return in a year's time. He goes back to the hall, which is now found to be fully inhabited, the first room that he comes to being crowded with knights occupied with decorative needle-work, who taunt him with his defeat. Then, when he passes through the town, this time it is filled with the citizens, who pelt him with bits of meat and call him coward. Garahes returns to Arthur's court and conceals the shameful experience of the garden, *sa honte del vergier*.[41]

This episode clearly corresponds to that of Pesme Aventure (pp. 199-201).[42] The knights made to undertake decorative needlework must be derived from the damsels of the Isle of Maidens woefully kept busy at it, an activity that they

40 *Descouneus*, 2533-44; *Lybeaus*, 1495-1500.
41 *Perceval*, First Continuation, 8608-9020.
42 Loomis, *op. cit.*, 321.

carry on happily at the Chastel as Puceles in the Second Continuation of *Perceval*.[43] We have the defeat incurring the penalty due in the Jousting for Hospitality in the tale of the Fair Unknown—disgrace and departure under a shower of refuse—instead of the hospitality with honour before the climactic encounter. And instead of the host we find the wounded knight and the Petit Chevalier.[44] As in *Yvain*, and differently from the Fair Unknown type, the meeting with the maintainer of the custom occurs after going through the deserted hall. But in common with both those other stories is a ride through the town, which appears in *Descouneus*. Here the hero crosses a bridge, enters through the gate into a fortified city and rides along the street to the castle. Similarly, in *Erec et Enide*, the hero crosses a bridge, passes through a gate into the fortified town and rides along the street.

Both Descouneus and Erec become the centre of interest for the inhabitants as they pass through the town, and cause much stir and discussion, but there is a notable distinction. The people of Galigan are looking forward with laughter[45] to the prospect of pelting Descouneus with refuse on his defeat, even as those of Synadoun are to be seen gathering it in readiness when Lybeaus arrives. Similarly, the people of the Chastel de Pesme Aventure receive Yvain shamefully, declaring that in this lodging-place he will suffer harm and shame, and as he heads towards the castle the crowd all shout aloud that such shame and woe will be done to him where he is going as he will never wish to recount (cf. Garahes).[46] But the scene at Brandigan, with the inhabitants admiring the hero, is comparable with that when Erec or Descouneus rides through the town of the Sparrowhawk Contest.[47] Yet the people of Brandigan also expect the hero to suffer harm in that place. They think it a pity that Erec is bound to die in the adventure for which the penalty for defeat is shame and death.

Before Descouneus reaches the castle in Galigan, Lanpart is met in the open playing chess, and he leads the hero into the place where the jousting custom is held.[48] The gate-keeper in *Floire et Blancheflor*, who is met at the foot of the Emir's castle in Babiloine, also plays chess, and with him the hero has a series of three contests held in the open before the castle (p. 148). He is the guardian of the entry to the castle within the city. From this type descends the adversary

---

43 *Perceval*, Second Continuation, 24521. The motif occurs with La Roche de Sanguin in *Perceval*, 8818 ff.:

> Maint bon vert drap riche et sanguin
> I tist on et mainte escarlate,
> Si'n i vent on molt et achate.

At the Chastel de Pesme Aventure, the maidens' toil enriches him for whom they work.

44 There are two figures at the corresponding point in the Fair Unknown type of tale (p. 147 f.).

45 On the adaptation of such material for the entry of Meraugis into the Cité sans Nom, see p. 217 below.

46 *Yvain*, 5106-35.

47 *Erec*, 747-73; *Descouneus*, 1655-84. Cf. p. 162 n. 10 above.

48 *Descouneus*, 2567-2614.

of the Encounter before La Roche, where the meeting occurs after the entry into the domain and before the gateway of the lady's stronghold, in *Papegau* the opponent leading the hero into the most beautiful meadow in the world, where they joust below the rocky height on which the fortress stands. In the equivalent Meeting with Guiromelant, who is found in a garden, Gawain is challenged to a duel at that very place, which is in the meadowland below the citadel of La Roche de Sanguin, and has been reached after encountering Orguelleus del Passage a l'Estroite Voie. And after his meeting with Sir Persaunte, who corresponds to Orguelleus del Passage, Gareth arrives at his destination and fights where Sir Ironsyde rides for the combat to be held, in a little vale under the lady's fortress (p. 152 f.). Again, in the Encounter at the Gateway of the Magician's Castle, the meeting occurs in *Wigalois* after the hero has passed through a gate on the bridge that lies below the gateway of Glois, before which he finds Adan von Alarie. At Chastel Perilleux, where the hero has seen before him the narrow bridge, the tower at the end of it, and the castle beyond, the encounter also happens after he has passed through a gate on the bridge, which is in that tower (p. 147 f.).[49]

But in *Lybeaus* the steward's tower (2096) is at the entry to Synadoun, and similarly the bridge-keeper in *Floire et Blancheflor*, who is met at the end of the bridge before his tower at Babiloine, is the guardian of the entry to the city. From my examination of The Rich Man at the Foot of the Castle (p. 147 ff.), it is evident that he has a close equivalent in Gornemant de Gorhaut in *Perceval* I, who is found on the bridge before a powerful fortress on a *roche naïve*. From this type descends the opponent in the Encounter at the Narrow Passage, who in *Papegau* is met in the open at the end of a pass, his castle being the entry to Ile Fort, where the lady's stronghold stands on the mountain behind (pp. 151, 198).[50] To the scene of the bridge-keeper sitting on a marble slab under a tree before Babiloine corresponds that of Adan von Alarie sitting on a step before the gateway of Glois and under a tree. Now which is the original, the guardian of the entry to the castle within the domain, or the guardian of the entry to the domain itself?

It can be seen, first of all, that the authentic picture is that of a meeting with the host before his own residence, for this is what we find with Lanpart, the bridge-keeper and the gate-keeper in *Floire*, Gornemant de Gorhaut, the boatman in *Perceval* II, and the adversary of the Encounter at the Narrow Passage. In the Encounter before La Roche the lady's stronghold has been made identical with the residence of the steward, and the Encounter at the Gateway of the Magician's Castle has amalgamated the combat from the Jousting for Hospitality with the guidance to the gateway of the castle where the hero is to accomplish his mission, which originally followed a night's lodging with the host-guide. This accounts for the meeting in these episodes being before the lady's or the magician's castle. Let us now shift our attention from the place of meeting to the

49 *Wigalois*, 6767-7194; *Papegau*, 72/34-73/38.
50 Cf. La Roche de Sanguin, on the cliff above the boatman's house (p. 143).

site of jousting. If Lybeaus is to be pelted throughout Synadoun after defeat, the field into which he rides for the jousting with the lady's steward (line 1561) cannot be outside the gate of Synadoun city, but outside the castle gate (line 1742) which must be that of the enchanted castle within. It follows therefore that an adaptation of the Jousting for Hospitality has retained a feature lost in tales of the Fair Unknown type that are extant, when the lady's steward, on the entry of Meraugis into the Cité sans Nom, rides with him through the town as the inhabitants gaze at the hero, talk together and look forward to the jousting, until the place is reached where the unavoidable custom begins (p. 217). There now becomes visible a reflection of the Jousting for Hospitality in the Approach to the Abandoned Castle, where the guide leads Wigalois from the entry of the land of Korntin to a marvellous and beautiful meadow that lies before the equivalent of the Cité Gaste (p. 210), even as in *Papegau* the opponent leads the hero for the jousting into the most beautiful meadow in the world before the gateway of the lady's stronghold. Thus the guardian of the entry to the domain is original, and the guardian of the entry to the castle within is his image, authentic in holding the contest with the hero before it but not in meeting him there.

In *Descouneus* not only is the steward's castle within a city, but the Cité Gaste is a separate fortress a day's journey away, which must be due to assimilation of the host's place to Brandigan, as indicated by the formation of the name Galigan. At Brandigan there is no meeting with a rich man on the bridge before the fortress, but within the city, as already with the gate-keeper in *Floire* (before 1170), the hero comes across the host before his own residence. But at Brandigan it is the King he meets, for the absence of the enchanted castle with its Queen promotes the host's residence to the chief habitation within the kingdom.

Hospitality with Honour

When they arrive, Evrain treats Enide with all the honour he can, and the guests praise their excellent reception. In the evening, they have everything in abundance at their meal that they could desire, fowl, venison, fruit, and several wines, but above all they receive friendly and pleasant treatment and are served with great joy. In the original, this was all due to delight at entertaining the champion fetched by the emissary from King Arthur, and fully tested. And stress was laid on this excellent hospitality. He who gains the victory in the jousting custom *ostel ara a grant honnor*, according to *Descouneus*, and from the fuller definition in *Wigalois* we see that he will have by way of amenity whatever he desires, for he will be given a good reception such as no-one would find elsewhere. Similarly, the boatman in *Perceval* II entertains Gawain to the best of his ability in his house, which is fit for a count to visit, at the evening meal Gawain is served with everything the host could provide, fowl, venison, and several wines, that night the hero has a host and lodgings such as give him pleasure, and he is greatly pleased with the service. The equivalent figure in

Perceval I, Gornemant de Gorhaut, is a rich host who treats the hero with great courtesy, and gives him a well-prepared evening meal at which there is plenty to eat and drink. With the rich host at the Chastel de Pesme Aventure, Chrétien asks his audience to hear now with what manner of hospitality the hero is received, and launches into a description of how he is lodged *a grant eise* and *grant enor*, as the master of the house orders. That night he is served at table with so many dishes that there are too many, and those who wait on him may well be exhausted with carrying them. In *Wigalois/Papegau*, it is the adversary of the Encounter at the Narrow Passage who has inherited the function of host along with that of the jousting condition (p. 151). Here, the Chevalier du Passage *les honnora et herberga moult aise tout a leur volonté, si furent bien servis et aise celle nuit,* while from Schaffilun they have a very good reception, and the host gives the hero a feast in the evening with an overflowing abundance of what he could have, as it suits him to take. From the excellent hospitality after the jousting in the original there also descends that in the Arrival at the Lady's Stronghold (following on the Encounter before La Roche), when Wigalois is welcomed with joy as the champion sent by Arthur, they deny him and the emissary neither amenity nor honour, and if they could devise anything more to please them it would have truly been carried out, for no knight delighted them better. At the evening meal greater honour has never been shown, neither before nor since, to anyone as is done there to the hero with pleasure. Most striking of all, however, is the parallel between what is served in *Erec et Enide* (cf. also *Perceval* II) and in *Floire et Blancheflor*, where to the host of the Fair Unknown type of story corresponds Daire, the bridge-keeper of Babiloine, whose hospitality is outstanding. At his house Floire is served richly (in vessels of gold and silver), there is great plenty of different wines, and an abundance of dishes with venison and several kinds of fowl, followed by fruits of every sort, for the city is well supplied with them.[51]

Floire, at the end of the meal given by his rich host, leaves off eating as he remembers his purpose in coming to the domain, and decides to speak to Daire of what he has at heart, just as Lybeaus, at the evening meal, broaches the subject of the adventure he has come to accomplish. There is parallelism here with Erec, but what is on the mind of Chrétien's hero is the gaining not of a lady but of the Joie de la Cort. Again, from the original hero Erec differs because he has not come to the domain in order to carry out a mission for which a champion had been sought, so that, like Gawain in *Perceval* II, and also Floire, he is zealous to undertake the adventure on his own initiative. The host tries to dissuade all three of these heroes from it, in contrast to what happens in the versions of the Fair Unknown type, but the agreement between *Erec et Enide*, *Perceval* II, and *Floire* suggests that in the common source the host,

51 *Descouneus,* 2529-32; *Wigalois,* 1944-50, 3337-41, 3468-74, 3973-4007, 4281-9; *Papegau,* 58/23-9; *Perceval,* 1549-78, 7473-93; *Yvain,* 5391-5439; *Floire,* 1485-1508.

distressed at the thought of death befalling the hero, first advised him not to undertake the adventure because of its danger, and then, when the hero showed his determination, agreed to see to the arrangement. However, Lybeaus, Gawain, and Floire are all told of the circumstances in the land,[52] while on the contrary Evrain gives away so little that the mystery in *Erec et Enide* is complete—the hero knows only the great peril, the glory to be gained, and the name of the adventure, so that significance resides in the way he is drawn on irresistibly.

ENCOUNTER WITH MABONAGRAIN[53]   (8 = VIII)

When he rises in the morning, Erec receives arms and armour from Evrain to wear, which he puts on. This seems to complete a motif from the source that *Erec et Enide* partially reflects in Guivret's gift of a rich palfrey to Enide (p. 195). An old, grey-haired man of rank bestows arms, armour, and a steed on Lybeaus, and the hero wears this armour for his next formal combat (p. 164 f.). If we take account of the shift of episodes to the beginning of the ride in the source of *Lybeaus*, this bestowal originally occurred just before the hero reached his destination (p. 157), so that the wearing of the presented armour by Lybeaus for the Sparrowhawk Contest corresponds to Erec doing the same for his combat with Mabonagrain.

In *Erec et Enide*, the host does not conduct the hero to the gateway of an enchanted stronghold, but leads him out of the fortress to a magic garden for the combat. The putting of a different picture within the frame taken from the Accomplishment of the Mission (p. 102 f.) is a phenomenon we have seen illustrated in Chrétien by the First Arrival at La Roche de Sanguin (p. 143 ff.) in *Perceval* II. What he has used in *Erec et Enide* for this purpose, while still preserving the theme of delivery from imprisonment in an enchanted place, I shall now investigate.

The Enchanted Garden

A close analogue to Chrétien's marvellous garden is that belonging to the Queen of Danemarche in the thirteenth-century *Le Livre d'Artus*.[54] The Queen possesses a very beautiful garden with all kinds of fruit-trees, which by magic is enclosed by air, as in *Erec et Enide*. It has only one entry and one exit, and grows some fruit that affects a man's capacity to leave the place. Chrétien's garden also has magic fruit, which can be eaten inside, but if taken with one the way out cannot be found. In *Le Livre d'Artus*, eating that fruit makes one lose all desire for chivalry or to leave the place, and causes one to find in it all the pleasures that can be imagined or devised. Here the magic fruit is on a tree laden at all seasons with attractive red apples—Chrétien describes his garden as having flower and fruit all the year round—and the lovely enclosure is full of knights and beautiful damsels.

---

52 *Lybeaus*, 1675-1734; *Perceval*, 7506-7647; *Floire*, 1509-1957.   53 *Erec*, 5624-6341.
54 E. Philipot, "Un épisode d'*Erec et Enide*: *La Joie de la Cour*—Mabon l'enchanteur", *Romania* XXV (1896), 272-5.

When knights penetrate the Queen of Danemarche's garden, they come to a tent under the enchanted apple-tree, where they are met by a tall knight with a very beautiful damsel (*la pucele du vergier*). She gives them the choice either oɪ undertaking combat with those who guard the place or of eating the apple she offers, and if they accept the fruit they will find themselves unable to leave. The enchantments can be destroyed by one who conquers the guardians. When this is achieved the prisoners of the garden are released, and the beautiful damsels who inhabit it are plunged in tears at the loss of their *amis*, the knights who have been conquered and killed.[55] In the similar account of the Val sans Retor in the *Vulgate Lancelot*, which is enclosed by air like a wall, the delightful spot is full of knights who have gone into it but thereafter can see neither the entrance nor the exit. The inability to leave stems from the nature of the knights, for other people can come and go without any trouble. In the Val sans Retor there is no delight that a knight should have that cannot be found, including the company of their *amies*. Within this beautiful vale the fay Morgain confines her own lover, and is found by Lancelot lying on a very beautiful and splendid couch in a tent. When he conquers the guardians of the place, that is the end of the imprisonment. The knights can now return to their close friends, who thought that they had lost them for ever, but Lancelot's action has harmed the damsels, since they have to do without the love-making in this convenient spot, and Morgain is annoyed at the destruction of the custom.[56]

In *Erec et Enide*, agreeing well with the tenor of such accounts are the damsel of the garden, found on a splendid couch under a tree, the lover whom she has confined in the delightful place enclosed by air, and her bursting into tears because the hour has come for her *ami* to leave the garden and return to his friends, to whom his release will give great joy.

Close to the enchanted garden in *Le Livre d'Artus* is the Queen's formidable castle on a *roche naïve*, with a large and splendid hall, and we are told that after the prisoners are released and the custom ended the place is handed over to the damsels of the garden and becomes the Fortress of Maidens. With its garden, it therefore corresponds to Maidenland in *Lanzelet*, which has a paradise of an enclosure that blooms all the year round as if in spring, and where the ladies who live there are full of happiness; those who spend any time in it never show sadness and always act with joy.[57] Brandigan is no Maidenland, but we have seen that it has much of the topography associated with this region, which was the destination of the hero's ride in the source (The Island Fortress, p. 197 ff.).

55 *Le Livre d'Artus*, ed. Sommer, vii, 170, 268, 298, 311-19.
56 *Vulgate Lancelot*, ed. Sommer, iv, 116-23.
The creation of these two places from which knights never return is by the ladies who possess them, to act as traps for knights. These localities are discussed by Loomis, *op. cit.*, 113.
57 *Lanzelet*, 202-8, 230-40.

That there was indeed a lovely enclosure walled by air in the lady's domain in the original story of the Fair Unknown type I can confirm from *Wigalois*, where it is found in the land of Korntin, which has the reflection of the enchanted castle (p. 198). Before the gateway of Korntin castle lies a beautiful meadow like a paradise, which is enclosed without a wall by a marvel ascribed to God, so that, though to the eyes it looks open, as in Chrétien the invisible wall acts as a complete barrier. A wonderful tree stands in the middle of the meadow, with delicious fragrance wafting from its flowers. In the Approach to the Abandoned Castle the animal guide enters this place, and its power is such that he becomes transformed into a man, the princess's dead father (a white-haired knight in *Papegau*), who instructs the hero about the mission, as the grey-haired guide Lanpart does before the gateway of the Cité Gaste (p. 102). The tree is in a country like a paradise in *Papegau*, full of sweet-smelling herbs, even as all medicinal herbs fill the garden at Brandigan. The guide leads the hero to the tree, one of the most beautiful that he has ever seen, with flowers of sweeter scent than anyone has known. The hero takes a flower from the tree, smells it, and its fragrance is so celestial that it fully satisfies him, and he has no desire to eat or drink. In *Wigalois*, the hero is given one of the flowers to protect him against the pernicious breath of a terrible serpent he has to destroy as part of his mission (instead of accomplishing the serpent-kiss).[58]

The lay-out at Korntin agrees with that at the castle of the Chastel de Pesme Aventure in *Yvain*, in the episode whose relation to the climax of the Fair Unknown type we have seen (pp. 199-201). The guide and Wigalois cross the bridge, pass through a gate, go along the road towards the castle and come to the beautiful meadow enclosed by an invisible wall, after which the way continues to the gateway of the abandoned castle. Similarly, when Yvain enters the castle by the gate he passes straight on and comes to the *prael*: this is enclosed by stakes, so that one can see inside, and it imprisons the damsels who belong to the Isle of Maidens. He searches for the entrance and, having found it, enters the *prael*, after which he continues to the deserted hall which lies behind.[59] There is no mention of an exit for the *prael*, but one must compare the garden walled by air at the Fortress of Maidens in *Le Livre d'Artus*, which has an entrance and an exit on the way to the castle, as well as the marvellous garden in *Erec et Enide*, with *une estroite antree* and *l'issue*.

Chrétien appeals to his source for the description of his garden, and a particularly close analogue is the garden of *la tour as puceles* at Babiloine, the place in *Floire et Blancheflor* (before 1170) which corresponds to the domain that is the destination of the ride in Chrétien's original (p. 201 f.). Babiloine seems to be meadowland from a distance, and its garden, like that at Brandigan, is full of birds of many kinds giving great pleasure with their song, spices in abundance and flowers at all seasons. It has every kind of fruit-tree, and he who is in the garden at Babiloine and scents the perfumes and hears the bird-song thinks

---

58 *Wigalois*, 4609-4746; *Papegau*, 65/1-66/31.
59 *Wigalois*, 4510-4858; *Yvain*, 5172-5341.

himself in paradise.[60] Erec receives an intimation of joy as he listens to the birds in the garden at Brandigan. But the most striking parallel is the passage which refers to the impossibility of passing the barrier if one cannot fly:

> Einsi que riens n'i puet entrer,
> se par desus n'i puet voler.
> > (*Floire et Blancheflor*, 1770 f.)
> Si que riens antrer n'i pooit,
> Se par dessore n'i voloit.
> > (*Erec et Enide*, ed. Foerster, 5743 f.)

In Chrétien it is the wall of air which thus encloses the garden, but in *Floire* we find the river Euphrates instead, by the process of assimilation to the garden of Eden that its author adopts. In the middle of the beautiful enclosure at Babiloine there surges a fountain under the loveliest tree ever seen, and this is *l'arbre d'amours*, which is all red, covered with rosy flowers at all seasons, with a bloom opening as soon as another falls.[61] The fountain is of magic power, and the flowers of the tree are endowed with enchantment.[62] Chrétien only speaks of a sycamore where the events take place in the garden at Brandigan, but the evidence points to a wonderful tree in his original, with marvellous flowers such as we see in *Wigalois/Papegau*. When in *Erec et Enide* we have the fruit that affects a man's capacity to leave the garden, this will derive from another account of the beautiful spot as the place which imprisons knights.

The Combat

Immediately after the description of the delights in the garden, Chrétien brings the hero face to face with contrasting horror, in the helmeted heads impaled on sharpened stakes, with one of them threateningly empty apart from a blast horn. The material now resembles that found in Gareth's combat with Sir Ironsyde in Malory, which Loomis and Schmidz, holding that the earliest form of the Fair Unknown type is the tale represented by *Sir Gareth*, explain as due to Chrétien drawing on the source of the latter (p. 120). As Loomis said, there are obvious analogies here between *Sir Gareth* and *Erec et Enide*: the hero is accompanied by a lady and a dwarf, and we have the ignominious exhibit of slain knights, a sycamore tree, the blast horn, the knight in red arms, his

---

60 Compare the garden in *Descouneus* which is assigned to the palace at the Ile d'Or, in the hero's unauthentic second visit (4289-4332). Like that at Babiloine, this beautiful garden is full of southern trees, spices of every sort, flowers that bloom at all seasons, and continuous song from birds of many kinds. The garden also has such perfumes that he who goes there thinks himself in paradise.

61 There is such a tree in the garden assigned to the Ile d'Or by Renaut de Beaujeu:

> Rosiers i ot d'itel nature
> Que en tos tans la flors i dure.
> > (*Li Biaus Descouneus*, 4321 f.)

62 *Floire*, 1645 f., 1744-1851.

surrender, and the excuse that his cruel custom is the result of a promise made to his lady-love.[63] There is a tiring after *none* has passed, with Mabonagrain alone in Chrétien, while in Malory both antagonists are so affected.[64] And we have a conversation of defiance between the hero and his opponent in both texts, with Mabonagrain objecting to Erec approaching his *amie*, even as Sir Ironsyde warns Gareth that Dame Lyonesse is his lady.

Loomis also pointed to the resemblance between the opening combats of the rides in *Sir Gareth* and *Erec et Enide* (a battle against a band of robbers, and another in which one of the opponents is met in a ford, overset in the water and drowned), and again held that this is due to a common source.[65] But the double battle of the Encounters with Marauders, as I have demonstrated (p. 172 ff.), was created by Chrétien. With this observation I have now accounted for all the adventures on Gareth's ride, and quite a medley they are as regards origin. First of all, opening battles based on those in *Erec et Enide*; then a core from the main source, a pattern of three repetitive encounters, with the Black, Green, and Red Knights (p. 264 f.); followed by a final perilous passage, the combat with Sir Persaunte of Inde, taken from the jousting with the guardian of the entry to the lady's domain in *conte d'aventure* X (p. 125 f.); and with the latter's good hospitality Malory's tale associates the coming of a damsel to the hero's bed, which was in the last night's lodgings of the main source (p. 266). Furthermore, Gareth's combat at the Pass Perilous with the Red Knight is clearly related to the Encounter at the Perilous Bridge (p. 87 f.), and of all the versions the closest is the First Encounter with Guivret in *Erec et Enide*. They come to a well-ditched castle whose lord looks out, sees them, wishes to joust with the knight errant, hastily arms himself and rides out to meet him. In the battle, both their steeds fall to the ground, a mutual unhorsing which distinguishes Erec's combat with Guivret from the corresponding encounter in the versions of the Fair Unknown type. When the adversary is overcome, he

---

63 Loomis, *op. cit.*, 181. To be rejected is an analogy alleged by Loomis which lacks logic: that while Brandigan is an island fortress, Dame Lyonesse's stronghold is near the isle of Avylyon.

64 Taking it to be a "solar trait", Loomis equated Mabonagrain's giving way after the hour of *none* with the statement in Malory that Sir Ironsyde's strength increases before high noon. The latter is a counterpart to the trait associated with Gawain since his battle with the Riche Soudoier, in which his strength doubles after midday (*Perceval*, First Continuation, 6247-54). Whereas the motif in Chrétien is that of a long battle with a redoubtable opponent whose strength fails after nones (about 3 p.m.), as in the duel with a Saracen in *Horn*, 3150 f.:

> Tresque none sonant dura la capleisun,
> Ke Rollac fud lassez.

In the most famous combat of a hero with a Saracen, that between Roland and Fernagu (mentioned in the Encounter with Mabonagrain, see *Erec*, 5729), the battle lasts *usque ad nonam*, when the adversary requires a respite (*Pseudo-Turpin*, 150 f.). Cf. *usque in horam nonam*, familiar in connection with the time after which Christ weakened at the Crucifixion (Mark, xv 33; Luke, xxiii 44).

65 Loomis, *op. cit.*, 128-33.

cries *"Merci, frans chevaliers"* in Chrétien, *"Mercy, noble knyght"* in Malory, and he invites the hero to stay with him in both texts.[66] Moreover, in the combat with Sir Ironsyde I can trace correspondence to the fulfilment of the mission in the main source (p. 266 f.), as well as matter from the Ile d'Or Episode (The Horn to be Blown as Challenge, p. 122 ff.), and also a limited equivalence to the battle before the lady's fortress in *conte d'aventure* X (p. 126). This adventure in *Sir Gareth* has a multiple origin that is symptomatic of the tale's synthetic nature, which is such that one must take account not only of *conte d'aventure* X but also of *Erec et Enide* as supplementary sources.

In short, far from *Sir Gareth* being the best version or the closest to the original from which descend the tales of the Fair Unknown type, and our being able therefore to use Malory's narrative to throw light on *Erec et Enide*, the situation is practically the reverse. *Sir Gareth* only bears on Chrétien's romance in so far as they both reflect material from stories of the Fair Unknown type; and as Malory's tale also draws on *Erec et Enide*, one can only employ *Sir Gareth* in support of evidence elsewhere for the shape of Chrétien's source, attributing to his influence any features of agreement in Malory with *Erec et Enide* against other versions of the matter in common. Thus, while confirming Brugger's inference that the combats with Mabonagrain and Sir Ironsyde make independent use of the battle at the Ile d'Or,[67] I introduce a modification, by taking account of *Erec et Enide* as a source for *Sir Gareth*.

Most of the features I have cited as analogues between the fights with Sir Ironsyde and the gigantic Mabonagrain are to be derived from the Ile d'Or Episode. The evidence collected under The Horn to be Blown as Challenge shows that the hanging of the horn on a stake in Chrétien is paralleled in *Floire et Blancheflor* (before 1170), by an element there from the Ile d'Or Episode; cf. the horn hanging on a pillar under a tree in *Li Chevaliers as Deus Espees*. In Malory however it is hung from a tree, as in *Durmart*, the common source being the Ile d'Or Episode in *conte d'aventure* X (p. 126). It can be seen that Malory's tale reproduces from the Fair Unknown type of story the hanging of the horn for use in summoning the antagonist, whereas in Chrétien the horn has no part to play before the combat. Furthermore, the combatants in Malory thrust not only each other but their horses as well to the ground at the first clash and lie stunned, as in the corresponding encounters between Descouneus and Malgiers, Gawain and Gernemant, Hector and Marigart, and Durmart and

66 Malory, VII, c. 10; *Erec*, 3653-3882. Gareth is wounded so sorely that his blood runs down to the ground. At the corresponding point, Durmart has a wound which streams with blood, but it is the opponent who is in this condition in the original story of the Fair Unknown type (p. 138 f.). *Conte d'aventure* X is the source of this kind of material not only in *Sir Gareth* but also in *Durmart* (p. 126); but the flowing of blood from Malory's hero may be due to blending of the Encounter at the Perilous Bridge with the First Encounter with Guivret.

67 E. Brugger, *ZrP* LXV (1949), 128, in his series entitled "Der Schöne Feigling in der arthurischen Literatur". It was Philipot who observed that there is ground in common between the Ile d'Or Episode and the Encounter with Mabonagrain.

Brun de Morois, indicating material from the Ile d'Or Episode, whereas in the fight between Erec and Mabonagrain the mutual striking to the ground of both man and horse does not occur immediately, and the knights are not stunned but quite unaffected.

This is because the opening of the battle reflects the Jousting for Hospitality, which is apt because its fighting has not taken place with the host, and Mabonagrain carries out *la costume male*. As Erec rides through the town to go outside, it is like his arrival run backwards, with the people passing comments on him and thinking it a pity that he should die, and the hero overhearing them (p. 204), while the scene is now closer to what I have indicated for the original Jousting for Hospitality (p. 205 f.). Evrain is with the hero, like the lady's steward who rides with Meraugis through the Cité sans Nom to the place where the unavoidable custom begins (p. 217); and the people watch the combat, which takes place outside the fortress in a marvellous garden enclosed by air, even as in the Encounter before La Roche there is a watched combat before the castle in the most beautiful meadow (*prael*) in the world, to which the opponent leads the hero in *Papegau* (p. 153), and as, in the Approach to the Abandoned Castle, the guide leads Wigalois to the marvellous meadow enclosed by an invisible wall, which is before the equivalent of the Cité Gaste (p. 210). In *Erec et Enide* the spectators sit under the trees,[68] just as in *Floire et Blancheflor*, in an equivalent of the Jousting for Hospitality, sitting spectators are present at the series of three contests which the hero has with his opponent in the open before the castle within the domain (p. 148). In the Jousting for Hospitality there is a series of three jousts, and it is not until the last of these that the hero fells the steward from his horse. Here both the antagonists smash their spears in each of the first two courses and are provided with fresh ones for the next joust, but in Chrétien we have no-one at hand to serve them with spears. However, he still conveys how the combatants at first make no impression on each other. Compare *Descouneus* (also *Papegau*, in the Encounter at the Narrow Passage) for the air of formality as the participants carry on *a droite joste*:

> Et quant cascuns ot fait son tor,
> N'i font demore ne sejor,
> Lances reprendent por joster
> Et laiscent tost cevals aler,
> Et puis durement s'entrevienent;
> Les lances alongnies tienent,
> Si se fierent de tel angoisse
> Que l'une lance l'autre froisse;
> Les esclices en font voler
> Si haut que on poroit jeter.
> De grant fin sorent bien joster.
>
> (*Li Biaus Descouneus*, 2651 ff.)

68 *Erec*, ed. Foerster, 5896 f.

Chascuns au plus tost que il pot
a sa lance sachiee a lui,
si s'antre vienent anbedui
et revienent a droite joste.
Li uns ancontre l'autre joste,
si se fierent par tel angoisse
que l'une et l'autre lance froisse.

(Erec et Enide, 5900 ff.)

With the mutual striking to the ground of both man and horse in the second course, the combat with Mabonagrain is shifted into the pattern of the fight in the Ile d'Or Episode, but the two designs are so merged together at this point that the antagonists, though their horses have fallen, remain unaffected in their saddles, as if still illustrating the motif of jousting for a while *avant que l'un eust l'autre remué de la sele (Papegau).* In the Jousting for Hospitality, the combat calmly comes to an end when the steward is toppled from his horse without injury,[69] but Erec and Mabonagrain rise and set to with the sword in a fierce battle as at the Ile d'Or.

The antagonist is overcome when the hour of *none* has passed not only in *Erec et Enide* but also *Li Chevaliers as Deus Espees,* yet it is only in Malory and Chrétien that there is a failing of breath after *none:*

And than thus they fought tyll hit was paste none, and never wolde stynte tyll at the laste they lacked wynde bothe.

(Malory, VII, c. 17)

ensi longuemant se conbatent,
tant que l'ore de none passe,
et li granz chevaliers se lasse
si que tote li faut l'alainne.

(Erec et Enide, 5948 ff.)

The really striking agreement between Malory and Chrétien, however, comes after the battle has ended. All the combats of the Ile d'Or type that I have listed (except in *Descouneus*) end with the adversary, in the hero's power, having his helmet unlaced or removed, and this is also what happens in Chrétien. But there is no menace made by the hero in *Erec et Enide,* whereas decapitation is in prospect or actually carried out with Gernemant, Marigart le Rous, Brun de Morois, and Sir Ironsyde, which is fitting when the opponent has the cruel custom of exposing heads.[70] But in Malory, as in Chrétien, the hero pardons his adversary for this crime. Above all, the opponent puts the blame for his maintenance of the custom on his lady only in these two versions.

69 For the combat of the Jousting for Hospitality, see *Descouneus,* 2633-94; *Lybeaus,* 1585-1638. Cf. the derivative in *Papegau,* 58/7-21; also *Wigalois,* 3519-60, but here the opponent is killed. See *Perceval,* 1491-1509 (derived jousting lesson).

70 Malory, VII, c. 16 f.; *Descouneus,* 2105-86; *Li Chevaliers as Deus Espees,* 4675-4734; *Vulgate Lancelot,* ed. Sommer, iv, 351 f.; *Durmart,* 4668-4788.

The Custom

A damsel he once loved made Sir Ironsyde promise to put all Arthur's knights he overcomes to a villainous death. This means that Sir Ironsyde's actions are doubly motivated, by two distinct women, one being Dame Lyonesse, for whom he has done many strong battles as her besieger and rejected suitor, and the other the former lady-love, the counterpart of the damsel in the wondrous garden who makes Mabonagrain carry out the custom for her. Thus one can trace conflation here.

Now the combat with Sir Ironsyde includes material from the Ile d'Or Episode, and in *Descouneus* we find Malgiers carrying out a custom similar to that imposed on Mabonagrain and Sir Ironsyde. However, let us examine the circumstances more closely. We have seen that the combat in *Li Chevaliers as Deus Espees* is derived from the Ile d'Or Episode in a source that agreed, against the *Descouneus/Lybeaus* version, with material in the battle with Sir Ironsyde which is from *conte d'aventure* X; and in that with Brun de Morois in *Durmart*, which is of the same origin (p. 126); while the fight with Marigart le Rous in the *Vulgate Lancelot* falls into this group (The Horn to be Blown as Challenge, p. 122 ff.). A comparison between Malgiers and Maugys (*Descouneus/ Lybeaus*), on the one hand, and on the other hand Gernemant in *Li Chevaliers as Deus Espees*, supported by Sir Ironsyde, Brun de Morois, and Marigart le Rous (the Poisson Chevalier in *Papegau* may belong to either side of the tradition), confirms that in the original story the adversary is, like Malgiers, a Red Knight and a tyrannical, unwanted suitor, hated by the lady and her people, and that this goes together with his being, like Maugys, her besieger (and a devastator of her domain, like the Poisson Chevalier), so that when the hero kills him he is welcomed in gratitude as the deliverer, which happens in every version of the Fair Unknown type, as well as in *Li Chevaliers as Deus Espees* and the *Vulgate Lancelot*.

The carrying out of the custom for the fay, because she has the habit of taking as her *ami* the knight who has killed her last *ami*, and of laying on him the same condition of defending the approach for seven years in order to marry her, is so intrusive in *Descouneus* that she would rather die than accept Malgiers, does not intend to do so even if he achieves the term, and when the hero slays him the custom vanishes, the fay waiving it when she offers herself to Descouneus.[71] It is a replacement, grafted into the context to serve the same end as the original motif, which could well have been that found in *Li Chevaliers as Deus Espees*, where a respite is set during which the besieger and rejected suitor will fight any knight who wishes to save the lady from her fate, on condition that if no-one conquers him the damsel will have to be his (p. 123).

The holding as prisoner of love and the imposition of the custom by the lady of the garden in *Erec et Enide* must therefore be distinguished from the Ile d'Or

71 *Descouneus*, 1949-2053, 2112-21, 2187-2276.

material, to which belong the heads placed on stakes for failure in the perform-ance of the task, to serve as warning to the hero when he sets out to accomplish it.[72] So the excuse given by Sir Ironsyde for his cruel custom is merely another instance of Malory's tale drawing on *Erec et Enide*. But the motif assigned to the fay in *Descouneus* cannot be derived from Chrétien, though its use may have been suggested by the similar feature associated by him with the exposure of heads. The original context from which the graft has been obtained for *Descouneus* would have to correspond to that in the contemporary romance of *Meraugis*.

Here it has also been put together with Ile d'Or matter, in a *conjointure* drawing upon such accounts as had provided elements for the Joie de la Cort episode, but arranged into a different pattern. Raoul de Houdenc is quite con-scious of Chrétien's treatment, as Meraugis declares on his arrival at the Cité sans Nom that he likes nothing so much as joy, and the general rejoicing is preceded by horn-blowing before he enters the town; but the material has otherwise not been taken from *Erec et Enide*. The entry of the hero into the seaport whose citizens come out and receive him with great joy is derived from the Ile d'Or Episode (p. 123). Meraugis is puzzled by this reception, and the mystery is obtained partly by the horn-blowing coming from the town, instead of from the hero to proclaim the victory, as in Chrétien, and partly by the omission of the combat which takes place before the entry in the Ile d'Or Episode. This battle is replaced in *Meraugis* by another of a different kind that follows the arrival and is introduced by an adaptation of the Jousting for Hospitality (p. 99 ff.).[73] The hero meets Meliadus, the lady's steward, who then rides with him through the town to the harbourside, where he tells Meraugis to enter a boat to cross over to the island within sight of the city, because it is a custom imposed on all who come to the Cité sans Nom, and if he is vanquished by the knight on the island they will do with him what they please. The joy turns out to be due to the prospect of *la joste*, even as in *Descouneus* the inhabitants look forward with laughter to the jousting and the hero's defeat, in both texts (as also in the Arrival at Brandigan) the people gazing at him and talking together as he rides past (p. 204).[74] But in *Meraugis* the custom itself is not that of the Jousting for Hospitality.

A knight had once asked the lady of the Cité sans Nom for her love, and she granted it to him, but through jealousy she held her lover captive with her on the island, where as her champion he carried out the custom of fighting all who came. After seven years in which he lived with her thus in a castle and slew

72 Motif H901.1 in S. Thompson, *Motif-Index of Folk-Literature* (1955).

73 On his way to the Cité sans Nom, Meraugis meets two ladies who warn him that he has passed the boundaries, and then he encounters a man who does the same (2828-61). This is paralleled at the equivalent point in material descended from the Fair Unknown type in *La Queste del Saint Graal* (p. 219 f.); cf. also *Perceval* II, in the Meeting with Greoreas (p. 136).

74 *Meraugis*, 2862-2980; *Descouneus*, 2567-82; *Erec*, 5445-81.

H

many opponents in the field, Gawain arrived, killed him, and had to take his place, to possess lady and castle and to maintain the custom till the day that his slayer would succeed to his office.[75] It is thus that Meraugis and Gawain come to fight each other on the island.

Though this is a valuable analogue to the imposition of the custom by the lady of the garden in Chrétien, for the closest we must go to a story in the Second Continuation of *Perceval*.[76] A Black Knight happens to enter the land of Avalon, where he comes across a beautiful damsel sitting by a fountain in a forest; he falls in love, and she agrees to be his in return for a promise to do whatever she requires. They travel together through the forest until they come to a lovely meadow where she wishes to remain, and he lies down and falls asleep. When the knight wakes up, he finds that the damsel has raised a marvellous castle, and she takes him outside to his steed and claims the boon. Henceforth he is to remain at the entrance in a tomb, which is all that passers-by will see, the castle being invisible to their eyes, and there he will attack those who utter certain words of defiance, not leaving his post until a knight comes who conquers him:

> Q'ainsint l'avoit an covenant
> A s'amie au cors avenant,
> Que de leanz ne se movroit
> Devant c'uns chevalier vandroit
> Qui par armes le conqueïst.
>
> (*Perceval*, Second Continuation, 20399 ff.)

Like Malgiers he is at his post all summer and winter, and is conquered after some years of this service. It is Perceval who arrives and defeats the Black Knight.[77]

There is a similar story in the thirteenth-century prose romance called the *Didot-Perceval*, as a replacement for the episode of the ford defended by the White Knight in the Second Continuation (p. 87). Urbain enters a forest, and as he passes through it he sees riding before him a beautiful damsel, whom he follows into a marvellous castle. He falls in love with her, she agrees to be his on a certain condition that she will specify, and he promises to do whatever she requires, before he knows what it is. She asks him to stay with her and go nowhere else, and tells him to do what we see the White Knight has done in the Second Continuation, to pitch a tent by the ford and defend it against any knight who comes there and waters his horse. The castle by the tent will remain invisible to other eyes. In similar fashion to the White Knight, if he defends the ford successfully for one year (it is seven years for the White Knight), he will achieve the greatest honour; he has almost completed the term when

75 *Meraugis*, 3123-87.
76 Cf. Philipot, *art. cit.*, 286.
77 *Perceval*, Second Continuation, 20359-583, 25070-298; cf. *Descouneus*, 1968-70, 2005-28.

Perceval arrives and defeats him, and he suggests that Perceval should take over the task, but the hero will not do so and the custom lapses.[78]

Such accounts suggest that there was a Breton lay in which a knight falls in love with a fay met in the forest, in return for her love engages to do whatever she wishes, before knowing what she will ask, and the unknown boon turns out to entail leaving mortal company and staying with her at a magic castle, while maintaining the custom outside until conquered by another knight. With this compare what Mabonagrain recounts to Erec after his defeat, how love grew up between himself and the damsel, and that one day she demanded a boon of him, but would not specify it, so that he promised it to her without knowing what she would ask.[79] Then, after he was knighted at the hands of Evrain in the garden, she claimed the boon and said that he had promised never to leave the place until conquered by another knight:

> Ma dameisele, qui siet la,
> tantost de ma foi m'apela
> et dist que plevi li avoie
> que ja mes de ceanz n'istroie,
> tant que chevaliers i venist
> qui par armes me conqueïst.
>
> (*Erec et Enide*, 6023 ff.)

A fairy-mistress tale, where the holding of the knight by the fay is achieved through his rash grant to her of an unknown boon, has been adapted to the situation in *Erec et Enide*, and its use explains why the power of the enchanted garden to affect one's capacity to leave does not require to be exploited.

The Blowing of the Horn

The Joy, as Mabonagrain informs the hero after his defeat, is to begin as soon as Erec blows the horn, and he urges him to do so. And when Erec sounds the horn rejoicing duly breaks out, not only among those in the garden but throughout Brandigan. At the Accomplishment of the Mission, the people of the country rejoice and come when they realize the glorious event has occurred, which in *Lybeaus* is because the hero has gone out of the palace and announced the news, while in *Papegau* the destruction of the Marshal is made known to the people of the region by the ringing of a bell at the top of the tower.[80] But we find a horn blown in an episode of *La Queste del Saint Graal*[81] (early thirteenth century), whose bearing on Chrétien's original is indicated by the location at a Fortress of Maidens going together with the imprisonment of its lady.

---

78 *Didot-Perceval*, 195-8.
79 The rash grant of an unknown boon is explained as due to love by the author's comment in both *Erec*, 6008-12, and *Perceval*, Second Continuation, 25156-9.
80 *Papegau*, 75/29-76/15.   81 Philipot, *art. cit.*, 261 n. 1.

Galahad enters a desolate chapel on a mountain, and while praying hears a voice telling him to go to the Fortress of Maidens and destroy the evil customs there. He departs, and soon sees from afar a powerful fortress down by the fast-running river Severn. On the way he meets an old man who tells him that it is the Fortress of Maidens, warns him that those there treat without mercy all who come, and advises him to turn back. Then Galahad comes across a company of maidens who warn him that he has passed the boundaries. But on neither occasion is the hero to be deflected from his mission. When he approaches his destination, he is faced with a squire despatched from the fortress to tell him that he is forbidden to advance further until his intention is known. "All I desire", says Galahad, "is the custom of the fortress." "You will be given it", the squire informs him, "and it is such that no knight errant has been able to accomplish the task." Then it continues as if the Jousting for Hospitality and the Accomplishment of the Mission have been rolled into one, for when the squire returns to the fortress there issue from it seven knights who are brothers and fight Galahad all at once. The battle continues till midday, when the hero's opponents are so exhausted that they have no further strength. They flee, Galahad goes to cross the bridge, and an old man with white hair meets him and presents the keys of the fortress. On entering the place, Galahad finds the streets full of maidens, who are all saying: "Welcome, sire! We have long awaited our deliverer! Blessed be God for sending you here!" They lead him to the castle and disarm him, and in the palace a damsel comes from a chamber carrying an ivory blast horn, which she gives to Galahad, informing him that if he wishes to summon those who from now on are his vassals he should sound the horn, which can be heard for at least ten leagues. In the editions of the French text Galahad gives it to someone else to blow, but in Malory he does so himself. In due course the fortress is filled with those who have come to realize what has happened, and they treat Galahad with great joy as one whom they hold as their lord.

It is explained to Galahad that the evil brothers came there ten years previously, when the lord of the domain was Duke Lynor, and the same night a quarrel arose between them and the Duke on account of his daughter, whom they wanted to have by force. They killed the Duke, imprisoned the damsel and subjected the land to their sway. She is now dead, but her younger sister remains alive, and to her Galahad hands over the fortress, seeing to it that the knights of the land render her homage.[82]

Here we have seven brothers instead of two, and none of them is killed, but this is just for the purpose of moral theology. The white-haired figure presenting the keys of the fortress after the hero's victory will be a reflection of the lady's steward in the Fair Unknown type of tale. The explanation of how the situation in the land arose is akin to that in this kind of story, where the magicians imprisoned the lady they wanted to have by force. In *Descouneus*,

---

82 *La Queste del Saint Graal*, pp. 46-51; also ed. Sommer, vi, 34-7; Malory, XIII, c. 14 f. Note the sister, cf. my comment, p. 126 n. 65.

the two brothers arrived after her father's death, but in *Wigalois* (where the imprisonment is replaced by the taking of refuge in an outlying fortress, and there is only one magician) the villain killed the father.[83]

Another account with such a horn at a Fortress of Maidens, and again related to the Fair Unknown type of material, appears in *Tristan de Nanteuil,* a fourteenth-century *chanson de geste.* The handsome hero, whose brutish Enfances make him more of a *vallet salvage* than Lybeaus, Carduino, or Perceval, in the forest meets the fay Gloriande, who promises him herself and the great treasure in her castle if he saves her from a horrible serpent.[84] On his victory over it, she tells him of his parentage and his name, even as Descouneus is informed of his by the lady of the domain when he has accomplished his mission. She takes Tristan to the magnificent castle, he enters the hall and sees more than thirty ladies carolling together in great joy and sweet song. King Arthur is there, and the hero is taken into a splendid garden where there is an ivory horn, which can only be sounded by *le plus preux qüe on püist trouver*; just as in Chrétien the man who succeeds in blowing the horn will acquire the greatest honour and fame, and the inhabitants have awaited the Joy of the Court for a long time, which now Erec has granted them. Tristan, like Erec, walks pleasurably through the garden as the birds sing. Then Arthur calls him forward, and tells him to hasten and sound the horn, which is like Mabonagrain. Tristan blows the horn three times, and at the blast, which makes the whole castle shake, all the fays hasten to the hero and show their joy with him, as the most valiant man in existence, and they convey him back to the palace. Tristan enjoys himself in *faierye,* and when he leaves, he turns round and finds that the castle has vanished.[85]

The blowing of the horn in the marvellous garden is thus a motif which was in Chrétien's original. He has then fused together two blast horns, one from the Ile d'Or Episode, there to challenge to battle the dreaded exposer of heads, and the other which is blown by the hero after the Accomplishment of the Mission, whose sound makes the inhabitants of the region hasten to the palace and rejoice.

This last function is bound up in *Erec et Enide* with another motif, that the prisoner is not to issue from the garden until the horn is blown, for it is then that the hero will have released him from imprisonment. In my material, the parallel to this is at the Chastel de Pesme Aventure, where Yvain's victory, over the demonic pair who are equivalent to Mabon and Evrain in *Descouneus,* delivers the wretched maidens from captivity in the *prael,* which they are not

83 *Descouneus,* 3319-22; *Wigalois,* 3666-3776.
84 The hero destroys a great serpent in *Wigalois/Papegau,* on his way to the magician's castle. Before the gateway of Korntin, the guide explains that the hero has to accomplish this deed (and not the serpent-kiss) in addition to the destruction of the magician, in order to save the land and win the princess (*Wigalois,* 4691-4706).
85 *Tristan de Nanteuil,* 8062-8759. The discussion of this episode by Brugger, *op. cit.,* *ZrP* LXIII, 128 ff., takes account of the related blowing of a horn in fairyland in the fourteenth-century *Le Bastart de Bouillon* (cf. Loomis, *op. cit.,* 183).

able to leave until the villains are conquered in battle (p. 201). In matter of the Fair Unknown type outside Chrétien we do not have imprisonment in the garden, and in the tale represented by the enchanted garden of the Queen of Danemarche and the Val sans Retor, on which Chrètien also drew in *Erec et Enide*, it is not the inhabitants who are captive. But at any rate, since the overcoming of the magicians does not in itself destroy the effect of their spells, as the original hero has to perform the serpent-kiss, the blowing of the horn may have been an act of general disenchantment, which is what the author of the Welsh redaction of Chrétien's story takes it to be in making it dispel a magic mist.[86]

The Joy of the Court

As the news spreads through Brandigan, the inhabitants hasten to the court from every direction, delighted by the event for which they have waited so long. At the Accomplishment of the Mission, in *Descouneus* all the people of the land similarly arrive when they hear the news that the prisoner has been released, and nothing prevents them from coming to the court (cf. *Erec*, 6126 f.), because of the joy which it gives them. But in *Descouneus*, though we might have some of the wording, we do not have borrowing of the theme from Chrétien, for tremendous joy at the recovery of one long imprisoned in an enchanted location is the climax of the Fair Unknown type of story. The inhabitants are hastening to their Queen, whom they have not seen for so long, and great is the emotion and never was such joy made when they see their lady who was lost. Great is the pure joy, when they have recovered their Queen. In *Lybeaus*, all the people of Synadoun throng to the lady, thanking God many times that their misfortune has been redressed, and lords do her homage, while in the Italian version, as in *Erec et Enide*, the great rejoicing is also directed towards the hero, the joy that the citizens manifest towards Carduino surpassing description.

86 In the episode of the Fortress of Maidens in the Second Continuation of *Perceval*, by sounding an instrument (as an insistent summons) the hero makes it spring to life with damsels and be transformed from the desolate place that it was at first (p. 199).

The sounding of an instrument, including the horn, is found in folk-literature of the British Isles as the means of revival from magic slumber, occurring with the return of long-lost persons whose coming is looked forward to. Many of these tales are of King Arthur. For instance, he lies asleep in a cave, and will not be roused until someone penetrates into it and blows Arthur's horn, which is a feat that would gain honour for him who achieves it (cf. Philipot, *art. cit.*, 261 n. 1). On these Arthurian legends, see E. K. Chambers, *Arthur of Britain* (1927), 222-7; also 319 in the 1964 reprint; and R. S. Loomis, in *Folklore* LXIX (1958), 15 f. In Gaelic, for a similar tale told of Finn mac Cool, see J. G. Campbell, *The Fians* (1891), 4. Cf. also the Last Trump (I Corinthians, xv 52): "In a moment, in the twinkling of an eye, at the last trumpet. For the trumpet will sound, and the dead will be raised."

The function of the horn in *Erec et Enide* as bringing honour to him who can sound it is a by-product of accomplishing the adventure. It is a test of prowess in *Tristan de Nanteuil*, while in the story of Havelok in Gaimar, *Estoire des Engleis*, 670 ff., the wonderful horn can only be blown by the true heir of Denmark.

Similarly, as we have seen, when the horn is blown at the Fortress of Maidens in *La Queste del Saint Graal*, after Galahad's victory over the villains who have kept its mistress prisoner, the fortress becomes filled with those who treat the hero with great joy as one whom they hold as their lord, and the knights of the land do homage to their lady.

The joy of the inhabitants is entirely at release from oppression in *Papegau*, where the lady is not a prisoner. Corresponding to the song composed by the ladies after Erec's victory, and called by them the Lay of Joy—Chrétien remarks it is no longer known—the damsels in *Papegau* sing words with joy, addressed to the knight who has delivered them from their oppressor. In similar fashion to *Erec et Enide*, people come from the region to see the hero and offer him homage, and he experiences the greatest joy that has ever been. They all go to the Queen and there is the greatest rejoicing and festivity, during which she receives homage from all. Similarly, in *Perceval* II, squires and damsels come and kneel before the hero as one they have long awaited and desired, and they are seen to honour him and offer their service. The princess declares that all the damsels will hold him as their true lord and are joyful to see him, the best of all worthy men, and Gawain has the greatest joy ever at the honour that God has given him.[87]

There is a basic distinction between this climactic joy in Chrétien's source and the earlier rejoicing at the Ile d'Or, in that in the former the site of the hero's victory is the palace, to which the people throng, whereas in the latter they escort him to it after coming in procession to meet him on his entry into the city (p. 123). It is the joy at the Ile d'Or which corresponds to the rejoicing in *Erec et Enide* on the hero's entrance into the fortress after his victory. There is a great press to welcome Erec already before he enters, the people showing their gratitude as they salute him, repeating continuously: "God save him through whom joy and gladness revive in our court! God save the most blessed man whom God has ever taken pains to make!" Thus they escort him to the court, and all kinds of musical instruments sound in accompaniment. In the Ile d'Or derivative found in *Li Chevaliers as Deus Espees*, as the people of the Port all come out in procession with the greatest joy to meet the hero, they express their gratitude and bless the hour that he was born, blessing him as well. When all the people of the Amoureuse Cité issue in procession to welcome the Chevalier du Papegau with great honour, the sound of musical instruments and rejoicing is deafening, even as in Chrétien the people of Brandigan abandon themselves entirely to joy and music. Similarly, at the port of the Cité sans Nom, when the inhabitants come out rejoicing to meet Meraugis and escort him into the city, all the ladies sing and maidens carol even more than at Mayday celebrations (p. 217).[88]

---

87 *Descouneus*, 3456-3503; *Lybeaus*, 2080-91; *Carduino*, ii, 66/1-8; *Papegau*, 75/21-77/30; *Perceval*, 7871-7949; *La Queste del Saint Graal*, p. 49 f.

88 *Descouneus*, 2187-2216; *Lybeaus*, 1396-8; *Papegau*, 19/2-20/2; *Li Chevaliers as Deus Espees*, 4740-83; *Meraugis*, 2880-2916.

That Chrétien should apply the term Joie de la Cort to such an occasion is perfectly understandable. The sense he ascribes to it agrees with that in the *Eructavit* (composed for his patron Marie de Champagne, quite likely in the 1190s), which as Nitze observed confirms Chrétien's *courtois* expression:[89]

> droiz est que chascuns s'atort
> Contre la joie de la cort.
>
> (*Eructavit*, 33 f.)

The term is here used of the wedding or coronation of a prince, which shows that Joie de la Cort means "the occasion when a joyful event is celebrated in the court". We have seen that in the Fair Unknown type of tale there are two occasions for such rejoicing, and that both are reflected at Brandigan. I shall now relate Mabonagrain's explanation of the Joie de la Cort to this double origin. When he says that Erec has given cause for great joy to the court, I can compare the Ile d'Or Episode. Here the course of the battle is watched by the lady and her damsels from the castle of the fortified town, and in the derivative episode of *Li Chevaliers as Deus Espees* the result of the hero's victory is that *la ioie est a la cort grans*, where *la cort* refers to the palace enclosure.[90] As a cause for the rejoicing, in Chrétien we do not have the delivery from a tyrant, though there is the exposure of heads associated with him. And the members of the court are not at the palace during the combat, because the King is the hero's guide to the enchanted location. Therefore, as they enter the garden with the hero, this is where the Joie de la Cort begins. On the other hand, when Mabonagrain says that all those who will come to the court will also rejoice, and so they who await this joy call it the Joie de la Cort, this occasion is analogous to that of the rejoicing at the Accomplishment of the Mission. But in *Erec et Enide* as yet neither the members of the court, nor the released prisoner, nor the hero are to be found at the palace. There they go, the prisoner leaving captivity in the garden like the maidens at the Chastel de Pesme Aventure, and they reach Evrain's palace by way of the rejoicing throng welcoming the hero into the city as in the Ile d'Or Episode. Then such is the Joie de la Cort at the release of the prisoner that there is a celebration for three days, during which the court honours Erec.

As the various elements come together, the imprisoning and magic garden enclosed by air outside the fortress at Brandigan is equivalent to more than one verdant spot in the source material. It corresponds to the site of the Jousting for Hospitality, which is held in the field before the castle gate in *Lybeaus* (p. 100), while we have a garden by the deserted hall for the derived jousting with the Petit Chevalier (p. 203 f.); and the derivative Encounter before

89 W. A. Nitze, "The Romance of Erec, Son of Lac", *Modern Philology* XI (1913-14), 468 n. 1.

90 *Descouneus*, 2116-21; *Li Chevaliers as Deus Espees*, 4242-9, 4740-6.

La Roche takes place in *Papegau* before the lady's castle and in the most beautiful *prael* in the world (p. 205 f.), even as we find a marvellous and beautiful meadow walled by air before the abandoned castle at Korntin and an imprisoning *prael* before the deserted hall at the Chastel de Pesme Aventure, which have a common source with the enchanted garden of the castle at Babiloine (p. 210 f.). And where impaled heads and a blast horn are seen outside a fortress and before a battle with a Red Knight, in the original Ile d'Or Episode, is reflected as a meadow or a garden in the combats with Gernemant, Marigart le Rous, and Brun de Morois (The Horn to be Blown as Challenge, p. 122 ff.). Again, it is a life of love that Mabonagrain leads, imprisoned within the magic garden, but the inhabitants of Brandigan are able to enter it, so that we have the atmosphere of a spot which affects people because of their own nature, like the Val sans Retor (p. 209). But what keeps Mabonagrain there is the necessity, as a rash boon to the damsel, to carry out the custom until defeated by another knight. Yet when Erec achieves this victory against him, it turns out to be the accomplishment of restoring joy to the land by the release of the prisoner, which the inhabitants have long awaited. Each of these elements contributes to Mabonagrain's personality. He is of more complex an origin than any other adversary in the romance, and the adventure is the summit of Chrétien's application of *conjointure*.

CORONATION AT ARTHUR'S COURT[91]

Erec, Enide, and Guivret go to Arthur, to whom the hero recounts his deeds, even as they are told by the emissary to the lady's steward in *Lybeaus*; correspondingly, Erec's account covers the adventures before the Arrival at Brandigan, and so does not refer to the climactic encounter at all.[92] Then the matter equivalent to the Wedding to a Queen (p. 104), partly fulfilled in the Wedding of Erec and Enide (p. 169 f.), is now completed, after the death of Erec's father. Continuing the exchange of roles between hero and heroine as compared with the source, it is Enide's parents who are sent for to attend the coronation. The return to Estregales, having already followed the wedding, is not repeated, the festivities bringing the story to an end.[93]

91 *Erec*, 6342-6878.
92 *Ibid.*, 6429-38; *Lybeaus*, 1666-71.
93 In *Floire et Blancheflor* (before 1170), where there is material corresponding to that in the Fair Unknown type of story (p. 201), the name of the hero, who has travelled incognito, is made known to the Emir, and the latter gives the heroine to him in marriage and offers a coronation. See *Floire*, 2706, 2864-3007. This is comparable with the giving by Arthur of the delivered lady in marriage to the hero whose name has just become known, at the coronation which takes place at his court. The description of the great festivity in *Floire* at the wedding is thus to be compared with that in *Erec et Enide* at the coronation.
Floire et Blancheflor and *Erec et Enide* adopt the same expedient for the raising of the prince-hero to king at the end of the romance (the heroine not being a Queen), with the arrival of messengers announcing his father's death.

The following tabulation brings out what I have so far established as basic material drawn on for each episode examined in this chapter (an asterisk indicates what maintains the sequence in the *conte Erec*, and italics the title given to an assumed *conte*):

FIRST ENCOUNTER WITH GUIVRET

> *Encounter at the Perilous Bridge
>
> invitation to a castle to have wounds healed (Encounter with a Huntsman)
>
> encounter with a dwarf-king (cf. *Huon de Bordeaux*)

MEETING WITH ARTHUR AND HIS COMPANY

> *unwitting encounter that ends in recognition (Encounter at the Perilous Bridge)
>
> invitation to stay in order to have wounds healed (Encounter with a Huntsman)

RESCUE FROM TWO GIANTS

> *Rescue from Two Giants

REFUSAL TO EAT AT LIMORS

> bitter lamentation at the fate of a knight who has fallen in a faint with blood flowing, and his transportation to a castle where he lies in this condition till evening (Encounter at the Perilous Bridge)
>
> *invitation to the meal that has been laid (Reconciliation Scene)
>
> marriage enforced on a presumed widow, who cannot be made to eat the meal after the wedding, and the return of her husband from supposed death to strike the villain down at mealtime and repossess his wife (cf. *Orson de Beauvais*)
>
> escape from the ruler with the compulsive desire to possess the beautiful person (Ile d'Or Episode)

RECONCILIATION SCENE

> *Reconciliation Scene (**RS**)

SECOND ENCOUNTER WITH GUIVRET

> *Attack by Three Avengers
>
> threatening army led from his castle by a lord, who clashes with the hero, the encounter ending abruptly by an immediate striking to the ground, which is followed by an invitation to a castle to have wounds healed (Encounter with a Huntsman)
>
> dwarf-king comes with an army in rescue (cf. *Huon de Bordeaux*)

STAY AT GUIVRET'S CASTLE

> midnight picnic, offered to the hero and his lady companion by a dwarf (Reconciliation Scene)
>
> *next morning, a departure for a castle, where a splendid horse is bestowed (Return of the Rescued Damsel)

healing by the end of a fortnight at the castle to which the hero is invited by his opponent (Encounter with a Huntsman)

ARRIVAL AT BRANDIGAN

*Jousting for Hospitality—but not the jousting scene

ENCOUNTER WITH MABONAGRAIN

*Accomplishment of the Mission

The Enchanted Garden of Maidenland as a Prison for Knights

heads impaled on stakes, blast horn, and a gigantic opponent in red arms, whose defeat causes a joyful reception of the hero on his entry into the city (Ile d'Or Episode)

Jousting for Hospitality—the jousting scene

The Rash Grant of an Unknown Boon to a Fay

opposition of real Cupid and pseudo-Cupid (*De planctu Naturae*)

final victory of the perfect creation over imperfections (*Anticlaudianus*)

CORONATION AT ARTHUR'S COURT

account of hero's deeds (Jousting for Hospitality)

*Wedding to a Queen (**WQ**)

the triumph of Nature and the Virtues (*Anticlaudianus*)

The inquiry has revealed how much of *Erec et Enide* is explicable from the Fair Unknown type of tale, as well as from Alain de Lille, which has made it possible to identify matter from supplementary sources. An important element, concerning the type of heroine, still remains to be explored.

II

Conte Sentimental

The beautiful maiden for whom the hero of the Fair Unknown type conquers the sparrowhawk does not wear ragged dress, but the finest raiment, and when she has the same white garment as Enide, which happens in *Durmart*, the *chainse* is of new and rich material. Nor does this kind of hero bring a poor damsel back to Arthur's court in order to marry her. And, though the framework for the adventure in the Fair Unknown type of tale is related to that of the ride in *Erec et Enide*, the hero's companion there is not his wife, nor even his love, from whom he is estranged through a breakdown in their relations.

Philipot therefore recognized that *Erec et Enide* is made up of a *conte d'aventure* to which has been attached a *conte sentimental* of the Griselda type, but he refrained from going into the question of this incorporation.[1] I can do so, however, now that it is clear what use Chrétien made of a *conte d'aventure*.

There is first to be considered the close relation between the Introduction in *Erec et Enide* and what is found in the story of Griselda, particularly in the version by Petrarch, who may have been conversant with the folk-tale on which Boccaccio based it:[2]

A poor man has a daughter who is beautiful in body, but incomparable in spirit, and faithfully performs her homely tasks. She draws the attention of a prince, who recognises her qualities, and by agreement with the father he espouses the maiden. Her shabby clothes are removed and she is arrayed in rich raiment, and her disordered hair arranged and a coronet set upon her head. Then, mounting her on a palfrey, the prince conducts her to the palace, and the nuptials are celebrated with much festivity.

We have seen how in Chrétien the rich vavasor that the original story apparently contained has been replaced by one sunk into poverty, and his poorly-dressed daughter made the contestant for the beauty prize. There are two rides side by side with the prince to whom she is betrothed by agreement with the father, one through the streets for the sparrowhawk contest, with her hair loose and wearing poor clothes—so unlike the beauty contestant in the original—and the other to the court for the nuptials, where she first has her shabby dress removed and is arrayed in rich attire, with a gold circlet set on her head.

1 E. Philipot, "Un épisode d'*Erec et Enide*: *La Joie de la Cour*—Mabon l'enchanteur", *Romania* XXV (1896), 264.
2 See D. D. Griffith, *The Origin of the Griselda Story* (1931), 16, 116-19.

In both stories there ensues a similar Preparatory Lull:

The maiden's virtues in married life and graciousness to her subjects endear her to all.

What we have is the folk-tale motif of the lowly heroine marrying a prince,[3] which is also in the Breton lay of *Le Freisne* by Marie de France, Chrétien's contemporary:

An abandoned child of honourable race is brought up by an abbess, grows to maidenhood with great beauty and moral perfection, and attracts the attention of a lord who persuades her to come and live with him in his castle, where he loves and cherishes her and all love and honour her for her simplicity.

But there is more than this to Enide. Let us try again:

She is of noble birth, yet living poorly, in a shabby dress, which is however fine, and she is not only beautiful and humble, but so morally perfect that she also possesses nobility of disposition. The hero sees her, wants to know about this maiden in old clothes, and he is told that she is highborn and what circumstances account for her condition. He wastes no time in declaring he will see she marries royalty and reigns. There is delight because she is to be a queen. She is taken to the palace and decked in rich attire, the wedding takes place, she and her royal husband have joy that night, and her social and moral perfection in married life is lauded to the skies.

This is Enide. But it is also Athanais, in the romance of *Eracle*, by Gautier d'Arras. An orphan whose father had been a senator, Athanais lives poorly with her aunt and wears an old *bliaut*. The hero, who recognizes her unique combination of great beauty, nobility, and humility, obtains her history from her aunt, looks at the maiden and finds not a single fault, has at last succeeded in discovering the perfect bride that he has been seeking for the Emperor. The story of Athanais is of Byzantine origin, being from the legend of Eudokia, Empress of Constantinople, which is found in sources close to folk-tale. Also in other respects Gautier's romance shows acquaintance with matters to be learned at Byzantium. As *Eracle* is attributed to 1176-81, and Gautier set to work on it for the princely family of Champagne, including Marie, who became Chrétien's patron, this analogue brings us to his very doorstep.[4]

3 Motif L162 in S. Thompson, *Motif-Index of Folk-Literature* (1955).
M. Wilmotte, "Une source historique de Chrétien?", *Romania* LX (1934), 195 ff., compares the union of Erec and Enide with that of Duke Robert and Arlette, *une fille de condition obscure* who is the mother of the bastard William the Conqueror in *Chroniques des ducs de Normandie*, by Benoît de Sainte-Maure. The contrasts are more convincing than the resemblances.
4 On *Eracle*, see A. Fourrier, *Le courant réaliste dans le roman courtois en France au moyen-âge* (1960), i, 185-257. The story of Athanais is in *Eracle*, 2589 ff.

That Enide should have a noble disposition from the start, and not just assume it with her new life, as Griselda does, is part of the contrast between noble birth and poverty, fine and shabby dress, and nobility and humility, which forms an element that is also present in Gautier's model of a perfect bride for the Emperor. It is blended with that of her undyed garment, its fine material and holes, and her superlative wisdom, which belongs to the beautiful girl in poor clothes called Prudencia.

Like Enide, after a period of love and content the heroine Le Freisne suffers disaster, when trouble comes upon her lord. But the criticism of his knights is that he should put her away and marry a noble lady. In the parallel event of the Italian story it is the prince who decides to do so himself, and he sends Griselda away. The Precipitation of Action is thus very simple in these tales, but in *Erec et Enide* it is not.

First we have Erec loving Enide so much that he falls into amorous indolence, and as a result neglects deeds of arms, until people call him recreant. In the crucial bedroom scene, Enide contemplates Erec's beauty, weeps tears that fall upon his breast as he lies asleep, and ends a lament, on how unfortunate she is to be the cause of his fall, with the exclamation: "How ill-fated you have been! (*con mar fus*!)" He wakes up and demands an explanation.

Before telling us what she says, Chrétien observes that in her anguish Enide has the misfortune to say what later she holds to be the words of a fool, though at the time she does not mean any harm. Chrétien does not limit himself to directing attention to her act in advance: he continues later in the romance to drive home how we should view it. The heroine bitterly regrets her fateful speech, which she regards as senseless and spoken outrageously in her arrogance. Enide blames and curses herself for those presumptuous and shameful words; she should have known very well that there is no better knight in the world than her lord. When Erec is apparently dead, and in her lament Enide hymns his praise, she also contrasts herself, blaming the tragedy on the mortal and poisonous words for which she deserves reproach. That grievous error has been the cause of his death, and all the fault is hers alone. Drawing the hero's sword, Enide goes so far as to try to take vengeance on herself for her transgression, and as such too it is regarded by Erec, for this is what he calls it when he pardons her at the reconciliation.

One must attend closely to that disastrous speech of hers, if one is to comprehend its effect. Enide informs Erec that he has lost his renown and is an object of derision whom all call recreant, which distresses her greatly. But she goes further, and says what causes her even more affliction is that she is given the blame, and people accuse her of having so entangled him in her net as to make him lose his prowess and desire no other occupation. Now he ought to think the matter over, and see how he might bring this reproach to an end and recover his knightly reputation. It is in answer to this demand that Erec sets out on the adventurous ride. When he treats her angrily, we can look for the cause in the unfortunate manner that Enide expresses to him her distress at being the instrument of his fall. It makes her demand seem due to concern not for him but herself, and her speech a casting of aspersions.

How much hangs on Chrétien's construction of the motive for the ride is to be seen from what happens in the Welsh redaction. Here the hero's lapse is not laid at the heroine's door in any way, for first he begins to indulge himself in ease, and then he finds eventually his greatest pleasure in dalliance with a woman. Thus, when Gereint loses his fame and prowess, the fault lies entirely within himself, excessive love of a woman being not the cause but the effect. Then, though the heroine feels grief in the situation, she does not warn the hero about his conduct, nor what people think of him, nor that she is blamed for his lapse. What she says in the bedroom scene corresponds only to her words at the beginning of it in Chrétien. She contemplates Gereint's beauty, weeps tears that fall upon his breast as he lies asleep, and exclaims: "Woe is me, if it is through me these arms and this breast are losing fame and prowess as great as was theirs!" Like Erec, Gereint is awakened by her words, but no conversation ensues. The heroine does not speak in a presumptuous manner, committing an act she comes to realize is a folly she bitterly regrets. Instead, Gereint jumps to a conclusion for which neither the story nor her words give him any justification whatsoever. In so far as he is distressed because she believes he has lost his prowess, and also by the thought that it is not out of care for him that she speaks, he may be compared with Erec. But not when he thinks this is because she is meditating love for another man in his stead and desires dalliance apart from him. Gereint sets out angrily on the ride with the heroine not as a result of any reproach or a demand to re-establish his reputation, but with the intention to punish her for the assumed desire to seek dalliance with another man, which makes him determined to see that she knows he has not so utterly lost his strength as she reckons. This makes him doubly unreasonable, for all she has done is to lament her share in his fall.

The Welsh redaction has retained the feature that the heroine does not mean to cast aspersions and the hero thinks she does, but it has failed to link this to her lamentation. It is in Chrétien that we see how the former stems from the latter, through the conversation that ensues, whereas in *Gereint*, where the heroine gets no further than her lament, we do not. The Welsh hero's jealousy is even more unwarranted than his anger at the imputation that he has lost his prowess, while on the contrary Erec's doubt of Enide's loyalty is understandable, again from that conversation. Thus the twin motivation makes sense in Chrétien, but that in *Gereint* does not, and the difference rests on the presence or absence of the conversation in the bedroom scene, without which the Action loses its mainspring. Then too the heroine's lament, which does not warrant the hero's reaction in the Welsh text, is not substantiated there itself, so much of a fossil is it from the source. *Gereint* does not trace the loss of the hero's valour to amorous dalliance, but the reverse, so that the theme of the lament makes as much nonsense of what precedes as what follows.

The heroine of the Welsh redaction is so utterly blameless that she is just like Griselda or Le Freisne, each of whom is put away by her husband and then sees to the arrangements for his wedding with the new bride, which gives full proof of her fidelity. But in Chrétien the rupture is the result of a transgression committed by the heroine during the bedroom scene. This element is related to another type of international popular tale, *The Search for a Lost Husband*.[5] Here a maiden is promised by her father to a supernatural bridegroom. The rest of this folk-tale type may be illustrated from the story of Cupid and Psyche in Apuleius, based on a Byzantine tale. The maiden is happy living at her husband's palace and has all she wishes, until she brings about disaster in a bedroom scene when she gazes on his beautiful form as he lies asleep: so does Enide, but her transgression does not lie in this act. Psyche lets a drop of hot oil fall from the light she holds over Cupid, which wakes him up: and Erec is also awakened by what Enide does, though it is not the tears that fall upon his chest which draw him out of sleep, but the sound of her lamentation. Psyche's act reveals the suspicion, planted by her sisters, that the husband who only comes to her in the dark is a monster; and similarly Enide, after reporting the slander that she has heard about Erec now that he does not display his martial gifts, also seems to imply that she believes it and requires proof of his nature, like Psyche taking to the light. As a punishment for the transgression, Cupid rejects Psyche and departs, leaving her in great distress. Before she can regain him, the depth of her devotion has to be proved by the trials undergone on a laborious search for her lost husband, until she finds and recovers him.

That *The Search for a Lost Husband* was known in Chrétien's day in some form appears from the contemporary romance of *Partonopeu*, where we find its Preparatory Lull and Precipitation of Action, with reversal of sex. Partonopeu enters into a union with Melior, the lady of a castle who comes to him in the dark, invisible. He lives happily there, but his mother thinks his beloved must be of devilish nature, and he is persuaded to inspect Melior by means of a light, whereupon he discovers not a monster but a most beautiful creature. Partonopeu is aghast at his folly, and distracted with grief to find that he has been responsible for the rupture of their union, as Melior upbraids him and makes clear that she will not pardon his transgression, which she regards as a betrayal. Rejected, he has to part from her, to fall into the depths of self-reproach for his disloyalty.

The evidence from *Partonopeu* may be supplemented from *Ille et Galeron*, a work composed shortly before Chrétien's romance and one which provides a partial bridge to it from the folk-tale type I have been considering. *Ille et Galeron* is derived from the tale found in Marie de France's *Eliduc*, but Gautier d'Arras modified the pattern of the Breton lay to bring his story close to *The Search for a Lost Husband*. Shortly after Ille and Galeron are married, Ille loses an eye and lies suffering his wound in a chamber. By his order Galeron is debarred from entering it, but she circumvents the prohibition, and we have a bedroom

5 Type 425 in A. Aarne and S. Thompson, *The Types of the Folktale* (1961).

scene comparable with that in *Erec et Enide*. When morning comes, Galeron looks upon her husband, weeps in anguish, Ille is awakened by her cry of lamentation and finds her in tears. There is a conversation and, fearing the loss of her love because of his infirmity, Ille flees, leaving his wife in great distress. Galeron sets out on a laborious search for him in which she suffers much, and reproaches herself that it was all her fault, pride in her was the cause why he reacted thus.[6] She eventually finds and recovers her husband just when he is about to marry a new bride, which also happens in *The Search for a Lost Husband*.[7]

In *Erec et Enide* the husband, fearing the loss of his wife's love because of his lapse, treats her demand to prove his nature as a betrayal, a transgression that deserves punishment by a break between himself and his wife, which greatly distresses Enide and causes her deeply to regret her thoughtless act, attributed by her to arrogance. There is no physical parting, however, though Enide thinks Erec is sending her into exile when he tells her to get ready to ride. But we have a theme rather like the search for a lost husband, being the regaining of his love and confidence by a wife who demonstrates fidelity to the full in undergoing trials on a journey towards their spiritual reunion.

The material reminiscent of *The Search for a Lost Husband* provides the heroine who, through her own fault, causes the breakdown in her marriage, and then, by sheer devotion to her husband, succeeds in re-establishing it. But in a story of the Cupid and Psyche type the transgression is a breach of a prohibition laid down by the spouse, whereas in *Erec et Enide* there is no such thing. Neither is it due to a wavering of fidelity. As in *Ille et Galeron*, but without breaking a prohibition, what the heroine does is due to her concern for the hero, and she is full of anguish at seeing the sad condition he is in. And yet Enide's act has an effect like that of a betrayal. This tragic irony fits the inauspicious time, when Enide sees Erec and herself as ill-fated, he in his disgrace and she for being the cause. Thus Chrétien has misfortune playing a part in her answer to Erec, so that a wrong note sounds, such as might occur with one in her situation under stress, while the anger that begins to show in him, as his wife tries to pretend she has been dreaming, and then his frightening reaction when she tells the truth, are further signs of how very much at this time they are both amiss. It is thus that with the logic of a human relationship there is achieved the same effect of reversal as at the turning point in *Anticlaudianus*, when Nature's perfect work, as soon as it has been created and endowed, comes under the assault of the Vices.

In respect of differences in the Precipitation of Action between *Erec et Enide* and the Cupid and Psyche type of story, and also *Ille et Galeron*, Chrétien's

6 *Ille et Galeron*, 1051-1302, 2268-2314.

7 This material in *Ille et Galeron* lends support to the view that *Partonopeu* has drawn directly from popular tradition rather than deriving matter from Apuleius. On the controversy over this question, see A. Fourrier, *Le courant réaliste dans le roman courtois en France au moyen-âge* (1960), i, 385 f.

romance is to be compared with the contemporary *Ipomedon* I, which is a tale of a Handsome Coward. Ipomedon grows up as a perfect young man, well spoken of by everyone, but when he goes to Calabria to serve La Fiere he relapses in one respect, devoting himself to hunting alone and not at all to arms, so that he is looked on as a coward and all find it sad that he lacks valour. La Fiere, who has vowed to marry the knight with the highest renown, develops an undeclared love for Ipomedon, and greatly laments that destiny has given him beauty but not prowess. She comes to realize that he loves her passionately, but because of her vow, and for his own good, she decides that it would be better for him to leave the country. Under cover of addressing another in his presence, she conveys advice to him by saying it is a fool who, before having gained renown, turns his thoughts to love: becoming amorous and pale, how he serves Love well, but Love will not confer on him anything of value, for he who devotes himself to Love loses all other ability. Ipomedon understands the hint and withdraws. La Fiere cannot sleep that night, regretting her words, blaming her action on her pride, and greatly distressed at the prospect of Ipomedon's departure. He cannot sleep either, thinking of those words which have struck him to the heart, and he makes up his mind to leave in the morning, sadly recognizing the justice of her rebuke. He departs, to win fame in many lands to merit the love of La Fiere, and she is overcome with grief when she learns he has gone.[8]

The lesson is that prowess is a prerequisite for true love, and that without it love is a sapping of man's strength. This is so, too, in Chrétien, but the falling away of Ipomedon is distinguished from that of Erec by not being caused by amorous dalliance, such as occurs with Durmart in the same part of his romance as the decline of the hero in *Ipomedon* I.[9] However, in common we have a love situation with the lapse in one respect of a perfect young hero who comes to devote himself to the occupation alone of hunting or of love, and not at all to arms, so that he is looked on as a recreant or coward and all find it a great pity that he lacks valour, a sad state of reputation that the heroine laments as she considers his beauty—Enide actually gazing on it. In both romances the heroine delivers a rebuke to the hero for his own good, as she advises him to see to his renown; and this is necessary for her sake, either to merit her love or to remove blame from herself. The heroine's words have a devastating effect on the hero, as he recognizes they are deserved and decides to make good his defect by leaving to seek exploits. She greatly regrets her act:

> "Lasse, cheitive, que pensastes,
> Quant vus od lui her seir parlastes?"
>
> (*Ipomedon*, 983 f.)
>
> "Ha! lasse, por coi fui tant ose,
> qui tel forssenaige osai dire?"
>
> (*Erec et Enide*, 2588 f.)

---

8 *Ipomedon*, 85-1613.   9 See p. 114 above.

The heroine blames herself for her pride, and is greatly distressed at the prospect of not seeing the hero again—in Enide's case because she expects to be banished.

In some respects Enide is like Ipomedon, for both begin their bedroom laments with the complaint that they have left their own country to come to such a bitter fate—Enide because she blames herself for Erec's lapse—and when asked to account for their lamentation and state of distress in bed they first explain it away as due to a dream but, when further urged, reveal the truth.

The most striking parallel of all is that in both romances the hero's decision to change his manner of life, from neglect of arms to the pursuit of exploits abroad, is precipitated by his overhearing what the beloved says about him, to which situation similar language is applied. Erec remarks that what Enide has said, as she lamented "*Amis, con mar fus!*", refers to him, not to another, for he has well understood to whom her words apply:

> "Por moi fu dit, non por autrui;
> bien ai la parole antandue."
>
> (*Erec et Enide*, 2518 f.)

She has not meant him to hear what she says, but in the comparable situation of *Ipomedon* I the heroine intends to be overheard, and the author comments that she did not speak for the person addressed, but rather for someone else, and he, for whom it was said, understood its obvious application:

> Ceo ne dit ele pas pur ly,
> Assez le dit plus pur autrui;
> Cil meymes, pur qi il fut dit,
> Mult apertement l'entendit.
>
> (*Ipomedon*, 905 ff.)

Later, in his bedroom lament, Ipomedon observes that she was referring to him: "*pur moy le dist*" (1152). In short, the crucial scene in which Erec and Enide take part is almost as if Ipomedon and La Fiere were put into the same bed.

In Chrétien, what one may call the Handsome Coward element expresses in relation to a marriage the Ile d'Or motif of the hero exposed to the riveting power of a beautiful woman's charms, but impelled by a rebuke to set off to accomplish his martial duty. It adds the theme of the perfect hero who first falls into derision, and then rises from this state to glory, which holds an important place in the master-plan of a marriage endowed with great gifts that is affected disastrously by human failings, and has to fight its way through to perfection.

When Enide conveys to Erec the necessity for him to put right his defect, his response is to order her to get out of bed immediately and prepare for a ride, a sudden command that alarms his wife, who departs in great trepidation to obey. She is already in tears when an attendant comes from Erec with the brusque message to hurry up: why is she taking so long, for her husband has been waiting outside a long time, fully-armed? Having previously supposed that she was about to be sent into exile, Enide is perplexed as to what Erec has in mind. She finds that they are setting off alone together, going they know not where, while what was implied by his abruptness comes out into the open, as he orders his wife to ride before him and not dare to speak, whatever she sees. Whenever she disobeys and warns him of opponents, Erec reacts angrily, and he accuses her of casting aspersions on his valour. However, though he certainly is harsh towards his wife, his treatment of Enide cannot be taken at face value. First we have a hint of affection for her when Erec makes arrangements with his father to look after Enide in case he himself fails to survive the ride. Later, after having been unaware of the first assailants until Enide puts him on his guard, on the second occasion Erec pretends that again he has not seen the opponents, so that from now on he is hoping she will warn him in spite of his threats to punish her if she speaks again. When Erec no longer doubts her devotion his menaces become less ferocious, and they are half-hearted as soon as he fully understands she has great love for him. Eventually Erec openly declares he is certain she loves him and assures Enide of his own love, telling his wife that he has fully tested her; and Chrétien later comments that the hero *bien l'a esprovee*. We have already seen that the evolution apparent in Erec's behaviour is related to the plan of the *bellum intestinum* that Chrétien's romance shares with *Anticlaudianus*, as well as to the pattern of the ride in the Fair Unknown type of tale. What remains to be considered is the relationship of the Action with international popular tale.

Erec demands from his wife on the ride not merely submission to his will, but utter compliance no matter what happens; this is also the position in the story of Griselda, where the heroine is required to promise not only full obedience but also that she will not be uneasy at any time, whatever her husband should say or do. In the general class to which this tale belongs, the husband deals cruelly with his wife at home, and she endures his acts without questioning them. The testing situation that Enide is called on to endure is not a domestic one, but tailored to the pattern of an adventurous ride derived from the Fair Unknown type of tale, Erec treating her as one who has maligned his prowess, and before whom he has to vindicate it on a journey during which warnings from her about opponents show nothing but doubt of his ability to vanquish them.

But the test which Enide passes is not the one that her husband calls on her to endure, for Enide is not made out to be a Griselda. In the ride situation created, a conflict is shown to arise within Enide between love and fear of her husband, and she dares to warn him of assailants. When he becomes aware of her state of mind, a corresponding tension develops in Erec, and it is clear he comes to realize that what he truly wants from his wife is not merely acceptance of his valour but active concern for him, which identifies the real point at issue with Erec about his wife's attitude when she reproaches him with his failure to maintain prowess. Now, while continuing with the apparent test of her fidelity, the proper one grows, as Erec looks for evidence of Enide's love and is affected by proof of devotion. That he fully tests her does not mean this was from the outset a deliberate course of action, such as occurs in the story of Griselda. *"Bien l'ai en la voie esprové"*, asserts the emissary; and yet she did not set out to put Descouneus to the proof, but evidence of his heroism accumulated and conviction dawned in spite of herself, as she observed how he would not be deterred by her from undertaking perilous adventures and that he conquers his opponents—even as Enide, despite Erec's threats, keeps on warning him and proving her loyalty.[10]

Thus the journey in Chrétien is in terms superficially of a Griselda-like situation fashioned from the ride of the Fair Unknown type, but truly of another, where the relationship of the hero and his companion in the source is reversed, and we have a Chevalier Mesdisant who persists in his behaviour until thoroughly convinced. This gives to Enide's agony a length that is as much a trial of devotion as Psyche's laborious search for Cupid, when he has severed their union as a punishment for her transgression, and the enormity of the betrayal felt by Erec is shown by the withdrawal of his love from Enide for so long.

But the transgressing is mutual in Chrétien, so that each makes the other suffer, as each seeks for the other's love that seems to have been lost:

> Tant on eü mal et enui,
> il por li et ele por lui,
> c'or ont feite lor penitance.
>
> *(Erec et Enide,* 5203 ff.)

They have to expiate their transgressions against each other, in a testing to the full which for both follows from the character of Erec as shown in the opening phase of the romance, where stress has been laid on his resolution. Side by side with Erec's determined pursuit of the ride to the very doors of death, for him Enide's loyalty remains on trial.

This careful development of the relationship on the ride is lacking in the Welsh redaction. To begin with, we cannot look to the Introduction to throw any light on Gereint's later behaviour, since it lacks the emphasis on that firmness which is so noteworthy a characteristic of Erec. As the Action sets in, Gereint does not arrange with his father to look after the heroine if he himself fails to survive the ride, and instead of ordering his wife to accompany him in her best raiment he tells her to bring the worst dress she has; which loses the point of the Encounters with Marauders, who in Chrétien are drawn to assault Erec by the richness of his wife's apparel and the splendid harness of her mount. Then, remaining like the Erec of the first combat, Gereint goes on swinging

---

10 A body of criticism has gathered round the subject of *Pourquoi Erec se décide-t-il à partir en voyage avec Enide?*, and Z. P. Zaddy made a study of this question in *Cahiers de civilisation médiévale* VII (1964), 179 ff. She rightly contradicted the former view that Erec sets out in order to test Enide, but went too far in denying that Erec tests her at all. A. R. Press, "Le comportement d'Erec envers Enide dans le roman de Chrétien de Troyes", *Romania* XC (1969), 529 ff., swings too far the other way in returning to the earlier conception. See p. 108 above.

from melancholia into fury whenever aroused by the heroine's warnings. Gereint is so unbalanced that when she puts him on his guard against opponents he accuses her of longing to see his death, and he is angry when his wife warns him of the amorous Count's evil intentions, at a time when Erec is impressed by Enide's loyalty. There is no question of Gereint pretending not to be aware of assailants, and far from showing any sign of affection lurking beneath his harsh exterior, or that he is seeking for devotion from her, he is engaged in a campaign of persecution.

When there takes place a change of heart, Gereint's mental alteration, so far as one can see, is a coming to his senses of a man who has been seized by a fit of madness. Overcome by grief, he suddenly realizes that the heroine is in the right. One would have expected him rather to feel that he is in the wrong, for his unwarranted suspicion that she desires dalliance with another man, but instead the passage reads as if the hero has been rebuked by her in the bedroom scene, which does not happen in the Welsh redaction. Here his conduct has been explained by jealousy, and yet signs of this vanish so quickly in the course of the ride that we see Gereint raising no objection to the amorous Count speaking privily to the heroine, at the point where Chrétien finds it necessary to inform us that Erec allows him to do so because he is not jealous.

In place of the picture that Chrétien gives, of how he who loves his wife comes to treat her harshly while he seeks to trust himself entirely to her, *Gereint* produces a botch, with a totally innocent wife persecuted by a husband gone mad with inexplicable jealousy. By its contrast, the Welsh redaction brings out elements of Chrétien's account on which is founded its essential nature as a *conte sentimental*.

The *conte d'aventure* that Chrétien used was the tale of Erec—so he informs us. But the title he gives to his own work is different. At the beginning of *Cligès* the poet declares that he is the man who composed the story of Erec and Enide. Guiraut de Cabreira, in his poetic catalogue of tales, thus speaks of the *conte Erec*:

> Ni sabs d'Erec
> com conquistec
> l'esparvier for de sa reion.
>
> (*Ensenhamen*, 73 ff.)

In Chrétien, when Erec brings Enide to Arthur's court, the Queen turns to the King and says:

> "Sire, si con je cuit et croi,
> bien doit venir a cort de roi
> qui par ses armes puet conquerre
> si bele dame en autre terre."
>
> (*Erec et Enide*, 1721 ff.)

Si bele dame instead of Guiraut's *l'esparvier*! In this change, the whole emphasis of the *conte d'aventure* has been altered in a most fundamental way. What the hero conquered *for de sa reion* in the original was only a sparrowhawk, but in Chrétien, through the same adventure *en autre terre*, he also gains Enide. Chrétien makes Enide what she is, and who she is we know—Nature's model, Nature's unique creation, the perfect being brought back for the completion of the project, a figure of moral quality, epitomized in her tattered robe, who has the role of the lowly heroine marrying a prince, she for whom the hero both loses and wins renown, the transgressor who discharges her penance, and the one whose love is put to the proof and overcomes all.

12

Conclusion

The results of this inquiry contradict what is a widespread view among Arthurians, that as much as possible of Chrétien's matter is to be explained from Celtic origins. Such inflation of the Celtic element in Arthurian romance has been partly carried out by assuming that three early Welsh tales do not derive from three of Chrétien's works, but from sources in common with them. As this hypothesis is fundamental to a large body of Arthurian studies, to blast away so much of this shaky foundation, by showing that *Erec et Enide* is a story of Chrétien's own creation, is to cause a wholesale collapse of theories, among them that a Welsh tale corresponding to a romance by Chrétien is evidence of ancient Welsh tradition present in his original:

> Assuredly, they were popular performances, with their Norman-French characteristics imposed on the old Welsh virtues, and appealing more to their sophisticated audiences than the earlier, ruder tales of Owein, Peredur and Gereint had done. So popular indeed, that the earlier versions have yielded before them and fallen from human memory.[1]

Besides such spinning of earlier Celtic versions of Chrétien's stories out of the Welsh romances, the bearing of other early Celtic texts on his material has been exaggerated. Loomis was not alone in detecting an Irish pattern in *Perceval* II in the following manner. Orguelleuse de Nogres, because she disappears while Gawain is dealing with the nephew of Greoreas, at a late stage of the hero's journey, is likened to the maiden messenger who comes to Bran, summons him to the Land of Women, and then disappears before he even starts. Furthermore, because Bran, after setting out across the sea, meets Manannan the sea-god coming over the waters, who announces that the Land of Women is not far, and Bran later departs from it over the waters by boat, the ferryman who meets Gawain in *Perceval* II is identified with Manannan, who possessed a magic coracle and was a rich and lavish host[2]—all this in spite of the Irish pattern being that of the hero voyaging in his own vessel. As we have seen, the boatman's role as a rich host is due to his origin in a personage belonging to the Fair Unknown type of story, whose lavish hospitality I have amply documented.

---

1 G. Jones and T. Jones, *The Mabinogion* (1949), xxx. The Welsh romances have even been derived from a continuous tradition in Welsh, without going through common French sources with Chrétien: see the summary of an article in *Llên Cymru* by R. M. Jones given in *BBSIA* XI (1959), 49.

2 R. S. Loomis, *Arthurian Tradition and Chrétien de Troyes* (1949), 444 f.

From the lady's steward in that type of tale also arises the hospitality of Evrain in *Erec et Enide*, which has again been explained from a Bran, but the Welsh one, by Loomis and one of his leading supporters. They claim that identifying Evrain with the Fisher King, called Bron in the *Didot-Perceval*, is helpful in elucidating the name of the adventure, the Joie de la Cort, and compare the situation at Brandigan with the joy to be produced by the discovery of the Rich Fisher's court in the *Elucidation* prefixed to *Perceval*. They are not at all disconcerted by the differences between the two subjects, not to say the contrast, since in one the joy is given to the court, but by the court in the other. And they go so far as to believe that Joie de la Cort was originally Joie del Cor, i.e. "Joy of the Horn", with reference to the horn of plenty attributed to Bran, and that this is why, after blowing the horn, "with joy was Erec well feasted and well served to his heart's desire" (*Erec*, 6138 f.). However, to take these lines as indicating that in an earlier version of the story there must have been feasting, and that here the food-providing horn of Bran has been transformed into a blast horn, has no justification whatsoever in the context. There the metaphor of being feasted on joy expresses Erec's gratification[3] at the rejoicing in contrast to the feelings of Mabonagrain's damsel, to whom it gives anything but pleasure. Thus the dilation of these scholars on the feeding of heroes at the Grail castle of Corbenic is pointless.[4] This inquiry shows clearly enough that the only question which can arise as to the connection of the adventure with Bran lies in the name of Brandigan.

The same commentators have seen "the numerous confusions and inconsistencies", "the many disharmonies" in the Joie de la Cort episode as due to the superimposition by the poet or source of one theme upon another, the pattern of Mabon's release from captivity obliterating many features characteristic of the visit to the castle of Bran.[5] But among the elements that have been brought together to form the Encounter with Mabonagrain one cannot include the captivity of Modron's son, Mabon, in spite of the long-standing identification of the two figures. This Mabon was one of the three famous prisoners of Britain, who in the Welsh *Culhwch and Olwen* is released from a fortress through an assault made by Arthur and his men. His imprisonment and the manner of his delivery are of quite a different nature from Mabonagrain's, and there is not the slightest evidence that the story of Mabon's captivity descended into Arthurian romance. Mabuz in *Lanzelet*, who is the son of a fay-queen, is an imprisoner of knights in an enchanted castle created by his mother, and Mabon, in the tale of the Fair Unknown, imprisons the lady in her own castle which he has himself enchanted.[6]

3 Cf. the figurative use of Latin *pascere*, to which the verb used by Chrétien corresponds.
4 H. Newstead, *Bran the Blessed in Arthurian Romance* (1939), 106-20; Loomis, *op. cit.*, 170-75.   5 Loomis, *op. cit.*, 175-8.
6 It is E. Philipot, "Un épisode d'*Erec et Enide*: *La Joie de la Cour*—Mabon l'enchanteur", *Romania* XXV (1896), 276, 284 f., who originally connected Mabon, son of Modron, and Mabuz with Mabonagrain.

Loomis thought there is a parallel between the ignorance of Mabonagrain's name outside Brandigan and that of the oldest animals disclaiming knowledge of Mabon, son of Modron, but what we have in the Welsh text is nothing but a folk-tale motif associated with the search for the prisoner,[7] and in Chrétien only a feature which comes from the hero of the Fair Unknown type, the youth who cannot give his name at court because he does not know it. Guinglain learns his name when he has accomplished his mission, and at the corresponding point of the story in Chrétien we find Mabonagrain revealing his own name and remarking that he was unable to give it where he was a youth, for it was unknown to him then.

It is thus futile to seek an explanation for the role of Mabonagrain in the Mabon contained in his name, other than that he is the hero's opponent in the climactic encounter at the enchanted locality, like Mabon in the tale of the Fair Unknown. Any later reference to Mabonagrain can only come from knowledge of Chrétien's romance, contrary to the opinion of Philipot and Loomis; they quoted the passage on "the fair son of King Urain, who was called Mabounain" from Potvin's edition of the First Continuation of Perceval, but now in Roach's edition we see that Mabonagrain is the nephew, as in Chrétien.[8] The form Mabonagrain is best taken as Chrétien's own extension of Mabon, with an Arthurian ring about it,[9] and a similar process may well account for the name Brandigan given to the kingdom.[10]

The mother of Mabon, Modron, was habitually drawn on by Loomis, and for Orguelleuse de Nogres in Perceval II he so dragged her in that one need not be surprised at failing to find any sign of her in the source material I have established for this damsel. On the grounds that Orguelleuse had once been the mistress of the falconer-knight Guiromelant, and later of Orguelleus del Passage, who guards the ferries of Galloway, it seemed likely to Loomis that she inherited these relationships from Modron, "the wife of Arawn, who was both a huntsman and a combatant at a ford" in Pwyll, the first branch of the Mabinogion. But Modron is not known as the wife of Arawn, and in any case Orguelleus del Passage could not be compared with this King of Annwn, for in Pwyll it is not he but his enemy Hafgan who opposes the hero at the ford. Loomis also went so far as to believe that the antagonists whom Gawain encounters beside La Roche de Sanguin (the nephew of Greoreas, Orguelleus del Passage, and Guiromelant) might descend from the three champions in

7 K. H. Jackson, *The International Popular Tale and Early Welsh Tradition* (1961), 76-9. Loomis also saw a sign of the mythic origin of Mabonagrain in a "solar trait", which I have already disposed of (p. 212 n. 64).

8 *Perceval*, First Continuation, 3773 f.

9 Cf. Godegrain (*Erec*, 1893). The form of the name Mabonagrain is generally explained as either the names of the two brother-magicians compounded together, or the original name for a single adversary which in the tale of the Fair Unknown has split to provide the names of two.

10 The name otherwise appears as that of a king in the Second Continuation of *Perceval*, 28011; cf. the name Dame Lyonesse, from the name of a region.

The Sickbed of Cuchulainn, whom this Irish hero, summoned by Liban to fight them to win possession of her sister Fand, slew in her beautiful island.[11] However, only one of these adversaries of Gawain forms part of the mission (which is shown to exist when the hero is at the boatman's house), and then only in the sense that he has the function of a knight guarding the passage, not one whose conquest achieves the mission.

But it is perhaps with *The Dream of Macsen Wledig* that the school of thought which is inclined on the slightest grounds to yoke Arthurian romance with what is Celtic outdoes itself. From this Welsh work Loomis explained the mysterious figure of a rich man with a highly-decorated artificial leg in *Perceval* II. *The Dream* gives a picture of a man sitting on a throne with the images of two eagles on it, and a board of gold before him like that for chess, and he is carving men for the game from a rod of gold. Chrétien or his source is said to have mistaken the words *eschaquier* and *eschac*, meaning chessboard and chessman, for *eschacier* and *eschace*, meaning respectively a man with an artificial leg and the leg itself; Chrétien's text is bent by taking *doler* to convey the sense of cutting pieces from something to use them, whereas it means to whittle, trim, or pare something down for use itself; and the bundle of rushes (*trossel de gles*) sat upon, which according to Loomis is puzzling—though rushes were then laid down when staying out of doors—he took to be "palpably a substitution for a *trosne aornee d'egles*".[12] This exhibits a curious need to explain away mystery in Chrétien as due to mistake. Such derivation in most dubious fashion from a Welsh work with which Chrétien has no plausible connection is not improved by Loomis's unconvincing attempt to identify the princess Clarissant with the Elen who is the subject of *The Dream*. He even saw this Elen as a partial prototype of the emissary in *Lybeaus*, who happens to be called Elene.[13] Another scholar, who operates a legitimate method when he relates *Perceval* I to the extant versions of the Fair Unknown type, does not do so in the least when he goes even further than Loomis to develop the claim that *The Dream* is a redaction of a lost Welsh legend about Caer Seint in Snowdonia, from which he derives the tale of the Fair Unknown, the hero who accomplishes his mission at Senaudon, whose lady is Queen of Wales in *Descouneus*. The legend is an unfounded hypothetical construction, and, having thus put Celtic material into the original tale of the Fair Unknown type which is not there, the scholar explains the Grail story of *Perceval* I from this second invention of his.[14] This is an instance of that approach to Arthurian romance which treats it as a do-it-yourself, make-your-own-myth-and-legend kit.

That so many possibilities for commentary of this kind on the origin of Chrétien's matter vanish into thin air, in the sources when they have been

11 Loomis, *op. cit.*, 441 f.   12 *Ibid.*, 445 f.   13 *Ibid.*, 458 f.
14 D. D. R. Owen, *The Evolution of the Grail Legend* (1968). The theory was in fact rejected by Loomis: see the discussion between him and Owen on "The Development of Arthurian Romance", *Forum for Modern Language Studies* I (1965), 64 ff.

identified, is a salutary lesson. It teaches that the contribution of Celtic material to Chrétien must be assessed more soberly than in the reckless manner which has been illustrated. And care must still be exercised when an analogue in Celtic story comes closer as a result of my findings, which is the case with *The Sickbed of Cuchulainn*, as will now be shown.

The text of this member of the Ulster cycle is a conflation of two recensions, one that is of the eleventh century (A), and another that has been interpolated from an earlier text (B), of the ninth or tenth century. According to Recension B, when Cuchulainn attacks two birds on a lake with a gold chain between them, he is overcome by sleep and has a fairy vision, in which a woman in a green cloak and another in a purple cloak come and smile at him and then strike him alternately with horse-whips. He wakes up to lie with a fairy sickness for a year. Then a man comes to him, declares he is Oengus, son of Aed Abrat (a fairy king), and tells Cuchulainn that his sisters Liban and Fand would heal him, and Liban would come to meet him at the spot where he had the vision. Cuchulainn returns there and sees the woman with the green cloak, who announces that she is Liban, come from Fand, whose husband Manannan has left her, and she has given her love to Cuchulainn. On behalf of her own husband, Labraid Swift-Hand-on-Sword, the best warrior in the world—his war-prowess is lauded in the poetry of *The Sickbed*—Liban summons Cuchulainn to come to the Plain of Delights and fight against Labraid's three fairy-king enemies for one day, in return for which he will be given Fand. Cuchulainn is unwilling to go, and sends his charioteer Loeg with Liban to visit the place. In a boat of bronze they cross a lake to an island where Loeg is welcomed at Labraid's house by a company of women, and by Fand in a room apart. As they are there, they hear the sound of Labraid's chariot coming to the island, and Liban greets him in verse praising his beauty and virtues, in addition to his war-prowess. Loeg returns and reports his tidings to Cuchulainn, who now goes to the island in his chariot with Liban and is welcomed by Labraid and all the women, Fand giving him a special welcome. Labraid immediately takes him to view the enemy host, and Cuchulainn tells him to go away now, leaving him alone by it. The enemy pursues him then, so that Cuchulainn does not find a place of safety in the country at their hands, but one day he wreaks on them much slaughter, and as Labraid returns the host flees. In Recension A, Cuchulainn then spends a month with Fand, but the outcome is that she surrenders her lover to his wife and returns to her own husband Manannan, which causes the hero to lose his reason, for a long time wandering through the mountains without food or drink, until he is healed by a drink of forgetfulness.

From this Irish tale, it is claimed, derive the stories of *Yvain* and *Sir Gareth*. As Loomis took this last to represent the original form of the Fair Unknown type, he thought one should also include the other Damoisele Mesdisant accounts, tracing to Cuchulainn's name that of Guinglain, and to the fairy isle of *The Sickbed* the castle beyond the river in *Perceval* II. It is by Liban's beating of Cuchulainn that he explained the humiliating treatment of the hero by the damsel in the romances.[15] But credulity is overstrained by this extraction of the emissary's behaviour towards the hero of the Fair Unknown type from the vision of two fays punishing Cuchulainn, and it is only the function of Liban as emissary that one may take into account, which does not seem to provide more than a general resemblance. On the other hand, now that Maidenland has been identified as the destination in the original story of the Fair Unknown type, the comparison with *The Sickbed* is underlined, for one can accept Celtic origin for this region, which is paralleled by the blissful fairyland of Irish story that appears in *The Voyage of Bran* and elsewhere, a delightful land of women.[16] In *The Voyage of Bran*, the Plain of Delights is profuse with flowers and splendours of every colour glisten, the island has an ancient tree in blossom, on which birds sing the Hours, and a fay brings a silver branch from "the apple-tree of Emain" to Bran, who falls asleep on hearing sweet music. We have seen that there is a marvellous tree in blossom as the prominent feature of the magic garden at the Castle of Maidens in *Floire et Blancheflor*, as well as of the wondrous meadow before Korntin castle in *Wigalois* and of the equivalent region by the abandoned capital of the Royaume aux Damoiselles in *Papegau* (the marvellous tree bears apples in the enchanted garden of the Fortress of Maidens in *Le Livre d'Artus*), and how the imagination of romancers plays with the delights or splendours of the places descended from Maidenland.

Again, if instead of *Sir Gareth* one takes the Fair Unknown type of tale and sets it against the Irish story, there comes to light some resemblance of the host-guide to the fairy king Labraid.[17] According to Recension A, Loeg reports to Cuchulainn that on his arrival at the fairyland he came to a wonderful place, to a mound where scores of companies were assembled, where he found Labraid. He found him seated on the mound, with weapons there, and a gold ball clasping his yellow hair. Labraid took him to his residence, which is that of two fairy kings, Failbe Find and Labraid. Loeg praises the magnificence of this house and tells of wondrous things, such as the marvellous tree of silver, from which music comes, that is at the entrance of the enclosure, and the trees which feed the whole household. As we have seen, the host of the Jousting for Hospitality in the original tale of the Fair Unknown type was a rich man of great prowess, splendidly dressed, who was found sitting in the open with a partner,[18] welcomed the hero when he arrived with the emissary,[19] took him to superlative lodgings, led him from his house to where the hero was to carry out the mission

15 Loomis, *op. cit.*, 129, 296-300, 303 f., 419, 439-42.

16 For this region, see Nutt's essay in *The Voyage of Bran*, and H. R. Patch, *The Other World according to Descriptions in Medieval Literature* (1950), c. 2.

17 There is some similarity in spelling between Lanpart/Lambard and Labraid, genitive Labrada.

18 For the scene, with its derivatives, see The Rich Man at the Foot of the Castle (p. 147 ff.).

19 On the relationship between the emissary and her lady, see p. 126 n. 65 above.

and by himself to sustain the assault of the enemy, and then hastened to him when the mission was accomplished, in a region associated with all kinds of fruit-trees.

But otherwise the role of the Plain of Delights and its inhabitants, and the nature of the hero's mission, so differ from the equivalent in the Fair Unknown type of tale that it is difficult to see *The Sickbed* as the source of the Arthurian story. The connection between the two is rather to be explained as due to the Irish tale resting on the same fairy lore as has given rise to the framework of the *conte d'aventure*. And it cannot be assumed that already in Celtic there existed this mythlike theme of joyous Maidenland plunged into misery and desolation, to be restored by the hero alone to a domain of happiness when he destroys the power of evil. In Chrétien one can still recognize some of the Celtic element embodied in this part of his original, but not in such an instance as when he uses the Encounter with a Huntsman, for he preserves hardly anything which makes this section of the Fair Unknown type of tale correspond to the first episode in *Pwyll*, where the hero has a confrontation with Arawn, who appears in a glade of the forest in pursuit of a stag whom he hunts with shining white hounds that have glittering red ears.[20]

The identification of sources has contributed significantly to knowledge of the relation between Celtic material and Chrétien. It has left several claims for Celtic origin high and dry, and the same is the case with some already doubtful analogies with Chrétien cited from later Arthurian romance. We have a combination of both approaches when Loomis treated the Meeting with Greoreas in *Perceval* II, the source of which he saw as in common with that of the episode in the First Continuation of *Perceval* where Garahes comes upon a recumbent wounded knight and the Petit Chevalier.[21] Loomis pursued this comparison to the identification of Greoreas and the hideous squire with the Welsh Bran and Beli, and to the disconcerting correspondence of an infamous character with the august Maimed King and an insolent one with the gracious Pelles. This is an example of Loomis's strong inclination not only to have a Procrustean bed of Celtic matter into which Arthurian romance must first be fitted, but also to construct common sources on the slightest provocation. Comparison between his work and my results shows how often he was wrong to conjure up the hypothetic tale, when no connection with the analogue had been established, or derivation from Chrétien was excluded on

20 On this equation, see Loomis, *op. cit.*, 125 f. *Pwyll* does not have the obtaining of the dog for a lady. This is found, without the hunt, in an episode of the *Tristan* by Thomas which seems to derive from the Encounter with a Huntsman (p. 91 f.). The dog Petitcru comes from Avalon and is very beautiful, shining with many colours; it bears a magic bell whose tinkling makes one forget sorrows. On seeing this dog Tristan is seized with a desire to obtain it from its owner, a Welsh duke, in order to give it to Isolt, and he gains it by combat (with a giant). Isolt then takes the dog along with her wherever she rides. See J. Bédier, *Le Roman de Tristan* (1902), i, 218 ff. The nationality of the dog's owner is no proof of Welsh origin for this account.

21 Loomis, *op. cit.*, 434-7. Compare pp. 136 ff., 203 f. above.

dubious grounds, or descent from a known story elsewhere was similarly rejected, as with the rescues in *Erec et Enide* and *Le Livre d'Artus* which go back to the Rescue from Two Giants in the Fair Unknown type of tale.[22] Loomis's procedure in such instances illustrates how his methods tended to rest on faith, not reason, when so often we have postulation without necessity which contravenes the principle of Ockham's razor.

Another lesson one learns is to be wary of basing ideas of antecedent Arthurian tradition on Chrétien, for we have seen how in relation to an original he is no mere gilder of base metal, but its transmuter into a different thing. Nor should wariness be relaxed when Chrétien appeals to the authority of a source. He remarks, when Erec is being attacked in the Escape from the Amorous Count, that this opponent is an excellent and courageous knight, according to what is told of him; but he is not referring to any such person in his original, only to the adversary of the Encounter with a Huntsman, which makes Chrétien's citing of an authority here as misleading as his mention of Macrobius for the description of Erec's coronation robe. This shows very well how one cannot take Chrétien's reference to a source to indicate that there is a genuine retelling.

How scholars can be misled by Chrétien may be illustrated by the manner in which the blend he concocted in Mabonagrain has blinded them as to the Arthurian tradition of the opponent who carries out the cruel custom of exposing the heads of slain challengers. Through believing in the authenticity of Chrétien's account in this respect, Philipot attributed to the original material a legend *d'un géant à la fois soupirant d'amour et coupeur de têtes, d'une fée qui le retient dans son île, et cependant assiste impassible à sa mort*, which he saw as basically the same type as that of Guengasouin in Raoul's *Vengeance Raguidel* (c. 1200), a knight kept by a fay on an island, given enchanted arms with which he slays Raguidel, and himself decapitated by Gawain. This romance also provides the separate analogy of the sinister Maduc le Noir, who kills knights and exposes their heads. The editor of the new edition of *Lybeaus* takes Maugys, who wears black armour, to be the same character as Maduc le Noir, who is a Black Knight, and the process of adaptation to a Saracen giant to include a change from the original situation in which like Malgiers in *Descouneus* the adversary defends a passage, in order to give proof of his desirability as a husband, to one in which he is a rejected suitor determined to win the lady by force. A similar conception was held by Brugger, who believed that the trait of Malgiers being hated by the fay in the Ile d'Or Episode is an alteration from the original story, which according to him provided both Mabonagrain in Chrétien and Sir Ironsyde in Malory with the direction by the lady-love as their excuse for the cruel custom. To the opponent in the Ile d'Or Episode he gave the appellation of *Fee-ritter*, associated the exposure of heads with this type of personage, and included under the designation not only Mabonagrain,

---

22 Loomis, *op. cit.*, 82-5, 160 f. See pp. 121 f., 164 n. 14 above.

Sir Ironsyde, and Maduc le Noir but also Marigart le Rous in the *Vulgate Lancelot*.[23]

However, not only is Malgiers a knight whom the fay is anything but willing to marry if he proves his desirability as a husband by battle, and who is no prisoner of hers but forces his suit on her, but also, as we have seen, his lack of popularity with the lady whom he wants is matched by his equivalents in Maugys, Sir Ironsyde, and Marigart le Rous, as well as Gernemant in *Li Chevaliers as Deus Espees*. And Maduc le Noir similarly practises his evil custom in a state of hostility with a lady because she will not love him but hates him, and thinks to gain her by destroying knights.[24] Every alleged *Fee-ritter* who exposes the heads of slain opponents is thus a suitor hated by the lady—except Mabonagrain. Once we do not accept the picture in the Encounter with Mabonagrain as authentic, the Arthurian tradition of the *Fee-ritter* is disentangled from that of the adversary in the Ile d'Or Episode, and defined as the motif which in Chrétien is represented in *Yvain*, where Esclados le Ros defends a fountain under a most beautiful pine not far from his wife's castle, and is killed by the hero, who marries her and assumes the custom.

At the basis of the methods I criticize, of which some illustrations have now been given, there lies some unfounded assumption that creates its own order out of the material. My own procedure has been different, allowing the evidence to lead me, and not only with regard to Arthurian sources. We have first seen how Chrétien shows the influence of certain contemporary works in Latin; and then, on looking there, I found the origin of such fundamental aspects of his story as its master-plan and the framework of the introductory section. This made me turn away from the Welsh *Gereint* and seek elsewhere for bearings on the genesis of Chrétien's tale. My findings on his material of Arthurian origin then made clear what further light could be thrown, from samples of story-telling fashion in Chrétien's day, or from the general store of international popular tale.

The Arthurian material itself has been handled by a comparative method that may be described in principle as seeking the logic responsible for the common ground between narratives, and in particular as observing shared patterns and seeing whether I can then come to conclusions—while bearing in mind that the significance of shared patterns varies—about the genesis of a story as a system comprising episodic material. Even when the evidence is insufficient for a positive conclusion, it may be possible to put it to use as a separator of patterns. Thus, there may be a certain similarity of structure, with some analogy between the situation of the heroes, but without significant congruence

23 Philipot, *art. cit.*, 270, 278-81, 285; *Lybeaus*, p. 232; E. Brugger, *ZrP* LXV (1949), 128 f., 132 f., 138 f., 146, in his series entitled "Der Schöne Feigling in der arthurischen Literatur".

24 *Vengeance Raguidel*, 1400-40, where the practice is explained as due to Maduc's hope that eventually Gawain, on whom the Dame de Gaut Destroit has fixed her love, and who is a knight he does not know personally, will be the one to suffer decapitation.

of episodes. This raises the question of some dependence of a later on an earlier text; but for my purpose I only required to use such resemblance of *Durmart* to *Ipomedon* (and *Fergus*) in order to mark out its framework and distinguish it from the Fair Unknown type, which left me to look for material of this kind in what fills the framework thus defined. Again, after noting the resemblances of *Ipomedon* II to the Fair Unknown type, I pointed to the distinction in the form of the hero's mission as well as the repetitive pattern of the encounters on the ride. Then, in Appendix B, I deal with its family, as a class of story allied to the Fair Unknown type, and through observation of this class lay a finger on the traits properly of the Fair Unknown type in the tales of Lore de Branlant in *Le Livre d'Artus* and of *Sir Gareth* in Malory.

As for the value of episodic parallels, this has been judged as follows. Conviction of a true relationship may result from the resemblances to any one episode being sufficiently detailed, or from the existence of analogues to more than one episode; and correspondence of order strengthens the evidence, which is all the stronger the longer a sequence of equivalents is maintained. There still remains the problem of how to decide on the nature of the relationship. Consider first the case of *Ipomedon* II, where we do not have a series of episodes in common with the related story. To the obvious structural resemblances of *Ipomedon* II to the Fair Unknown type, and the coincidence of a name, which are transparent analogies, I added parallels with its episodic material which, as they have been missed by those who have looked for them, I shall describe as opaque. My decision was that since motifs dispersed over a repetitive pattern in *Ipomedon* II are concentrated together naturally in the Fair Unknown type, all this amounts to evidence for derivation from the latter. It became evident that tales of the family of *Ipomedon* II, whose narrative structure is allied to that of the Fair Unknown type, have attracted features from this kind of story. In the tale of Lore de Branlant, the parallels with the structure of the Fair Unknown type are limited, and sufficiently accounted for from the family of *Ipomedon* II; but there are agreements with the episodic material of the Fair Unknown type which are striking enough to betray its influence in these respects. And in the tale of *Sir Gareth* there appear elements properly of the Fair Unknown type which are so distinctive that I can point to their source in a definite version.

I am able to do this with *Sir Gareth* partly on the ground of sequence, finding significance in the location of the reconciliation scene and the succession of two combats that are related to two that follow each other in the same order in a version of the Fair Unknown type. In *Durmart*, where we have one adventure that is a transparent analogue to the Fair Unknown type, there occur other parallels which are located within a series that becomes a factor in my identifications. Again, obvious analogy with the Fair Unknown type is comparatively restricted in *Erec et Enide* and *Perceval* II, and at the same time a principle of following the original order operates, more strongly than in *Durmart*. It is the existence of this principle that has made the matching of material in sequence an important aspect of my comparative method, by means

I

of which I determine the correct framework of reference within which the analogues can find their right place. The detailed analysis in relation to the sources will then depend for much of its conviction on a sequential logic, where some equivalences, taken by themselves, would have been weak, but they resist breaking because the chain has the strength of its strongest links.

It is the tracing of a sequence in relation to the tale of the Fair Unknown, through analogues both transparent and opaque, that set me on the right track to follow with *Erec et Enide*. By this means the order of episodes in the common original (*conte Erec*) was indicated, and so how to construct a table of descent for the versions of the Fair Unknown type. Support for my table was found in material of this kind recovered from other tales, and then confirmation from a comparison of *Perceval* II with the earlier narrative lines of the Fair Unknown type as they had so far been laid out. With matter descended from the original form of the Fair Unknown type in this way assembled and correctly arranged, I brought it to bear on *Erec et Enide* in a process of recognition, the latter's mirroring of the *conte Erec* being judged from those other reflections in contemporary and later texts. This made me see how Chrétien not only follows the course of the lost *conte Erec* but also draws simultaneously from any other part of his source, so that one of his episodes could combine matter from three in the original. The results of this systematic comparison were so striking as to leave no room for doubt that Chrétien's source was indeed what I have made it out to be, and that my conclusions, though subject to correction in detail, are in the main right about the way in which he handled it. After *Erec et Enide* had thus been explained from the *conte Erec* as far as this could be done, elements of different origin stood out in relief.

This particular comparative method, with its advance step by step to the unravelling of the *conjointure*, has been made possible by the existence of a group of romances (the Fair Unknown type) whose relation gives scope for reconstruction, whose sustained bearing on Chrétien's work can be shown, and which has provided a solid core from which fragments can be recognized. A firm basis was thus made available for the discovery of what must unavoidably be compared, for the interrelation of analogues by proper criteria, and for the realization of the truth about Chrétien's use of source material. The method of derivation in *Erec et Enide* is exactly that declared in the prologue. Chrétien says that he draws a *conjointure* from the *conte Erec*, and we see that he rips it apart for fragments, which are often bits of episodes and may even consist of merely a motif, to inspire his own quite different putting together, ingeniously related to the original.

The fusion of elements may produce features which intrigue the reader, as we see in particular from the Encounter with Mabonagrain. Feelings of wonder and horror are evoked by the scene of a beautiful damsel on a rich couch in the midst of a magic garden, accompanied by a knight who has the habit of impaling heads on sharpened stakes, which makes him a terrifying figure to oppose; and when the couple are brought within the orbit of human nature their residence in the garden remains singular, and his practice seems to go beyond what was necessary. However, one should not be surprised to find strange things in an enchanted place. On the other hand, its power is not explicitly exerted upon him, and others enter the garden without being similarly affected. Yet its enclosing wall of air is fittingly associated with an imprisonment which is subjective, because accepted by the knight as a duty. But his retention in a magic locality, carrying out the custom until defeated by another knight, mystifies when required by a mortal woman. Then, when the condition for his release is fulfilled, his liberation is not complete until the hero blows the horn, but why? And how is it that his return from the life in the garden is to give such tremendous joy to all, and they look forward to it with the expectation that would be warranted with the return of King Arthur to the Britons? And why then was the rejoicing, when the longed-for event takes place, entirely directed at the hero? Such mystifications have given rise to the view typified by the dictum of Gaston Paris:

Il est clair qu'on se trouve en présence d'un vieux conte mal transmis, que le poète français ne comprenait plus et qu'il a rendu encore plus inintelligible en essayant de l'expliquer.[25]

But what has been shown by the unravelling of the *conjointure* is that the view is untenable which holds that Chrétien was dealing with an account which came to him in corrupt form or which he misunderstood. On the contrary, it was perfectly clear and straightforward, and there was no mystery in it, but only magic. And the deliberation with which Chrétien proceeds in *Erec et Enide*, as he creates his *conjointure* of diversities from the *conte Erec*, may be illustrated by his managing to sustain the sequence in the source, the fitting into a *plan d'ensemble* based on a contemporary Latin work, and, of the various means of deriving from an individual element, above all the astounding relationship of the Encounters with Marauders to the material in the *conte Erec* to which it corresponds. Chrétien could not have started composing *Erec et Enide* only with the *conte Erec* in hand and a general idea in mind of what he was going to do with it, for in the process of construction that has been traced there lies the proof for the preparation beforehand of a detailed design. Fantasy together with a certain inconsequentiality makes for the effect of myth, giving an extra dimension not quite within human understanding. The maker of the myth entitled the Joie de la Cort was Chrétien himself, its qualities are those he chose for it, and the mystifications, which suggest the existence of some deep significance, result from his own manipulation of the elements he put into it, as certainly as the responsibility is his for withholding particulars about the adventure to come, and charging the narrative with intimations both of peril and of joy.

25 G. Paris, *Romania* XX (1891), 154, in a review of the edition of *Erec et Enide* by W. Foerster (1890).

I*

The next Arthurian romance, Chrétien's *Cligès*, is acknowledged to be an artificial composite of his own making, where "he has taken widely separated details and brought them into a new combination",[26] in other words where he operates a form of *conjointure* as well. Indeed, in *Cligès* there is quite a resemblance to the method in *Erec et Enide* if:

> la manière constante de Chrétien consiste à faire en quelque sorte éclater les épisodes du *Tristan* et à en utiliser les données en une constellation toute autre, dans l'invention de laquelle s'affirme précisément son génie.[27]

Such a principle of construction would create difficulties through the clash of disparate elements, as Fourrier remarks of one place in *Cligès*:

> N'est-ce point la preuve des difficultés qu'éprouvait Chrétien à souder de façon parfaite, dans sa transposition, des éléments empruntés à un récit où ils figuraient déjà, mais dans un ordre différent, plus simple, plus cohérent?[28]

This question could well be asked, for instance, about the puzzle in Enide's name becoming known the first time for her wedding, when in *Descouneus* the corresponding motif is clear, straightforward, and appropriate. And certainly in the Joie de la Cort, the supposed *vieux conte mal transmis*, Chrétien set himself a veritable challenge to coherency with the complexity of his *conjointure*. But here it is particularly suitable, as productive of intriguing overtones in an adventure located in a marvellous part of the Arthurian world. Raoul de Houdenc showed some understanding of the principle when he followed Chrétien's example with his own *conjointure* of diversities in the adventure experienced by Meraugis at the Cité sans Nom.

In *Perceval* II, the tone of burlesque that plays such a great part, blended with other effects such as mystery, surprise, pathos, or engaging appeal, is already well illustrated in comparable amalgams in the first half of the romance. The handling of *Perceval* II shows as much ease and confidence, and is just as much in harmony with the flow of Chrétien's late masterly style as those earlier scenes of the work. Of a piece with this surface manner is the approach to the source material in *Perceval* II, which is ironic, humorous, and witty. We see strange things happening to the original matter, and what one becomes aware of is the aiming at a narrative which is new but cleverly related to the source. It seems to be a case of playing with the original, with a conscious, deliberate, and controlled freedom that creates a different story by various methods of derivation, like those of musical composition with its techniques that make variation a sophisticated art. Everything goes to show that we should attribute to Chrétien, and not to some intermediary, the treatment of the source material that has been revealed.

26 J. D. Bruce, *The Evolution of Arthurian Romance* (2nd edn., 1928), i, 119.
27 A. Fourrier, *Le courant réaliste dans le roman courtois en France au moyen-âge* (1960), i, 143.
28 *Ibid.*, i, 151.

Here Chrétien pursues the method of thus interlacing matter from three originals, and even, as he follows one, draws on another at the same time, as when he brings Gawain along with the host-guide to the enchanted palace, and then sets up the image of a sitting figure that the hero comes across before the double-gated entrance. The intended creation of mystery is evident, when our attention, along with Gawain's, is directed by the host asking what is thought of this man with a richly-decorated artificial leg, who sits silently whittling a staff, seen but not seeing, and taking no part in the action. The scene epitomizes the kind of creative process which is definitely fertile in Chrétien, who so often—as we have seen—responds to a moment in his source as to a little picture, which he reinterprets. This unleashes his inventive powers, of which, as well as of the general verve of his imagination, we have ample illustration in *Perceval* II. It does show up the solemnity with which so much that should be attributed to Chrétien's own hand has been swallowed as representing authentic Arthurian tradition, or even traced to Celtic origins.

From *Erec et Enide*, *Cligès*, and *Perceval* II we learn the practice in half of Chrétien's writing in the Arthurian genre, that he did not operate at all like the literary hack that Loomis in particular would have him be, putting into verse and prettifying the tales of others, sometimes barely understanding what they meant or misreading what they wrote, and pursuing his source through thick and thin and with resigned bewilderment, under the handicaps it imposed.[29] On the contrary, we see him doing what he tells us he does with his source as he embarks on his Arthurian career, that he constructs from it what will demonstrate how it is best to give free rein to one's skill, which is as near as a medieval romancer could come to a claim to be a creator, who does not fashion *ex nihilo* but resorts to something to produce the work.

This result has obvious implications for the rest of Chrétien's production, and cuts the ground under much that has been written about the formation of Arthurian romance. Its nature has been misunderstood, and the history of its growth distorted, when originals have been assumed which are in fact ghosts conjured up from Chrétien's work. We have heard how for two generations anthropology suffered under the dead hand of Frazer and *The Golden Bough*, and for fifteen hundred years medical concepts stagnated under the compelling plausibility of Galen's theory of the four humours. Literary appreciation of Chrétien has had to struggle against theories of origin, taking his matter in the most literal way as derivative, which have been seductive as powerful manifestations of imagination, far greater than any that were allowed to the romancer.

As illustrative of the contrast between the new Arthurian traditions, established by Chrétien, and the old ones of the existing *contes d'aventure*, we can now take the differences between *Erec et Enide* and *Perceval* II on the one hand and, on the other, the versions of the Fair Unknown type whose shape

29 Loomis, *op. cit.*, 466 f.

in his day has been clarified. In this way we have gained much insight not only into Chrétien's methods of composition, but also into the *matière de Bretagne* as it lay before him, in which the Fair Unknown type of tale held such a central position that to Brugger the majority of extant Arthurian romances which relate the adventures of a hero (including those now only existing as incorporated into compilations and cycles) seemed to be its descendants.[30] A basis has thus been laid for further Arthurian exploration. This must not be allowed to bury the truth in a clutter of assumptions without foundation, as has happened conspicuously with the Celtic element,[31] but should employ comparative methods that ensure properly-orientated comparison of the truly comparable. I set out to find ways of doing this with the first Arthurian romance, and among my workings there are procedures which will surely prove of service elsewhere. Advance is possible, so long as one demands of Arthurian studies the same standard of evidence as prevails in other fields of scholarship.[32]

If this book's claim to reach such a standard is justified, then we have managed to peer over Chrétien's shoulder as he makes pictures whose relation to the original is remarkable and unexpected. We have been watching him while he lends tones to matter which did not have them. And we have caught him at work giving a shape to his romance which will project ideals. His stories on the courtly love of Lancelot and Guinevere and on the mysterious Grail were to have such pervasive influence on Arthurian romance that to us these themes typify the genre. To obtain a true conception of the creative process that was working at the very outset of the career that so affected the course of literature, and by this means to strike right at the root of the problem that has threatened to paralyse Arthurian studies, this has been the object of the quest.

---

30 Brugger, *op. cit.*, Z*r*P LXIII, 125.

31 Cf. A. J. Bliss, "Celtic Myth and Arthurian Romance", *Medium Aevum* XXX (1961), 19 ff., who concludes that "the cause of scholarship would benefit more from a careful sifting out of the grain from the chaff than from the endless multiplication of improbable conjectures".

32 For an approach, applied to fragmentary versions and translations, which has produced results with regard to the structure and genesis of a lost thirteenth-century Arthurian prose romance, see F. Bogdanow, *The Romance of the Grail* (1966).

APPENDIX A

Dating the Allegories of Alain de Lille

THE DATE OF *DE PLANCTU NATURAE*

De planctu Naturae does not have the maturity of *Anticlaudianus*, and stylistically it follows more closely the rhetorical precepts taught by Matthew of Vendôme,[1] whose *Ars versificatoria* has been dated by Faral shortly before 1175. It is also affected by the Latin songs, mostly belonging to the 1170s, that were composed by Walter of Châtillon, and Strecker, whose judgement is to be respected, observed that the style of *De planctu Naturae* suits the period 1175-80.[2] In turn it exerted influence on the last book of *Alexandreis*, for Walter of Châtillon, who probably finished the epic in 1181,[3] here has Nature descending in order to make a complaint against unnatural acts.[4] *De planctu Naturae* must also be responsible for the Nature topos early in *Ille et Galeron*,[5] not long before what appears to be a reflection of events in 1181.[6]

Alain infuses the cosmological role of Nature with moral force, conveying that what is to do with the world and human nature is intrinsically good if governed by natural law, and the work exalts marriage, looking upon the sexual act in this condition as honourable and of God's purpose. Alain's conception of Nature therefore militates against Catharism, the heresy of the Albigensians, which held that what is to do with the world and the body is intrinsically evil and must be purged from man, and his allegory has the effect of attacking the heretical denigration of marriage and its carnal relations.[7]

The struggle against these heretics became particularly fierce from late in the 1170s. In 1177, the Count of Toulouse asked for missionaries from Cîteaux and also wrote to the Pope for help. Henry II of England and Louis VII of France decided to take measures against the heretics in 1178, a papal legate,

1 G. Raynaud de Lage, *Alain de Lille: poète du XIIe siècle* (1951), 147 ff.
2 K. Strecker, "Walter von Chatillon und seine Schule", *Zeitschrift für deutsches Altertum* LXIV (1927), 164-6.
3 See p. 259 below.
4 F. Pfister, "Die Klage der Natur im Alexanderlied des Walter von Châtillon", *Neue Jahrbücher für das klassische Altertum* XXVII (1911), 520 ff.
5 See p. 6 above.
6 See p. 36 above.
7 The anti-catharist trend of *De planctu Naturae* has also been observed by A. D. Scaglione, *Nature and Love in the Late Middle Ages* (1963), 34 f., and P. Piehler, *The Visionary Landscape* (1971), 55-62.

255

archbishops, bishops, and the Abbot of Clairvaux being sent to Toulouse, accompanied by many ecclesiastics. The Lateran Council of 1179 condemned the beliefs of the Cathars, and declared excommunicate both them and their protectors. In 1181 the Pope entrusted a new mission to Henry of Clairvaux, now cardinal and legate. According to report, Alain de Lille attended the Lateran Council with the Abbot of Cîteaux—the Cistercians were active as missionaries against the Cathars, and Alain joined their order—and there destroyed the arguments of the heretics.[8] To refute them he wrote the first book of his *Contra haereticos*, dedicated to Guillaume VIII, lord of Montpellier from 1172.

The dating of *De planctu Naturae* to the period 1178-80 would satisfy stylistic considerations, fit the time when its influence first appeared,[9] and suit the way in which the work seems particularly relevant to the struggle against the Cathars, providing a case opposing them on philosophical grounds, even as one is framed by *Contra haereticos* on the basis of theology.

THE DATE OF *ANTICLAUDIANUS*

For the dating of *Anticlaudianus* one can refer to an article by Hutchings,[10] but as there remain various corrections and additions to be made, and the matter is crucial for the determination of the period when Chrètien de Troyes was active, it will be discussed at some length and the nature of the evidence demonstrated.

Near the beginning of Alain's poem there is a description of the palace that is Nature's home, decorated by the painter's art rendering the ways of man, with inscriptions making plain the pictured story. There are portraits of the great men Nature had created, men of genius and men who were heroes, but also of men in whose creation one might think she had amused herself or gone astray. This passage provides evidence for the date of *Anticlaudianus*:

> Illic pannoso plebescit carmine noster
> Ennius et Priami fortunas intonat; illic
> Mevius, in celos audens os ponere mutum,
> Gesta ducis Macedum tenebrosi carminis umbra
> Pingere dum temptat, in primo limine fessus
> Heret et ignavam queritur torpescere musam;
> Illic precipiti Nero fulmine concutit orbem,
> Indulgens sceleri, cogit plus velle furorem,

---

8 *Anticlaudianus*, p. 12.

9 Unless one accepts the view of M. T. d'Alverny, *Alain de Lille: textes inédits* (1965), 34, who holds that in *Sentences* written before 1176 there is an echo of some phraseology in *De planctu Naturae* applied to *solutio quaestionis*.

10 C. M. Hutchings, "L'Anticlaudianus d'Alain de Lille: étude de chronologie", *Romania* L (1924), 1 ff.; reviewed by Raynaud de Lage, *op. cit.*, 20-4.

Quam furor ipse velit; quicquid distillat ab illo
Nequicie sese totum partitur in orbem;
Illic dives eget, sitit aurum totus in auro
Midas, nec metas animo concedit habendi.
Militis excedit legem plus milite miles
Ajax milicieque modus decurrit in iram.
Fractus amore Paris, Veneris decoctus in igne,
Militat in Venerem; dum militis exuit actus,
Damnose compensat in hac quod perdit in armis.
In Davo propriam miratur noctua formam
Et vultus peccata sui solatur in illo.

(Anticlaudianus, I, 165 ff.)

(There our Ennius demeans himself in ragged poetry and bawls of Priam's fortunes. There Maevius, daring to set his dumb mouth in the skies, while he tries to depict the deeds of the Macedonian general with the faint traces of obscure verse, is stuck exhausted at the outer threshold, and complains his languid muse grows listless. There Nero shakes the world with his hurled thunderbolt, and, addicted to evil, whips up Frenzy to want more than Frenzy itself would wish; whatever wickedness exudes from that man spreads throughout the world. There rich Midas suffers want, thirsts for gold in the midst of gold, and allows no limits to his passion for possession. Ajax, more warlike than a soldier, goes beyond the bounds of a soldier's duty, and his manner of warfare degenerates into fury. Paris, his spirit broken by love, and ruined in Venus's fire, takes love-making to be his war; while he casts off the role of soldier, he ruinously makes up in love for what he loses in warfare. In Davus the owl admires its own image, and in him finds solace for the faults of its own appearance.)

Maevius was an Augustan poet ridiculed by Virgil and Horace, and there is no need to guess who is meant (even as Matthew of Vendôme in his *Ars versificatoria* attacked a contemporary under the name of Rufus or Rufinus), for the person whom Alain aims to satirize is indicated by his citation of *Gesta ducis Macedum*, the opening words of *Alexandreis*, the epic by Walter of Châtillon. This work is dedicated at the beginning and end to Guillaume de Champagne as Archbishop of Rheims, where he was installed in 1176. The opening dedication suggests that the poem was undertaken for him:

Huc ades, et mecum pelago decurre patenti,
Funde sacros fontes, et crinibus imprime laurum,
Ascribique tibi nostram patiare camoenam.

(Alexandreis, ed. Migne, ccix, 465)

(Be present in this, sail with me on the sea which lies open, pour forth the sacred streams, press the laurel crown on your hair, and suffer our muse to be ascribed to you.)

The preface declares that the author laboured on the work for five years, and at the end of Book V, halfway through the poem, at the point where Alexander makes a triumphant entry into Babylon, there is a historical allusion:

> Si gemitu commota pio, votisque suorum
> Flebilibus, divina daret clementia talem
> Francorum regem, toto radiaret in orbe
> Haud mora, vera fides, et nostris fracta sub armis
> Parthia baptismo renovari posceret ultro:
> Quaeque diu jacuit effusis moenibus alta
> Ad nomen Christi Carthago resurgeret, et quae
> Sub Carolo meruit Hispania solvere poenas,
> Erigeret vexilla crucis, gens omnis, et omnis
> Lingua *Deum* caneret, et non invita subiret
> Sacrum sub sacro Remorum praesule fontem.

(If, moved by the loving sighs and weeping prayers of his people, divine mercy give such a King of France, the true faith would without delay shine throughout the world, and Parthia, shattered by our arms, ask of its own accord to be restored through baptism; Carthage, which for a long time has lain with scattered walls, would rise aloft again to receive the name of Christ; Spain, which deserved to suffer punishment under Charlemagne, would raise banners of the Cross; and every race and every tongue would hymn the name of God, approaching the holy font not unwillingly under the venerable bishop of Rheims.)

This pious hope that a King of France would achieve such crusading success will apply to the young Philippe Auguste, who was crowned on 1 November 1179—his father Louis VII died in September of the following year.

In his study of *Alexandreis*, Christensen decided this allusion is probably to be dated to the beginning of 1180, and came to the conclusion that the poem was begun not long after the Archbishop came to Rheims, say 1178, was completed about 1182, and published a few years later, because the preface states it has been on the author's hands for a long time after completion.[11]

However, the beginning of 1180 was an inappropriate moment for Walter to refer to Philippe Auguste in these terms. After his coronation he took over the rule of France from his sick father and turned against his mother's family, the house of Blois-Champagne, driving her out of his dominions and persecuting her brothers, among them the Archbishop of Rheims. On the other hand, 1179 would be an apt time for Walter's allusion. In this year Henri le Libéral, Count of Champagne and brother of the Archbishop, departed in charge of an expedition to the Holy Land after Louis VII had failed to mount a Crusade. Instead, the King summoned the nobles of France to attend the crowning of his son by the Archbishop of Rheims on 15 August, but Philippe fell ill, and it was not until the autumn that the nobles were summoned again, this time for

11 H. Christensen, *Das Alexanderlied Walters von Châtillon* (1905), 7-13.

1 November. Against the background of this year, the allusion in *Alexandreis* is seen to imply disappointment in the old King while it expresses hope of fulfilment in his successor. I may therefore take it that the passage was written at a time when the coronation of Philippe was in prospect, and if I put its composition as early as the original summons, and assume the second half of the poem took two and a half years to write, then the epic was finished late in 1181. One also obtains 1181 by adding five years to the time when Guillaume de Champagne was installed at Rheims, which is how Hutchings computed the earliest possible date for the completion of *Alexandreis*.

Hutchings concluded that this gives a *terminus a quo* in 1181 for the date of *Anticlaudianus*, but I prefer 1182, in order to take account of the statement in Walter's preface (at which, as Hutchings observed, Alain will be aiming when he has Maevius stuck exhausted at the starting-point, complaining that his languid muse grows listless) that for a long time he has had it continually in mind to suppress the work on which he had laboured for five years, either completely destroying it or keeping it private.

For the *terminus ad quem*, Hutchings brought to bear Jean de Hanville's *Architrenius*, a poem which shows resemblances to *Anticlaudianus*, in addition to the influence of *De planctu Naturae*.[12] Early in the first book, *Architrenius* is dedicated to Walter of Coutances, Bishop of Lincoln, when he had been called to the archbishopric of Rouen. The election of Walter to Rouen was confirmed by papal letter dated 17 November 1184, but he was not allowed to go there for some time.[13] Jean de Hanville conveys at some length that Rouen is waiting expectantly and with great longing for Walter's instalment, which suggests it was imminent. According to Hutchings, the dedication points to November-December 1184, but it must be dated a little later, shortly before the enthronement of the new Archbishop on 24 February 1185.[14]

This is not long before the time when the troubadour Bertran de Born, shortly after about 1185, composed *Domna puois de mi nous chal*,[15] in which he imagines a *domna soisseubuda*, a woman fashioned with qualities collected from the best ladies he knew. This conception is related to the creation in *Anticlaudianus* of a perfect human summing up in one work the individual gifts bestowed by Nature here and there on others.

Judging by *Alexandreis* and *Architrenius*, Hutchings placed the composition of Alain's poem within the limits of 1181-84, but I have modified the *terminus a quo* to 1182, and, because the dependence of *Architrenius* on *Anticlaudianus* has not been convincingly demonstrated, I adopt c. 1185 as the *terminus ad quem*.

12 The resemblances to *Anticlaudianus* are summarized by Hutchings from the study by E. Bossard, *Alani de Insulis Anticlaudianus cum divina Dantis Alighieri comoedia collatus* (1885), c. 2. On *Architrenius* and its use of Nature, see Piehler, *op. cit.*, 86-94.

13 See the note by Stubbs in *Chronica Rogeri de Hoveden* (Rolls series), ii, 284.

14 The date that Hutchings adopted for the dedication must rest on the entries for the translation to Rouen and from Lincoln in P. Gams, *Series episcoporum ecclesiae catholicae*.

15 S. Stronski, *La Légende amoureuse de Bertran de Born* (1914), 96.

I**

The other literary allusion, in the passage we have been considering in *Anticlaudianus*, makes Ennius write on the Troy story. The target of Alain's shaft was already identified early in the thirteenth century as Joseph of Exeter, composer of *Ylias*—the twelfth-century epic that stands beside *Alexandreis* for fame—by the gloss on *Anticlaudianus* attributed to William of Auxerre.[16] Near the beginning of *Ylias* there is a dedication to Baldwin, Archbishop of Canterbury, and Hutchings observed that if Alain knew the poem in its complete form *Anticlaudianus* would have to be composed after May 1184, but that since some lines in the epic speak of Henry II's eldest son, Henry, as still alive, it was finished by 1183, apart from the dedication, and could have been shown to Alain while Joseph of Exeter was in France.

In fact, Baldwin was inducted to Canterbury in May 1185. Furthermore, the allusion in the prologue of *Ylias* to the imminence of a Crusade in which Baldwin is to take part indicates that the dedication is no earlier than 1188. This is accepted as the date of Joseph's epic by its recent editor, Gompf.[17] But surely the prologue and epilogue, with their references to an epic Joseph of Exeter was to compose on the Crusade, were added to a completed work which had already given its author a reputation as an epic poet, for he was evidently commissioned in 1188 by Baldwin to write that poem on the expedition to the East.[18] Thus *Ylias* may well have been composed before 1188. The limiting date is then set by the mention of young Henry in the text, which is wrongly taken to refer to him as still alive,[19] for the passage is comparable with one in *Topographia Hibernica*, III, xlix, by Giraldus Cambrensis, who similarly lavishes praise on the martial prowess of the young prince, but certainly after he was dead. The lines on him in *Ylias*, which complete Book V (the work is in six books), are therefore to be dated after the middle of 1183, which indicates a time before which Alain would not allude to *Ylias*.

Now, if in the case of both Ennius and Maevius we have literary allusions to contemporaries, then, as Hutchings pointed out, the rest of the passage in *Anticlaudianus* is likely to contain historical references of this kind. Alain seems to hint that all the errors of Nature which are portrayed have to do with the present or the recent past: *Postremos subtristis habet pictura penates* (*Anticlaudianus*, I, 155), "a very sad picture occupies the final position in the hall". And Hutchings goes on to argue that Nero, Midas, Ajax, Paris, and Davus are identifiable with Henry II and his four sons, and that the structure fits this, because Nero is marked off from the rest by having the first four lines devoted to him while the others are given two lines each (in Bossaut's edition, Paris actually has three lines), and follow a sequence which corresponds to that of their ages if they stand for the English princes.

It is obvious how apt these identifications are. Henry II was a despotic

---

16 Raynaud de Lage, *op. cit.*, 20.
17 L. Gompf, *Joseph Iscanus: Werke und Briefe* (1970), 19-22.
18 The references to this epic are given by Gompf, *op. cit.*, 61.
19 Gompf also rejects the claim that the text refers to young Henry as still alive.

king with a large empire and a vast system of alliances, and during his reign he had relations with every state and ruler in Christendom. He almost succeeded in opening a way to the Mediterranean from Aquitaine through Toulouse, and was even alleged to have aspired to the position of Holy Roman Emperor. His moments of fury led to such occurrences as the murder of Thomas Becket, whose killers went unpunished. Thus he corresponds very well to the picture of a Nero who shakes the world with his hurled thunderbolt, whips up Frenzy to want more than Frenzy itself would wish, and spreads his evil throughout the world. His eldest son Henry, the Young King (crowned during his father's reign), was not suffered to govern Anjou and Normandy—as Richard governed Aquitaine and Geoffrey did Brittany—and trouble arose between him and his father because he demanded territories and was refused. Thus young Henry, who spent money like water, instead of maintaining himself from his own domains had to depend on the allowance provided by his father. He made a habit of escaping to the King of France or the Count of Flanders, who would entertain him or furnish the prince with the means of surrounding himself with a retinue of knights, and when he fled in 1182 to Philippe Auguste, Henry was only persuaded to return by his father's promise of a magnificent pension. Here, then, is our rich Midas suffering want, and a thirst for gold that could not be quenched by his ample supply of gold. Richard began to be like a ferocious Telamon-Ajax in the later 1170s, when he besieged and razed castles in Aquitaine, and his duchy continued thenceforth to feel the weight of his heavy hand as he undertook the suppression of his unruly vassals. And Geoffrey was courteous, charming, and well-versed in military affairs, but without the reputation of his elder brothers. Hutchings claimed that the allusion to success in love is due to Geoffrey's marriage to Constance of Brittany in 1181, but it is preferable to turn instead to *A totz dic*, the lamentation by Bertran de Born over the death of the prince in 1186, and observe the line which exclaims that lovers have lost their leader: *Perdut an lor capdel li drut*.[20] This throws light on his character as a courtly lover which enables one to respond fully to the force of the irony in a poem by Bertran de Born addressed to Geoffrey in 1183. In the sirvente *Senher en coms, a blasmar vos fai*, he conceives of Limoges as a lady waiting for Geoffrey to arrive for a rendezvous she had arranged while he had been with her.[21] As Bertran mockingly puts it, a lover should not keep a lady waiting. Thus Geoffrey would be suitably represented by Paris—the name is applied to the courtly lover-knight in *De Phyllide et Flore*[22]—while Davus is a symbol for one who is contemptible and repulsive, and would do for John.

Hutchings made out a case for a particular period as providing apt correspondence with these historical allusions in *Anticlaudianus*. According to him, the Young King was led to compose his differences with Richard in return for

20 See the translation by R. R. Bezzola, *Les origines et la formation de la littérature courtoise en Occident*, iii (1963), 233.

21 C. Appel, *Bertran de Born* (1931), 34 f.

22 T. Wright, *The Latin Poems commonly attributed to Walter Mapes* (1841), 258 ff.

the pension in 1182 from Henry II, thus abandoning his rights for gold, and laying himself open to the reproaches of Bertran de Born for coming to terms because of money. Richard would not submit to his brother Henry, and continued hostilities, burning and pillaging, at the end of 1182, says Hutchings, who also has Geoffrey submitting in 1182 to his father. In 1183 Geoffrey surrendered to Richard, after the death of his brother and ally Henry, and so lost militarily. On these grounds Hutchings dated *Anticlaudianus* to the second half of 1182, or the first half of 1183. Raynaud de Lage accepts his arguments, and sees the passage in Alain's poem as belonging to 1182, at latest 1183, but holds that because of the work's length we should not be far from the truth if we date the publication of *Anticlaudianus* to 1184.[23]

With the year starting in January, these events mentioned by Hutchings, apart from the bestowal of the pension on young Henry late in 1182, are in fact entirely in 1183. But, as it happens, we have to keep in mind the situation in both years.[24] The Aquitanians could not bear the firm hand of Richard, and intrigued for him to be replaced by the gracious Young King, the landless prince to whom the idea of possessing such a rich domain was irresistible. Both he and Geoffrey entered into collusion with the Aquitanian league to destroy Richard's power, with a deviousness intended to deceive Henry II as to their intentions. In the spring of 1182 the Aquitanian rising was in full career, and Henry II hurried to the aid of Richard. Eventually we find that Geoffrey, too, is there with his father. Then the Young King made up his mind to advance into Aquitaine, and he was joyfully received at Limoges. Nevertheless, he joined his father and brothers at the siege of Périgueux, and the Aquitanian cause received a sharp reverse with its surrender in July. The sudden end of the war left Aquitaine in a dreadful state, with mercenaries released to wreak havoc all over the country. Young Henry then made a demand for a share in his father's territories, was refused and fled to the court of France; and his eventual return, to accept the gold for which he had such a thirst, was followed by this scene at Caen on 1 January 1183. Of his own accord, the Young King confessed to his father that he had pledged himself to the league of Aquitanian barons in the struggle with Richard, and he offered to make peace with his brother. It was now that Bertran de Born made his reproaches in *D'un sirventes nom chal far lonhor guanda*, where he upbraids young Henry for submitting to his father and ending his opposition to Richard[25]—and he jeers at his dependence on Henry II for his means. The King went with Henry, Richard, and Geoffrey to Angers, where he made them take an oath of obedience to him and peace with each other, and tried to have Richard pay homage to the Young King. But the only result was that Richard refused, left for Aquitaine in a temper, and his father blew up in one of his famous rages, calling on Henry

---

23 Raynaud de Lage, *op. cit.*, 22, 24.
24 There is an excellent account of this period by K. Norgate, *England under the Angevin Kings* (1887), ii, 222-31, by which my own is guided.
25 Appel, *op. cit.*, 30 f.

and Geoffrey to subdue their brother. They responded with alacrity. A fierce war ensued between Richard and the Aquitanian league under the leadership of the Young King, using Limoges as his headquarters from early in February and aided by his brother Geoffrey. Richard appealed to his father, who, seeing how dangerous the situation had become, advanced into Aquitaine on Richard's side and invested Limoges on 1 March. Before 17 March the Young King ran out of means to pay his mercenaries, and robbed the citizens of Limoges, seizing their wealth. Then, to the great shock of the Aquitanian chronicler, Geoffrey of Vigeois, he proceeded to strip the shrine of their patron St. Martial. He went to secure Angoulême, and on his return the citizens of Limoges pelted him off with stones. He led his army to the venerated religious house of Grandmont and took all its treasures, and then to Rocamadour, the most famous holy place, where he stripped the shrine of St. Amadour as well. Then the Young King died at Martel on 11 June, the citadel of Limoges soon fell, Geoffrey seems to have fled, and the Aquitanian rebellion, apart from some further resistance from Bertran de Born, suddenly collapsed.

It may well be that at this time Alain de Lille was in Southern France. He dedicates works to Guillaume VIII, lord of Montpellier from 1172, Ermengaud, Abbot of St. Gilles from 1179, and Henri de Sully, Archbishop of Bourges from 1184, while his interest in the Cathars would be connected with the increase in activity against them in Southern France from 1178, and his association with Cîteaux possible from 1179, when he may have accompanied its abbot to the Lateran Council. It is also known that he spent some time at Montpellier. Thus his antagonism against the English royalty is quite likely due to the southern bitterness against Henry II and the whole of his brood during the Aquitanian war. This existed in the second half of 1182, with the exasperation at the failure of the league against Richard; it rose to a height at the beginning of 1183, with the Young King's betrayal of his secret alliance with the Aquitanian barons; and then, when he and Geoffrey openly came over to their side, eventually there was shock at the forcible laying of hands on wealth with which to pay mercenaries. At the second and third points there are circumstances which particularly suit the Midas allusion, but I cannot preclude its application to the general situation of the Young King. Thus, a reference to this prince in *Anticlaudianus* could have been made as early as the second half of 1182. On the other hand, the Young King's death is not itself a *terminus ad quem* for the dating of the Midas allusion, which could have been written after he died, in a portrait of the recent past.

The period thus indicated for the allusions is from the second half of 1182 to not long after the middle of 1183. If one added the identification of the Ennius allusion as a reference to *Ylias*, this would leave "not long after the middle of 1183" as the date of *Anticlaudianus*. I do not take account of this in arriving at the earliest likely date of publication, which will be 1183.

The Relation of *Sir Gareth* to *Ipomedon* II

In both these romances of similar basic structure and allied to the Fair Unknown type, the cause of a scornful attitude towards the hero is exaggerated, Ipomedon being disguised as a fool and Gareth being made a kitchen boy. The Black, Green, and Red Knights, who have a further brother in the blue knight, Sir Persaunte (an addition from *conte d'aventure* X, see p. 125), and are defeated in succession by Gareth, are to be compared with the three opponents encountered on Ipomedon's ride, i.e. Malgis, Creon, and Leander, each a cousin, nephew, or brother of the fourth antagonist (the besieger Leonin). The repetitive pattern of the encounters differs in the two romances; that in Malory's tale is paralleled in the story of the Dame de Roestoc,[1] which is found in the *Vulgate Lancelot*. This must also be classified with *Ipomedon* II, as a story allied to the Fair Unknown type but in which the emissary is sent for a champion to save her lady by combat with the rejected suitor who besieges her with an army, and with a series of repetitive encounters on the hero's ride to his destination. Here, the motivation of a scornful attitude towards the hero is also exaggerated:

The Dame de Roestoc is besieged by her rejected suitor Segurades, a tall and formidable knight, who devastates her people and her land by war, and whom she will not have for all the world, but she proposes the respite of a year during which he should engage in single combat with all who dare to champion her cause against him, and thus the matter would be settled either by his conquest of all, or his defeat by one. These conditions are accepted by Segurades, but there is a contradiction of the motif, as he and his men then guard all passages to the land, so that no knight errant can enter. The valiant Hector is with his *amie*, the cousin of the Dame de Roestoc, and a hunchback dwarf who is the *amie*'s uncle, when a damsel arrives with a letter from the lady saying that the term of respite has drawn near its end, and asking the dwarf to go to Arthur's court and obtain Gawain as her champion. This is regarded as a difficult task, Hector is not allowed by his *amie* to undertake the combat with the formidable Segurades, and the upshot is that the dwarf engages an unknown knight—in fact, Gawain himself—who happens to be with them. But the dwarf despises and insults the hero, because he is deceived by his pretence of cowardice, and Gawain

---

1 *Vulgate Lancelot*, ed. Sommer, iii, 277-309. Discussed by E. Brugger, *ZrP* LXIII (1943), 323 n. 2, LXV (1949), 121, in his series entitled 'Der Schöne Feigling in der arthurischen Literatur".

bears his rudeness in silence. On the way to Roestoc, while it is Hector who fights and conquers the adversaries, in three successive encounters where knights and their men bar the passage, Gawain is treated by the dwarf with growing contempt, the situation here being that the hero displays no prowess before he achieves the mission—another knight does so instead—so that his lack of promise makes the lady in distress very despondent about her fate.

Gawain here shows the same patience with the scornful dwarf as practised by the hero of the Fair Unknown type in the face of the emissary's *mesdisance*. On the other hand, Gawain is just like Ipomedon, because by his pose he deceives both the Mesdisant figure and the lady in distress, who in Hue de Rotelande's romance is also thrown by the hero's behaviour into despondency about her fate. And as in *Ipomedon* II the encounters on the journey are three in number, with ties existing between the lady's besieger and the hero's opponents on the ride. But in as much as a succession of perilous passages is passed, the story of the Dame de Roestoc goes with *Sir Gareth*.

This pose of the hero's as a coward, coupled with a framework for the tale like that in *Ipomedon* II and *Sir Gareth*, is also found in the story of Lore de Branlant,[2] which is in *Le Livre d'Artus*:

A lady with a dwarf attendant comes as emissary to Arthur's court on behalf of her mistress, and asks for a champion to fight in single combat against a cruel knight who makes war on her to possess her by force. Gawain demands the mission from King Arthur because it is the first *"que ge i uoie"*, and pretends that he is Daguenet le Coart. The emissary and her dwarf leave without him. Gawain's pretence throws her mistress Lore de Branlant into despondency, she receives the hero badly when he arrives, and the members of the court, consoling her, sound like the dwarf when he pleads with the emissary on behalf of the Fair Unknown type of hero as they leave Arthur's court (that Descouneus may well turn out to have valour). When Gawain gives proof of his prowess in a battle, Lore de Branlant begs his forgiveness for her treatment of him, and there is a reconciliation.

It can be seen that these stories carry to excess the theme of the dwarf's plea to the emissary:

> "On ne doit ome blamer mie
> Dusc'on sace sa coardie:
> Tel tient on vil que c'est folor,
> Que Dius donne puis grant honnor."
> (*Li Biaus Descouneus*, 309 ff.)

In *Le Livre d'Artus* the encounters are not of the repetitive kind,[3] while in the story of the Dame de Roestoc, where they are, we do not have such a series of night-lodgings as occurs in Malory's tale, after each of the encounters

2 *Le Livre d'Artus*, ed. Sommer, vii, 74-8, 84-107.
3 On the nature of the adventures in the story of Lore de Branlant, see p. 121 f. above.

with the Green Knight, the Red Knight, and Sir Persaunte of Inde. This agrees with the doubly repetitive pattern of *Ipomedon* II, where lodgings are taken on three evenings, and there has been an encounter each day with one of Malgis, Creon, and Leander. But in *Sir Gareth* the hospitality is given by the vanquished knights themselves, which is a feature that Brugger recognized as passing back along the tale from Sir Persaunte through the force of analogy.[4] The last of these night-lodgings, when Sir Persaunte's daughter is sent to the hero at night—but he talks to the maiden gently and will not deflower her— may be compared with the last night's stay in *Ipomedon* II, when the damsel Ismeine comes to the hero's bed, and in the course of a conversation he refuses her advances courteously.[5]

Immediately before the combat with the besieger Sir Ironsyde, Gareth stays overnight at a hermitage, and so does Ipomedon before his battle with the besieger Leonin. In Malory, the dwarf goes to the lady's castle and gives news of the hero's arrival and a report on him and his deeds, while both the emissary and the dwarf enter the lady's castle in *Ipomedon* II, and Ismeine discusses with her mistress the hero and his deeds. The squire of Leander, one of Ipomedon's adversaries on the ride, had already reported to Leonin that his lord had been slain by a knight accompanied by a damsel, and Leonin realized that the emissary had come with the awaited champion, of whom he had already heard that he also conquered Malgis and Creon. Similarly, the besieger in *Sir Gareth* receives news of the hero's arrival and his overcoming of the opponents on the way. The dwarf falls in with Sir Ironsyde and tells him the emissary has come with the champion fetched from Arthur's court, who has killed or vanquished the knights at all the perilous passages.[6]

When the hero arrives at the place of combat before the castle, in both romances there is first a conversation in which the besieger warns him that the heroine is his lady and the hero denies this and declares that he loves her; which is unexpected in Malory's tale, since we have no love theme here until its sudden emergence at this stage, motivated only by the sight of Dame Lyonesse at a window in the castle above. Whereas Ipomedon is in love with La Fiere throughout the romance. Both heroes fight the antagonist in full view of the people and the lady in a fortress by the sea, which we find elsewhere, but then the stories basically agree in an odd course of events: the hero sojourns in his adversary's camp (briefly in *Ipomedon* II, ten days in *Sir Gareth*), and after the opponent has left the scene the hero goes to the entrance of the lady's castle, speaks to her from the outside and then departs from the place. The difference is that Gareth fully expects to be received, but is dismayed to find the entrance of the castle closed against him, with Dame Lyonesse unaccountably

---

4 Brugger, *op. cit.*, Z*r*P LXV, 125.   5 Malory, VII, c. 12; *Ipomedon*, 9159-9212.

6 Malory, VII, c. 14; *Ipomedon*, 9025-64, 9217-70. In the story of the Dame de Roestoc, after the perilous passages the hero spends a night at one of the lady's castles (just as the hermitage in *Sir Gareth* belongs to the lady), and the dwarf sends word to her what kind of knight he is bringing.

refusing to have him until he has won a reputation, in spite of what he has done for her, whereas Ipomedon continues in character by pretending to be the besieger Leonin in his black armour, and says that now La Fiere has to have him, which greatly upsets her, because she will not have Leonin at any price.[7]

At this point the chain of parallels is broken, as the two texts diverge. Ipomedon is disappearing into the forest, when King Meleager's nephew Capaneus arrives and intercepts him, and there is a combat in which the identity of the hero is eventually revealed. The end is more complex in Malory's tale: the hero finds his way to another castle nearby, that of Sir Gryngamour at the isle of Avylyon, and here he meets Sir Gryngamour's sister, whom he does not recognize, but she happens to be Dame Lyonesse, who in the meantime has transported herself there. It is also peculiar how, when they have become lovers and Gareth hears that Arthur is seeking his whereabouts, he arranges with Dame Lyonesse to advise the King to proclaim a tournament for her hand, so that the hero sets his own lure from his hiding-place. These odd twists are connected with the delivered lady turning up at the hero's place of resort, instead of going to Arthur's court after the hero has left the scene. Compare the story of the Dame de Roestoc, where the hero also departs after conquering the besieger and stays at another place with a brother (Helain de Taningues) and sister. She heals his wounds and is given a love gift, while the Dame de Roestoc goes to Arthur's court and frets over the disappearance of the champion she has fallen in love with. In the story of Lore de Branlant, the hero similarly disappears from the scene after he has accomplished his mission, leaving the delivered lady in love with him. He goes to the realm of Escavalon, where he is welcomed by the King and his daughter Floree. As in *Sir Gareth* at the equivalent point (p. 131), a bed is prepared for the hero, and when all have retired for the night the lady rises and comes to his bed; though she does not enter it but returns to her room, to which she invites him and where they consummate their love,[8] so that one is reminded of Frustration 3 and the Consummation in The Night Scenes at the Ile d'Or (p. 132 ff.).

The tourney in Malory is of the same nature as the Three Days Tournament that completes *Ipomedon* I, where it is held for the hand of La Fiere, and each day the hero appears disguised in arms of a different colour, jousts spectacularly, and disappears from the field at the end of the day. But in *Sir Gareth* it brings about the *dénouement* in similar fashion to the tourney in the early thirteenth-century French romance of *Fergus* by Guillaume le Clerc, which has been claimed to rest on the same scenario as Malory's tale, the name of Dame Lyonesse being taken to stand for Dame de Loenois and her domain identified with Lothian, the lady of which is the heroine of *Fergus*.[9] Here we also have the

---

7 Malory, VII, c. 16 to c. 19; *Ipomedon*, 9435-9952. The identity of Gareth is similarly mistaken for that of a Black Knight, but on the ride.

8 *Le Livre d'Artus*, ed. Sommer, vii, 106-10.

9 H. Newstead, "The Besieged Ladies in Arthurian Romance", *PMLA* LXIII (1948), 803-8; R. S. Loomis, *Arthurian Tradition and Chrétien de Troyes* (1949), 115 f., 365 f.

hero fighting the besieger in full view of the lady in her castle, and allowing him to keep his life. However, in comparison with *Ipomedon* II the resemblances of *Fergus* to *Sir Gareth* are restricted, and, apart from the end-pattern with the motif of the tournament proclaimed by Arthur for a lady's hand, in order to lure the hero from the place to which he has disappeared after rescuing a lady by fighting as her champion, *Fergus* is closer than *Ipomedon* II to *Sir Gareth* only in such a detail as its hero requiring the vanquished besieger to submit himself to the lady and make amends, and then to go to Arthur's court.[10]

It is the resemblances of *Fergus* to *Ipomedon* II that are the more striking. Just like Ipomedon, Fergus emerges from the forest to fight an adversary who has been waiting, with the lady already in despair at the prospect of her champion failing to appear, he conceals his identity from her, and after his victory plunges back into the forest. When Fergus completely disappears, this classes him with Gawain in the story of the Dame de Roestoc, which, as we have seen, belongs to the family of *Ipomedon* II, and has a hero who remains incognito and gives the lady in distress good cause to be despondent about her fate. Another instance where *Fergus* corresponds to *Ipomedon* II is when its hero departs from Arthur's court on a quest that requires single combat with a formidable Black Knight, and Fergus comes to the castle of Lidel where his host's niece, Galiene, falls in love with him and at night enters his chamber, offering him her love, which he puts off. This bedroom scene has been compared to one in *Sir Gareth*, on the last of the three night-lodgings with a knight, when Sir Persaunte's daughter comes to the hero and he will not deflower her,[11] but the agreements are with the equivalent of this in *Ipomedon* II, where it is the emissary Ismeine who has fallen in love with the hero. In *Fergus*, like *Ipomedon* II (spread over the last two nights of the three lodgings in the latter), the lovesick damsel debates with herself, hesitates to declare her love, but cannot refrain from going to the hero's bedside, where she puts her hand under the bedclothes, kneels by his bed in distress and declares her love, and the hero puts her off on the ground that he must carry out the combat he has undertaken. Fergus affirms he will then return to her, while Ipomedon placates her by saying that if successful he will do whatever she wants.[12] The next day, both heroes accomplish their quests by a victory over a knight in black armour. Evidently, there is matter in *Fergus* which has descended from *Ipomedon* II, and if *Fergus* did not draw directly on this but on the source of Malory's tale, then that source conformed even more to *Ipomedon* II than *Sir Gareth* allows us to see.

The evidence which has been laid out shows that *Sir Gareth* goes back to a source close to *Ipomedon* II, from which that source may indeed in turn have been derived.

---

10 The besieger, in the story of the Dame de Roestoc, also has to submit himself to the lady, and then they both depart to King Arthur.

11 The comparison with a scene at Avylyon in *Sir Gareth*, also made by Newstead, must be rejected. This coming of a lady to the hero's bed is quite different, see p. 131 above.

12 *Fergus*, 41/25-55/12; *Ipomedon*, 8685-8898, 9111-9212.

Bibliography

This list expands the abbreviated references which have been given, and generally excludes works of which sufficient bibliographical detail has already been provided in the notes. Place of publication for books mentioned here is London unless otherwise specified.

Abbreviations

BBSIA	*Bulletin bibliographique de la Société Internationale Arthurienne*
CFMA	*Les Classiques Français du Moyen Age*
EETS	*Early English Text Society*
JEGP	*Journal of English and Germanic Philology*
PMLA	*Publications of the Modern Language Association of America*
SATF	*Société des Anciens Textes Français*
ZrP	*Zeitschrift für romanische Philologie*
ZfSL	*Zeitschrift für französische Sprache und Literatur*

Studies

Frequently-cited works bearing on the question of source material for *Erec et Enide*:

Brugger, E., "Der Schöne Feigling in der arthurischen Literatur", *ZrP* LXI (1941), 1 ff.; LXIII (1943), 123 ff., 275 ff.; LXV (1949), 121 ff., 289 ff.; "Nachtrag", LXVII (1951), 289 ff.

Loomis, R. S., *Arthurian Tradition and Chrétien de Troyes* (New York, 1949).

Mills, M., "The Huntsman and the Dwarf in *Erec* and *Libeaus Desconus*", *Romania* LXXXVII (1966), 33 ff.

Philipot, E., "Un épisode d'*Erec et Enide*: La Joie de la Cour—Mabon l'enchanteur", *Romania* XXV (1896), 258 ff.

Saran, F., "Ueber Wirnt von Grafenberg und den Wigalois", *Beiträge zur Geschichte der deutschen Sprache und Literatur* XXI (1896), 253 ff.

Schofield, W., *Studies on the Libeaus Desconus* (Harvard Studies in Philology and Literature 4: Boston, 1895).

Texts[1]

This list omits Classical Latin works, and some texts of marginal interest.

---

1 Where more than one edition of a text is given, unless otherwise specified the citations are from the first edition mentioned.

(A) Collections

Cohen, G., *La "comédie" latine en France au XIIe siècle* (Paris, 1931).
Jones, G. and T. Jones, trans., *The Mabinogion* (Everyman's Library 97: 1950).
Migne, J. P., *Patrologiae cursus completus. Series latina* (Paris, 1844-64).
Sommer, H. O., *The Vulgate Version of the Arthurian Romances* (7 vols. and index: Washington, 1908-16).
Wright, T., *The Anglo-Latin Satirical Poets and Epigrammatists of the Twelfth Century* (2 vols., Rolls series: 1872).

(B) Individual Writers and Works

References to collections in List (A) are abbreviated to the surname(s) of the editor or translators.

Aimon de Varennes, *Florimont*. Ed. A. Hilka (Gesellschaft für romanische Literatur 48: Göttingen, 1932).
Alain de Lille, *Anticlaudianus*. Ed. R. Bossuat (Textes Philosophiques du Moyen Age 1: Paris, 1955).[2]
De planctu Naturae. Ed. Wright, ii, 429 ff. Also ed. Migne, ccx, 431 ff.[3]
Alexandre, *Athis et Prophilias*. Ed. A. Hilka (Gesellschaft für romanische Literatur 29, 40: Dresden, 1912-16).[4]
Alexandre de Paris, *Roman d'Alexandre*. In vol. ii of the Princeton edition, for which see *Roman d'Alexandre*.
Andreas Capellanus, *De amore libri tres*. Trans. J. J. Parry, *The Art of Courtly Love* (Records of Civilization, Sources and Studies 33: NewYork, 1941).
Baudri de Bourgueil, Poems. Ed. P. Abrahams (Paris, 1926).
Benoît de Sainte-Maure, *Roman de Troie*. Ed. L. Constans (*SATF*, 6 vols.: Paris, 1904-12).
Bernardus Silvestris, *De mundi universitate*. Ed. C. S. Barach and J. Wrobel (Bibliotheca philosophorum mediae aetatis 1: Innsbruck, 1876).
Bertran de Born, Lyrics. Ed. A. Stimming (Romanische Bibliothek 8: Halle, 1892).
Carduino. In *Poemetti Cavallereschi*, ed. P. Rajna (Bologna, 1873).
Le Chevalier du Papegau. Ed. F. Heuckenkamp (Halle, 1896).
Li Chevaliers as Deus Espees. Ed. W. Foerster (Halle, 1877).
Chrétien de Troyes,[5] *Le Chevalier de la Charrete*. Ed. M. Roques (*CFMA* 86: Paris, 1958).
Cligès. Ed. A. Micha (*CFMA* 84: Paris, 1957).

2 There is a poor translation of *Anticlaudianus* by W. H. Cornog (Philadelphia, 1935).
3 *De planctu Naturae* has been translated by D. M. Moffat (Yale Studies in English 36: New York, 1908).
4 Unless the T text is specified, the citations are from the main version.
5 There is a translation of four romances by Chrétien de Troyes in Everyman's Library 698.

Erec et Enide. Ed. M. Roques (*CFMA* 80: Paris, 1952). Also ed. W. Foerster (Romanische Bibliothek 13: Halle, 1896).

Guillaume d'Angleterre. Ed. M. Wilmotte (*CFMA* 55: Paris, 1927).

Perceval. Ed. W. Roach (Textes Littéraires Français 71: 2nd edn., Geneva and Paris, 1959).

Philomena. Ed. C. de Boer, *Ovide Moralisé*, ii, 337 ff. (Amsterdam, 1920).

Yvain. Ed. M. Roques (*CFMA* 89: Paris, 1960).

La Cote Mal Taillie. Fragment. Ed. G. Paris, *Romania* XXVI (1897), 276 ff. This tale is otherwise cited as incorporated in the *Prose Tristan*.

Cristal et Clarie. Ed. H. Breuer (Gesellschaft für romanische Literatur 36: Dresden, 1915).

Culhwch and Olwen. Trans. Jones and Jones, 95 ff.

Didot-Perceval. Ed. W. Roach (Philadelphia, 1941).

The Dream of Macsen Wledig. Trans. Jones and Jones, 79 ff.

Durmart le Galois. Ed. J. Gildea (2 vols.: Villanova, Pennsylvania, 1965-6).

Erex saga Artuskappa. Ed. F. W. Blaisdell (Editiones Arnamagnaeanae, Series B, 19: Copenhagen, 1965).

Eructavit. Ed. T. A. Jenkins (Gesellschaft für romanische Literatur 20: Dresden, 1909).

Flamenca. Ed. M. J. Hubert and M. E. Porter (Princeton, 1962).

Floire et Blancheflor. Ed. M. M. Pelan (Publications de la Faculté des Lettres de l'Université de Strasbourg, Textes d'Etude 7: new edn., Paris, 1956).

Floovant. Ed. S. Andolf (Uppsala, 1941).

Gaimar, Havelok episode of *Estoire des Engleis*. Ed. A. Bell, *Le Lai d'Havelok and Gaimar's Havelok Episode* (Publications of the University of Manchester, French Series 4: Manchester, 1925).

Gautier d'Arras, *Eracle*. Ed. E. Löseth (Bibliothèque Française du Moyen Age 6: Paris, 1890).

Ille et Galeron. Ed. F. A. G. Cowper (*SATF*: Paris, 1956).

Gereint, Son of Erbin. Trans. Jones and Jones, 229 ff.

Giglan. *L'Hystoire de Giglan filz de messire Gauvain* (Lyon, 1539).[6]

Giraldus Cambrensis, *Descriptio cuiusdam puellae*. In *Opera*, i, 349 ff., ed. J. S. Brewer (Rolls series: 1861).

Topographia Hibernica. In *Opera*, v, 3 ff., ed. J. F. Dimock (Rolls series: 1867).

Griselda. Apart from Boccaccio's *Decamerone*, X, x, there is Petrarch's version, ed. W. F. Bryan and G. Dempster, *Sources and Analogues of Chaucer's Canterbury Tales*, 296 ff. (1941).

Guillaume de Poitiers, Lyrics. Ed. A. Jeanroy (*CFMA* 9: Paris, 1913).

Guillaume le Clerc, *Fergus*. Ed. E. Martin (Halle, 1872).

Guiraut de Cabreira, *Ensenhamen*. Ed. M. de Riquer, *Les chansons de geste françaises*, 342 ff. (2nd edn., Paris, 1957).

---

6 Not paginated; all references are to the signatures.

Hartmann von Aue, *Erec.* Ed. E. Schwarz (Darmstadt, 1967).

Hue de Rotelande, *Ipomedon.* Ed. E. Kölbing and E. Koschwitz (Breslau, 1889).

Protheselaus. Ed. F. Kluckow (Gesellschaft für romanische Literatur 45: Göttingen, 1924).

Hugh of St. Victor, *Didascalicon.* Ed. Migne, clxxvi, 741 ff.

Huon de Bordeaux. Ed. P. Ruelle (Université Libre de Bruxelles, Travaux de la Faculté de Philosophie et Lettres 20: Brussels, 1960).

Jaufré. Ed. C. Brunel (*SATF*, 2 vols.: Paris, 1943).

Jean de Hanville, *Architrenius.* Ed. Wright, i, 240 ff.

Joseph of Exeter, *Ylias.* Ed. L. Gompf, *Joseph Iscanus: Werke und Briefe* (Mittellateinische Studien und Texte 4: Leiden and Köln, 1970).

Lidia. Ed. E. Lackenbauer, in Cohen, 211 ff.

Le Livre d'Artus. Ed. Sommer, vol. vii.

Lybeaus Desconus. Ed. M. Mills (*EETS* 261: 1969).[7]

Malory, Thomas, Works. For convenience I have used the edition by E. Vinaver in the Oxford Standard Authors (1954 and 1969). The standard edition of Malory by Vinaver is in 3 volumes (2nd edn.: Oxford, 1967).[8]

Marie de France, Lays. Ed. J. Rychner (*CFMA* 93: Paris, 1966).

Matthew of Vendôme, *Ars versificatoria.* Ed. E. Faral, *Les arts poétiques du XIIe et du XIIIe siècle,* 106 ff. (Bibliothèque de l'Ecole des Hautes Etudes 238: Paris, 1924).

Milo. Ed. M. Abraham, in Cohen, 153 ff.

Miles gloriosus. Ed. R. Baschet, in Cohen, 179 ff.

Narcisus. Ed. M. M. Pelan and N. C. W. Spence (Publications de la Faculté des Lettres de l'Université de Strasbourg 147: Paris, 1964).

Orson de Beauvais. Ed. G. Paris (*SATF*: Paris, 1899).

Partonopeu de Blois. Ed. J. Gildea (2 vols.: Villanova, Pennsylvania, 1967-70).

Perceval, First Continuation. Ed. W. Roach, *The Continuations of the Old French Perceval of Chrétien de Troyes,* vol. iii, part 1, The Short Redaction (Philadelphia, 1952).[9]

Second Continuation. Ed. W. Roach, *The Continuations of the Old French Perceval of Chrétien de Troyes,* vol. iv (Philadelphia, 1971).

Piramus et Tisbé. Ed. C. de Boer (*CFMA* 26: Paris, 1921).

Prose Tristan. As analysed by E. Löseth, *Le roman en prose de Tristan* (Bibliothèque de l'Ecole des Hautes Etudes 82: Paris, 1891).

Pseudo-Turpin. Ed. C. Meredith Jones, *Historia Karoli Magni et Rotholandi* (Paris, 1936).

Pwyll, Prince of Dyfed. Trans. Jones and Jones, 3 ff.

La Queste del Saint Graal. Ed. A. Pauphilet (*CFMA* 33: Paris, 1923). Also ed. Sommer, vol. vi.

---

7 Unless otherwise specified, the line numbers are cited from the C text.
8 I give the traditional book and chapter numbers of *Morte Darthur,* preserved by Vinaver to facilitate reference to Caxton's edition.
9 The line numbers are cited from the A (SPU) text.

Raoul de Cambrai. Ed. P. Meyer and A. Longnon (*SATF*: Paris, 1882).
Raoul de Houdenc, *Meraugis de Portlesguez*. Ed. M. Friedwagner (Halle, 1897).
Raoul (de Houdenc?), *Vengeance Raguidel*. Ed. M. Friedwagner (Halle, 1909).
Renaut de Beaujeu, *Li Biaus Descouneus*. Ed. G. P. Williams, *Le Bel Inconnu* (*CFMA* 38: Paris, 1929).
Roman d'Alexandre. Ed. E. C. Armstrong *et al.* (Elliott Monographs 36-41, 6 vols.: Princeton, 1937-55).
Roman d'Eneas. Ed. J. J. S. de Grave (*CFMA* 44, 62: Paris, 1925-31).
Roman de Thèbes. Ed. G. Raynaud de Lage (*CFMA* 94, 96: Paris, 1966-8). Also ed. L. Constans (*SATF*, 2 vols.: Paris, 1890).
Roman van Lancelot. Ed. W. J. A. Jonckbloet (2 vols.: s'Gravenhage, 1846-9).
The Sickbed of Cuchulainn. Ed. and trans. M. Dillon, *Serglige Con Culainn* (Columbus, Ohio, 1941).
Sir Gareth of Orkney. Malory, VII.
Sir Gawain and the Green Knight. Ed. J. R. R. Tolkien and E. V. Gordon (2nd edn., revd. N. Davis: Oxford, 1967).
Thomas, *Horn*. Ed. M. K. Pope, *The Romance of Horn* (Anglo-Norman Texts 9-10, 12-13, 2 vols.: Oxford, 1955-64).
Thomas, *Tristan*. Fragments. Ed. B. H. Wind (Textes Littéraires Français 92, 2nd edn.: Geneva and Paris, 1960).
Tristan de Nanteuil. Ed. K. V. Sinclair (Assen, 1971).
Ulrich von Zatzikhoven, *Lanzelet*. Ed. K. A. Hahn (Frankfurt a. M., 1845).[10]
The Voyage of Bran. Ed. and trans. K. Meyer and A. Nutt (Grimm Library 4, 6: 1895-7).
Vulgate Lancelot. Ed. Sommer, vols. iii-v.
Walter of Châtillon, *Alexandreis*. Ed. Migne, ccix, 459 ff.
William of Blois, *Alda*. Ed. M. Wintzweiler, in Cohen, 107 ff.
Wirnt von Gravenberg, *Wigalois*. Ed. J. M. N. Kapteyn (Rheinische Beiträge und Hülfsbücher zur germanischen Philologie und Volkskunde 9: Bonn, 1926).

---

10 *Lanzelet* has been translated by K. G. T. Webster, revd. R. S. Loomis (Records of Civilization, Sources and Studies 47: New York, 1951).

Index

* A hero or heroine whose name provides the title of a text, or a hero whose name is coupled with that of the heroine in a title, is not normally indexed separately from the title. The name of a personage of comparable function in a text, but which does not enter in this way into the title, has been similarly treated. Indication of such inclusion is given after the title heading, and where necessary the name is cross-indexed to the title.

THE FAIR UNKNOWN TYPE

A. The Type   B. Episodes   C. Extant versions

110-13, 180, 265; emissary, 87-8, 90-92, 99-100, 126n, 171-2, 196; her *mesdisance* and repentance, 86, 89, 105-11, 113, 125, 139, 151-2, 171-2, 237; dwarf, 112-13, 116-18, 137, 139, 162n. In stories of Lore de Branlant and Dame de Roestoc, 264-5. Further refs., with *Erec*, 92, 160-62, 192-193, 195-6, 211; *Perceval* II, 127, 137, 139-41, 154, 156

Arthur, champion required from, 86, 103; defeated opponent to report to, 88, 92, 98, 115, 137, 189; hero welcomed as champion sent by, 85, 100, 107-8, 206-7; informed of hero's name, 169; arrival and departure from, wedding and coronation at his court (Wedding to a Queen), see *Episodes*. Motifs not of F.U. type: proclaims tournament to lure hero, 104, 133; as hero, see *Papegau* in *Extant Versions*; his nephew, 139

B. Episodes

E Enfances, 84, 166-7, 182; with ref. to *Tristan de Nanteuil*, 221

AA Arrival at Arthur's Court, 85, 111, 115, 126n, 166-7

DA Departure from Arthur's Court, 105-6, 111, 115-16, 118n, 160, 172, 196, 265; analysis, 86-7

1 = IV Encounter with a Huntsman, 115, 130, 144n, 184-5, 188-90, 194-6; analysis, 91-2. Relation to Visit to Escavalon, 129-130, 156; *Sir Gawain*, 155-6; *Pwyll*, 246. Further refs., with Chrétien, 246; *Erec*, 83, 92, 159n, 160-61, 165, 247; other romances, 119-20, 152-3, 246n

2 = V Sparrowhawk Contest, 111-12, 116, 118-19, 128-9, 157, 162-82, 196nn, 204; analysis, 92-8. Further refs., with *Erec*, 83, 160; other romances, 115-16, 119-20, 122, 159

3 = VI Ile d'Or Episode, place in series, 85, 137; analysis, 98-9; combat, 112-13, 116-117, 122-4, 126, 211-17, 225, 247-8; arrival, 123-4, 132, 159, 167-8, 170-72, 183, 202n, 223-4; night scenes, 132-5, 170, 173-9, 184; escape, 183-4. Relation to Avylyon episode, 135-6; Visit to Escavalon, 135-6, 156; *Sir Gawain*, 155-6. Further refs., with *Erec*, 170, 184, 192, 195, 221, 235; other romances, 112, 119-20, 122n, 142, 179n, 201, 217, 267

4 = I Encounter at the Perilous Bridge, 90, 117, 137-40, 188-92, 196, 212; analysis, 87-8. Further refs., with *Erec*, 185n, 193, 194; other romances, 119, 122

5 = II Rescue from Two Giants, 89-91, 113, 117-18, 121-2, 140-41, 164, 179-80, 247;

analysis, 88. Further refs., with *Erec*, 83, 190-92, 195; other romances, 112, 119 **RS** Reconciliation Scene, 107-8, 111-13, 180, 192, 195; analysis, 89. Further refs., with *Erec*, 90-91, 193. For X variant, see below

6 = III Attack by Three Avengers, 85, 89, 113, 117, 139, 141, 172-3; analysis, 90-91. Further refs., with *Erec*, 194; other romances, 112, 119, 122, 138

RRD Return of the Rescued Damsel, 122, 157, 164-5, 195, 208; analysis, 89

7 = VII Jousting for Hospitality, analysis, 99-101; island fortress, 142, 197-202; enchanted garden, 208-11; rich man at foot of castle, 147-9; meeting with host, 203-6, 217; jousting, 142, 153n, 214-15, 224-5; hospitality, 206-7. Relation to The Sickbed, 245-6. Further refs., with *Erec*, 225; other romances, 143, 220

8 = VIII Accomplishment of the Mission, 143-5, 199-201; analysis, 102-4; Cité Gaste, see main Index; blowing of horn, 219-22; joy, 222-4; hero's name known, 169, 221, 242. Further refs., with *Erec*, 208, 225; *Floire*, 148n, 201-2. For X variant (**VIIIa**), see below

WQ Wedding to a Queen, 169-70; analysis, 104. Further refs., with *Erec*, 225; other romances, 148n, 150, 201, 225n

Special X Development

VIIa Encounter at the Narrow Passage, 119, 125, 149, 151, 198, 205, 207, 212, 214-15 **RS** Reconciliation Scene, 89, 125, 154, 156 **VIIb** Encounter before La Roche, 100, 126, 147, 149, 153, 205-6, 213-14, 224-5 **ALS** Arrival at the Lady's Stronghold, 100, 107, 143, 145-7, 150, 154-5, 197, 207 **AAC** Approach to the Abandoned Castle, 154, 198, 206, 210, 214, 225, 245 **VIIc** Encounter at the Gateway of the Magician's Castle, 142, 147-50, 205 **VIIIa** Accomplishment of the Mission, 102-103, 142, 150, 197-8, 223

C. Extant Versions

Carduino, with this hero, 84-5; position in table of descent, 109-10, 113, 118, 120, 126n, 137, 156. Emissary and dwarf, 86, 89, 103; emissary, 106n, 107n, 126n, dwarf, 90, 101-2, 113, 117-18, 180n. E, 166-7, 182; **AA**, 85; **DA**, 86; 3 = **VI**, 99, 133-4, 177; 4 = **I**, 87, 90, 139-40; 5 = **II**, 88, 109n, 113, 117; night meal, 89, 113, **RRD**, 89; 8 = **VIII**, 101-3, 142, 144-5; 222; **WQ**, 104, 170. Motifs of F.U. type lacking, 98n, 102, 106nn, 107n, 203